VILLARD

THE LIFE AND TIMES
OF AN
AMERICAN TITAN

PORTRAIT OF HENRY VILLARD,
C. 1880–90, BY ELEANOR BELL.
Courtesy of the University of Oregon Museum of Art.

Gift of Oswald Garrison Villard.

VILLARD

THE LIFE AND TIMES
OF AN
AMERICAN TITAN

Alexandra Villard de Borchgrave
and
John Cullen

NAN A. TALESE
Doubleday
NEW YORK   LONDON   TORONTO   SYDNEY   AUCKLAND

Published by Nan A. Talese

An imprint of Doubleday
A division of Random House, Inc.
1540 Broadway, New York, New York 10036

DOUBLEDAY is a trademark of Doubleday, a division of
Random House, Inc.

Library of Congress Cataloging-in-Publication Data
de Borchgrave, Alexandra Villard
Villard : the life and times of an American titan /
Alexandra Villard de Borchgrave and John Cullen.
—1st ed. in the United States of America.
p.   cm.
Includes bibliographical references (p.) and index.
1. Villard, Henry, 1835–1900. 2. Capitalists and financiers—
United States—Biography. 3. Journalists—United States—Biography.
4. Railroads—United States—History—19th century.
I. Cullen, John, 1942– II. Title.

HG172 .D4 2001
070.92—dc21
[B]   00-061545

Book design by Lee Fukui

In Loving Memory of

HENRY SERRANO VILLARD (1900–1996), C. 1905.

Alexandra Villard de Borchgrave Private Collection.

Contents

Preface

THIS BIOGRAPHY of my great-grandfather Henry Villard is the ful-
fillment of a promise to my father, the late Henry Serrano Villard.

Shortly before my father died, on January 21, 1996, he took my
hand in his and said, "You are the only member of the family I can
count on to tell your great-grandfather's story. Promise me you will."
While I may have looked confident as I gave my word, I trembled in-
wardly at the enormity of the task before me.

Henry Villard had loomed large in my upbringing. His legendary exploits as an intrepid correspondent who had known President Lincoln and had covered many battles of the Civil War,
mounted on his imposing black horse; his love for the only daughter
of the fiery abolitionist William Lloyd Garrison; his unshakable belief in Thomas Edison's early experiments in electricity; and the en-
trepreneurship that drove him to complete the Northern Pacific
Railroad not only constituted riveting bedtime stories but also gen-
erated intense family discussions around the dinner table.

I was seven when I was first shown Henry Villard's stately brownstone mansion, known as the Villard Houses, on Madison Avenue
(he occupied the south wing, the others to be sold to five other families). But it was only much later, when the houses were deemed a national landmark, that I came to understand the tragedy connected
with the legacy my great-grandfather had left. For despite his outstanding qualities of courage, determination, perseverance, and
benevolence, Henry Villard was also overly optimistic, disinclined to
focus on details, and prepared to risk all for the sake of a worthy but

shaky enterprise—shortcomings that eventually would lead to financial disaster and the loss of his corporate empire.

Throughout my youth, the house stood as a symbol of Henry Villard's greatest dreams and deepest pain, and I felt the excitement of his accomplishments as well as the humiliation and embarrassment of his downfall each time I passed the cobblestone courtyard.

Now, with its enduring presence, the mansion continues to remind me that it is possible to suffer ruin, to rise on the strength of friendship, and to once again implement an unparalleled idea. The pride I feel today in Henry Villard's comeback more than compensates for the sadness of his darkest hour.

From the moment I started the research, I yearned to do justice to the adventure, the joy, and the heartbreak Henry Villard experienced in his lifetime. In that regard, I would like to express my gratitude to John Cullen, my gifted coauthor, who, in bringing not only his exceptional talent as a writer but also his knowledge of German to bear on the manuscript, made this book a reality.

Henry Villard believed in America. To this day, our country offers unique opportunities to anyone with the courage and determination to realize a dream. It is my hope that this book will serve as an inspiration to those with such a dream.

Alexandra Villard de Borchgrave
WASHINGTON, D.C., JUNE 2000

Acknowledgments

FROM THE BEGINNING, I realized that it was going to take years
to complete this project.

There were so many excellent books to be read in which Henry
Villard was mentioned, such as *Lincoln* by David Herbert Donald,
Yankee Reporters 1861–1865 by Emmet Crozier, *The Bohemian Brigade*
by Louis M. Starr, *Edison: A Biography* and *The Robber Barons* by
Matthew Josephson, *Union Pacific: The Birth of a Railroad 1862–1893*
by Maury Klein, *Frederick Billings* by Robin W. Winks, *The Villard
Houses* by William C. Shopsin and Mosette Glaser Broderick, and innumerable books on Henry Villard's rivals, such as J. P. Morgan, Jay
Gould, and James J. Hill. There were history books on the German
revolution of 1848, New York in 1853, the Civil War, Reconstruction,
and the Gilded Age. There were volumes of newspaper articles covering each period, many of them on microfilm at the Library of Congress, and hundreds and hundreds of letters written by Henry
Villard, Fanny Garrison Villard, William Lloyd Garrison, Frank Garrison, and Wendell Garrison, among many others, that had to be
read.

I knew early on that a successful conclusion to the task lay in finding appropriate help. To this end, I am immensely grateful, first, to
my dear friend Lucky Roosevelt, who introduced me to my respected
agent, Georges Borchardt; to Georges, who saw the potential in the
story; to John Bowers, whose invaluable expertise on the Civil War
and American history brought the subject into focus; to Nan A.
Talese, my nonpareil editor, whose interest in Henry Villard gave life
to the project; to the librarians at Harvard's Houghton Library, es-

pecially the infinitely courteous and patient Tom Ford, and the librarians at the Harvard Business School's Baker Library; to Margrit Beran Krewson, former curator of the German Collection at the Library of Congress, who gave me so much of her time and guidance; to James H. Billington, librarian of congress extraordinaire, who was unfailingly helpful; to Paul A. Mahon, my great literary counsel; to Roger Williams, who ably assisted me in editing the first draft; to Caitlin Shetterly, who meticulously checked the facts in the first draft; to Leitha Schwiesow, who found essential documents at the Houghton Library; to Stephanie Lanz, who unstintingly helped translate German family papers; to Sinclair Hamilton and Stanley M. Stefan, who cheerfully spent many tedious hours photocopying; to Sirio Maccioni, dynamic owner of the world-famous Le Cirque, in the New York Palace Hotel, who always made me feel warmly welcome in my great-grandfather's former home, and to his charming assistant, Tanya Boudakian; to Anita Cotter, the former director of public relations, and to all the courteous staff of the New York Palace Hotel.

I am singularly indebted to those special friends whose extraordinarily gracious and generous support helped make this book possible: Nemir A. Kirdar and Richard M. Scaife, who contributed to the grant established at the Heritage Foundation through the kind effort of Edwin J. Feulner Jr.; Abdullah Alireza; Joan K. Davidson of Furthermore, the J. M. Kaplan Fund publication program; John L. Loeb Jr.; Jane B. Owen; Janet and Arthur Ross of the Arthur Ross Foundation; and Taki Theodoracopoulos, who contributed to the grant established at the New-York Historical Society through the kind efforts of Betsy Gotbaum, president, and Paul Gunther. I would especially like to thank Paul Gunther and the staff at the New-York Historical Society for all their assistance in completing this project. A special thank you also goes to Eric Peterson at CSIS for his expert help in drafting the grant proposal.

Suzanne Burris at the Burlington Northern and Sante Fe Company, Susan Sanborn Barker at the Sophia Smith Collection at Smith College, Mary Beth Kavanagh and Nicole Wells at the New-York Historical Society, Chris Hunter at the Schenectady Museum, Jean Nattinger at the University of Oregon Museum of Art, Elaine James at the Dudley Branch of the Boston Public Library, and assistants at the Library of Congress and the National Archives all have my deep appreciation for providing rare photographs. The outstanding work done by Chrome Photographic Services also deserves particular recognition.

The kindness of relatives, most especially Joachim and Alice Hilgard in Berlin and Katharine N. Villard, Judy Mann Villard, and others in New York, California, and Massachusetts, who searched their files and closets for family photos and articles, can never be forgotten. My gratitude also extends to accomplished author Kurt E. Armbruster, for his helping hand.

I am truly grateful to all the friends who have shared this long journey with me and who have forgiven me for the time I have had to spend away from them.

Most of all, I want to thank the two most important men in my life—my beloved, inspirational husband of thirty-one years, Arnaud, and my treasured, talented brother, Dimitri Villard—for giving so freely of their time and judgment. Their unwavering support, encouragement, wise counsel, and love made me stay the course.

Alexandra Villard de Borchgrave

FRANZ MORITZ JOSEPH PFEIFFER,
Henry Villard's maternal grandfather, c. 1816.
Alexandra Villard de Borchgrave Private Collection.

Rebellion

*Sometimes I think America's
A place I might set sail for:
The freedom-barn, where every lout
Is equal to his neighbor.*

*It scares me, though—a land of such
Tobacco-chewing goons,
Where they bowl without a kingpin
And they spit without spittoons.*

HEINRICH HEINE,
"Where to Now?"

The fledgling revolutionary, called upon to lead the class in prayer, rose and stood beside his desk. Tall for his age—he was barely fourteen—he had not yet grown into his body, which seemed almost too thin to support his large head. But his will was stout; he was convinced of the justice of his cause; there was no faltering either in his voice or in his resolve. The prayer he was reciting was a standard one, invariably pronounced at the beginning of the two periods of religious instruction that he and his classmates received every week. One section of this prayer besought divinity on behalf of royalty, imploring God to maintain a special regard for the welfare of "His Majesty, our most gracious King and Lord, anointed in Christ," and the entire royal family. When the boy came to this "reactionary sentence" (as he was later to call it), he calmly skipped over it, moving without pause to the closing supplications. His classmates, likewise pledged to this act of defiance, unanimously followed his lead; but Dr. Krieger, the religion instructor, who also happened to be the city pastor, could not allow such an impious omission to go un-challenged. "What's the meaning of this?" he asked sharply.

"The monarchy has been abolished," the young rebel said. "How can we pray for the king?"

True to his name (it means "warrior"), Dr. Krieger welcomed this opportunity to do battle for the right and established order of things. It was his devout belief that divinity doth hedge a king, however be-set by rabble or slighted by youthful insolence. "I insist that you re-cite the petition for the welfare of the king and his family!" he thundered.

"I will not," the boy said firmly, and stared Authority in the face.

With mounting rage, Dr. Krieger ordered six more members of the class to say the prayer for the king. They refused, one after an-other, each as calm as the first. "This is open rebellion and contempt for religion, for the king's majesty, and for myself!" the pastor yelled. "I shall give this class no further instruction!" For a long, silent mo-ment, he contemplated his adversaries. He was searching for vacilla-tion or guilt; he saw before him only obstinacy and conviction. Then he stalked out of the room.

A resounding blow had been struck for democracy. Savoring their triumph, the mutinous adolescents gathered around their leader, young Heinrich Hilgard, who had just changed the course of his life.

     ▦   ▦   ▦

The French Revolution was an earthquake whose aftershocks shook Europe for generations. As the momentous events that be-gan in 1789 grew increasingly sanguinary ("Let unclean blood soak our furrows!" shouted the singers of the "Marseillaise"), the nobles and clergy of other lands resolved to combat the spread of danger-ous republican ideas beyond the borders of France. The result was the French revolutionary wars (1792–1802), which plunged much of the continent into chaos, made the career of Napoleon Bona-parte, and led directly to the far greater chaos of the Napoleonic wars (1803–15). After the guns fell silent at Waterloo, ending a generation of upheaval, the exhausted nations of Europe welcomed a period of relative calm. Constitutions were proclaimed here and there, there were a couple of minor revolutions, but in most countries the nascent republican movements languished. In France, where it had all begun, Bourbon buttocks were once more commodiously ensconced on the Bourbon throne.

But in 1830, a new French revolution sent tremors throughout Europe. This time the French installed as their ruler a man they called, somewhat misleadingly, the "citizen king," and the republican movements in many lands, particularly Germany, grew murmurous again. Then in 1848, yet another French uprising, the February Revolution, overthrew the monarchy. Louis Philippe, the citizen king, conforming to the republican zeitgeist, left Paris in a hansom cab, and the Second Republic was proclaimed. These events set off a massive chain reaction; counting the small German states, the Italian states, and the provinces of the Austrian empire, more than fifty revolutions broke out in Europe in 1848. Republicans were everywhere in arms; and everywhere, after an appropriately heady, though brief, period of success, they failed. In France itself, which had as usual given the signal for the general tumult, the upshot of it all was the Second Empire and the reign of Napoleon III. In the various kingdoms, grand duchies, duchies, and other principalities of Germany, hereditary rulers breathed a sigh of relief as their republican opponents underwent arrest or execution, emigrated, or withdrew into obscurity to gnash their teeth and bide their time.

Thus the short-lived republican triumphs all over Europe in 1848–49 were mirrored in the intoxicating but ephemeral victory of the apprentice radicals, led by young Heinrich Hilgard, in Dr. Krieger's religion class. The setting for their revolt was the gymnasium, or preparatory school, in Zweibrücken, an old town in the region of southwestern Germany known as the Rhenish Palatinate, between the west bank of the Rhine River and the French border. This proximity to France made the Palatinate particularly sensitive to events there, and it had in fact been conquered and incorporated into France during the French revolutionary wars. In 1815, when the Congress of Vienna set about the rezoning of post-Napoleonic Europe, the Palatinate had been assigned to the kingdom of Bavaria and was thenceforward called Rhenish Bavaria. And so it was the king of Bavaria from whom Heinrich and his classmates dared to withhold the benefit of their prayers in May 1849.

· · ·

Heinrich Hilgard, the future Henry Villard, was born in Speyer, in the home of his maternal grandparents, on April 10, 1835. Speyer, a medieval city picturesquely situated on the west bank of the Rhine, was at that time the capital of Rhenish Bavaria. His mother, Katharina Antonia Elisabeth Pfeiffer, known as Lisette, was the daughter of a hero of the French revolutionary wars, the former captain Franz Pfeiffer. Often wounded and even more often decorated during his long service (1790–1801) in the counterrevolutionary army of the prince of Condé, he laid down his arms, began collecting his pension, and turned to the comforts of domestic life and the security of a bureaucratic career, eventually rising to the position of chief administrator of the Bavarian government's salt monopoly.

In his grandson's eyes, Franz Pfeiffer achieved almost mythic proportions, like the heroes of the romances Heinrich was so fond of reading. His grandfather's "noble, finely chiseled features," complemented by his "stately bearing," made him the epitome of "masculine beauty," while his heroic past and generous heart were the attributes of a chivalric ideal, the knight *sans peur et sans reproche.*

Georg Friedrich Hilgard, Heinrich's other grandfather, was a different matter. Embittered by the Bavarian government's abrupt termination of his civil service career while he was mayor of Speyer, and much occupied with the numerous new family that resulted from his second marriage, Black Fritz—so called because of his black hair and dark, burning eyes—lived in retirement in his country house, the Klosterhof, near the remote village of Kirchheim-Bolanden. Heinrich spent much less time with this rather cold grandfather than he did with his warm and loving Pfeiffer grandparents, but one of Black Fritz's sons, Robert Hilgard, Heinrich's half uncle though only two years his senior, became his friend and played an important part in his life.

Heinrich's father, Gustav Leonhard Hilgard, was descended from a centuries-old line of theologians, country pastors, and minor civil servants in the Palatinate. Gustav's father held various important government offices, and his mother, Charlotte Henrich, who died when Gustav was eleven, came from a well-to-do family of bankers. Gustav himself, after a brilliant academic career, entered the legal service of the kingdom of Bavaria. He received a series of official appointments in the Palatinate and settled with his family (Heinrich had two sisters, one older and one younger) in Zweibrücken in 1839.

Heinrich Hilgard was thus the scion of a most respectable, socially prominent, highly educated upper-middle-class family. Although there were no nobles nestled among the branches of the family tree, the presence of so many high-ranking magistrates and civil servants conferred upon the family a sort of *noblesse de robe,* and Gustav Hilgard naturally had great expectations for his only son. As sometimes happens, the son had expectations and ideas of his own.

Religion played a notable part in the courtship and marriage of Gustav Hilgard—gifted, intelligent, hot blooded, and extremely handsome (according to his son), with curly brown hair and deep blue eyes—and the blond, blue-eyed, beautiful, and charming Lisette Pfeiffer. The Catholic authorities decreed that Gustav must agree in writing to raise all future children as Catholics before Fräulein Pfeiffer, his childhood sweetheart, could become his wife. Jealous and headstrong, Gustav had already fought one duel over Lisette, and although he was by no means a zealot in matters of religion, as the descendant of quite a few Reformed Church pastors he was more than willing to take on the papists. Lengthy negotiations by post with Lisette's father resulted in the latter's proposing that sons of the marriage be raised as Protestants and daughters as Catholics. At first Gustav refused to countenance so abject a compromise, and then, when he had at last agreed to it, the Catholic authorities declared that it was out of the question. The maiden herself, though she was the designated object of these maneuverings, seems to have been little consulted about them. Finally, after three years of dogged controversy, the exasperated Gustav announced that he was ready to withdraw his offer of marriage unless his terms were met. The church capitulated, and Gustav led his hard-won bride to the altar in 1833.

One gathers that Lisette, who looks frank and good humored in an old photograph, immediately set about her lifelong task of raising the spirits of her intense, scowling husband. She also immediately began producing children in a rapid succession of pregnancies, three in four years, that permanently affected her health.

Heinrich had a happy early childhood, marked by nothing more unusual than the severe case of measles that laid him low for many weeks in his sixth year (a portent of the sudden debilitating illnesses that would assail him all his life). He and his sisters, Anna and Emma, were close enough in age to be companions as well as siblings; and the faithful setter Feldmann, who had been a mere puppy when Heinrich's parents laid him next to their son in his cradle, grew up with him and never left his side. Heinrich was not quite four years old when his family moved to Zweibrücken, where they eventually settled into a large, spacious apartment in an elegant building. The apartment's many rooms, and especially the two abandoned structures in the courtyard—former stables, storerooms, and servants' quarters filled with all manner of fascinating junk—provided an ideal setting for the free play of childish fantasy.

Opa and Oma Pfeiffer insisted on having one of the young Hilgards, their only grandchildren, with them at all times, so Heinrich and his sisters took turns making extensive sojourns in their grandparents' big house on the Königsplatz in Speyer. During one such stay Heinrich attended the local school, but he hated having to sit next to the poorly clothed, unwashed lower-class children who were his fellow pupils. He tells us that he tried, without success, to overcome this "aristocratic sensitivity." Though certainly not the "born aristocrat" his father was, Heinrich would always have difficulty conforming absolutely to the republican motto, much as he subscribed to it in principle. Liberty? Yes, indeed, as much as possible. Equality?

Ah, there was some room for quibbling. Fraternity? A figure of speech, open to interpretation.

This natural aloofness was compounded by a sense of alienation, and it made him an uncommonly shy child in the presence of strangers, including other children. From the familiar security of his grandparents' house and garden, which lay on a large, tree-lined square, he would peek wistfully at the romping bands of youngsters that filled this public space, but he could never bring himself to join them. His shyness would in time disappear without a trace, but his image of himself as the loner standing apart would linger in the background of his personality.

In school he was a better than average student, doing well in reading, rote learning, and arithmetic, and poorly in penmanship. Except on rare occasions, his undifferentiated headlong scrawl remained quite difficult to decipher all his life. In autumn 1843, at his own urgent request, Heinrich was allowed to leave the grammar school in Zweibrücken and enroll in the lowest class in the gymnasium. He was only eight and a half years old and not yet academically equipped for the rigors of German preparatory school education, but his friends, all of whom were two or three years older than he, were scheduled to enter the gymnasium in the fall, and Heinrich didn't want to be separated from them. (Later on it seems to have occurred to no one that having essentially skipped two or three grades, he might without disgrace or loss repeat a gymnasium year.) Latin and Greek were especially troublesome, as his foreshortened grammar school career had not allowed him to acquire the solid foundation in the ancient languages that was required for success at the secondary level. Henceforth he was in general an indifferent student, and during his first four years at the gymnasium he was rather less than that, to his father's great, and plainly expressed, disappointment.

Despite his shortcomings in the classroom and his relative youth, Heinrich distinguished himself among his fellows for vivacity and mischievousness; though the youngest in his class, it soon became clear that he was also the boldest. Frequent illnesses, including an eight-week bout of scarlet fever, could only temporarily slow him down.

In August of 1847, King Ludwig I of Bavaria made a state visit to Speyer. Heinrich's burgeoning republican tendencies were outweighed by his love for his grandfather Pfeiffer, a man whose body bore the marks of his service to royalty, and the two of them were garlanding the upstairs windows in anticipation of the royal procession. The boy eagerly answered the call for the midday meal, but when his grandfather failed to follow him, he was sent back upstairs to fetch the old man. Heinrich found him lying on the floor beneath the window, unmoving, his eyes wide and his face blood red, dead of a stroke. This was Heinrich's first glimpse into the abyss, his first realization of the terror and suddenness of death.

Also in 1847, Heinrich passed from the lower division, or Latin school, to the gymnasium proper—roughly from grammar school to high school, though within the same institution—thus dodging by the skin of his teeth his father's threat to apprentice him to a tradesman if he should fail to be promoted. Nevertheless, it was by this time apparent that there was a widening rift between Heinrich and his father. Nominally attributed to Heinrich's lackluster performance in school, the growing dissatisfaction and resentment between the two actually sprang from much deeper and less mutable causes. Father and son were too different from each other in areas that might lead to harmonious relations, such as values and interests, and too alike in traits inimical to harmony—obstinacy, intolerance—to be able to limit the range and intensity of their disagreements.

The February Revolution, the flight of Louis Philippe, and the ensuing republican agitation were a source of great distress to Gustav Hilgard and his friends and colleagues in the service of the royal government. The Revolution of 1789 had provoked bitter consequences for all Germany, particularly the lands west of the Rhine; a new surge of radicalism from the same source could not bode well for Gustav and men like him.

His son, on the other hand, was galvanized by the prospect of revolution, which would lead to the new and better world of democracy. Among the Hilgard family, leftist—that is, antimonarchical—tendencies were hardly an aberration. Henry Villard would later declare that the events of 1848 permanently politicized him, but like some of his other characteristics, his intense interest in politics might be considered part of his inheritance as a Hilgard. His great-grandparents Jakob Hilgard and Maria Dorothea Engelmann, ardent supporters of the French Revolution of 1789, underwent years of privation and persecution because of their radical sympathies. A high level of political consciousness and distinctly democratic convictions were included in their descendants' patrimony. All four of Heinrich Hilgard's paternal uncles, his father's four younger brothers—liberal, dissident, and dissatisfied—turned their backs on kings and kingdoms and emigrated to America.

All the Hilgards and Engelmanns in the Palatinate shared these advanced political ideas, with one crucial exception: Gustav Hilgard. Perhaps in reaction to the ideological unanimity of his family, Gustav embraced patrician principles at an early age and never let them go. He believed that popular self-government was an impossibility and thought that some men—for example, the king of Bavaria—were born to rule over others.

The acknowledged political leader of the Hilgard-Engelmann clan was Heinrich's great-uncle Theodor Erasmus Hilgard, the brother of Heinrich's grandfather Fritz. Theodor Erasmus was a legal scholar and appeals court judge in Zweibrücken. In 1834, his opposition to the creeping oppression of the Bavarian monarchy led him to terminate his brilliant legal career and resign his judgeship. In September of the following year he emigrated to Illinois, at that time on the Western frontier of the United States. He carried along with him his protesting wife, their nine children, and the bulk of the family furniture, including the piano. In a letter to his former colleagues on the court of appeals, Theodor Erasmus explained his motives for taking these drastic steps, declaring that he "considered it an inestimable gain to make my descendants freemen."

Theodor Erasmus's decision was the result of long, careful meditation. He had weighed the difficulties and dangers that he, his wife, and his children would suffer from so thorough an uprooting and so utter a change in their way of life against the free institutions, immense spaces, and (as he thought) boundless opportunities to be found in the United States. Observing the failure of republican movements all over Europe, most spectacularly in France, their country of origin, Theodor Erasmus had concluded that the dream of a democratic Germany would not come true, at least not in his lifetime, and he began to advocate emigration as the solution for his entire extended family.

The chosen destination of the many Hilgards and Engelmanns who followed Theodor Erasmus's advice—and after 1835, his example—was Belleville, Illinois, the site of a numerous German colony, most of whose members were natives of the Palatinate. Filled with the spirit of German Romanticism and, like many of his countrymen, more comfortable plying abstract ideas than grasping concrete realities, Theodor Erasmus had constructed for his relatives and himself an ideal vision of life on the American frontier that corresponded only partially to what he and they found there, and he was to return to Germany in 1855. But many of those whom his exhortations had persuaded to emigrate remained in America, including almost all of his children; and his descendants, as he had wished, were freemen.

For his part, Gustav Hilgard did his best to dissuade his brothers, all four of whom eventually emigrated, from their adherence to their uncle's views. He had the satisfaction of seeing three of them return, never having adjusted (as he had predicted they would not adjust) to the exigencies and deficiencies of life on the edge of civilization. Their democratic, antimonarchical sentiments underwent no change, however, and Gustav continued his political isolation within his family, the sole island of monarchism in a democratic sea.

Henry Villard believed that the emigration of his relatives to America was the decisive factor in the course of his own life, but the sequence of events that began with the February Revolution of 1848 was of nearly equal importance. These events focused young Heinrich's precocious political interests and provided a broad, clearly outlined area where he and his father could never meet.

In the early months of 1848, the revolutionary fires were burning high all over Germany. In the Palatinate, the very air hung charged with anticipation, hopeful or dreadful, depending on one's views. Normal school activity in the Zweibrücken gymnasium was virtually suspended. No one had any time or thought for scholastic accomplishments. There was but one topic of discussion before, during, and after classes: would revolution come to the German states, particularly Bavaria? The Bavarian government, taking the threat seriously and wishing to palliate it, announced a series of measures granting freedom of the press, freedom of assembly, and the arming of the citizenry; furthermore, a Zweibrücken attorney and member of the legislative assembly known for his liberal views was called to Munich and appointed minister of justice. These bloodless liberal successes, though they elated Heinrich, disgusted his father, whose attitude toward the revolution and the canaille it advanced grew increasingly reactionary.

Gathering tensions were momentarily alleviated by Heinrich's confirmation at age thirteen in the old Speyer cathedral. Now, religion was an area in which father and son held compatible views, though this fact does not seem to have brought them closer together. In his later years, Henry Villard would remember the impressive scene in the cathedral, the ceremony that confirmed him as a member of the Protestant church, as the last time he felt anything like a religious impulse. On another occasion, referring in his memoirs to the numerous clergymen on both sides of his family, of whom he was the direct descendant, he wonders, "Whether I've done honor to my ancestry in this regard?" The answer, as he knew, was no. He explained his lack of religious inclinations by recalling his father's complete indifference to religious customs and his frequent railing against "the parsonry." Gustav bowed to kings, not pastors, and produced a son who bowed to neither. Formal religious instruction at school and the pressure to participate in religious observances eventually turned Heinrich against everything that had to do with the church. He hated services, especially in winter, and his "unchurchly attitude" seems to have lasted throughout his life.

Politics was altogether more absorbing. Heinrich became an avid newspaper reader, anxious to keep abreast of the rush of events. His democratic enthusiasms at the time no doubt derived more from the zeitgeist than from any deep consideration of the issues—he was, after all, still in his early teens—but the spirit of 1848 informed his thinking until he died.

Zweibrücken's citizens availed themselves of their new right to bear arms. A local militia, five hundred strong, was organized. This force was seen as a democratic gesture, and most government officials tested the prevailing winds and joined up too. One of the few who refused to enlist was Gustav Hilgard. He let it be known that he considered such trimming a contemptuous lunge for popularity and that it was abject self-abasement for a royal official to join ranks with shopkeepers and workmen. Though he was partially right—politicians, as we know, want people to like them—nobody could accuse *him* of courting popularity. His reputation as a reactionary grew.

The militia drilled thrice weekly and afforded Heinrich and his friends a profuse source of delight, not because of their republican sympathies but because the sight of the respectable burghers of Zweibrücken bumping bellies, knocking heads, and spinning about in all sorts of uncommanded directions was exactly the sort of thing—Adults at Play—that high-spirited adolescents could watch for hours.

In May 1848, a national assembly of specially elected representatives from all over Germany convened in Frankfurt am Main. This assembly, known as the Frankfurt Parliament, had been called by a group of liberal leaders in response to the wave of revolutionary sentiment that was rolling through the German states, but the members in attendance represented all political points of view and included the most famous and influential figures of the time. The avowed purpose of the Parliament was to lay plans for German unification and to determine how a newly unified Germany would be governed.

Heinrich Hilgard eagerly read newspaper accounts of the daily proceedings in Frankfurt and burned to attend them in person. His chance came in the form of a fortuitous invitation from his half uncle Robert Hilgard, who was then living in Frankfurt. Gustav's initial reaction to this plan was a contemptuous refusal, but Heinrich recruited his mother as an ally and the two of them were able to persuade Gustav to give his consent, if not his blessing, to the journey. At thirteen and a half, Heinrich was surely among the very youngest of those who observed the proceedings of the Parliament; he attended many sessions, saw most of the famous members of the assembly (their names were familiar to him from his avid reading), and returned home a more convinced leftist than ever.

One of the most conspicuous and vehement of the radical republicans in the Parliament was Friedrich Hecker. He came from the grand duchy of Baden, the most liberal of the German states, where he had made a name for himself as a leftist agitator. During the revolutionary period of 1848–49, the common greeting throughout the Rhineland was *"Hecker hoch!"* (Up with Hecker!), and the *Heckerhut* (Hecker hat) he affected, a cocky piece of headgear adorned with a long red feather, became a much-admired, much-copied symbol of the revolution. By carefully husbanding his travel funds, Heinrich was able to buy himself a *Heckerhut* before leaving Frankfurt. The young revolutionary wore his new hat home, apparently hoping to provoke the wrath of the authoritarian against whom he was chiefly in revolt—his father—but was both disappointed and relieved to encounter a relatively mild reaction. Gustav, who found his son's defiance almost but not quite beneath contempt, contented himself with remarking, "There are many people making fools of themselves in this way, and if you want to join them, I have no objection."

The subsequent career of Friedrich Hecker exhibited certain parallels with that of his admirer, the future Henry Villard. Hecker eventually lost his seat in the Parliament and was forced into exile. He emigrated to Illinois, bought a farm, became an ardent member of the Republican Party, fought in the Civil War, and gave antislavery speeches that were famous among all the German-speaking people in the United States.

Heinrich was encouraged in his revolutionary views by the various radical relatives (all from the paternal side of his family) who paid visits to the Hilgard home in Zweibrücken, despite their glaring differences with his father. At school, he associated himself with the most radical (and least disciplined) elements and began to get in trouble.

The struggle between the left and the right in Germany, in which (not for the last time) the forces of reaction were to triumph, entered its final phase in March 1849. The Frankfurt Parliament, having moved steadily rightward, voted a proposed federal constitution that provided for German unification, parliamentary government, and a hereditary emperor. King Friedrich Wilhelm IV of Prussia was offered the crown, but he disdained to receive it from such an assembly. How could a ruler by divine right accept appointment and authority from ordinary mortals who held their positions by popular election? The Parliament collapsed in futility, and many leftist leaders saw no recourse but violence.

The revolution's dawdling, however, had given the rulers of many German states, particularly Prussia (the biggest and strongest), time to recover from the effects of the uprisings of March 1848. In the Palatinate, a rather slovenly revolt—Engels, who fought in it, was disgusted by its "amateurishness"—declared the Bavarian monarchy abolished and established a provisional government. All state officials were required to declare their allegiance to this new government; rather than do so, Gustav Hilgard took an early holiday, going into what he correctly judged would be a brief exile. By way of contrast, his brother Friedrich, who had returned from the United States, participated in the revolution and was a leading member of the government it set up.

It was in these circumstances, therefore—with his father gone from the Palatinate, Uncle Friedrich in the highest circles of the new order, and democracy bursting out all over—that Heinrich felt emboldened to defy Dr. Krieger in his religion class and refuse to pray for the king. But as Henry Villard would write, "Brief was the democratic dream in Germany." The Prussian army marched into Rhenish Bavaria; there were a few lopsided clashes, after one of which an older gymnasium student who had joined the Zweibrücken militia lay among the dead; the army of the provisional government was driven across the Rhine into Baden and dispersed. Dreams of civil liberties gave way to the realities of power, order was restored, royal authority returned, and so did Heinrich's father.

We can imagine how enthusiastically Heinrich greeted the vindicated royalist's return. This first in a series of increasingly disagreeable scenes was followed by a public denunciation from the city pastor, Dr. Krieger himself, who accused Heinrich of being "a ringleader in the impertinent mockery of His Royal Majesty" and gave him a choice: either expulsion from the gymnasium or repetition of the school year. Crushed, Heinrich brought his father the bad news.

In a seething rage, Gustav announced to his son that his formal education was over, that the humiliation of repeating the year was not to be thought of, and that he now had two further choices: he could be apprenticed to a merchant or he could be apprenticed to a craftsman.

Young Heinrich Hilgard was as liberal as the next scion of the *haute bourgeoisie*, but he was both ambitious and aware of class prejudices, and he knew that the only way to real success in Germany lay along the elite educational track: first the gymnasium, then the university. Abandoning all hope of a gymnasium education meant a "lifelong degradation" to the artisan or merchant class. Desperate, he thought of a possible solution, a French boarding college some fifty miles away, where well-to-do Zweibrücken families sometimes sent their problem sons. Resorting once again to his surest rhetorical strategy, his mother, Heinrich succeeded in winning his father's grudging approval of this banishment. It was decided that Heinrich would depart a month early, thus gaining time to bring his French up to speed.

The college, a semimilitary academy with a strict regimen, was located in the Alsatian town of Phalsbourg, which lies on a high plateau in the Vosges Mountains above Strasbourg. In September 1849 Heinrich traveled unaccompanied to this foreign land and his new life. He romantically envisioned himself as a political exile, and on his way to the school he visited another political exile, his uncle Friedrich Hilgard, late of the Palatinate provisional government and now residing, with good reason, in Alsace.

When he reached Phalsbourg, the young martyr to the revolution was appalled by the conditions he found in the school. It was dirty, dilapidated, and primitive, and it promised to be quite cold during the imminent winter. There were communal troughs where all personal washing took place, and what he had heard about "the omnipresence in France of certain vermin" (probably bedbugs) turned out to be all too true. Moreover, his first night's stay provided him with an object lesson in democratic principles. The dormitory was not yet ready, so he was given a single room. Led by his upbringing to expect the equivalent of room service, he placed his muddy boots and soiled traveling clothes outside his door. The next morning they were still there, where and as he'd left them.

Heinrich's stint in the Phalsbourg college was dismal, hard, uncomfortable, but strangely satisfying and unarguably successful. Despite his low opinion of some of his teachers, he did well and learned much in his courses—classical languages, mathematics, French grammar and literature, singing, drawing, gym, and religion—making great strides in French, at last understanding mathematics, and even discovering that he was not helplessly behind in Latin and Greek, as he had been in Zweibrücken. He found the food revolting and the conditions insalubrious, yet he grew several inches, went from puny to strapping, and remained comparatively healthy for a couple of years. He considered his classmates unsavory ("As everyone knows, the French do not distinguish themselves by their personal hygiene") and morally objectionable—in later life, he never seemed so exquisitely, purblindly, paranoidally Teutonic as when he complained of "French complacency," of the way the French felt "superior to Germans"—yet he was proud to achieve a certain standing among his fellows and to act as the leader in several pranks, the best of which was the definitive plugging of the dreaded trumpet used to blast the sleeping students into consciousness every morning. When he returned home for Easter vacation, he was the object of universal admiration, astonished his father with his French, looked smashing in his school uniform, and could perhaps be forgiven for a bit of self-satisfied preening. Gustav, visibly proud, went for walks with his son and promised to send him to the gymnasium in Speyer for the next school year. Political subjects were not discussed.

Heinrich sailed through his final exams at Phalsbourg and returned to the Palatinate brimming with self-confidence. He had escaped a commercial career, averted educational and social disaster, and mollified his father. In the autumn of 1850 he left for Speyer, where he would complete his preparatory school education while living with his widowed grandmother and spinster aunt in the beloved old house on the Königsplatz.

Henry Villard was to look back on these two years in Speyer as "perhaps the happiest I ever spent." Although he achieved only a moderate degree of academic success, he still managed to remain on good terms with his father, and he grew increasingly pleased with himself and his prospects for the future. He formed no close friendships in the gymnasium in Speyer, just as he had formed none in the college in Phalsbourg. He could be happy without the right friends; he couldn't be happy with the wrong friends. He would recall giving up a friend because of "certain revelations" about his moral character. Heinrich was (and remained) too choosy, too critical, too demanding to be easily satisfied. His standards were so impossibly lofty and his expectations so unrealistically high that he was inevitably doomed to disappointment. Another way of looking at the matter is that he was breathtakingly priggish and snobbish. Any close friend of his had to combine good looks, proper manners, enlightened views, and "inner purity."

What he was looking for was ideal friendships, of the kind exalted in the boys' tales and bildungsromans of the German Romantic period, wherein it was possible to find physical, mental, and moral perfection all united in a single character. What is noteworthy is not his failure to find a friend like this but his belief that he was somehow worthy of such a paragon. Heinrich had won his own good opinion, and despite some doubtful moments he would never really lose it. These two happy years, spent just out of his father's reach in the home of his adoring grandmother and aunt, were for him a particularly complacent phase, during which he was constantly overestimating himself. He spent a lot of time in idealistic dreams, filled with notions for improving the world while professing complete contempt for it.

Heinrich's maturing interest in literature during this time led him to read many of the works of such renowned German authors as Goethe, Schiller, and Heinrich Heine. He loved most of all Schiller's intense, high-minded dramas, passionate meditations on personal and political freedom, and he was almost equally struck by Heine's lyrical and satirical poems, with their mingled sweetness and pungency and their evocation of disillusioned exile. He also admired the popular contemporary author Karl Gutzkow, whose rambling, windy, vaguely liberal novels and plays today seem badly dated but were widely praised in his lifetime.

Like many of his countrymen, Heinrich appears to have taken a few steps toward the political right during this time. Many factors can have contributed to this shift: the ignominious collapse of the republican movement throughout Germany; Heinrich's growing class consciousness; the familial, academic, and social success he'd achieved by toeing the line; his contentedness with the present state of things. For whatever reasons, his attitudes and behavior took on a distinctly aristocratic air. He became something of a dandy, much occupied with fancy dress and society balls. He took lessons in "the horseman's noble art" and worked to improve his dancing skills. He developed a crush on one Elise Mühlberger, a captivating fifteen-year-old from "a middleclass but well-to-do family," as he described her in his memoirs, using that "but" to justify his setting his sights on a mere daughter of the undistinguished bourgeoisie. He suffered all the pangs of adolescent love—loitering around her house, trying to catch a glimpse of her at a window, or laying careful plans for a "chance" meeting with her and her family in a park or pleasure resort—but had to give her up because he could not bridge the gap of their difference in class. The fortunate Elise knew nothing of her suitor, nor of his withdrawal of his suit, for social barriers had prevented Heinrich from securing an introduction to her and they had never exchanged a word. At a dance he met two sisters, apparently of the right class and famous for their beauty and political radicalism, but he "found their emancipated ways repellent." Most telling of all, he lobbied unsuccessfully to invite to his graduation ball the ex-king of Bavaria, Ludwig I, who had been forced in 1848 to abdicate in favor of his son. Heinrich thought the old man's presence would give the proper cachet to the festivities.

During his last year at the gymnasium, Heinrich wrote an essay that won a prize. Never one to underestimate his prospects of success in any endeavor, he immediately saw opening up before him a glowing future as a famous German author. Heinrich was certain that he had the ability to make a living with his pen, and as he later rather smugly pointed out, the future was not to prove him completely wrong. Literature had always had great appeal to him; now writing became his chief ambition.

Some of Heinrich's other activities in his senior year were rather less edifying. Along with students from several prominent families, he joined a forbidden fraternity and developed a taste for carousing that did little honor to his idealism. On one evening the carousing was followed by vandalism, relatively minor but sufficiently serious to put the police on the case. Heinrich denied his involvement, but this patent lie earned him a stiff punishment: one day in the local jail, with nothing on the menu except bread and water. So great was his shame that he had his first thoughts of emigrating to America. To his surprise, however, he did easy time (friends smuggled in food) and received indulgent treatment from his parents. His mother even seemed pleased that her son was moving in such refined circles.

Heinrich and his parents engaged in lengthy discussions on the subject of his university career. Theology and medicine were out of the question; law was an outside possibility, but it bored him, and besides, his lawyer father advised against it on the grounds that advancement in the legal field was unacceptably slow. Heinrich proposed to study the subjects that most interested him—literature and fine arts—and suggested that his father could support him until literary success made him financially independent. Gustav replied to this naive proposal by declaring that he had two other children and could not in conscience deprive them of their rightful inheritance by subsidizing an "aesthete"; moreover he didn't believe in "aesthetics" anyway. He made it clear that Heinrich was a burden that he, Gustav, was determined to lay down as soon as possible, and to that end he wanted the boy to decide on a course of study that would lead, smoothly and quickly, to a paying profession.

They concluded, rather wearily, that the way out of this impasse passed through the *Polytechnikum,* the technical university in Munich. German industry was at that time in the course of its first great expansion; the Hilgards had many acquaintances whose sons had got their degrees from the technical university and gone on to fill important industrial positions. Heinrich liked the idea of filling an important position, but polytechnical schools were a social notch below the university, where all his friends were going, and despite his aptitude for mathematics, the thought of studying industrial subjects left him cold. The last word, however, was not his, and in November 1852, after a stern lecture from his father, the two of them set out for Munich, where Gustav wanted to oversee his son's enrollment in the *Polytechnikum* and find him proper living quarters. Heinrich wept when he left the family home in Zweibrücken, and he would have wept harder had he known that he had set foot in it for the last time, and that he would never see his mother's loving face again.

*   ▪   ▪   ▪

Father and son Hilgard stayed ten days in the "best guesthouse" in Munich, and Heinrich, always ready to be impressed by the best inn or the best society, marveled at the size and grandeur of the place and thrilled to the noble names in the guest book. Gustav found the boy rooms in a respectable boardinghouse, secured him entrée to some of the better families, delivered a final lecture, and bade his son farewell. Confronted by the solitude of his sudden autonomy, Heinrich wept again.

After a few months of conscientious application to his studies, he took a few heedless, but at some level purposeful, steps on a road that led straight downhill. A noted psychoanalyst has observed that "the crisis in a young man's life may be reached exactly when he half-realizes that he is fatally overcommitted to what he is not." Thrust into a situation requiring a degree of responsible behavior for which his immaturity, inexperience, and inclinations left him totally unprepared, and precipitated by his peremptory father into a struggle for his own identity, Heinrich proceeded to stumble and writhe until, at a terrible cost, he bought his freedom.

He began by enrolling in the University of Munich and signing up for courses with a well-known poet and a respected art critic, naturally neglecting to inform his father of this bold move. Two months of technical studies had been almost more than he could bear; now he abandoned them altogether. His next step was far worse. Heinrich became a *Korpsstudent,* a member of Franconia, the most fashionable and most expensive of the student corps, or societies, then much favored by the sons of the German upper classes. So completely had Heinrich lost faith in his ability to communicate with his father that he neglected to inform him of this step as well, even though Gustav himself had belonged to such a fraternity in his student days.

These corps, apparently formed to allow university students to emulate some of the worst aspects of military life, were a strange outgrowth of German society. Life in a corps was highly regimented and ritualized, and there were two main areas of concentration: the *Mensur,* or student duel, and the alcoholic debauch. A duel to the death was well-nigh impossible—thick pads covered every part of the duelist's body but the face, left bare to facilitate acquisition of the prestigious dueling scars—but the frequent, carefully scheduled benders, which one sardonic historian calls "the more dubious half of the corps' prescription for personal enrichment and noble cast of mind," could pose a genuine hazard to one's health.

Part of Heinrich recognized these time-wasting, reprehensible inanities for what they were, but another part loved the panache, the high spirits, the camaraderie, the prestige, the uniforms, and the access to the "better levels" of society. His idealism, his unfadingly rose-tinted lenses, his almost endearing faith that whatever he did was by definition valuable prevented him from seeing that his membership in the Franconia was a turning point, the beginning of the end of his university career.

Although Heinrich no doubt participated in the odd duel, his face remained unscarred. His funds, on the other hand, badly nicked by his registration fees and then thrust through by his corps expenses, were close to death. His bills and his debts mounted. Guilt, shame, the dread of inevitable discovery, broken resolutions to do better, and moments of insight into the paltriness of his life began to weigh on his mind. A fever that was circulating among his fellows (no doubt weakened by their manifold exertions) struck him down, so heavily that he checked into the hospital. He wrote to his parents, who worried and wrote to his landlady; she replied at generous length, complaining about Heinrich's unpaid back rent, his irregular life since joining the student corps, his neglect of his studies. Puzzled and angry, Gustav contacted the *Polytechnikum,* where Heinrich hadn't been seen for months, and then the jig was all the way up. Heinrich wrote a full confession and apology, the furious reply to which was that he must leave Munich within forty-eight hours and return home.

Heinrich thought again about emigration, but instead recruited a family friend to intercede with his father and arrange a meeting in Speyer. There Gustav once more relented, but on his own terms: he would not carry out his threat to put Heinrich in the army; Heinrich could continue his university career, but at the more sedate University of Würzburg, where he must study law; his days as a *Korpsstudent* were over; and he must pay all his debts. Gustav must by now have regarded his former objections to Heinrich's studying law as beside the point, which was to get the boy educated and off his hands. Advancement in the legal profession was slow, but it was better than no advancement—and no profession—at all.

By April 1853, refreshed and repentant, Heinrich was settled in Würzburg and ready to start his new life. For a while, as before, he lived simply and studied hard, but soon his legal studies became as obnoxious to him as those at the *Polytechnikum.* Scheming to find a way to study literature, he started neglecting his courses and returned to his reading of the German classics. A fellow student at this time remembered him as sober and quiet, reading avidly and spending little, but not studying law. Heinrich worked on various literary projects, planning to justify himself by early success. His self-confidence remained impregnable; his time, however, was running out.

August was approaching, and with it the end of the semester. By now he owed his landlady for months of room and board, and it was impossible to return home so deeply in debt. He tried unsuccessfully to borrow money from a couple of contemporaries, setting out his plight in excruciating detail. When there was no response, he realized his miscalculation and turned to a distant but rich older relative, a kind of second cousin–in-law. After some hesitation, this kindly gentleman agreed to the loan, but insisted that he must tell Heinrich's father when next they met, a matter of a week or ten days. In a cold sweat at the thought of what he had to do, Heinrich saw that his only chance was to flee; he was certain that his father, as soon as he learned about all this recent backsliding and begging, would carry out an oft-repeated threat and deliver him, incorrigible young recidivist that he was, into the untender hands of the Bavarian army.

By now quite disconnected from reality, Heinrich tried a last, ludicrous ploy: a sudden dash to Dresden, home of the author Karl Gutzkow. Heinrich would produce some of his manuscripts; the famous writer would at once recognize their worth; Gustav would bow to this expert validation and allow his son to embark on a literary career. Heinrich paid off his landlady, packed some clothes, books, and about a hundred manuscript pages containing some poems and his observations on a variety of "physical, literary, and philosophical questions," and set off to dazzle the unsuspecting Gutzkow.

Arrived in Dresden, and realizing that the point of borrowing money is to use it, Heinrich checked into one of the very best hotels. He then spent a couple of days admiring the art and architecture of that once beautiful city. Early the following afternoon, he gathered up his manuscript, focused his will, and presented himself at the door of Gutzkow's apartment. The famous man was in his early forties, chronically ill and hence somewhat cadaverous, soft voiced, and mild mannered. As Heinrich, at some length, was declaring his purpose, he saw on the writer's face the beginnings of an indulgent smile. Still smiling, Gutzkow asked Heinrich to state his age and education; the response to this made him smile even more broadly. When he asked how he was supposed to judge Heinrich's talent, the boy recognized his cue and brought forth his manuscript, where-upon the writer at last laughed aloud: "Aha, of course, in the usual way, with the first fruits of your labors!" Then, without so much as touching the manuscript, which remained clutched in Heinrich's hands, Gutzkow made a gentle but unequivocal little speech. He received at least one such visit a week, from young people all over Germany. He was flattered by Heinrich's high opinion but he felt obliged to tell him, manuscript unseen, that he was as yet too young and too little educated to be able to produce valuable work. Heinrich's wisest course would be to complete his studies at the university; by that time the degree of his talent would be clearer to him as well as to others. And lastly, writing was a miserable, precarious profession, a lifelong struggle even for the successful, an unquenchable source of dissatisfaction and despair. "No bread," said he, "is harder than a German writer's." That was one more dream dashed; Heinrich caught the next train to Hamburg.

Hamburg: an open door, so to speak, through which one might walk into another world. Heinrich checked into the usual first-class hotel and considered his options. He could go home to Zweibrücken and throw himself upon the mercy of his stern and wrathful father, and then like a mass of wet clay be slapped and pummeled into yet another unnatural shape, or he could get on a boat and put many thousands of miles between himself, on the one hand, and his father and the Bavarian army, on the other. A third option, offering his literary services to a Hamburg newspaper, lasted no longer than it took to get a quick rejection. A count of his dwindling funds shocked him deeply, even inspiring him with the luminous idea of moving to a cheaper hotel. Then he got down to studying destinations. Australia? North, South, or Central America? After three days of pondering, he chose the United States. He rejoiced in its democracy, he admired its beauties in the travel books, he considered his many relatives who were there, but what really decided him was the price—the United States was the cheapest ticket of all.

Heinrich bought one, which gave him the right to a second-class passage from Hamburg to New York on a three-masted clipper, the bark *Nordamerika*. Remembering tales of the winters in the northern

United States, he sold his summer clothes, some books, and a watch to buy a winter coat. The next day, August 27, 1853, he embarked, bringing with him the new coat, the suit on his back, a second pair of pants, some underwear, six books, his manuscript, and one and a half Prussian thalers.

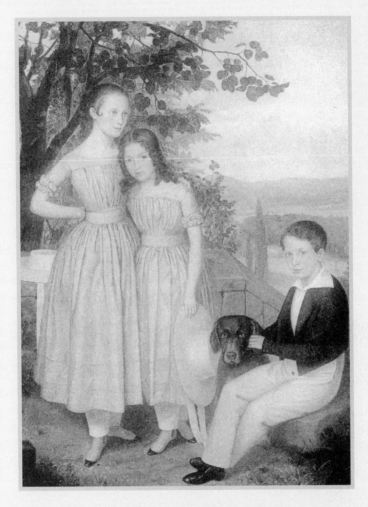

ANNA, EMMA, AND HEINRICH HILGARD,
C. 1844, BY HOFFMANN.

Photograph of an oil painting of Henry Villard (Heinrich Hilgard) with his sisters.

Alexandra Villard de Borchgrave Private Collection.

2

The Sorrows of Young Henry

There is a time in every man's education when he arrives at the convic-
tion that envy is ignorance; that imitation is suicide; that he must take
himself for better or worse as his portion; that though the wide universe
is full of good, no kernel of nourishing corn can come to him but
through his toil bestowed on that plot of ground which is given to him
to till. The power which resides in him is new in nature, and none but
he knows what that is which he can do, nor does he know until he has
tried.

RALPH WALDO EMERSON,
"Self-Reliance"

The voyager was eighteen years old, and he had chosen to abandon his homeland and his family. Furthermore, he had notified no one of his whereabouts or of his imminent departure,
not any of his friends, not even his sisters. He had pulled himself out
of his past as one pulls a knife from a sheath, completely free and
clear. Filled with changing fantasies that resembled one another
chiefly in their impracticability, he knew nothing about what he
would become except that he would choose it for himself.

He had, however, one absolute certainty: he had done those closest to him, particularly his mother, a terrible wrong. In Gutzkow's
Aphorisms, a compilation of more or less pithy moral, philosophical,
and literary reflections, there occurs the following sentence: "Mis-
treating a mother's heart is robbing a church." If Henry Villard ever
came across this pronouncement from the pen of the man he had
once wildly envisioned as his mentor and protector, it must have

given him pause. For the time being, however, there was no pausing; the *Nordamerika*, scudding and bobbing, pitching and rolling, moved steadily westward, and during the early days of the voyage the young landlubber's stomach was queasier than his conscience.

Before long, both had settled down and were ready for the long haul. Although Heinrich well knew that his actions were difficult to forgive, the self-confident enthusiasm with which he always began every new undertaking cut short his sojourn in the enervating precincts of guilt. As a mature man, he was able to look upon his decision to leave home and country and sail to America as a "charitable stroke of luck." What he had needed for his "moral rescue," he wrote, was the pitiless and unyielding discipline that he was to undergo "in the long, painful struggle for material existence." But now, despite the taint of filial guilt, Heinrich was the picture of innocence—youthful, eager, inexperienced, and trusting. Dreams shrouded the means he would use, but he saw his end clearly enough: to prove his father wrong about his character, to achieve rapid material success and thus justify himself in his father's eyes.

A quintessential figure of German Romanticism is the wanderer between two worlds. The romantic young wanderer Heinrich Hilgard, as he traveled from one world to another, arrived at a new identity as well. He was not so dreamily alienated as to have lost all practical sense; determined to remain untraceable and therefore unmilitarized, he judged it necessary to change his name. He had had a schoolmate at Phalsbourg, a Belgian, one Henri Villard, whose name was close enough to "Heinrich Hilgard" to cause a minimum of wrenching. So Heinrich took it as his own, slightly anglicizing it, and by the time he stepped ashore in New York, he was calling himself Henry Villard.

Meanwhile, the first of his trials was the voyage itself. During one stretch the ship lay becalmed for two weeks; this tedium was succeeded by an extended period of heavy gales. Meteorological vicissitudes, however, were as nothing beside Heinrich's other discomforts, all of them rooted in the unacceptable but irreversible fact that he was traveling in second class. He and his fifteen fellow second-class passengers occupied a single large stateroom, furnished with sixteen beds and, in their midst, a long table, whereon all meals were taken; all eating, sleeping, dressing, and undressing took place in this room. Washing was carried on yet more publicly, on the deck, in metal washbasins. Soap rations were exiguous, and there was never enough water. Linen was even scarcer; the beds featured bare mattresses and uncased pillows, and no napkins or tablecloths were ever seen. The food was wretched, carelessly served, unfairly shared, and scanty. Worst of all were Heinrich's fellow passengers, an uncouth, quarrelsome, vulgar lot far inferior to him in social class, education, refinement, and intelligence. A lawyer and a landowner were the only two exceptions to this general loutishness. Spending nearly eight weeks surrounded by people so common, so far below his station (as he later described them), proved to be more than he could bear, so Heinrich sought the company of the twelve first-class passengers. The 230 souls crowded into steerage accommodations remained, for the most part, invisible and unthought of.

Heinrich's search for better shipboard society did not prove to be an unmitigated success. Among the first-class passengers was a Russian who introduced himself as a doctor. Upon learning that Heinrich had been suffering for some time from an aching tooth, the doctor offered to pull it for him. Heinrich must certainly have been in a great deal of pain, because he assented to this suggestion, which involved unanesthetized dental surgery performed upon him by a stranger on the open sea. To the younger man's lifelong chagrin, however, the doctor pulled the wrong tooth. Heinrich was left with a doubly aching jaw and, perhaps, mixed feelings about the Russian elite.

He spent a great deal of time on board perusing guidebooks and elaborating schemes. He felt most attracted to "the mighty rivers, the endless forests, the measureless prairies, and the towering mountain ranges" of the American West, the vast region between Missouri and the Pacific Ocean. It was these Western states and territories, the guidebooks asserted, that offered the most possibilities and the most promise. This appealed to Heinrich's youthful adventurousness, his curiosity about the unknown, his energetic imagination. He fantasized about striking gold and returning to his family in triumph, and was sorely tempted by the invitation of one of his traveling companions, a young lawyer, to accompany him on his way to California. Heinrich's lack of funds—he was down to a few pennies—and proper clothing prevented him from accepting. Despite his naturally sanguine temperament and the inconveniences of the voyage, Heinrich began to dread the end of it, and his heart was in his throat as he walked down the gangway to one of the many piers along South Street, at the southeastern tip of Manhattan Island, on October 18, 1853. He had some cause for concern: he was a mere boy, eighteen and a half years old, without experience or discernible skills in any sort of work; he could neither understand nor speak a word of English; his net worth was a few cents; and the only people in the country who knew him and might help him were his relatives in southern Illinois, a thousand miles away.

■   ■   ■

When Henry Villard (as we shall call him from now on) stepped ashore in New York, he entered one of the most astounding, intimidating, multifarious, bustling, and chaotic places on the face of the earth, a city of immense, often inharmonious diversity and fierce, often unfocused energy. Then as now, but even more conspicuously, the most abject poverty and ignorance existed alongside great wealth and refinement.

In 1853 only about 25 percent of Manhattan, the southernmost quarter of the island, was occupied. Buildings thinned out north of Fourteenth Street, and above Twenty-third Street there was open country. As more and more people, both immigrants and Americans, poured into the city, its elite citizens beat a stately but constant retreat northward, moving "uptown"—which seems to have started around Washington Square—and leaving lower Manhattan to the rabble and stain of commerce, to gouging landlords, their agents, and their victims (who, of course, were mostly immigrants), to the filthy tenements, immigrant slums, and insalubriousness of the city's poorer sections.

The assault on the senses, especially in the poorer and commercial districts of the city, must have been overwhelming. The dense traffic in the surrounding waters, served by the band of wharves, piers, and docks that went right around the southern rim of the island, meant that the activity of loading and unloading, delivering and picking up, was unceasing. The sidewalks boiled with people, and the streets were packed with all manner of conveyances, each of them adding its bit to the general cacophony: the clash of iron hooves and iron-rimmed wheels on stone, the creaking and groaning of springs and chassis, the shouts of irate drivers. Every weekday, an average of fifteen thousand vehicles clattered and banged past the corner of Broadway and Fulton. Only a small portion of the city had sewers, and the pervasive, mephitic stench of fetid sumps and overflowing privies was an aspect of everyday life that is, fortunately, difficult for us to imagine.

Germans made up about a third of the more than 3 million immigrants who arrived in New York between 1840 and 1860. Only the Irish landed in greater numbers. Most immigrants passed through the city to other destinations, but enough remained to cause a steady expansion in the population, which by 1853 had moved well past six hundred thousand and was increasing daily. As a result of this inundation, by 1855 two of every three adults in Manhattan had been born outside the United States.

The population wasn't the only feature of New York life that was growing explosively during the early 1850s. A great economic boom was producing a wealthy elite that included dozens of millionaires by 1855 (there had been only two, ten years earlier) and thousands of individuals and families with substantial fortunes, especially when we consider that all dollar amounts should be multiplied by a factor of at least thirty in order to arrive at a rough estimate of their equivalent value in 2000.

By 1853, New York City was the third-largest German-speaking metropolis in the world, surpassed only by Berlin and Vienna. As in all immigrant groups, most of the Germans who arrived in New York were poor, and many were also unhealthy, unstable, and in need of public assistance. These were the people who had come to the New World for economic reasons, driven from home by bad harvests and the same potato blight that caused the even more numerous Irish emigration. In addition, however, the German exodus included a goodly number of political emigrants, leftists, and radicals whose revolutions had failed. Some of them were well-educated professional men, much given to stating their passionately held political opinions in public. Others lower in social rank felt just as passionately, for example one Frederick Bultman of Hanover, who decided to emigrate at age thirteen when he went to the tax collector's office to pay his father's taxes, saw the gilded royal coach, and realized that artisans like his father had financed this royal display. For a great many German immigrants, "the United States was first and foremost the land of *kein König da,* 'no king there.' "

German immigrants in general—Henry Villard was no exception—were highly politicized in comparison to other groups, and less conservative in their social and religious views. Freethinking intellectuals, socialists, and outright Marxists were among the German community leaders in New York City, and German-Americans, including the great majority who passed through New York and settled among the large German communities in Pennsylvania, Ohio, Indiana, and Illinois, tended to line up on the left, or liberal, side of the political issues of the day, first and foremost among which was slavery.

A related phenomenon among immigrants from Germany derived from their extreme socialization, their inborn fondness for clustering together and for group activities, especially as carried on in taverns and restaurants, political clubs, singing societies, sporting groups, and the like. What better setting for ardent political discussions than a large, noisy beer hall, what better stimulus than a brimming stein? German life and activity in New York City was centered in *Kleindeutschland,* Little Germany, a compact but sizable area in the eastern part of lower Manhattan, comprising much of the Bowery and significant portions of what would later come to be known as Little Italy, Chinatown, and the Lower East Side; the changing names reflect the constant ethnic flux that characterizes New York to this day. Nearby William Street and its surrounding neighborhood formed the hub of German commercial activity in the city.

Henry Villard's plight, therefore, was serious but not quite desperate; a large, homogeneous section of New York, conveniently close to his landing place, was filled with tens of thousands of people whose native language was his own, as well as with innumerable German businesses, shops, and societies of every kind, including one, the well-organized, efficient German Emigrant Society, specifically constituted to help people in his condition. There were dozens of German newspapers, one of which, the *New Yorker Staats-Zeitung* (its editor had fought on the barricades in Vienna in 1848), claimed the largest circulation of any German-language newspaper in the world.

Three months before Henry's arrival, President Franklin Pierce had inaugurated, on a site near what is now Bryant Park and the New York Public Library, the Crystal Palace at the first United States World's Fair. Conforming to the ephemeral nature of many large structures in New York, no matter how impressive, this one, "a slightly smaller model of the famous exhibition hall in London," was to burn to the ground in October of 1858. During its five-year existence it attracted millions of visitors from all over the world, who came to New York to admire the latest marvels produced by science, technology, and industry in a period of stunning technological progress.

Newspapers from October 18 to October 20, 1853, Henry Villard's first three days in America, give some idea of what New York offered its more prosperous inhabitants. Hotels and rooming houses advertised room and board at prices ranging from $5 to $10 dollars per week. A recent performance of Verdi's *I Lombardi* at Niblo's Garden was soundly panned and the composer characterized as "one of those unfortunate men of genius who fail to excite the sympathy of a general audience." A concert held at Metropolitan Hall on the night of Henry's arrival promised an all-Mendelssohn program of daunting length, with the *Scotch* Symphony, excerpts from the oratorio *Elijah,* the violin concerto, and the incidental music to Shakespeare's *Midsummer Night's Dream* forming part one of the two-part program (admission was fifty cents; reserved seats cost a dollar). The "new and wonderfully successful dramatic version" of the best-selling novel of the nineteenth century, *Uncle Tom's Cabin,* was beginning a long and successful run at the National Theatre. For less highbrow tastes, Wood's Minstrels and Negro Delineators were performing at 444 Broadway; up the street at the Stuyvesant Institute, Signor Blitz, "Professor of Natural Magic," was dazzling the crowds with his ventriloquistic skills and his "500 LEARNED CANARY BIRDS"; the multicultural Chinese Assembly Rooms featured Buckley's Ethiopian Serenaders.

For the present, however, such diversions were beyond Henry Villard's ken, and well beyond his possibilities. Avoiding the packs of his countrymen whose profession it was to pounce like wolves on new arrivals from Germany and fleece them bare with promises of cheap lodging, employment assistance, gemütlichkeit, and the rest, Henry attached himself to a group of first- and second-class passengers who were going to a highly recommended hotel, the Stadt Constanz, a few blocks down Maiden Lane and right on William Street.

After boldly checking into the hotel (room and board $5 a week), Henry fell into one of the depressive states that were part of a discernible pattern in his life. The wings of his self-confidence would bear him beyond reality or reason, he would take an incredible chance, bet all he had, and then somehow he would realize how far he'd gone, how much he'd gambled, how disastrous his predicament was, and this realization would plunge him into despair, his faith in his luck would crumble away. And yet, no matter how steep his descent, nor how deep the abyss, it would rarely take more than a glint of hope, a tiny glimmer, to restore all his conviction and all his faith.

His shipboard friend the California-bound lawyer noticed Henry's gloom—the youngster may not have been at pains to conceal it—and having learned a thing or two about Henry in the course of a nearly eight-week voyage, knew full well the cause of his dejection. He generously offered a loan of $20, which Henry accepted with a whole heart. In his view, he now had at least three and possibly four weeks of room and board secured, and his relief allowed him "to look the future straight in the face." He made two resolutions: to start seeking employment immediately and to try to contact his relatives in the West.

He began carrying out his resolutions the next day. Though he had come to the United States without knowing the addresses of any of his Hilgard relatives in Illinois, he knew that a distant cousin, Dr. George Engelmann, was a prominent physician in St. Louis. Henry wrote a letter to his uncle Theodor Hilgard, in Illinois, and sent it to Dr. Engelmann with a request to forward it. Then Henry strode forth from his hotel and joined the busy throngs, blending in easily with the hundreds and hundreds of young people who were doing exactly what he was doing: pounding the sidewalks of New York, looking for a job.

While on this quest, Henry saw much of the city and was struck by "the intense commercial activity" and by the black servants who waited on the guests lounging in some of the best hotels. The finest of all the hotels was the Astor House, on Broadway near City Hall, "the nation's most prestigious hostelry." Henry and some of his fellow boarders from the Stadt Constanz decided to dine at the Astor House and see this world-famous establishment, "one of the wonders of the age," for themselves. Their splurge, alas, brought them little satisfaction. The hotel staff spoke neither German nor French, only English; the bill of fare was likewise written in that incomprehensible tongue; the dining room was neither so large nor so richly decorated as those in certain large continental hotels; and the food, revoltingly enough, was served American style, all at once and in great abundance. Stunned and embarrassed, the unfortunate Europeans couldn't enjoy anything, finished as quickly as they could, paid their seventy-five cents apiece, and "withdrew in disgust."

Things were different at the Stadt Constanz. The landlord, Max Weber, was yet another ex-revolutionary, a former officer in the army of the grand duchy of Baden who had been forced to emigrate after participating in the 1849 uprising. Almost every evening, in the tap-room of Weber's hotel, large groups of German refugees held loud political discussions in authentic, old-country beer-house style. Henry eagerly attended these sessions, but he was discouraged in his hopes because many of the participants (some of whom had never ventured outside of *Kleindeutschland* and knew no Americans at all) railed vociferously against the United States and called its vaunted liberty a sham.

William Street contained many other German establishments—boardinghouses, hotels, taverns, and dance halls. One nearby hotel, run by another former revolutionary, a jovial barrister from Baden, had a "low character" and was filled with "adventurers of both sexes." The dance halls, however, offered an even "lower grade of entertainment" and were staffed by "suspicious-looking female attendants." We may wonder in vain whether Henry Villard, when he wrote down these warily virtuous observations as a respectable middle-aged man, was accurately reporting the feelings that his nineteen-year-old self had harbored toward such hardworking girls. We have nothing but his words to guide us.

Henry was determined to find work. He applied without success to the Bavarian consul, the emigrant society, mercantile firms, drugstores, restaurants, even a couple of beer halls. He had no experience, no references, and no English. He fancied that his "perhaps too genteel appearance" worked against him, but the other factors were probably decisive enough. Nearly three weeks went by, and his efforts, though persistent, availed him nothing; his money was fast disappearing. Then, at last, the letter that he was waiting for arrived.

It was from Uncle Theodor, and its contents were both good and bad. On the one hand, Henry's notions of visiting his relatives in Illinois received a distinct rebuff. Theodor, like his brother Gustav, was a stern man unswayed by consanguinity or compassion; he told his nephew to stay well away from Belleville until his relatives "clearly understood the reason" for his coming to America. On the other hand, the letter contained a bank draft for $50.

Saved once again, Henry repaid his loan, bought a cheap but warm winter suit (his overcoat wouldn't be enough for the swiftly approaching winter), and set out for Cincinnati, chosen because of its large German population. The trip was long and unpleasant. One traveled by riverboat, rail, and ferry to Philadelphia, by rail to Pittsburgh, and then by steamboat to Cincinnati. Henry bought the cheapest tickets possible and suffered from discomfort, odors, hunger, and the presence of his lower-class fellow sufferers. At last the *City of Pittsburgh* docked in Cincinnati, the Queen City of the West.

By now back down to $3, Henry had to settle for almost totally objectionable accommodations in an inn that was "the worst-looking tavern" he had ever seen but offered room and board for $2.50 a week. To his great relief, he was able to wash up, and then he set off for a walk in the city.

Henry headed for the part of town with the densest concentration of Germans, who made up about a third of the inhabitants. In the bar of the Hotel Palatinate, run by a man he had known as a policeman in Zweibrücken, Henry met several other Rhenish Bavarians who had emigrated to Cincinnati. Among them were political refugees who had fled the Palatinate after the 1849 revolution, an editor of the leading German newspaper, a medical doctor who had been Gustav Hilgard's fellow student at the University of Würzburg, and other respectable gentlemen, all of whom offered Henry a great deal of advice but little hope of obtaining gainful employment. As members of the educated upper middle class, they deplored the notion that one of their own might be reduced to performing manual labor, yet they agreed that Henry's education was too general to be of use to him in finding a suitable job. The wisest course, they unanimously suggested, would be for Henry to go to his relatives in southern Illinois, spend the next two years learning English, and then look about him for employment befitting his station.

Henry was too ashamed, or too proud, to admit to these counselors that his relatives had no intention of receiving him, so he limited his demurrals to the truthful observation that he had not enough money to pay his way to Illinois. Finally, the day before his hotel bill came due, Henry's father's former fellow student gave him an envelope containing $15 and a letter to a steamboat agency that guaranteed his passage down the Ohio River to its mouth at Cairo and then up the Mississippi to St. Louis, across the river from

Belleville. Thanking the older man profusely for the loan, which he promised as always to repay at the earliest possible moment, Henry took his leave.

Now Henry found himself in a serious quandary. He naturally felt an obligation to follow the program recommended to him by his benefactor, but his pride revolted at the idea of appearing as a beggar before his relatives. And even if they should receive him, what then? Wouldn't that put an end to his freedom? And wouldn't this surrender serve only to confirm what Henry most wanted to confute, his father's low opinion of him? Henry had not yet suffered enough to contemplate such a capitulation seriously. A fellow passenger on the *Nordamerika,* en route to his brother's farm in Indiana, had invited Henry to visit him and implied (or so it seemed to Henry) that there would be a place for him, and work to be done. Snatching at this vague hope, Henry decided to disregard his ticket to St. Louis, travel instead a few miles down the Ohio River to Lawrenceburg, Indiana, and from there take a train to the vicinity of his shipmate's brother's farm.

With this stubborn decision, Henry condemned himself to a year of wandering, hardship, humiliation, and travail. A few of his adventures seem like picaresque escapades; more often, however, his struggle for survival offers a sobering glimpse into the soul-crushing drudgery and primitive living conditions that were the lot of unskilled laborers in provincial America in the mid–nineteenth century. Under the bludgeonings of necessity, Henry's fastidiousness, his consciousness of his superiority, and his faith in the intangible promise of the future all underwent significant modification; throughout his ordeal, however, his luck, like his optimism, though they might occasionally wobble, never failed him altogether.

When the teenaged immigrant, lightly burdened with his meager possessions, stepped off the train from Lawrenceburg at a stop somewhere in southeastern Indiana, he felt "like Robinson Crusoe, stranded in the wilderness." The narrow platform he stood on was new and rudimentary; there was no station building, nor any other building of any description; before and behind him stretched the empty tracks; and all around him, except for the narrow swath hacked out for the railroad, encroached the primeval forest. No other human being, not one habitation, was in sight. A stranger in a strange land, he picked up his bag and set off down the tracks.

The brothers, when he finally found them, had sold their farm and were planning to seek their fortune west of the Mississippi River. Henry was forced to take lodgings in a country inn "of a very primitive character" run by a German farmer. This place, a forerunner of the truck stop, featured a continual traffic of teamsters arriving and departing, community sleeping in a dormitory (under necessity, guests were expected to double up), passable food, and extremely low rates.

With winter nearly upon him and his money gone, Henry entered, for a while, a sort of fatalistic trance. His desultory ramblings in the surrounding forest and farm country had wrecked his boots and emphasized his isolation. The little work available was farmwork, for which he deemed himself unsuited, and in truth this part of the state was too sparsely populated to offer many opportunities. By Christmas 1853 Henry was homesick, lonely, ill shod, inadequately clothed, and in arrears with his room and board. A week later, after New Year's, Henry confessed his plight to the farmer, his landlord, who was not surprised but reproved him for his long silence. He declared that Henry must seek work farther afield. Shivering, with blistered feet, sometimes having to fight his way through snowdrifts, Henry began walking every day to the nearest towns—the closest of which was twelve miles away—to look for a job, returning at night to his inn and an atmosphere laden with mistrust and reproach.

Henry's method in these towns was to look for concerns with German signs and inquire within. Although to us, a century and a half later, it is amazing how many German-speaking individuals, groups, and entire communities Henry encountered in his travels, his lack of English was a constant impediment during his first year, and every position he sought in these small towns required at least some knowledge of the official language of the country. At last, increasingly desperate, he met a doctor from the Palatinate who mentioned the only position he knew about in town: two German coopers, men whose business it was to make barrels and casks, needed an apprentice. "But you will hardly want to learn a trade, especially one such as this," the doctor told Henry.

Notwithstanding the truth of this observation, early in 1854, and with a heavy heart, Henry Villard indentured himself for three years to the proprietors of a cooper shop in a town he called Pennsylvaniaburg (unlocatable on present-day maps) in southeastern Indiana. He was far from convinced that his future lay in barrels, but he felt that he had no other choice.

Henry hated this situation from the start. The terms—room and board plus $50 the first year, $70 the second year, and $100 the third year—seemed to him liberal enough, so low had his expectations fallen, but to be bound for three years to "one of the lowest trades," to face "social and intellectual degradation"! He had to summon all his fortitude, not to do the work, which consisted of menial domestic labor and light help in the shop, but to endure the discomforts and outrages of his daily life. He, his two bosses, and the wife of one of them shared a small cabin made of rough-hewn logs. Henry's sleeping quarters, where the bachelor partner also slept, was a low garret, his mattress and pillow were sacking stuffed with corn husks, his covering two coarse, dirty blankets. Privacy in these cramped quarters proved impossible. The wife was a termagant given to rages that bordered on insanity, and her husband, by way of surviving these, drank heavily. Violent scenes were a daily occurrence. Furthermore, his employers were stingy and disagreeable. They refused to give him an advance for a new pair of boots, they shared "the inclination, so common with the German lower classes in this country, to seize eagerly every opportunity to make those who stood socially above them in Germany feel that they are now their equals or betters." Apparently more imbued with democratic principles than their young hireling, his employers nevertheless made him miserable with their low-life behavior, and after five weeks of "serfdom" he was about to snap.

The inevitable breakup of this misalliance came one day when, fresh from an unusually harsh scolding and sulkily drunk, Henry's uxorious boss took exception to some "trivial oversight" and insulted him with a torrent of abuse. Henry retaliated, he later claimed, by calling his employer a "low boor." We may surmise that this is but a euphemistic translation of the form of words he actually used, which were pointed enough to provoke the older man into coming at him with a stave. Henry, a well-made six-footer with youth and sobriety on his side, threw his opponent to the ground, his other employer joined the fray, and a general punch-up ensued until Henry was able to escape through the door of the shop. He left behind his overcoat, his other belongings, and his indenture.

A local pastor tried to get back Henry's things for him, but the incensed coopers refused, claiming them as damages for his broken contract. The subject of cash payment for his five weeks' work was not to be thought of. The kindly pastor gave him $2, all he could afford, and sent him on his way. Henry headed in the direction of Lawrenceburg and spent that evening in a pleasant village inn. Early the next morning he was back on the road again. It was late February, and Henry had nothing at all but the clothes on his back, yet as he strode along he was buoyant, "released from bondage," filled once again with great expectations.

Thoroughly drenched after walking nearly twenty miles in a frigid downpour, Henry finally came to the outskirts of Lawrenceburg, where luck smiled on him through the rain. The landlord of the first inn he came to was not only a native of the Palatinate but an acquaintance of Henry's family. At first, and quite reasonably, the bedraggled apparition aroused his suspicions, but once these were allayed he treated his miserable young guest with great solicitude. Thanks to his host's provision of good cheer, dry nightclothes, and a warm bed, the sometimes fragile balance of Henry's health withstood the severe trial it had undergone.

The landlord liked the young man and sympathized with his plight. Soon, despite Henry's linguistic shortcomings, he was working in the barroom attached to the inn. His generous countryman offered him new clothes, new boots, room, board, and $15 a month. More comfortable than he had been in months, and filled like the air with the promise of spring, Henry could be relatively content, even though the realization that he had now adopted "the low calling of a bar-tender" made him blush with shame.

He was not required to blush for long. He learned the simple tricks of the trade quickly and was well liked by his landlord, the latter's partner, and their German customers, but these accomplishments were not enough. When the barroom filled up with clamorous Americans, workingmen who liked a bit of repartee with their "spiritous liquors," Henry was at a loss. After ten days, his landlord reluctantly announced that he and his partner were afraid of losing their anglophone customers and had decided to let Henry go. He could take with him his new clothes, $7—more than he'd really earned—and several letters of recommendation to potential employees in Cincinnati, where there would be more opportunities for him.

Somewhat daunted at the probability of encountering the benefactor who had financed his departure from Cincinnati in the first place, four months ago, and who believed him to be in Illinois, Henry nevertheless traveled up the river to Cincinnati in early March 1854, took lodgings rather better than those he'd resorted to in November, and began looking for work. One of his ex-landlord's letters recommended him to a firm of German publishers. Upon applying there, Henry was immediately engaged as a salesman and assigned to peddle songbooks and "colored lithographs of a humorous character" to the German-Americans of Cincinnati. He had found, for a change, an occupation that left his self-respect relatively intact, and he threw himself into his work with great determination, assiduously canvassing German stores, saloons, restaurants, barbershops, and meeting halls. While hawking his wares at a meeting of the local freethinkers' association, he was asked to include among them a lithographed caricature of the papal delegate, who was then visiting Cincinnati and who was a notorious reactionary, despised for his persecutions of liberal leaders after the risings of 1848–49. The caricature, a reminder of the revolutionary fervor of his younger days, became part of Henry's inventory, and he sought to supplement his income further by soliciting subscriptions to a German illustrated newspaper published in New York.

For all his ambition and enthusiasm, however, sales in Cincinnati petered out after a few weeks; his publishers suggested that he take to the road. By the beginning of May, a few weeks past his nineteenth birthday, he was a drummer, walking from town to town in the nearby districts of Indiana and Ohio, trying to lighten his load of books and prints. As had been the case in the city, however, his reception was "generally ungracious," not to say rude, and few of the people he called upon had any interest in books and prints, no matter how humorous in character. By the end of two weeks, he had spent the money advanced to him for expenses as well as most of what had accumulated from his infrequent sales. He was not only nearly broke, but also in debt to his firm, the owners of which grew nervous and demanded an accounting.

Stalling for time, Henry redoubled his efforts, but in vain. Toward the end of May, while staying at an inn in Hamilton, Ohio, he met a young man from Speyer—a cooper, of all things—five years in America, thoroughly "americanized," and so affable and considerate that Henry failed to reflect on his social level or the humble nature of his trade. The cooper took a liking to Henry, saw that he was in trouble, and set about putting his mind at rest. He was prosperous, he said, and he could assist Henry until he found some means of support. Soon he would go to Quincy, Illinois, a town of abundant opportunity, and set up in business there; if Henry would wait, they could go together. The cooper then confided to Henry that he was in love with their landlord's niece, she returned his affection, and soon he planned to obtain her rich uncle's consent and marry the girl before going west.

Two weeks passed, and with them nearly all the rest of Henry's money. His sales had long since dwindled to nothing, his expenses continued to mount, his friend the cooper remained optimistic but vague. Then one morning Henry heard a "great commotion" downstairs. Just last evening, it seemed, the landlord—the source and center of the commotion—had curtly rejected the earnest cooper's suit. But the old man had underestimated both his niece's willfulness and her suitor's enterprise; the amorous young couple had eloped in the night; and the discovery of the abduction from the inn had set the landlord roaring. This rush of events surprised Henry as much as anyone, but as the cooper's intimate friend he was under suspicion of complicity and unceremoniously thrown out of the house. There was, however, a bright side: the landlord's rage consumed him utterly and drove from his mind all thought of Henry's overdue room and board charges, which the young man had no means of paying. Once again, Henry decamped via the next train. This one took him to Richmond, Indiana, some twenty-five miles away.

Now began "the hardest experiences" Henry had in America, harder even than the wretched winter he had just endured. In Richmond there was only one German inn, run by a butcher with a dirty wife and a still dirtier sister-in-law. Henry remained there for several days, more grieved by watching the landlady mix the salad with her unwashed hands than by the fact that he had no money to pay for his room and board. He regarded with aristocratic disdain the common laborers, German and Irish, who frequented the inn. The landlord, however, upon learning that Henry could not settle his bill, was little inclined to make class distinctions in his favor. He subjected Henry to a "torrent of abuse," not even sparing the lad's soft hands, which in the irate butcher's opinion proved him to be "nothing but a genteel loafer." Early the next morning Henry was sent, or perhaps chased, to a nearby brickyard, where he was engaged as a "general helper" at $1.25 a day. Time, experience, and hunger had combined to dull somewhat the sharp edge of Henry's disdain for manual labor, and he was glad of this opportunity to make some money, even if only "in the sweat of my brow." Sure of his mettle, he took on his first wheelbarrow load of prepared clay and began to propel it across the yard, a distance of some 150 feet, over planking and up a slight incline.

Alas, he was wearing his traveling salesman's clothes—which were, in fact, his only clothes, a suit and a starched shirt. As the suspicious foreman watched and the mighty sun of June climbed high, Henry grew weaker; each trip across the yard halved his strength. His shoulders and arms began first to ache, and then to lose all force. The foreman reprimanded him for his slowness, hustling him along, and Henry spilled his next barrow load all over the planking, capsizing himself in the process. Fired on the spot, and afraid to return to his boardinghouse, he struck out across the fields with no money and no prospects.

In a community of Pennsylvania Germans, who found his *Deutsch* as hard to understand as he did theirs, he learned that the grain harvest had begun. While the afternoon gradually deepened into dusk, Henry walked from farm to farm, seeking work. He had no luck, but shortly after sunset, after trudging for miles, he found an abandoned, crumbling cabin. There he spent the night, stretched out on the floor, looking up at the stars, and pondering a hard, undeniable truth: he had "now reached the state of actual vagabondage."

The next morning he was stiff and hungry, but before long he came to a farm where help was wanted. Henry was put to work as a binder, one who practiced the ancient occupation of gathering up the stalks of harvested grain and tying them into sheaves. The work was arduous, requiring long, backbreaking hours spent stooping and straightening under the broiling sun. The pay was $1.50 daily, plus room and board. The food, as always at harvest time, was tasty, nutritious, and abundant. The hands slept in a large garret, two to a bed, but by bedtime Henry was too exhausted to be discomforted by this arrangement. After ten very full working days, the harvest was over. Proud of himself for having labored hard and well, Henry now felt qualified as a general farmhand. He was out of work again, but he had $15 in his pocket, and already he was dreaming of becoming a farmer.

Henry, who during this period of his life was quite often inappropriately dressed, had worn the same hot, uncomfortable outfit during ten consecutive days of sheaf binding under the sun of late June. Disgusted by himself, and embarrassed, no doubt with cause, by his aura, he headed for the nearest village to buy some clothes. He couldn't find what he wanted, but he found a train station, and Indianapolis was only forty miles away.

In a German store in Indianapolis, for $6, Henry bought socks, underwear, a work shirt, a coat, a pair of pants, and a piece of soap. He then walked through the "well-built, smart-looking city of about 20,000 inhabitants" to the banks of the White River, at that time on the outskirts of town. There he bathed himself, at long last, and washed the few articles of his old clothing that he wished to salvage. He lay them out to dry in the bright sun and then stretched out beside them. His self-respect was back; things were looking up.

Henry had learned many things in the past eight and a half months, but English was not among them. Without much effort, however, he located cheap German lodgings. After settling in and looking a little more around Indianapolis, Henry found that he was well content. Though his money was down to $5, still he thought he'd rest for a day in this pleasing city "before carrying out my plan to return to the country to become a regular farmer."

As a matter of fact, Henry's agricultural adventures were over. The next day, while he was out strolling in the neighborhood of his boardinghouse, the sharp sounds of his native tongue caught his attention. They came from a lumberyard, and Henry stopped to look inside. Despite his American clothes and what he thought of as his genteel bearing, both his nationality and his condition must have been readily apparent to a discerning eye, for the man who was directing the work in the yard called out to him at once: *"Suchen Sie Arbeit?"* Yes, Henry replied, he was looking for a job, and the next day he began loading and unloading lumber for $7 a week. Since this was more than double what he was paying for room and board, Henry felt that he could accumulate some savings; besides, the city was more congenial to his tastes than the country, and his farming fantasies began to fade.

Paradoxically, Henry was both proud of his ability to perform manual labor well and ashamed of the work itself. He hadn't been "a breadwinner by my hands long enough to feel at home among" his fellow workers in the lumberyard—they were all north Germans, and therefore alien to begin with—but he was at pains to conceal from them his superior origins. Since class comparisons, almost exclusively in his favor, seem to have been a principal activity of his consciousness, especially when it came to his countrymen, one wonders how successful Henry was in keeping the other laborers from discovering his background. He had nevertheless progressed far from the days when he refused to consider jobs that were beneath him.

This one didn't last long. Henry's unpredictable health had survived the rigors of a cold winter compounded by the dangers of bad nutrition, exposure, and inadequate clothing, but now he was struck down by the "fever ague," a malady common in Indianapolis during the summer. Its symptoms resembled those of malaria, and the usual remedy was quinine pills; Henry was to have frequent recourse to them for the rest of his life. These could not prevent him, however, from becoming incapacitated for more than two weeks, and when he was finally strong enough to return to the lumberyard he was told that his position had been filled.

Undaunted, he commenced yet another search for employment, and after three days he found his first railroad job, working as a helper on a wood train for the Indianapolis & Madison line. Perhaps as a portent of things to come, this proved to be both the highest-paying work he had yet done—his salary was $35 dollars a month—and the easiest, consisting mostly in traveling by train from one point to another to load or unload locomotive fuel. After nearly three weeks of steady work, however, the symptoms of his illness returned with a vengeance. Violent shaking, a leaping fever, and chills that seemed to originate in his bone marrow struck him down for many days and left him so enfeebled that his recovery took nearly as long. By the time he could work again, his long absence had cost him his job.

He had recourse, most reluctantly, to bartending, an occupation so "utterly repulsive" to him that he "could not help feeling degraded" by it. However déclassé it may have been, dispensing strong drink to the intemperate enabled Henry to save a little money and to form a new plan. He would go to Chicago, a city that was, like himself, very young and very promising. On October 18, 1854, one year to the day after his arrival in the United States, Henry got off the train in the Windy City. His arduous *Wanderjahr* was over.

※　　　※　　　※

Chicago in late 1854 was a shambling, vigorous city built almost entirely of wood, a fact that would cost its citizenry dearly seventeen years later, when Mrs. O'Leary's legendary cow kicked over the fateful lantern. For all its unpaved streets, its wooden sidewalks and buildings, and its thorough lack of refinement, however, Chicago exuded a rude health, a rough cosmopolitanism, and a boundless vitality that appealed to the energetic young Henry Villard as he roamed through the unfamiliar streets.

In one such street he came upon a German boardinghouse with a sign bearing the name of the proprietor, Bernhard Norkin. Believing this to be the name of a man from Speyer, a playmate's elder brother who had emigrated to the United States many years before, Henry entered the house and made inquiries.

Henry's guess was right; it was the same man. Emigrés from the Palatinate were apparently quite thick on the ground in those days. The difference in their ages was too great for Norkin to be able to recognize Henry, but upon learning the identity of his young visitor, the older man immediately extended to him the hospitality of the house. This proved somewhat disappointing to Henry, for the place was soon revealed to be nothing more than an emigrant hotel, with perfunctory decor, minimum comfort, and cramped dormitory-style rooms where strangers slept in adjoining beds. There was a big turnover in guests and frequent new arrivals, most of them fresh from Germany, or as fresh as the sea voyage and the trip from New York could leave them. The sight of such countrymen left Henry cold, for "emigrants in those days were no more attractive in respect to cleanliness and otherwise than to-day." Perhaps by now he no longer thought of himself as an emigrant.

Although he was unhappy in such plebeian surroundings, he decided to stay. He was helped in his decision by the obvious desire of the Norkins, man and wife, to be of service to him, and by the thought that Norkin's many long-established connections might be helpful to him in searching out a job. That the Norkins were offering him free room and board was probably taken into consideration as well.

Norkin did indeed know several influential people, including a publisher and an editor of the city's leading German newspaper, the *Illinois Staats-Zeitung*, but they gave Henry nothing except wise counsel. For his part, he went to employment bureaus, shops, and business establishments, and even advertised in the *Zeitung*, to no avail.

Weeks passed. Fortified by his host's assurance that he could stay all winter if necessary, Henry disregarded such unsatisfactory positions as saloon waiter and delivery wagon driver, which were the only sort of openings he could find. One morning Norkin, visibly surprised, handed Henry the *Zeitung* and pointed to a notice addressed to Heinrich Hilgard, an urgent request to contact the undersigned in Belleville, Illinois. The signer was Henry's half uncle, schoolmate, and friend, a favorite of his mother's, Robert Hilgard, who Henry had believed was still in Frankfurt.

Even though no one in his family knew where he was, or even whether or not he was alive, Henry was sure that Robert had come to America specifically to find him. Replying to him would break Henry's resolution not to tell his family of his whereabouts until he could do so with the triumphant announcement that he did not need their financial support. As Henry struggled with his pride, Norkin, who knew nothing of his young guest's estrangement from his family but knew dithering when he saw it, told Henry with a smile on his face that if he—Henry—didn't write to Robert at once, he—Norkin—would do it for him. Chagrined, thwarted, Henry sat down to write the first letter he had sent to any member of his family in more than a year.

Henry told Robert where he was, alluded to some of the lesser horrors of the past year, stressed his confidence in the future, and asked for news of his family in Zweibrücken. Eight days later, returning to his boardinghouse after another fruitless search for acceptable work, Henry found the reply to his letter in the sitting room: Robert Hilgard, in person.

Robert brought him much news. Like Henry, though rather less drastically, he had come to America to seek his fortune. Before leaving Germany, he had visited the Hilgards in Zweibrücken. Henry's parents and sisters were all well, though naturally troubled and saddened by his flight from home. They were fairly certain that he had gone to America—perhaps news of him had filtered back to them from one of Henry's numerous chance meetings with his countrymen—and Lisette, Henry's mother, had extracted a solemn promise from Robert to find and help her wayward but no less beloved son.

And Uncle Theodor (Henry's uncle and Robert's half brother), though he could not approve of Henry's behavior, had authorized Robert to offer Henry a home with his family.

Understandably apprehensive about the kind of welcome he could expect from his uncle, and probably a little ashamed of himself, Henry capitulated when Robert emphasized his mother's anxiety; her loving concern for him would not cease to torment her until she knew that he was safe. Henry, reduced to tears, put himself in Robert's hands.

The next day they started for St. Louis, arriving there at noon on the day following. Visits to various more or less distant relatives in and around St. Louis took up the next few days, and then the time had come. Robert and Henry crossed the Mississippi and spent the night in Belleville. Early the next morning they set out for Theodor Hilgard's farm, some five or six miles out of town. Having touched bottom, Henry was on his way back up, but he was going to make the next phase of his climb under the auspices of someone very like his father.

Drawing of the farm near Belleville, Illinois, owned by
Theodor Engelmann (1808–89), first cousin of
Henry Villard's paternal grandfather, Georg Friedrich Hilgard.
Courtesy of the St. Clair County Historical Society.

3

The Lure
of the Law

Still added days went by. Whether Bartleby's eyes improved or not, I could not say. To all appearance I thought they did. But when I asked him if they did, he vouchsafed no answer. At all events, he would do no copying. At last, in reply to my urgings, he informed me that he had permanently given up copying.

"What!" exclaimed I; "suppose your eyes should get entirely well— better than ever before—would you not copy then?"

"I have given up copying," he answered, and slid aside.

HERMAN MELVILLE,
"Bartleby the Scrivener"

The center of Belleville, in St. Clair County, Illinois, lies about a dozen miles from the eastern bank of the Mississippi River as it bends around St. Louis, Missouri. The town is situated on bluffs that form the eastern rim of the river's floodplain; to the east and north, a strip of fertile upland, six to ten miles wide, stretches for a hundred miles. In the late 1820s, many German immigrants were attracted to Belleville by the discovery of coal nearby, but these first arrivals constituted a mere stream compared to what was to become a mighty tide of German immigration to Belleville and its surroundings. From the mid-1830s on, St. Clair County was "the major German center of Illinois," extolled in dozens of German guidebooks and thousands of letters home. Ten percent of the population of Rhenish Bavaria had been lost to emigration between 1849 and 1856, and Belleville had attracted an especially high concentration of Henry Villard's countrymen from the Palatinate. Many of them shared characteristics so distinctive that they came to be seen as an unusual, not to say peculiar, group unto themselves.

Because these men had all received the best that Germany had to offer in terms of classical education, with its emphasis on the languages of ancient Greece and Rome, they were called *die lateinische Bauern*, the Latin Peasants or Latin Farmers. In a letter written from Belleville and dated October 8, 1843, Henry Villard's great-uncle Theodor Erasmus Hilgard, who had emigrated to Belleville in 1835, sought to disabuse his concerned mother of the notion that he and his family were spending all their time farming. "I can truthfully say that never in my life have I been so occupied with things of the mind, with the ancient classics, with modern literature, with language study, with pondering the more serious political questions and opinions, and finally with writing poetry, as I am here." He went on to discuss the progress of his translation of Ovid's *Metamorphoses*. Such reflections and such an avocation might have seemed unusual for most farmers, but not for these.

The Latin Farmers were "noblemen, doctors, lawyers and judges, former university professors and school teachers, as well as business men of a fine type"; there were even a few musicians. What they had in common, along with progressive political attitudes and heterodox views of religion, was an extremely high level of education, culture, intelligence, refinement, and accomplishment—Theodor Erasmus had been a justice of the Bavarian Supreme Court and a prolific, respected writer and scholar—and an extremely low level of knowledge related to the business of farming, which they proposed to take up.

As one would expect from such an extraordinary group, many of the Latin Farmers of Belleville achieved distinction in their adopted country. Among them was one of Heinrich Hilgard's boyhood heroes, Friedrich Hecker. Belleville's most prominent political exile, a symbol of the uprisings of 1848–49 in Germany, Hecker played an important role in American politics as well, and was one of the few Latin Farmers to make a real success of his farm. Another distinguished member of the colony was Gustav Koerner. Like Hecker, he was a political fugitive, but his revolutionary misstep had taken place fifteen years before Hecker's. In 1833 Koerner took

part in an ill-considered putsch in Frankfurt that left him a
wounded, wanted man. Disguised as a woman, he managed to get
across the French border and reach Le Havre. There he joined a
group of a hundred emigrants from the Palatinate, among them
many members of the Engelmann family. One of these Engelmanns
was Koerner's coconspirator and fellow fugitive; another was his future wife. Gustav Koerner was thus distantly related to Henry Villard
by marriage; he would give the younger man much generous assistance during his early years in the United States and remain his lifelong friend. Like Hecker, Koerner would serve with honor in the
Union Army and enjoy political success as a leading member of the
Republican Party.

Rich or poor, educated or not, the vast majority of German immigrants in the United States were opposed to slavery, and very few
of them ever owned a slave. (Slaves in America were given family
names that reflected the English, Scottish, French, Spanish, or Irish
origins of their masters, and more recently many African-Americans
have taken Arabic or African names, but it is rare indeed to come
across a black American with a German last name.) Almost all Germans disliked slavery; the Latin Farmers found it repellent and appalling, and they were vociferous in their denunciations. These
veterans of the struggle for liberty, these idealists, these refugees who
had fled their homes in search of freedom, could never get over the
irony of having come to the land of golden promise, the land, indeed, of the free, only to find that men, women, and children were
hobbled, penned, and sold like cattle there, *under the protection of the
law!* Of course, they had known before they emigrated that the
United States was divided into slave states and free states, but reading about slavery and actually seeing it in practice were two quite distinct modes of knowing. Some of Koerner's group had thought at
first of settling in Missouri, a slave state; the sight of a white woman
beating a black girl in a St. Louis rooming house had sent them flying across the river to Belleville and the free soil of Illinois. It is likely
that Henry Villard saw slaves for the first time while he was on his way
to Belleville, perhaps during his own stay in St. Louis, and it's safe to
say that his reaction was similarly unequivocal.

Even in a free state, the evil of slavery had a way of making its presence felt, and Missouri was too close for comfort. In 1837, in Alton, Illinois, a town on the Mississippi River not twenty-five miles from Belleville, a mob surrounded the printing office of an antislavery newspaper. Its editor, Elijah Lovejoy, had moved his operation to Illinois after losing three consecutive presses to mob violence in Missouri. This time, standing on free soil, he chose to defend his property and was murdered in front of his family; firebombs destroyed his press as he lay dying. This and similar incidents only served to reinforce the natural inclinations of the Belleville community; its members knew that slavery was a disease that made everybody sick, and they eagerly joined the abolitionist movement.

One of the characteristics that distinguished the Latin Farmers from most of their fellow German immigrants, and for that matter from most Americans, was the way they felt about religion. All of these scholarly agriculturists had participated in, or at least sympathized with, the revolutionary movement in Germany; all had carefully examined the power structure against which they rebelled; and all had noted the glittering adamant bands that linked rulers by divine right to the anointed agents of that selfsame divinity. This complicity between churchly authority and the reactionary political leaders they despised led most of the highly politicized Latin Farmers to be extremely wary of religion, particularly of the organized kind. There were many rationalists, anticlericals, and freethinkers among them, including some who continued, for reasons known only to themselves, to attend church. A German Evangelical pastor in Belleville declared that the Germans in that part of the country were "most all infidels or rationalists calling the Bible an old rusted book." An American preacher agreed completely, complaining that the German church in Belleville was "almost entirely made up of skeptics and loose moralists." To illustrate his point, he recalled the time when he offered to sell a Bible to a member of the German congregation, who had responded, "I want no Bible; I have the great book of the world. I want to know nothing about Jesus Christ; I have the guide of my own reason."

Like most of the European immigrants who came to America in

the nineteenth century, the Latin Farmers mightily resisted the pernicious effects of the temperance movement. (Henry Villard could recognize much more easily the evils of slavery than he could those of a glass of good wine.) In 1855, the citizens of Illinois voted on the so-called Maine Law, a law patterned after one recently passed in that state that prohibited the manufacture and sale of alcoholic beverages. St. Clair County voted 4,408 to 909 against the Maine Law, an 83–17 percent split. This lopsided tally contributed to the defeat of the law (by 54 to 46 percent) in Illinois, and the Latin Farmers—many of whom, including Henry's uncle Theodor, were engaged in the cultivation of vineyards—toasted their victory.

This, then, was the community that Henry Villard was about to enter in the fall of 1854. "Outwardly Belleville looked like a typical German village with its German signs and its German beer gardens," and inside the houses "domestic life was still precisely like that which he had left . . . in the Palatinate." Henry's flight from home had led him on a journey that covered fifteen months and many thousands of miles, yet now, in the middle of the North American continent, he was returning to a kind of Germany: a concentrated, rarefied version of his homeland, free from political repression and populated by a liberal intellectual elite. As a discrete community, these Germans held certain republican ideals in common with the general population. A broader view of the matter, however, reveals that their political, social, and religious convictions estranged them from their contemporaries, who considered these Germans odd beyond comprehension. For their part, the Latin Farmers found their new countrymen too uninformed, too unintellectual, too provincial to be interesting, and almost too unrefined to bear; for educated Germans, the American habit of spitting tobacco juice—anywhere, anytime—symbolized the kind of behavior with which there could be no reconciliation. (Ironically, time and democracy, levelers of all things, would smooth out these discrepancies as well.) The world of the Latin Farmers was to provide Henry Villard with a familiar, pleasurable, welcome, but slightly unreal rest period in his uphill struggle. Eventually he would have to leave his homeland once again and return to reality.

■　　　■　　　　■

Theodor Hilgard welcomed his nephew "rather stiffly" to his hundred-acre farm on the rolling prairie northeast of Belleville. Henry's aunt, Emma, however, greeted him with exceptional warmth, won his heart immediately, and proceeded for the rest of his stay to give the motherless adventurer something he sorely needed: loving-kindness, maternal affection. Henry's oldest cousin, Gustav, was away at school, but the remaining seven, who ranged in age from six to seventeen, provided him with ready-made generational allies. Relations with his uncle began to thaw somewhat when Henry, experienced as a manual laborer, volunteered to help with the chores and showed himself willing to do everything from pig feeding to snow shoveling. Safe, warm, and secure in the midst of a loving family, Henry was able finally to relax, and a feeling of "inner peace" came over him for the first time in many years. Christmas was a festival "in true German style," and the thought of his previous, decidedly unmerry Christmas stung his eyes with grateful tears.

New Year's Day 1855, came quickly, and then the winter deepened and there was little farmwork to be done. Henry spent much of this time making excursions with his aunt and uncle, calling on people in town and on the surrounding farms. They visited dozens of relatives and friends, pillars and leaders of the community. Delighted to be once again in the company of intelligent, educated people, he grew more and more content.

Shortly after his arrival, at the friendly but insistent urging of his aunt, Henry had worried from his pen—it took him three days—the long-postponed letter to his family, his first attempt to contact them in well over a year. At the end of January, to everyone's relief, a packet of thick envelopes arrived from Zweibrücken. Henry's mother and sister sent him affectionate, newsy letters, encouraging him in all his endeavors and, most lovingly of all, making hardly an allusion to his past. His father, however, apparently unable to countenance writing directly to his son, addressed himself to Theodor instead. After effusively thanking his brother for taking the prodigal into his care and promising to reimburse all the expenses Theodor might incur in this dubious cause, Gustav, about to be appointed justice of the Supreme Court in Munich and ever the judge, moved on to an assessment of his disappointing son's moral character. Heinrich's past made him impossible to trust; it would require a long, uninterrupted period of good behavior on his part to change his father's opinion. Nevertheless, Gustav offered to make a moderate contribution to his son's support until such time as he could earn his own living.

The subject of this harsh reply was little troubled by it; its offer of financial assistance was more than he had expected. As for the rest—his low standing in his father's estimation, his father's willingness to broadcast his paternal chagrin—Henry was used to all that.

Driven by a desire for genuine independence and impatient to prove himself, Henry began to cast about for work. As usual, the search was coupled with a motley collection of fantastic schemes. He read a book, *Many Ways to Make an Easy Living,* and for a while was taken with the idea of peddling "Cologne water." During his travels he had identified in many places a real need, and therefore a large potential market, for agreeable scents. Besides, the book included a recipe for preparing the cologne, so all the problems and inconvenience of importing it could be avoided.

Since he knew that he wasn't qualified to do anything but manual labor, Henry wanted to find work somewhere away from Belleville; inflexibly class conscious no matter what class he was in, he didn't want to diminish the social standing of his uncle's family by performing menial tasks in their neighborhood. A cousin informed him of an available position in Carlyle, the seat of Clinton County, Illinois, some fifty miles east of Belleville. Mr. Zophar Case, clerk of court and recorder of deeds in Clinton County, was in need of an assistant to copy deeds into the county records, a job for which Henry seemed peculiarly unqualified: the legal instruments were executed, naturally, in English, and the scrivener must have a neat hand. Henry conscientiously pointed out to his cousin his deficiencies in English and penmanship, but these were set at naught and inquiries sent as to wages. Twenty-five cents a page, was the reply, whereupon Henry tried his hand at such a page in another cousin's law office. He found he could do one in less than an hour, writing very carefully; this rate seemed to him sufficient to secure a living wage, and on March 23, 1855, he got off the train in Carlyle bearing a letter of recommendation from Gustav Koerner, then lieutenant governor of Illinois.

Zophar Case turned out to be a large, stained, uncouth, lazy man, an accomplished raconteur and expectorator of tobacco juice, streams of which he would send slurping into the office spittoon from a considerable distance. Henry quickly mastered the prescribed copying procedures and did not shrink from providing some much-needed janitorial services. Delighted at the boy's industry and neatness, the clerk turned over more and more of his clerical duties to this new assistant, thus freeing himself to spend the day chatting with whoever came into his office to ask a question, file a deed, or pass the time. Henry received $3 a week extra for taking charge of every other aspect of the office routine, and before long he was making as much as $65 a month.

Meanwhile, for the first extended period of time since his arrival in the United States, Henry was immersed in the English language, which he copied, heard, and was compelled to speak all day and practiced systematically at night. He talked as much as he could, particularly to his landlord's pretty daughter, who willingly assisted him in his linguistic efforts. His comprehension improved so greatly that he started attending court sessions "and listened for the first time to examples of forensic eloquence." There were other, less edifying courtroom spectacles as well, including several trials where counsel pleaded their causes despite the impediments of an advanced state of intoxication, and one memorable instance when the judge, lounging at ease with his feet on the desk before him, interrupted a lawyer in the midst of a fiery argument in order to sponge a chaw of tobacco.

Eventually Henry copied himself right out of a job; once he had eliminated the backlog of unrecorded deeds, there weren't enough new ones to pay his way. Having obtained his uncle's consent to his proposed return, in about the middle of August Henry left Carlyle and went back to the farm outside Belleville. He had a new summer wardrobe, $60 in savings in his pocket, and little regret about having left a place with few attractions and no possibilities.

He also had a new scheme for his future. His months in Carlyle had taught him the immense power and importance of the American legal profession, and he determined to become a lawyer himself. He discussed his decision with his uncle, and Theodor agreed to write to his brother on Henry's behalf; direct communication between these two still seemed to be out of the question.

While waiting for Gustav's reply, Henry fell back into the pleasant routine that characterized life on his uncle's farm, but the letter from his father arrived promptly. Gustav assented to the proposition and offered in support a modest annual sum, which he would provide for two years and which, he said, would allow his son to devote all his time to study. Henry was hot with enthusiasm, already imagining a brilliant legal career capped by political success, but a visit to Koerner cooled him down.

It transpired that Gustav's offer was niggardly; Henry could neither commence university law studies with so little support nor complete a degree in so short a time. The less preferable alternative, Koerner suggested, was the one usually followed in the West: Henry could take a job as a clerk in a law firm and learn theory and practice simultaneously.

He disliked this solution, but it was the only one available. Koerner recommended him to a prominent Belleville lawyer named George Trumbull, brother of Lyman Trumbull, a distinguished U.S. senator from Illinois. The choice of an American lawyer was deliberate, as Henry's English was still far from perfect, but it soon became apparent that he would be able to absorb but little English and even less of Blackstone's *Commentaries* in Trumbull's office, in which clients, idlers, and gossips, all speaking German, convened throughout the day. Henry practiced English with an American tutor several hours a week, but these efforts availed little because all the rest of the time he spoke and heard nothing but German. A renewed applica-

tion to Koerner secured him a place in the offices of Manning &
Merriman, a law firm in Peoria, where Henry arrived near the end of
November.

His duties at his new firm consisted mostly of copying, his current forte, and the rest of the time he was, in theory, free to study his
law books. Of the two partners, Henry preferred Mr. Manning, who
drank too much but was good humored and witty, to Mr. Merriman,
a devout Christian who annoyed Henry by his frequent attempts to
convert him to true belief. Henry always resisted any endeavor, however well meaning, to mold his identity, and this one was no exception. Finally, having run out of polite ways to ward off his employer's
unwelcome ministrations, Henry resorted to outright scoffing, but
the undaunted proselytizer's efforts continued.

Religion was a problem for Henry in the pious community of
Peoria. If he revealed his lack of faith and aversion to churchgoing,
the people he met either set about his conversion with the most
pressing urgency or shunned him like a leper. He had letters of introduction to only one family in town, but when they found out that
he was a freethinker they cut him permanently. Not going to church,
Henry realized, "is a great social obstacle in this country." Thus os-
tracized, he felt isolated and lonely, especially when he recalled the
comforting Christmas he had spent with his uncle's family the previous year.

As the months passed, Henry realized that he was making little
progress with his law books. The firm's other student allowed that he
had reached the same conclusion, and the problem was easy to iden-
tify: as had been the case at Trumbull's, the offices of Manning &
Merriman provided a constant spectacle of bustle and chatter. Henry
was fascinated by the political discussions and amused by Mr. Manning's adroit way of handling his clients, especially when the subject
of fees arose, but continual distractions and lack of privacy made
study impossible.

While contemplating his next move, Henry, who still retained all
his old literary ambition, made his first venture into journalism. He
wrote a couple of essays that, he later explained—still overweening
after all those years—were "of a partly descriptive and partly philo-

sophic-aesthetic character," boldly signed his youthful effusions, and sent them to the editor of the *Belleville Zeitung*. This gentleman, who knew Henry, complimented his work and published it forthwith. Unfortunately, with a monumental tactlessness not wholly attributable to his youth, Henry had discoursed in one of his essays upon "German philistinism," especially as manifested in Belleville, Illinois, where he had arrived in an advanced state of wretchedness little more than a year before and where his numerous relatives and their neighbors had welcomed him cordially. His article offended many members of the community and brought him several reproving letters, including a distinctly testy note from Uncle Theodor. Henry was sorry to have caused bad feelings, but on the other hand, all the attention flattered his vanity. Journalism, he saw, was work that he could perform without shame.

In the meantime, he was coming ever more incontrovertibly to the conclusion that his adviser, Koerner, had been right in the first place: for a thorough grounding in the law, one should go to a university, not a law office. Since his father would not provide sufficient support for him to attend a university, Henry would simply have to make enough money to put himself through law school. As he pondered the best means of accomplishing this, he saw a series of advertisements in the newspaper. These ads, placed by a Chicago-based bookselling firm, promoted a new and imposing work, an *Encyclopedia of American Literature,* to be published in three large volumes at $5 apiece. Glowing reviews from literary eminences filled the ads, which ended with an invitation to "enterprising young men of good address" to contact the firm. If deemed suitable, they would be assigned certain designated areas of the country, within which the young canvassers would enjoy exclusive rights to sell subscriptions to the three-volume set and thus earn liberal commissions.

This, Henry thought, was the right thing. The books were highly recommended, obviously important, and most desirable; there would be no competition in selling them; he would see more of the country and keep improving his English; and through the power of his will he would tap, in the cities, towns, and villages of America, the thirst for culture that would pay his way to Harvard Law School.

GEORG FRIEDRICH HILGARD, MAYOR OF SPEYER,
Henry Villard's paternal grandfather, c. 1815.
Courtesy of Mark C. Hilgard.

4

The Solitary Salesman

Young man, I have no skill to talk with you, but look at me; I have risen early and sat late, and toiled honestly and painfully for very many years. I never dreamed about methods; I laid my bones to, and drudged for the good I possess; it was not got by fraud, nor by luck, but by work, and you must show me a warrant like these stubborn facts in your own fidelity and labor, before I suffer you, on the faith of a few fine words, to ride into my estate, and claim to scatter it as your own.

RALPH WALDO EMERSON,
"The Conservative"

Too impatient to wait for an exchange of letters, Henry requested a week's leave of absence from Manning & Merriman, packed his trunk, and took a train to Chicago. There he went immediately to the headquarters of the bookselling firm and was shown to the office of the man in charge of subscriptions. Seeing before him a youth whose good sense was no match for his enthusiasm, this considerate gentleman offered Henry a realistic assessment of a canvasser's lot and prospects. The young man's response was to boast of his experience in the canvassing business—perhaps he was temporarily oblivious of the way that experience had ended—and to declare himself up to the challenge. The bemused bookseller agreed to employ him on a trial basis, assigned him the "entirely unexplored and very promising" city of Milwaukee, equipped him with the three volumes of the *Encyclopedia,* a stack of subscription books, and some circulars, and wished him successful selling. That night Henry wrote to his law firm, explaining his decision to give up the law for a while in favor of an excellent business opportunity. The next morning he left for Milwaukee.

Once again, he had allowed himself to be carried away, both literally and figuratively; he was traveling one hundred miles due north in the dead of winter to a place he had never seen, whose inhabitants he would persuade to purchase subscriptions to books he had not read; and he would flog these ponderous tomes, written in American English and dealing with American literature, to a largely immigrant population. How can such behavior be explained?

Like all questions concerning motive and desire, including one's own, this one is at bottom unanswerable. Let us try, nevertheless, to examine our young man as his train chugs northward along the shore of Lake Michigan. He is ambitious, energetic, fond of impossible dreams. His personality exhibits many characteristics that seem essential to success if one is to convince people that they should buy what one has to sell. Physically imposing—tall, strongly built, with a cleft chin, piercing blue eyes, and golden highlights in his brown hair—he is quite conscious of the impression that he makes and confident in his powers of persuasion. He is attractive, charming, earnest, eager, gregarious, absolutely unencumbered by shyness or modesty or diffidence; and most important of all, he has the true salesman's indispensable gift: unaffected sincerity. He believes without reservation in the value of what he's selling, just as he believes in the value of everything he puts his mind to, in the feasibility of every plan, the realization of every dream. Indeed, he will go on to a career driven to great (though sheer) heights of success by his firm faith in his vision and by his ability to convey that faith to others. His dreams and visions will alter their shape, change beyond recognition; his faith will abide. Its current object, the *Encyclopedia of American Literature,* will not weigh him down for long.

Milwaukee's large and comparatively cultivated German population had earned it the nickname of *Deutsch-Athen,* the German Athens. Its cultural assets included accomplished orchestral, choral, and chamber music societies, various clubs that sponsored lectures and debates, and an excellent German theater. Henry immediately took lodgings at the Hotel Welstein, "the best German inn in the

United States," and began to work this fertile cultural soil by introducing himself to the leading Germans in the city.

Contrary to his expectations, however, his educated countrymen—among whom he had counted on finding the majority of his customers—showed little interest in American literature and even less desire to improve their acquaintance with it. Moreover, Henry discovered to his chagrin that they "had not become sufficiently emancipated from their feelings of caste" to discern in him anything other than a lowly book peddler. After three weeks of constant humiliations, blinding snowstorms, frigid weather, and paltry sales (mostly to Americans), he returned to Chicago. He had laid out several more dollars than he had taken in, and his experiment with the dissemination of culture had come to a disheartening end.

Within a few days, however, he had a new job and new hopes. A want ad in one of the Chicago newspapers led to a successful application for a position with a recently established real estate firm. Henry was hired as a salesman and put in charge of attracting German clients, both buyers and sellers. The agency had impressive offices on the courthouse square, Chicago was going through a period of enormous expansion, and Henry was looking forward to a bright future when he celebrated his twenty-first birthday, on April 10, 1856.

Since leaving Belleville, he had made significant progress in English, and for many months now his avid newspaper reading had included at least as many American publications as German. His interest in politics had always been keen; now it absorbed almost all his spare time. Although he was not a United States citizen and was therefore ineligible to vote, he plunged into political activity, formed opinions, took sides, attended meetings and rallies, shouted, cheered, paraded, put his heart into his cause. People all over the country were doing the same thing; political apathy was not an American problem in 1856.

       ▪   ▪   ▪

For several decades the great edifice of the United States, built astride the fault line of slavery, had shifted and shuddered. How could it have been otherwise? The men whose noble words blare out like trumpet calls at the beginning of the nation's history—the man who cried, "I know not what course others may take; but as for me, give me liberty or give me death!"; the man who wrote, "We hold these truths to be self-evident; that all men are created equal; that they are endowed by their Creator with certain inalienable rights; that among these are life, liberty, and the pursuit of happiness"; many of the men who signed that statement; and the man who led the revolutionary armies to victory and freedom from the British tyrant—these very men were all slaveholders. Slaves worked their fields, built their houses, lived and died on their estates, were bought, sold, and punished according to their will. There was a gaping discrepancy between the ideals of liberty and equality that the Founding Fathers had so eloquently expressed and the protection of slavery that they had incorporated into the Constitution. The great edifice rested upon this contradiction as upon a foundation cracked from the day it was laid.

Over the years, there had been many attempts to remedy a situation that seemed increasingly irremediable. By 1801, all the Northern states had abolished slavery within their borders. Its expansion into the territories was restricted in the Missouri Compromise of 1820 and fudged anew—to cover the vast tracts of land recently acquired, by a sort of international armed robbery, from Mexico—in the Compromise of 1850. But the essentially violent nature of slavery, which depends for its existence on the constantly implicit threat of physical harm, seemed to guarantee that nothing so bloodless as a compromise could resolve the matter.

The Fugitive Slave Act, a fundamental component of the Compromise of 1850, aroused Northern antislavery sentiment to new levels of virulence, which in turn confirmed Southerners' belief that the North was out to destroy their economy, their institutions, and their liberties, especially the liberty to enslave. In 1852, the year before Henry Villard arrived in New York, Harriet Beecher Stowe's sensational best-seller, *Uncle Tom's Cabin,* exacerbated the spread of hostile opposition to slavery in the North and aroused deep resentment in the South.

In January 1854, while Henry was unhappily learning the cooper's trade, the wily and ambitious Senator Stephen Douglas of Illinois, a rather unscrupulous man despite his honorable office, introduced the Kansas-Nebraska Act in the Senate. In May, just about the time when Henry was evicted from his lodgings under suspicion of having been an accessory to elopement, a revised and more Southern-friendly version of Douglas's bill was voted into law. Henry was at the beginning of the worst six months of his life; the country had begun its final slide into chaos.

The Kansas-Nebraska Act created the territories of Kansas and Nebraska, repealed the Missouri Compromise, and provided that the people of the two territories, prior to statehood, would decide whether or not to allow the institution of slavery to exist within their borders. This cynical piece of legislation touched off what amounted to civil war in Kansas, a small foretaste of the real thing to come; throughout 1855 settlers, agitators, and murderers representing both sides of the slavery question started to pour into the territory, gathering themselves for the spectacular acts of violence that would inspire the press to name the future state "Bleeding Kansas."

The situation worsened in the election year of 1856. During one period of about eight days in May, proslavery "border ruffians" sacked and burned the free-soil town of Lawrence, Kansas; in revenge, John Brown, a patriarchal slaughterer of the unrighteous in God's sight who seemed to have sprung directly from the pages of the Old Testament, murdered (with the help of some of his many sons) five proslavery settlers who had had nothing to do with the raid on Lawrence; and in the hallowed precincts of the United States Senate, Congressman Preston "Bully" Brooks of South Carolina took exception to a vituperative speech by Senator Charles Sumner of Massachusetts and caned him into unconsciousness—"plantation discipline," someone said.

       ■   ■   ■

Such was the noxious political atmosphere in the barely united States when Henry Villard reached man's estate in 1856 and became politically engaged; the country was going through the turbulent, doom-laden early years of the most catastrophic decade (1855–65) in its history. The Whig Party, wrecked by the Kansas-Nebraska Act, was fading away, and in its place a new political force was taking shape and starting to call itself the Republican Party. Though the more radical opponents of slavery considered the Republicans unscrupulous opportunists whose antislavery stance resulted not from moral indignation or belief in racial equality but from political expediency, the new party rapidly grew in numbers and strength. The Republicans attracted many people like Henry Villard, people morally and rationally opposed to slavery as the greatest evil in American society and therefore opposed to the vast majority of Democrats, North and South, who tended to genuflect before the interests of the slaveholders.

There were plenty of reasons, some better than others, for hating slavery, and it was perfectly possible to oppose it vehemently and to be a racist at the same time. It's easy to imagine that Henry Villard, so convinced of his own superiority, so quick to make distinctions of class and condition, was moved to denounce slavery more by compassion for the slave than by any sentiments of egalitarianism or universal brotherhood. After all, slaves belonged by definition to the lowest class, and there weren't any freedmen with a gymnasium education. His racial attitudes, however, like those of a great many Americans—first and foremost among them Abraham Lincoln—would evolve considerably over the course of the next ten years.

The first campaign that captured Henry's attention and considerable energy was run by candidates for various municipal offices in Chicago, including that of mayor. Though conducted in the free state of Illinois and involving only local offices, this contest was nonetheless fought, and bitterly fought, over the issue of free soil versus slave soil. Like a clot, the slavery question had moved to the heart of American politics.

Henry's commitment to the cause, which it would be more accurate to call anti-Democrat than Republican at this point, was characteristically wholehearted. He loved the meetings, the cheering, the torch-lit processions, the controversies, the contagious excitement of political engagement. For him the issues were clearly drawn, and he could not imagine how anyone who considered rightly of the matter could reach a conclusion different from his own. Great was his indignation, therefore, when he reflected that there were Germans on the Democratic ticket and that it was supported by prominent Germans and a leading German newspaper. He could understand it if the "ignorant, priest-ridden Irish" supported Democratic candidates, but Germans? On election day, though he could not vote, he worked at the polls and saw for the first time the democratic process in action: altercations, fistfights, even riots broke out throughout the day.

In the end, all Henry's efforts were in vain, and his absolute faith shattered; the Democrats won decisively. During the weeks that it took him to get over this "unutterable humiliation," this "grievous disappointment," he consoled himself with the thought of the many political contacts he had made through his enthusiasm and dedication.

While recovering from postelection shock, Henry decided to bid farewell to the real estate business. His agency and its salesmen, including him, had failed to secure enough clients to remain afloat, and his employers made the decision easy for him by proposing that he forgo his salary and work strictly on commission. This seemed like a step in the wrong direction, and besides, he had bigger things on his mind.

Henry had conceived a new scheme, a scheme on the grand scale. He would persuade young Germans living in Illinois and the other states of what was then the Northwest to form a society, with himself as its head. This society would raise capital, obtain a large tract of land in Kansas, and found there a German free-soil community, a "vanguard of liberty." He had caught the feverish belligerence of the time; he and his young associates would declare themselves ready and willing to fight, if necessary, for the cause of free soil in Kansas. In fact, before he began to elaborate his scheme, he had considered joining one of the companies of riflemen that were forming with the purpose of exercising in Kansas what Senator Douglas had styled "popular sovereignty."

This plan allowed Henry both to apply his powers of persuasion—he liked selling, liked charming and cajoling people into seeing things his way—and to put his political beliefs into action. He had no difficulty in finding a number of interested young German men, but they, like him, though high in enthusiasm, were low in capital. Deciding to go where the money was, he called on several well-known and suitably rich opponents of slavery in Chicago and succeeded in getting a dozen subscriptions of $100 or so.

This wasn't enough capital to buy land, but it was enough to cover traveling expenses. The support he needed would be easier to solicit in the larger cities in the East; on the way, he'd stop in Washington, D.C., where he could see about obtaining a federal or congressional land grant. His associates, now organized into a society with a treasury and a printed prospectus, approved his plan, authorized his trip, and supplied him with travel funds.

Washington was a thoroughly unsatisfactory place, its clutch of stately public buildings rising above a mass of rickety houses, shacks, and other mean structures, its broad streets a perpetual sea of mud. Apart from the imposing seats of patriotism and government, the city was distinctly shabby; especially in the heat of July, it gave the impression of a slow and sleepy town in the rural South. As was his wont, Henry spent his first day seeing the sights in this new city. They left him unimpressed.

The next day, fingering his letters of introduction, he gained access to Lyman Trumbull, the junior senator from Illinois and brother of George Trumbull, in whose office Henry had made his first swipes at the legal profession. Kindly received, he submitted his promotional material and made his pitch, which ended with an unabashed plea for government assistance. Smiling at such unspoiled naiveté—Henry must have been reminded of his interview with Karl Gutzkow—Trumbull told his young visitor that his efforts were wasted, his plan illegal, and his timing, at this crucial moment in national politics, unsurpassably bad.

This "cold-water douche," as he called it, left him "crestfallen," but the very next day he adjusted his crest and waited (for two hours) on the other Illinois senator, Stephen A. Douglas himself. The "Little Giant"—he was very short and very broad, with a mane of black hair and a stentorian voice—glanced at Henry's letters, asked him to summarize his prospectus ("My time is so limited that I cannot read it"), and interrupted him before he was well launched with a flat refusal.

Henry, who hadn't seen the last of Senator Douglas, proceeded to Philadelphia, where his letters of introduction and his talent for locating the right people gained him access to many wealthy gentlemen who shared his political beliefs, including the senior member of the famous Drexel and Company banking firm. Several of these gentlemen, particularly Mr. Drexel, closely examined Henry regarding his plan—which he had by no means worked out in detail—and pitilessly pointed out its various flaws and omissions, for example, the fact that it included no provision for offering investors a return on their investment. Henry was asking for charity; these were businessmen. After a rather mortifying week, he left for New York, deflated, discouraged, still stalwart.

Back in New York for the first time since his inauspicious departure in the fall of 1853, nearly three years before, Henry settled in at a top-notch hotel, the Prescott House, a well-known resort for Germans "of the better classes" from all over the United States as well as Germany itself. Almost at once, he made the acquaintance of a character named Colonel Blenker, the former leader of an independent radical battalion during the 1849 uprising in the Palatinate. This force had distinguished itself more by its revolutionary emblems than by its military prowess, and now the colonel, to his clearly articulated disgust, made his living as a small farmer in Rockland County; he supplied the Prescott House with produce in exchange for dinners and wine, particularly the latter. He was a large, loud, cantankerous, red-faced man, much given to vehement denunciations of his adopted country, where his obvious merits had yet to be recognized. Despite these dissatisfactions, Blenker was to play in the American Civil War a rather more glorious role than he had played in Germany in 1849.

Before long, as in Philadelphia, Henry began to meet many politically influential people, leaders of the new and rapidly organizing Republican Party. Among them was Friedrich Kapp, a lawyer and political activist who would remain his close friend for life. Kapp advised Henry to stop trying to raise money for nothing and to organize a joint stock company.

The young entrepreneur had as yet but an indistinct idea of what such a company was, and no idea at all of how to set about organizing one. What was painfully clear, however, was that he had neither the influence nor the means to bring about such an organization, and that even if he should somehow manage to form a company his lack of capital would exclude him from any possibility of controlling it. He began, grudgingly and reluctantly, to realize that he was out of his depth and his mission a failure; meanwhile, he remained several weeks in New York, enjoying the energy and the lively political scene. He went to Republican meetings and receptions, frequented Republican headquarters, hobnobbed with Republican chiefs; he even shook hands with the Republican presidential candidate, John C. Frémont, and his wife, Jessie. Soon Henry abandoned his Kansas plan altogether, but the charms of New York life, and the thought that he had now disbursed in traveling expenses all the money he'd collected in Chicago, made him reluctant to return there and face his associates, who were waiting patiently for news of his success.

An angry letter eventually summoned him to Chicago, where, after a "stormy session" that included much distasteful dickering over his travel expenditures, Henry resigned his position. Settling accounts with his associates had left him in a familiar but unwelcome state—"pecuniary embarrassment"—and he began to cast about for some new project, some new source of hope and income.

As was so often the case with him, the solution to his problem came to him quickly and fortuitously. The Republicans in Racine, Wisconsin, on the railroad line between Chicago and Milwaukee, were attempting to wrest the German vote away from the Democrats. As part of their strategy, they proposed to purchase the Democratic German newspaper and change its affiliation. They were looking for someone to supervise this transition and to guide the newspaper along the paths of true Republicanism.

When a friend at the *Illinois Staats-Zeitung* casually mentioned this opening to Henry, he saw at once that he was incontestably the man for the job. Racine, he was sure, would be the beginning of a distinguished career that would combine his literary talents and his fascination with politics. Neither his youth nor his foreign origin seemed to him to present any obstacle to his understanding of the great political issues confronting the United States, and he was convinced that his energy and enthusiasm would supply whatever was lacking.

Whenever Henry Villard thought he was reasonably close to a good opportunity, he liked nothing better than taking a train to meet it. Having extracted from his surprised informant a letter of introduction to the Republican executive committee in Racine, Henry got on the next train. This one, he knew, was taking him in the right direction.

COL. FREMONT

PLANTING THE AMERICAN STANDARD ON THE ROCKY MOUNTAINS.

COL. JOHN CHARLES FRÉMONT,

c. 1856.

Courtesy of the Library of Congress.

5

Quest for Recognition

What historic denouements are these we are approaching? On all sides tyrants tremble, crowns are unsteady, the human race restive, on the watch for some better era, some divine war. No man knows what will happen next, but all know that some such things are to happen as mark the greatest moral convulsions of the earth. Who shall play the hand for America in these tremendous games?

WALT WHITMAN,
"The Eighteenth Presidency!" (1856)

Now an adult and on the way to his first serious job, young Mr. Villard arrived in Racine, Wisconsin, near the end of August 1856, about four and a half months past his twenty-first birthday. With its scenic location on the western shore of Lake Michigan and its modest population (twelve thousand people, about a third of them Germans), Racine bore some comparison to the beloved towns where he had grown up, Zweibrücken and Speyer, and he felt comfortable there at once. As he admired the grand views of the lake, the fine harbor, the attractive homes on shady streets, he was more than ever determined to get the job he'd come for. Upon his arrival in the offices of the Republican committee, he was pleasantly surprised to discover that the chairman was not some jaded veteran of the political wars, heavy with accumulated experience and set in his ways, but a young, bright, activist lawyer. Moreover, this personable gentleman was obviously delighted to see him, not least because Villard was the only applicant for the job. The aspiring editor's relief upon learning that no one else had taken advantage of this opportunity quickly gave way to apprehension when the chairman determined to convene a meeting of the committee members on the spot. Bracing himself for the inevitable questions concerning his journalistic experience, Villard was amazed when the introductions were followed immediately by congratulations; he was hired at once, no questions asked, for the "princely" salary of $18 a week—far more money than he had ever earned before.

While the committee, highly satisfied with their appointment, took immediate steps to exercise their secret option to buy the German newspaper from its publisher, the chairman helped Villard look for a place to live. This quest too was speedily accomplished; the new editor took a room in the home of "a genteel private family" for $5 a week, including all meals. Not twenty-four hours after leaving Chicago, Villard found himself "at anchor in what appeared to be a permanent haven of rest and promise. A feeling of security and hopefulness came over me which I had not experienced to the same degree since I landed on American soil." During the next several days—that is, until the sale of the newspaper was finalized—he was in a euphoric state, pleased by everything he saw in the town and looking forward to the commencement of a great career.

Reality soon reined in the sprinting coursers of Villard's imagination. The offices of the *Volksblatt* (the "People's Paper") were dingy, its obsolescent, hand-operated printing press painstakingly slow, its type scanty and exhausted, and its appearance wretched. The news it printed had apparently been selected so as to engage the minds of its readers as little as possible, and its few editorials were amateurish and ungrammatical. It was, in short, a rag, cobbled together without care, skill, judgment, or taste. The list of subscribers was correspondingly small, fewer than four hundred, many of them rural folk who either had not paid their subscription for years or had paid it in kind, with butter or chickens or potatoes.

Though Villard's own education had remained incomplete, he always considered himself a member of the educated class and sought the company of those he thought of as his intellectual equals, people with discernment in literature and art and cultivated political views. Much chagrin, therefore, attended his discovery that there were but two highly educated men, both physicians, among the *Volks-blatt*'s subscribers. He realized that any display of his literary talent would be tossing pearls before swine, or in some cases swineherds.

The task before him would have daunted a more unassuming man. The very idea that he could appeal successfully to an unedu-cated Democratic readership with a new, refined Republican news-paper, sprung upon the said readership without warning from one issue to the next, indicates the level of Villard's self-assurance, matched in this instance by that of the young and confident Repub-lican Party.

He set himself to work with a will, learning the trade as he went along, rewriting his editorials again and again, laboring night and day to produce a respectable paper with inadequate materials. The few German-language Republican papers in the state applauded his efforts; the many German Democratic journals, however, appalled by the *Volksblatt*'s volte-face, railed against this Republican treachery and its putative mastermind, Henry Villard, abusing him "with much wrath and unanimity of feeling." For the first time, but by no means the last, he perceived that freedom of the press is a mixed blessing: at the same time that it gives you the freedom to speak your mind as you choose, it gives others the freedom to write just about anything they like about *you*. Villard was denounced as "an adventurer, an im-ported hireling, an ignorant greenhorn," this last the most unkind-est cut of all. His replies, or rather retaliations, flowed easily from his pen, for he found that he took great pleasure in this sort of combat.

Naturally, Villard lost more than half of his subscribers. The Re-publican campaign, however, took as many copies as he could print every week, so new subscriptions were not a pressing concern. Mean-while, he was so caught up in the political fervor that swept the coun-try in the presidential campaign of 1856 that the *Volksblatt* alone could not satisfy his appetite for partisan activity. He founded a Ger-man section of the local Republican club, persuaded a respectable number (more than fifty) of his countrymen to join, and for the first time engaged in public speaking. Not surprisingly, he quickly got over his first embarrassment, winning applause from his hearers and enjoying himself immensely. He even gave a couple of brief, well-prepared addresses in English at general meetings of the Republican club. His success made him think that, with practice, he could "make my mark on the rostrum." The club also gave him the opportunity to hear many prominent speakers, both local and national, who addressed mass rallies. The most eloquent local leader was Judge Doolittle, later a United States senator.

Amid all this dedicated activity, Villard still found time to broaden the scope of his journalistic endeavors. During his time in New York, he had made the acquaintance of the editors of the *Neue Zeit*, an eminent, extremely literate German weekly. Shortly after his arrival in Racine, he submitted to them a long article on the general political situation in the Northwestern section of the country. To his delight, the editors accepted his submission at once and requested more. Thus, by knowing the right people, identifying a marketable area of investigation, and—on his own unresting initiative—producing competent work in that area, Villard became a Western political correspondent for the *Neue Zeit*. The pay ($5 each) was disproportionate to the amount of time he spent preparing his freelance articles, but it was so much added to his income, and by his reckoning the prestige of writing for such a high-toned journal as the *Neue Zeit* more than compensated for its parsimony.

As the presidential election approached, Villard worked himself into a frenzy of anxious excitement. From morning till midnight he solicited, rallied, met, marched, debated, argued, buttonholed, organized, chanted, and cheered, all to no avail. The Democratic candidate, James Buchanan—nicknamed "Old Public Functionary" because of the many offices he had held in his long political career, and even more inclined to support and appease the proslavery forces than either of his decidedly conservative predecessors—comfortably defeated the Republican candidate, Frémont, and an ex-president, Millard Fillmore, the candidate of the American Party. Not only did Buchanan win all the states of the South, he also triumphed over his opponents in several Northern states, including Illinois and Pennsylvania (though not Wisconsin).

Villard took the defeat of his candidate and his cause the only way he could—highly personally. He was thrown into a condition of humiliated, antisocial disgust, and more than a week passed before he was able to emerge from this private pit. As always, he had hoped too hard, believed too utterly in the rightness of his own perceptions; and his reaction to disappointment, to having been proved wrong, was commensurately intolerable. Fortunately, it was also brief; his character made him incapable of inhabiting a state of despair, no matter how thorough or intense, for very long.

Besides, the *Volksblatt* clearly required all his attention. With the end of the campaign came the withdrawal of the party's campaign subscriptions, and the *Volksblatt*'s 250 subscribers, many of whom had remained on the list despite the provocation of the paper's political somersault, were not enough to keep the publication in existence. Advertising income had also shrunk; the printing equipment, especially the type, was in urgent need of renewal; and the Republican Party officials, recognizing a sinking ship when they saw one, canceled the weekly subsidy they had provided during the campaign. Villard accordingly received "my first lesson in that common experience in this and every other free country, that there is the greatest difference between the promises of politicians before an election and their fulfilment after it."

Further developments reinforced Villard's apprehension of this dispiriting truth. It turned out that the Republican committee had not bought the *Volksblatt* outright from its former Democratic owner; since they had had no intention of devoting any more money than necessary to keeping this operation alive beyond its usefulness, they had merely made a down payment of 25 percent and taken a six-month mortgage on the rest. In the same spirit, having shrewdly gauged their young editor, they made him a conspicuously refusable offer, which he mulled over for a few days and then, against all odds, accepted. They agreed to turn over ownership of the paper to him, magnanimously waiving any claim to a reimbursement of their down payment and requiring only that the *Volksblatt* continue to support the Republican Party. For his part, Villard took upon his inexperienced shoulders the burden of the mortgage (which was now due to expire in four months' time), the prospect of doubling the subscription list (which was the only way to insure the paper's survival), and the responsibility of editing and producing the newspaper (which included writing editorials and articles).

All this proved too much even for Villard's abundant energies, but he didn't go down without a struggle. Although he solicited advertising assiduously and canvassed feverishly for new subscriptions, traveling out to the countryside and the nearby towns and even going as far as Milwaukee, and although he performed his writing and editorial duties deep into the night, meeting deadlines with minutes to spare, the odds against him were too great. One can smile at his hubris and lack of any real clues concerning his own limitations, but his conduct throughout this struggle shows that he was not utterly naive and that he had the instincts proper to the lone-wolf entrepreneur that he would become. What he didn't yet have was the nerve, perhaps because the stakes weren't high enough. He managed to avoid indebting himself personally for type and other business expenditures; his ideas about generating additional sources of income for the paper, including opening a job-printing service, were sound enough, but impracticable because his time was so short; he performed the paper's business at the paper's expense, making sure that he and his compositors were paid on time; and he knew when it was time to quit.

In January 1857 he advised the Republican committee of his plight, and they authorized him to turn the newspaper over to its former owner, who accepted it with great reluctance and immediately changed its affiliation back to the Democrats. (It seems that subscribers to the *Volksblatt* were expected to exhibit some elasticity in their political views.) This once and present owner threatened but did not pursue legal action against Villard and the Republican committee. He nursed his grudge, however, and in 1881, at the height of Villard's prosperity, wrote him an irascible letter claiming that taking back ownership of the *Volksblatt* had ruined him and demanding some acknowledgment of his distress. Villard's sense of duty and standard of ethical behavior were unusually high, despite the high-finance world in which he operated, and besides, he loved the grand gesture; he sent this querulous man $1,000.

V illard found himself in congenial surroundings, with savings enough to last a few months, and free from the obligation of making frantic efforts to keep the sinking *Volksblatt* afloat. Resolved to stay where he was for a while, he continued throughout the winter and spring of 1857 to submit articles and essays, all of them readily accepted, to the *Neue Zeit*. He had a bit of leisure and was enjoying relative, though fleeting, prosperity, so there was an opportunity for some serious pondering on the subject of his future.

The editor and readership of the *Neue Zeit* obviously appreciated his work; it was clear, therefore, that his long-cherished belief in his ability to succeed as a German writer was well founded. Unfortunately, this dream was no longer enough. Despite its millions of immigrants, a significant percentage of whom were Germans, the United States was an English-speaking country. Villard saw that he could achieve real prominence (something he very much wanted) as a journalist in America only if he wrote in the official language. He had made great linguistic strides; now it was time to cross the finish line. Much of his spare time and energy went into learning to write correct, fluent English, using a painstaking method of his own devising that involved memorizing and reproducing various randomly chosen texts. His progress after a few months emboldened him to write an article in English—an essay on European politics—and to offer it to the *Daily Advocate,* the local Republican paper.

This was his modest debut as an American journalist. To his heady delight, the editor of the *Advocate* accepted his article and asked him for more of the same. Soon he was writing one or two English articles a week for this newspaper.

Meanwhile, Chief Justice Roger B. Taney of the United States Supreme Court, belying the frailty of his eighty years, had given the country a powerful push on its way down a steep, dark road. In 1846, a Missouri slave named Dred Scott had sued his master's widow for freedom for himself and his family on the grounds that, while in the service of his master, he had lived for years on free soil, including the state of Illinois. At first Scott lost the case, then won it, together with his freedom, then lost both on appeal, then appealed to a higher court; steadily accumulating weight and significance, this "simple freedom suit" gradually made its way to the highest court in the land. Seeing its opportunity, the Supreme Court's Southern majority chose to use its decision in *Scott v. Sandford* to make a definitive statement on the vexed questions of black citizenship and the government's power to limit slavery.

On March 6, 1857, a mere two days after President Buchanan's inauguration, the court handed down its decision in the Dred Scott case: by a 7–2 majority, Scott's claim to freedom was denied. Nor was this all. In a thick, sweeping opinion, Taney enunciated the most extreme proslavery arguments ever to issue from the United States Supreme Court: slavery was under the protection of the Constitution; the government had no power, by the Missouri Compromise or any other enactment, to keep slavery out of the territories; and the guarantees of the Declaration of Independence and the Constitution did not extend to Negroes, who were to be regarded as "so far inferior, that they had no rights which a white man was bound to respect."

Far from settling the matter, this ferociously partisan decision served only to raise political tensions in the country to nearly intolerable levels. The proslavery forces, seeing the moral and constitutional justice of their position confirmed by the highest authority in the land, became more inflexible and aggressive; those who opposed slavery, shocked by the blatant injustice of the decision, grew increasingly convinced that only some awful cataclysm could put an end to the national nightmare. While Henry Villard sat in Racine and worked on his prose style, the country kept up its steady march toward disaster.

Young, gregarious Mr. Villard did not spend all his days and nights toiling over his newspaper articles and perfecting his English prose. For the first time since he had landed on American soil, he was able to conduct, in a setting that greatly appealed to him, a social life undistorted by pressures of time, money, employment, family duty, class differences, or linguistic inadequacy. As though under the influence of a natural law, he gravitated toward the socially, politically, and intellectually prominent citizens of the town: civic leaders, successful businessmen, college professors. With his good looks, natural charm, youthful vitality, cosmopolitan background, and aristocratic manners, Villard was a welcome addition to the social circles of Racine, and he received many invitations. He was impressed by "the neatness, order, comfort, peace, and quiet that, as a rule, characterize the American home"—could these qualities have been missing from the homes of the families he knew, particularly his own, in Germany?—but what he found most striking in the homes he visited was the women.

While no one would mistake Henry Villard for a feminist, his views on the subject of the opposite sex were unusually enlightened for his day. It was during his stay in Racine that he first began to appreciate the female citizens of his adopted country, and this appreciation, later ratified and exalted by his marriage to an extraordinary woman, remained undiminished for the rest of his life. After Racine, he would always believe "that American women of any social position have not their equals in any other country for brightness, tact, and true womanhood, and that they are as intelligent as American men and superior to them in all other respects—except, of course, knowledge of practical life." Quaintly phrased, perhaps—one flinches a little at what "practical life" might be taken to mean, to say nothing of "true womanhood"—but expressive of genuine regard.

Delighted as he was by the young ladies of Racine, one of whom nearly captured his available heart, and comfortable as he generally felt in his surroundings, Villard could not ignore what was for him the single great drawback to the enjoyment of American society in general and the community of Racine, Wisconsin, in particular: it was pervaded by religion. Everyone belonged to a church; the fact that Villard belonged to none was considered a blemish, though some allowance was made for him as a foreigner. Not satisfied with such tolerance, he managed to let his freethinking views be known. He thought he noticed, after this, "a certain shrinking" from him, but he was too provoked to regret his frank speech, for he had attended a couple of revivals. Church services were bad enough, but these spectacles appalled him, repelled him, and probably made him recall with some nostalgia the staid rituals of the Reformed Church he attended in Zweibrücken. He found it incredible, inexplicable, that the sober, well-mannered ladies and gentlemen he met socially were capable of such public exhibitions of violent religious frenzy. Most shocking of all was the noted orator and future senator Judge Doolittle, "gesticulating and jerking his body into all sorts of attitudes like a madman and exhorting the crowd around him to do likewise in 'professing the Lord!' " as his young admirer and fellow Republican activist watched in horror. For Villard, this was the religious equivalent of tobacco spitting, an offensive American practice that he could never accept.

By May 1857 Villard's dwindling savings, insufficiently enhanced by the sporadic income from his freelance pieces, made it necessary for him to leave Racine. He did so with distinct reluctance, having on the whole spent a pleasant, profitable, and professionally useful ten months there, but it was obvious that his goal of success as a writer of newspaper editorials would have to be pursued "in the intellectual centres of the East." Packing his few belongings and the manuscripts of six long articles (three in German and three in English) on a variety of subjects, he bid a sorrowful farewell to the many friends and acquaintances he had made in Racine and started on the long eastward journey. Better armed and more confident than ever before, he turned his back on the provinces and set out for his third try at storming the forbidding, indifferent citadel of New York City.

Through connections established the previous year, abetted by wearisome hours of "antechambering," Villard was able to get introductions to various editors at the leading daily newspapers in New York—the *Tribune,* the *Herald,* the *Times,* and the German paper, the *Staats-Zeitung.* Only at this last, however, did he receive any encouragement. His application was but one out of many, yet the owner of the *Staats-Zeitung,* Mrs. Anna Uhl (widow of Jakob Uhl, its founder), received him kindly and passed along a couple of the young man's articles to her literary editor; throughout all the vicissitudes of the past years, Villard had maintained his interest in reading and in forming opinions about what he read.

Before long the *Staats-Zeitung* notified him that his articles had been accepted for publication. Although its politics were "abominable"—it was a Democratic newspaper—and its rate of payment mortifying, particularly when he compared it to the amount of time he spent laboring over his articles, Villard pocketed his fees and wrote gamely on. Other German newspapers, including the faithful *Neue Zeit,* accepted occasional pieces from him, but in no case was he a regular contributor. As for the American papers, he had to lower his aim. Giving up, at least temporarily, the dream of leaping out of nowhere onto the editorial pages of the English-language dailies of New York, he began sending them actual reportage, mostly brief items concerning goings-on among the German population of the city.

About half of his submissions were accepted—the rest represented hard work wasted. Yet again, circumstances compelled his retreat into a precarious existence; yet again, he began living from hand to mouth on a small, uncertain income, too poor for any sort of social life and reduced to solitary brooding. By the end of July he began to find his situation intolerable and resolved to change it.

With each passing day, each underpaid article, each flat rejection, Villard looked upon his decision to seek his fortune in New York as a more serious mistake. As he would often do in the future, he sought a remedy for his difficulties in the West. He cast about for a means of returning there and conceived the idea of persuading one of the American newspapers to send him as a correspondent to the territory of Minnesota, where controversy was raging between Democrats and Republicans at the convention then meeting to frame the constitution of the future state. After some hedging, the managing editor of the *Tribune,* Charles A. Dana (later assistant secretary of war under Lincoln), consented to give him the assignment. The terms could have been more advantageous—for example, Villard had to pay his own traveling expenses—but he was quick to discover that various perquisites were attached to such a job.

One of the best of these came to him through the good offices of Thurlow Weed, editor of the *Albany Journal.* Continuing to build up an extensive network of influential acquaintances, particularly among journalists and politicians, Villard applied to Weed, a perfect stranger, for assistance. The older man responded at once, helping Villard obtain a pass that entitled him to free travel by rail and water from Albany to Prairie du Chien, Wisconsin, the westernmost terminus of the railroad in Wisconsin at that time. It took four and a half days to get to Prairie du Chien, followed by a twenty-four-hour voyage on a passenger steamer up the Mississippi to St. Paul, where Villard disembarked on a bright, hot day in the middle of August.

St. Paul had begun as a town of narrow, crooked streets built on hills overlooking the Mississippi River a few miles upstream from its confluence with the Minnesota. Incorporated but three years earlier (1854) and numbering only about seven thousand inhabitants, St. Paul was destined to grow hard and fast. Sensing this bursting energy, Villard responded favorably to it, as well as to the town's lovely setting and the advantages of its location. But a series of events, partly calamitous and partly comic, shortened his stay in Minnesota. Against all expectations, the Democrats and Republicans compromised their differences, finished their appointed task in good order, and adjourned the convention before the eager correspondent had been on the scene for two weeks. Hungry for material (he was being paid by the column), Villard started visiting other parts of the territory. He and a group of young men scheduled a two-week hunting party in the wild country northwest of the city—Villard apparently planned some descriptions of untamed nature for the *Tribune*'s readers—but the overly sanguine hunters bogged down in a tamarack swamp, lost several pitched battles with great clouds of mosquitoes, and turned their welted faces back in the direction of St. Paul after an awful day and a half. On another trip, this time to a town forty miles south of St. Paul, Villard lost an equal amount of blood to the thirsty Minnesota mosquitoes, but he was able to make a few connections and put together a few stories once he reached his destination. To his chagrin, however, upon his return to St. Paul he found a letter from the editor of the *Tribune* canceling his assignment.

Back he went to New York, forming along the way the rather drastic scheme of persuading some newspaper there to send him to cover the Sepoy Mutiny, then bloodily raging on the Indian subcontinent. The idea of being a war correspondent appealed to him, but his time had not yet come, and no paper would consider paying his way. Meanwhile he was quickly running out of money; the severe depression of 1857 struck New York City as it did the rest of the country, causing banks to fail, trade to stand still, and jobs to dry up; any notion of raising sufficient funds for a passage to India vanished.

In fact, Villard's funds were not even sufficient for daily existence. By the end of October, harsh necessity had driven him to a German boardinghouse in Jersey City, where one of his fortuitous meetings saved him from total disaster. He discovered, among his fellow lodgers, a married couple from the Palatinate; the man was a skilled stonecutter whom Villard had known in his youth, and the wife was a former servant of the Hilgard family. These kind people supported the penniless young man for many weeks, thus earning his lifelong gratitude, which he was pleased to demonstrate quite amply in more prosperous times.

The depression deepened; Villard kept writing. The streets of New York, where he regularly ventured in mostly vain attempts to sell his articles, were thronged with the unemployed and the homeless, and he wondered how close he was to joining them. An advertisement in a Pennsylvania German newspaper, picked up by chance, announced openings for schoolteachers in several counties in the southeastern part of the state. The prospect of a schoolteaching career was not one of those that filled our young man with fantasies of fame and fortune. But he was desperate, and regular employment, considering his other choices, seemed extremely desirable.

Having made up his mind, Villard characteristically chose the railroad as the quickest way to his fate, whatever it might be; letting his fate come to him was not in his line. On October 31, carrying the valise that contained his few belongings, he took a train to Reading, Pennsylvania, there to persuade the appropriate people to hire him for a position for which he had, as far as he could tell, neither qualifications nor training. The county school commissioner in Reading had no openings and sent Villard on to his colleague in Lebanon, the seat of the adjoining county. There the commissioner, charmed by the personable young applicant, gave him an ad hoc oral examination for the required teaching certificate, coaxed the answers out of him, and directed him, certificate in hand, to Jonestown, six miles distant.

Villard walked to Jonestown the next morning. Like many Germans, he loved tramping through the countryside. He had braved the pathless Minnesota wildernesses (he would brave others), insects and all, largely for the sake of the picturesque woodlands, the oak-fringed lakes, the contact with the unimproved, untainted natural world, but he was fondest of landscapes that combined natural beauty with the harmonious, ameliorating imprint of man. Here, along the road to Jonestown, he found much to admire as he rambled through the rolling, fertile country with its prosperous farms, its green valleys, and its swift streams running down from the nearby Blue Mountains. In the neat little village of Jonestown, he was directed to the village doctor, who was also the chairman of the local school board.

This gentleman, after an hour's pleasant chat, told Villard he was "altogether too well educated"—and by implication, too upper class—for the people he would be dealing with, but the resolute young man stressed his lack of choices and was assigned to teach two terms of three months each at the village school. For this labor he was to receive $30 a month, more than he'd expected, and free room and board. Unappetizingly enough, this latter perquisite was to come to him at the hands of his pupils' families, who were supposed to take weekly turns putting him up.

Villard had a week to prepare himself for the latest addition to his multifarious résumé. He moved into the most attractive of the three hotels situated on Jonestown's elm-shaded public square, bought the required textbooks, and began to cram. Between study sessions, he made sure to meet the leaders of the little community and to indulge his delight in the autumn finery of the surrounding countryside. On a morning in early November 1858, he set out for the little schoolhouse, forty-five minutes' walk from the village, and his first pedagogic adventures.

He had sixty students, no more than forty of whom came to class on any given day, ranging in age from five to eighteen. They and their families, descendants of Palatinate peasants who had come to

Pennsylvania as indentured laborers a hundred years before, spoke a literally outlandish dialect of German and hardly any English at all; Villard's High German, which must have sounded quite aristocratic to their ears, was the language of instruction. None of the pupils exhibited a very high level of academic accomplishment, so (except in the matter of penmanship) Villard felt adequate to his task and conscientiously tried to instill in them some systematic knowledge. The children were shabby and dirty but healthy, ignorant and badly schooled but intelligent, and Villard, though stunned by how little they knew ("I seemed to be among veritable German peasant children"), enjoyed the reverence verging on awe that they showed him. Conduct was not a problem, but he did have to deal sternly with laziness, "especially on the part of the older girls." Their languor, perhaps, was due to the anticipation of being scolded by their handsome young instructor.

Rather less diverting were his living conditions. His hosts, though generally kind, were far too coarse and unpolished for him, and far too reminiscent—in their cooking, their furniture, their general domestic life—of the degraded peasantry of his homeland. They even slept on and under featherbeds, just like peasants in the Palatinate, and Villard had to submit to this indignity as well. A century in America had civilized the families of Jonestown somewhat, but almost all of them remained "sadly ignorant, narrow, and low," uncouth in their table manners and "still innocent of the use of handkerchiefs." Their lives were so circumscribed and their curiosity so meager that most of them had never seen a railroad, "though they lived within six miles of one!"

Henry Villard, who was curious about most things and naturally drawn to railroads, could not comprehend lives so deadened by apathy. Eating and conversing with such people, spending evenings and weekends in their domestic circles, and then going off to sleep with the male farmworkers tried him sorely. After Christmas, however, he started boarding exclusively with the family he liked best, the Umbergers, and things improved.

Despite the drawbacks of his situation, an occasional glance at a newspaper sufficed to assure Villard that he had made the correct choice. The financial crisis was causing deepening distress in large cities all over the country, while he had a steady job, a regular income, and a great deal of free time. Every Saturday he went to the schoolhouse, fired up the stove, and spent the day writing pieces for sale to the New York newspapers. He met the usual resistance from the American dailies, but the *Staats-Zeitung* accepted some descriptive sketches and even a short story. Villard spent the rest of his leisure time seeking out company, calling on people in Jonestown and Lebanon (where he struck up an acquaintance with the editor of the "leading local paper"), and joining the loungers around the stove in the various taverns.

This pleasantly detached existence continued until the end of May 1858, when the closing of the schools for the summer put an end to Villard's appointment and freed him for yet another attempt on New York City. This time he would get inside the citadel; a distinguished ten-year journalistic career was about to begin.

LINCOLN AND DOUGLAS IN A PRESIDENTIAL FOOTRACE.
Published by J. Sage & Sons, 1860.
Courtesy of the Library of Congress.

6

The Reporter
and the
Rail-Splitter

That is the real issue. That is the issue that will continue in this country when these poor tongues of Judge Douglas and myself shall be silent. It is the eternal struggle between these two principles—right and wrong—throughout the world. They are the two principles that have stood face to face from the beginning of time; and will ever continue to struggle. The one is the common right of humanity and the other the divine right of kings. It is the same principle in whatever shape it develops itself. It is the same spirit that says, "You work and toil and earn bread, and I'll eat it." No matter in what shape it comes, whether from the mouth of a king who seeks to bestride the people of his own nation and live by the fruit of their labor, or from one race of men as an apology for enslaving another race, it is the same tyrannical principle.

ABRAHAM LINCOLN,
Lincoln-Douglas debates (October 15, 1858)

Although Jonestown had clearly been just another dead end, Villard left it with some reluctance; he had lain there as in a quiet bed, not luxurious or notably comfortable but thoroughly peaceful. Now he had to arise and return to the waking world, to the active, adventurous life he craved, with all its promise and all its uncertainties. There was a sad parting with the Umberger family and other friends, none of whom he would ever see again, and then he turned toward the future. He was twenty-three years old. He had a "moderately replenished" wardrobe, about $60 in cash, nearly as much again due him from the *Staats-Zeitung*, excellent health, a great desire for fulfilling work, and "fully regained and unbounded confidence."

Villard went directly to the offices of the *Staats-Zeitung*, where he was warmly received by the publisher, Oswald Ottendorfer, and by Mrs. Anna Uhl, the proprietress, later to become Mrs. Ottendorfer. They complimented him on the freelance work he had done for the paper in the past and looked forward to further collaboration with him. The *Staats-Zeitung*, the country's leading German newspaper, had an impressive nationwide circulation. Mrs. Uhl and Ottendorfer proposed to employ their eager applicant in the dual capacity of canvasser and correspondent, assigned to travel through Ohio, Indiana, Michigan, and Illinois, collecting for old subscriptions and soliciting new ones while writing regular "descriptive" pieces for the newspaper. For a trial period of three months, a period filled with potential as far as he was concerned, Villard would receive a weekly salary of $15 plus expenses.

The cub reporter accepted this proposition without hesitation, pocketed the fees due him plus a sizable advance for his expenses, and left for Ohio on the following day. For five weeks he crisscrossed the state, with mixed success. The weekly dispatches he wrote were appreciatively received and duly published, but his performance in the other aspects of his job satisfied neither his employers nor himself. Collecting proved painstakingly difficult, and his attempts to win over new subscribers to the paper were not merely unsuccessful; they subjected him to frequent rudeness.

As he cast about for a solution to this latest predicament, he was struck by an inspired idea. The newspapers were full of stories about the upcoming series of debates to be held between the Democratic senator from Illinois, Stephen Douglas, and a forty-nine-year-old Springfield lawyer and former congressman named Abraham Lincoln. Douglas, though only forty-five, was campaigning for his third consecutive term in the Senate as another step in what many, including himself, considered his irresistible march to the presidency; his rival, Lincoln, in his own peculiar and deceptively shambling way, had emerged as the leader of the young Republican Party in Illinois, but he was little known outside the state and very few people, not including himself, thought of him as presidential material.

Alert and sensitive to the political conditions in his adopted country, Henry Villard was among those with sufficient insight to discern that the contest between Douglas and Lincoln would be of historical importance and that Illinois, though far from the corridors of national power, was about to become the focal point of American politics. He persuaded his employers to change his job description, and soon he was on his way to Chicago as the *Staats-Zeitung*'s correspondent (no soliciting required), assigned to cover one of the most significant political confrontations of the nineteenth century.

*   *   *

With the good timing essential to a successful journalist, Villard reached Chicago in early July, just before the triumphant arrival of Douglas and his entourage from Washington. Villard's brief and unsatisfactory meeting with the Little Giant two years previously now provided an opportunity that he seized with characteristic boldness. He called upon the senator in his hotel; Douglas recognized him at once—people seemed to have no trouble remembering him—welcomed him cordially, declared his entire willingness to have Villard accompany him on his travels through Illinois, and introduced him to various friends and associates. Most impressive of all was the senator's regally beautiful young wife, who charmed the susceptible bachelor reporter utterly.

Douglas and his opponent, Abraham Lincoln, had first met in the 1830s and had been rivals of one sort or another for more than twenty years; Douglas had even courted Mary Todd before Lincoln married her. Throughout the 1850s, and particularly after Douglas conceived and championed the notorious Kansas-Nebraska Act in 1854, Lincoln's speeches "constituted one long running rebuttal to what Douglas said and what Douglas did." For Douglas, slavery was a morally neutral institution whose chief drawback was that the controversy it aroused interfered with progress, with the settlement and development of the country, with economic expansion. His popular-sovereignty doctrine asserted that slavery should be allowed or forbidden in the territories—and therefore in whatever new states were admitted to the Union—according to the will of the people who lived there. Douglas thought the democratic process would dissolve this annoying problem, the Union would be preserved, and the nation could turn to the real business at hand.

As an unabashed white supremacist, Douglas was largely indifferent to conclusions about the morality of slavery. Lincoln, by contrast, held staunch antislavery views—"If slavery is not wrong, nothing is wrong," he said—and he was disgusted by Douglas's popular-sovereignty nostrum, which made slavery and freedom ethically equal and reduced the difference between them to mere economics. Lincoln was no believer, at least not at this point, in racial equality, and if he had been, admitting as much would have been tantamount to committing political suicide in the profoundly racist America of the mid–nineteenth century. For a long time he thought wistfully, ludicrously, of colonizing the former slaves in Africa as the best cure for the slavery disease, but he never engaged in race baiting, as Douglas did, and he could never be brought to believe that the rights of black Americans, bound or free, were any narrower, or any less inalienable, than those of the whites. Villard, whose views on this subject were still in the formative stage, quoted Douglas's position in his dispatches with guarded approval.

In the four months that preceded the November elections (after which the newly elected state legislature would in turn choose one of them as U.S. Senator), Douglas and Lincoln spoke their minds in almost every county in the state of Illinois. Apart from the seven debates, they delivered hundreds of separate speeches and traveled a total of ten thousand miles. Their campaign made journalistic history: it was the first to be reported by correspondents who traveled with the candidates, and Henry Villard was among the innovators. Both Douglas and Lincoln employed a variety of special conveyances and reached their destinations amid all the fanfare their supporters could muster. The unusual appointments in Douglas's personal railroad train included, mounted on a flatcar, a small cannon, with which the senator forestalled the potential ignominy of arriving unsaluted in a town by saluting himself. Lincoln, as befitted both his young party's financial resources and his homely, downbeat style, traveled and arrived with less pomp but quite as much circumstance.

Henry Villard was often a passenger on Douglas's train, where the endlessly reiterated explosions of the Little Giant's little cannon were followed by the roars and shrieks of the greeting crowds, the rumble and bang of fireworks, the brassy blare of band music. By the time the senator arrived at the venue for the first debate (Ottawa, in north central Illinois), on August 21, 1858, he had already delivered some seventeen separate speeches all over the state—Lincoln, with twelve, was not far behind in the mass production of words—and public interest in the coming clash of the titans verged on hysteria.

Like the other debates, the one in Ottawa presented a spectacle that we can perhaps visualize if we imagine a combined carnival parade, major sporting event, and music festival. Conveyed by every means from trains to mules, including Illinois River canal boats, people came from miles around, more than doubling the population of the town, clogging its streets, and filling its biggest open space, the public square. Lincoln and Douglas, the stars of the occasion, entered the square in separate elaborately decorated carriages at the head of long processions of chanting, celebrating supporters. Great crowds of people, some of them perched in trees or on rooftops, lined the streets and cheered the candidates as they passed. Others turned the event into a picnic, bringing their families and their lunches or buying food and drink from the many vendors in and around the square, whose offerings included roasted meats, corn, ice cream, and abundant alcohol. Hours before the speaking began, people began jockeying for the spots closest to the platform—there were no seats—and a bit later a few boisterous souls, elevated by a mixture of political fervor and hard liquor, climbed onto the roof of the speakers' stand and crashed through to the platform itself, shattering several planks and sending a shower of splintered lumber upon the heads of the reception committee assembled below.

But this unbridled festive scene was overlaid by an atmosphere thick with evil omens and dark forebodings. Martial symbols and accoutrements were everywhere—cannons, fireworks, marching companies, military bands—and press accounts of the proceedings were laced with such words as "volley," "combat," "battlefield." Illinois itself, as Villard perceived, might be considered a miniature model of the United States as a whole: mostly antislavery and Republican in the North, mostly proslavery and Democratic in the South, evenly divided and volatile across the center. In spite of their courteous behavior toward each other, the two candidates represented, in microcosm, the powerful and dangerous differences that were splitting the country in two. Before many years were to pass, the issue of slavery would be resolved by wholesale slaughter; in Illinois, in the late summer and early fall of the year 1858, two eloquent and impassioned speakers tried to settle it with words. Their equally impassioned but less inhibited audiences—ten thousand in Ottawa, as many as sixteen thousand at a couple of the later debates—crowded around the platform, shouted questions and comments, howled, groaned, cheered, argued with the candidates and one another, and frequently resorted to blows. And standing in front of many of those crude platforms, nudged and jostled by the throng as some particularly committed constituents traded punches in the dust, our young German immigrant watched American democracy in action, listened, took notes, and tried to make sense of what was taking place. If he failed to do so, he was not alone—the forces at work had already moved beyond the power of rationality to grasp them—but he realized, instinctively and acutely, that he was bearing witness to something momentous.

As a Republican (though not yet a citizen), Villard was in something of a delicate position. He was writing for a Democratic newspaper, and the newspapers of his day were unabashedly partisan; neutrality or objectivity had no place in political reporting. To a reporter from another Democratic newspaper, Douglas's "countenance" at Ottawa was aglow with "that particular intellectual and demolishing look that he is so famous for," while a Republican newsman had "never seen a human face so distorted with rage. He resembled a wild beast in looks and gesture." Villard was expected to take sides with similar vigor.

It is difficult to determine exactly how much of the reports printed in the *Staats-Zeitung* jibed with the dispatches Villard actually wrote—the paper used no bylines, and there seems to have been a good deal of editorial revising—but on the subject of Lincoln, Villard was a hostile reporter writing for a hostile newspaper. He was able to justify this apparent party disloyalty by aligning himself with those Republicans who saw an opportunity in the fact that Douglas's pragmatic indifference to slavery offended many proslavery Democrats, particularly Southerners, for whom nothing less than militant advocacy of slavery was acceptable. Such Republicans, no friends of Lincoln, believed that Douglas's reelection, preferably unopposed, would help bring about a definitive split between the antislavery and proslavery wings of the Democratic Party.

Besides, Abraham Lincoln was not Henry Villard's type. Even though Villard saw that Douglas was a master rhetorician arguing for "a wrong and weak cause" and Lincoln "a thoroughly earnest and truthful man, inspired by sound convictions," he admired the Democrat's orotund dignity and found the Republican both impossible to like and personally distasteful. Always impressed by physical attractiveness, Villard could discover none in the "indescribably gawky" Lincoln, whose outsized features gave his unlovely, cadaverous face the aspect of a melancholy clown. Lincoln was largely indifferent to his dress and appearance, as many of his portraits reveal, and when he spoke he tended to jerk and bounce awkwardly by way of emphasizing his points. Worst of all, he offended the fastidious young reporter with his well-known fondness for coarse anecdotes and off-color jokes, especially those of his own invention. Villard met Lincoln frequently during the course of the campaign and always found him "most approachable, good-natured, and full of wit and humor," but the Republican candidate's incorrigible tendency to pepper his conversation with "risky" stories repeatedly shocked the young man. In fact, the backwoods American "Rail-splitter" (so called because of one of his youthful occupations, whacking timber into fence rails) so repelled the aristocratic foreigner that at first Villard, as Carl Sandburg wrote, "couldn't make out Lincoln at all." Eventually, Villard acknowledged Lincoln's greatness, admitting that "there was nothing in all Douglas's powerful effort that appealed to the higher instincts of human nature, while Lincoln always touched sympathetic chords." But first impressions remained strong, and Villard could never forget those jokes.

Nor could he forget the "ludicrous sight" of Lincoln after the Ottawa debate, carried most reluctantly from the platform on the shoulders of a couple of strapping farm boys, a "grotesque figure holding frantically on to the heads of his supporters, with his legs dangling . . . and his pantaloons pulled up so as to expose his underwear almost to his knees." Despite the way Lincoln rose to the unfathomable challenges of his presidency, despite the soulful profundity of the Gettysburg Address, despite the legend that shrouded the martyred president in a mythic glow, whenever Henry Villard thought about him his mind's eye glanced disapprovingly at a pair of absurdly exposed long johns.

An unexpected and intimate meeting with Lincoln, however, served to mix Villard's feelings about this unattractive but oddly compelling man. Some time after the second debate, at Freeport on August 27—probably in the early days of September—Villard arrived at a flag railroad station twenty miles west of Springfield and found there, waiting alone on the platform, the candidate himself. There were no handlers, no aides, no supporters; Lincoln had been, for a change, unceremoniously dropped off, and like Villard he was waiting for the Springfield train. It was nine in the evening, the air was hot and sticky, both travelers were stained by the omnipresent dust, and the train was late.

They exchanged greetings and a few perfunctory pleasantries, slight acquaintances not particularly overjoyed at this surprise meeting. The usually loquacious Villard recoiled a little in antipathy, Lincoln had other things on his mind, and both men were tired. The heavens, however, conspired to penetrate their barriers. Instead of the train, a thunderstorm came up; the bare platform offered no shelter of any kind; the two beat a concerted retreat to a side track and clambered into an empty freight car. There they squatted on the floor, and for an hour, sometimes shouting at one another above the crashing thunder and the rattling rain, their faces occasionally lit by flashes of lightning, these two men, the Sucker (the Illinois equivalent of Hoosier or Buckeye) and the *Pfälzer* (Palatinate German), utterly different in background, manners, and sensibilities, got to know each other.

First, like a good reporter, Villard drew his man into talking about himself, and what Lincoln said was modest and disarming. When he was a country store clerk, he declared, his greatest ambition was to be in the state legislature. And now, look at what his friends had got him into. It made him laugh to think of it. He hadn't considered himself qualified to be a United States senator, and it had taken a long time for those friends to convince him, and for him to convince himself, that he was. "Of course," he said, with another of his shrill, peculiar laughs, "now I'm sure I'm good enough, but in spite of it all, I say to myself every day, 'It's too big a thing for you, you'll never get it.' " This paradox obviously struck him as comic, because mirth grew in his voice as he revealed the curious fact that his wife, Mary, had no such reservations. "She insists that I'm going to be Senator and President of the United States, too." Lincoln clutched his pointy knees and rocked with laughter—what could be funnier than his wife's ambition? "Just think," he chuckled, "of such a Sucker as me as President!"

Then, like a good politician, Lincoln started asking his own questions. Where was Villard from? What was his family? How had he learned such fluent English in so short a time? And was it true that most educated Germans were "infidels"? "Well," the young infidel said, "it's true that you don't see many of them in church."

This didn't surprise Lincoln. "My own inclination is that way," he revealed, meaning he didn't fancy the inside of churches either. Raising the ante, Villard replied with a frank exposition of his views on religion, stressing his disbelief in Christianity, the existence of God, and the immortality of the soul. Lincoln's public utterances suggest, and most historians believe, that he was a profoundly spiritual man, but on this occasion he did not commit himself. Villard got the impression, however, that Lincoln shared his opinions; it is an impression that Lincoln *would* give, and Villard *would* get. At last they heard the whistle of the train, and together they splashed across the tracks to flag it down. Soon they were clanging into Springfield, where, wearily but cordially, they parted.

In the elections of November 2, Douglas managed, not without difficulty, to retain his Senate seat. Lincoln and his supporters were quite cast down, but as far as Villard was concerned, the right man had won. Still, the closeness of the race and the nationwide attention it received—attention that reporters like Villard helped to focus— made Lincoln a national figure and set him firmly on the path of his dramatic destiny.

For Villard, too, the Lincoln-Douglas debates marked a kind of turning point. The packed trains, the bad roads, the primitive towns, the wretched accommodations, the awful food, the constant travel, the repeated shifts from exaltation to exhaustion and back again, the pressure of deadlines, the hours spent standing in the sun and dust listening to the same speeches for the tenth or twentieth time—all these difficulties were surmountable, or at least endurable, and by the end of the four-month ordeal, Villard had served his apprenticeship. Now, at long last, he had a profession, one that fulfilled his long-cherished dream of making his living by his pen while at the same time offering as many opportunities for discovery and adventure as even his restless heart could crave.

His coverage of the Lincoln-Douglas debates not only broadened his experience; it also immensely widened his circle of acquaintance. Starting with the two principals, Villard had made many professionally and personally important contacts among politicians, leading citizens, and colleagues. He had done his job well, satisfied his employers, and assured himself for possible future use an entrée into the highest levels of government. He had also met a man who would be his lifelong friend and associate—Horace White of the *Chicago Press and Tribune*—but there were now plenty of other talented, influential people who knew and liked the young journalist Henry Villard. William T. Campbell, the future founder of Texaco, was so taken with him at this point that he named his firstborn son Henry Villard Campbell. As the new year, 1859, approached, Henry Villard could be proud of his accomplishments and more certain than ever of his bright future.

HORACE GREELEY.

Photograph by Mathew Brady.

National Archives.

7

All That Glitters

It's four long years since I reached this land
In search of gold among the rocks and sand,
And yet I'm poor when the truth is told,
I'm a lousy miner,
I'm a lousy miner, in search of shining gold.

"LOUSY MINER"
(American folksong)

With the elections of 1858 over and the year drawing to a close, Henry Villard, now in possession of a career, began to make career moves. He was more than ever determined to become an American journalist writing in American English—he always exhibited a wholehearted desire to be as thoroughly American as he could—but he wisely decided to focus his efforts on the Western press this time and to make his breakthrough there. The *Cincinnati Daily Commercial*, he thought, showed the kind of ability and enterprise he'd like to be associated with, so he took a train to Cincinnati, where he went directly to the office of the publisher. This gentleman referred him to the news editor, Murat Halstead, a distinguished young journalist (Villard's senior by only five years) who would go on to become proprietor and editor in chief of the newspaper.

"When I first saw Villard," Halstead wrote, "he was a stalwart, handsome youth of good manners." The young man "spoke English and German with equal facility and a strong simplicity that always characterized his style of expression." The applicant arrived well armed with specimens of his work in English, and Halstead found this same quality of "strong simplicity" on the page. Halstead's description of Villard's writing is almost a sketch of the man himself: his work "had the merits of terse statement, evident sincerity, and reliability. The style was not ambitious and the meaning not obscure. He had a keen eye for the essential points of a complex state of facts."

After a few interviews, Halstead hired Villard as a correspondent and assigned him to report on the upcoming session of the Indiana state legislature, which promised to be highly controversial because both Democrats and Republicans claimed majority status. Early in January 1859, Villard arrived in Indianapolis and dutifully began attending the august deliberations of the legislature and filing reports. Now writing for a Republican newspaper, and liberated from the conflict that his personal dislike for Lincoln had caused, Villard felt free to express himself with his wonted frankness; that this often bordered on tactlessness was not the kind of consideration he was likely to dwell upon.

In any case, Villard had written only a few articles for his newspaper before producing one in which, using strong, simple terms with evident sincerity, he roundly insulted one particular Democratic senator. The reporter's words prickled in the honorable gentleman's brain like a burr in his underwear and produced a drastic reaction. The senator had the offending article read, with great indignation, into the records of the Senate, denounced the reporter from the floor "in very violent language," and rammed through a motion to withdraw his press privileges and expel him from the chamber. This would not be Villard's last journalistic conflict with legislators, but it ended his brief career as a legislative reporter.

As far as Halstead was concerned, Villard's offense had been "to tell the truth and stick to it." The editor vigorously defended his reporter in the editorial columns of the *Commercial* and considered the affair a "test of manhood" that the young man had passed with flying colors; but Villard, with his Germanic inclination toward solemnity, especially regarding official authority, could not take so indulgent a view of what felt to him like public humiliation. Halstead thought "his German education had not stimulated him to be humorous

about the thunders of authority," and so Villard "was not immediately inclined to see the humor of his expulsion."

Although it probably never became a joking matter, the Indianapolis incident and the brief period of depression that followed it
quickly faded into the past, because the future had turned to gold.
Even before his Indiana assignment, Villard had hearkened with
much interest to the reports of gold strikes that were coming out of
the West with increasing frequency during the latter months of 1858.
The reports centered on the vast, wild, mountainous country in the
vicinity of Pikes Peak and the upper courses of the South Platte River,
in what is now Colorado but was then a little-explored wilderness,
mostly frequented, if at all, by nomadic Indian tribes.

Villard's natural curiosity and spirit of adventure spurred him to
propose that Halstead assign him to discover the truth about this El
Dorado in the Rocky Mountains. The editor agreed, and at the end
of February Villard left Cincinnati and began his long journey west.
He had read and heard much about the California gold rush of 1849
and the great wealth that had come to a few lucky forty-niners, and
already visions of fame and fortune were dancing in his head. He
dreamed not merely of striking it rich but of becoming a founder of
cities and states, a hero of the wilderness, a benefactor of mankind.

The motives of virtually everyone else who headed in the direction of Pikes Peak in 1859 were rather less idealistic. The lingering
effects of the severe depression of 1857 were partially responsible,
for they led men to seek desperate remedies for their miserable lot;
but the abiding cause of this new westward stampede was that peculiar kind of avarice—gold lust—which drives its wild-eyed devotees to
extremes beyond the comprehension of those unaffected by it. Villard was plunging into a movement that was both typically American
and archetypal, combining as it did the pioneer spirit with a quest
whose object was the very symbol of materialism.

A few days after leaving Cincinnati, Villard found himself on a
riverboat, steaming up the Missouri past the straggling hamlet of
Kansas City to the bustling town of Leavenworth, Kansas, the best
starting place for the trip to Pikes Peak. Although this was still early

in the rush, which would reach flood proportions in the spring, Villard's boat was crowded with eager Pikes Peakers, all fitted out for mining and feverish with gleaming dreams. There were already a thousand of them in Leavenworth, with more arriving every day.

Villard's pockets were as usual stuffed with letters of introduction, and he quickly met the important and knowledgeable people of the town, including the editor of the local newspaper. Everyone had an opinion or a story, or both, about the exclusive topic of conversation, Pikes Peak gold, but facts were hard to discern beneath the myths and fairy tales that were being circulated and sworn to. So many people had faith—in the gold if not in the fairy tales—that a freight company had decided to establish a line between Leavenworth and the new settlements along Cherry Creek, in and near the center of what is now Denver. When Villard arrived in Leavenworth, this enterprise—calling itself the Leavenworth and Pike's Peak Express Company—was busily setting up relay stations at twenty-mile intervals all along the six-hundred-mile route. The first stagecoach would leave for Cherry Creek in about two weeks; the fare was a whopping $200, but Villard was granted a 50 percent journalist's discount and bought the first ticket.

When, three weeks later, amid the cheers of a thousand spectators, the red-painted, canvas-covered Concord Coach left Leavenworth on its maiden run, our intrepid correspondent was the only passenger. For some the price was too high; others were concerned for their scalps, for the coach would travel many long, desolate stretches through Indian country; and most thought they'd just wait and see how things turned out. So Henry Villard, just past his twenty-fourth birthday, sat alone and stared out of the window as the heaving, slamming, springless carriage bounced across a beautiful empty landscape, rolling prairie as far as his eyes could see. At Fort Riley he slept in the last bed he would enjoy for six months and made the acquaintance of half a dozen cavalry officers, several of whom he was destined to meet again, not long hence, on the battlefields of the Civil War.

The coach covered the five hundred miles between Fort Riley and the Cherry Creek settlements in six and a half days, climbing slowly but steadily, passing over ridges and across plateaus, guided by stakes or piles of stones, buffalo bones, and dung, set up by the company's scouts; there was no road, and the passenger was thoroughly contused. For days they drove through one immense buffalo herd after another, the vanguard of the vast summer migration from Texas to Canada. It took an hour to traverse these herds, the red coach rattling past the shaggy monsters as they placidly grazed, so close that Villard could look into their piggish, incurious eyes. At length the coach climbed past the buffalo grass, and the landscape grew more arid; vegetation was scarce, and water was to be got only by digging. As he lay on the ground at night, wrapped in his buffalo robe and gazing up at millions of stars, Villard drew in great lungfuls of the pure, bracing air.

He had become a pioneer, and no discomforts, no ghastly tales of cannibalism and survival, no threat of savage beasts or murderous Indians could diminish the joy he took in his adventure. On the sixth day the great mass of Pikes Peak began to loom in the distance, a sight Villard found thrilling and exalting. From the crest of the last and highest ridge, he rejoiced in "one of the grandest sights to be beheld anywhere in the world": the broad valley of the South Platte River and its tributaries, surrounded by the rugged, seemingly impenetrable rampart of the Rocky Mountains, anchored by Pikes Peak in the south and Longs Peak in the north. The last fifty miles of the journey ran downhill, and by the light of a majestic sunset the coach at last came to a halt in front of the log house that was company headquarters in the settlement of Denver.

There were tents, wigwams, dugouts, adobes, and rough cabins scattered all along both sides of Cherry Creek, with the greatest concentration near the point where the creek poured itself into the South Platte. Denver, on the right bank, contained only about a dozen structures of any kind and seemed likely to be dwarfed by Auraria, on the left bank. Auraria could boast of many more inhabitants and included all the business establishments, for example, taverns, a tailor's shop, a shoemaker's, a printing office (which had recently begun producing a weekly paper, the *Rocky Mountain News*), and even— a touch of refinement—a little cabin where a watchmaker kept shop.

All of these enterprises were, of course, quite raw, and the buildings that housed them were of the most rudimentary kind.

Diversions were few along Cherry Creek; the unexpected arrival of the coach brought out the entire population of the settlements. By popular demand, the sole passenger, fresh from the States and doubly qualified as a news source by virtue of his profession, climbed onto a log and regaled the multitude for half an hour with the latest news from the U.S.A. It is agreeable to imagine young Henry Villard, bruised and slightly unsteady after being jolted from Kansas to Colorado, standing in the midst of this dirty, grizzled throng of settlers, prospectors, adventurers, and assorted desperadoes and delivering a thirty-minute German-accented current events bulletin. His efforts were gratefully received, and he became at once a familiar and welcome member of the community.

Villard stayed in a log cabin a few miles up Cherry Creek. Like every other structure in the vicinity (hardly a building, or a settler, had been in the area for more than six months), this one had no windows (glass was not available), no chairs, and no beds; there was a roof of sorts, but no floor. Although these primitive conditions resembled nothing that his civilized European upbringing had prepared him for, he adjusted to them rapidly and seemed comfortable amid the rough and rowdy men with whom he was in daily contact. They shared in common with him a thirst for adventure, a natural preference for activity over passivity, and romantic dreams of sudden, spectacular success. As for women, there was a total of five (and seven children) in the settlements, rarities of the local fauna, seldom seen curiosities. Along Cherry Creek, the ruling passion was the lust for gold.

In point of fact, however, that object of desire remained coyly obscure. New seekers were arriving daily, in ever increasing numbers, drawn as by a magnet by the hope of finding gold. They came from every direction and by every conceivable means of transport, especially wagon trains. There was also an unfathomably large number of handcarters—doughty, desperate souls who shoved and hauled their belongings in little carts across the vast short-grass prairies of the Great Plains. Many such men pushed their carts directly into the next world, never to reach Cherry Creek, while others, more fortunate, were picked up "in the direst distress" by one or another of the wagon trains. But despite this swelling population and its massed assault upon the landscape with picks, shovels, and prospecting pans, no one was finding what he was looking for, and Villard had little gold news to report. The discoveries of 1858 that had precipitated the rush in the first place had proved to be scattered and insignificant, and no new strikes had succeeded them.

The gold fever was subsiding in the settlements, and many a brilliant hope died of inanition. The influx of newcomers was somewhat counterbalanced, though not matched, by a mounting number of departures. Every day dozens of disillusioned settlers pulled up their stakes, literally, and started to make their weary way back home. One Sunday in May, Villard and several others were sitting around the express office, gloomily discussing how weary, stale, flat, and unprofitable all the uses of gold prospecting seemed to be, when in walked a dust-caked, heavily bearded miner like a prophet come down with glad tidings from the mountain. Refusing to fall in with the mood of the company, he declared himself a firm believer in the presence of gold in the ribs, bowels, and streams of the Rockies, particularly around the headwaters of Clear Creek. After a minimum of urging, the miner produced ocular proof: a bottle of "flour gold," or gold dust, and several large chunks of rich gold-bearing quartz.

This happy news spread through the Cherry Creek settlements like a brushfire. In the twinkling of an eye, general lamentation changed to general rejoicing, and despair gave way to wild anticipation; greed once more had reason to live. Five days later, a scout who had accompanied the miner back to his claim returned with five ounces of gold, and the fever reached epidemic proportions. In the following days there was a general exodus from the settlements to the site of the strikes, a tributary of the South Platte about thirty miles from Auraria and Denver. Everyone left, including the doctors, the lawyers, the sheriff, the judge, the tavern keepers (pioneers of free enterprise, they loaded their stock into their wagons, anticipating a brisk business at Clear Creek), and Henry Villard.

The reporter set out on a borrowed mule, hot on the trail of breaking news, carrying with him his bedding, his carefully wrapped buffalo robe, and "three days' supply of hard bread and bacon, and ground roasted corn, which, mixed with water, furnished a very cooling nourishing beverage"; he was rapidly transforming himself into a frontiersman. Exhilarated by the mountain air and his prospects, he rode through the breathtakingly perpendicular landscape, through blooming mountain meadows, across rushing streams, over foothills, and up a steep mountainside to the large encampment at Clear Creek, almost ten thousand feet above sea level. Night was falling hard, and Villard had to unpack his weary mule hurriedly in the fading light. Although nearly exhausted himself, the reporter managed to locate the leader of the original Clear Creek expedition, John Gregory, who had been prospecting there with his party—the place was now known as Gregory Gulch—since the end of March. Gregory kindly offered Villard a spot in the corner of his big tent, and in a few minutes the young man was sound asleep.

He awoke refreshed, chewed his way through a miner's breakfast, and began his search for gold and rumors of gold. In the process, he interviewed many miners, starting with Gregory himself; visited all the leads and mines in Gregory Gulch; examined the newly constructed sluices and slides, the newly dug ditches and shafts; entered the miners' tents and pine-branch huts; and watched men digging and delving in the mountainside, hauling quartz and rocks, washing out pans of pay dirt, catching the gold with quicksilver in the riffles of the sluices. He "washed out many a pan" himself, gaining therefrom nothing but experience; nevertheless, he saw enough gold to convince him "that the new Dorado had really been discovered." After a week he returned to Denver to write his dispatches and spread "this great news."

The Cherry Creek towns were now busy and booming. Gold was circulating, building was starting up again, people and provisions were arriving around the clock. Although most newcomers headed straight for the mountains, a pair of distinguished gentlemen alighted painfully from the express company's stagecoach in Denver and sought lodgings in town. They were newspapermen, older colleagues of Villard's: Horace Greeley, the renowned editor of the *New*

York Tribune, and Albert Richardson, a senior correspondent for the *Boston Journal.* The appearance, among the lean-tos and log cabins of Denver, of these two high-ranking representatives of the Eastern press was an indication of the way the news from Pikes Peak—apolitical, uplifting, the stuff of pleasant fantasies—was beginning to divert the country's attention from its descent into political and societal disaster.

Both of the gentlemen from the East were injured, particularly Greeley, and the stagecoach itself was badly damaged. It had been attacked, not by hostile Indians but by a band of angry buffalo. As the driver was gingerly maneuvering his vehicle through one of the immense herds grazing its way across the prairie, the fearsomely massed animals—as though sensing the presence of the sage whose famous advice, "Go west, young man," would contribute so much to the near extinction of their species—had charged his coach and overturned it.

Greeley was afforded several further opportunities to regret having heeded his own counsel. He was carried to a new hotel called the Denver House, a large log cabin with a canvas roof, dirt floors, no interior walls, and a half dozen guest rooms, which were partitioned off by more of the ubiquitous canvas nailed to seven-foot frames; the beds were unfinished boards. The proprietors of the Denver House had obviously elected to concentrate on the chief attractions of their establishment, liquor and gambling, which could be enjoyed twenty-four hours a day in the well-equipped barroom and gambling parlor that occupied most of the space in the big cabin. Bawdy songs, roaring celebrations, cries of despair, drunken brawls, even the occasional gunshot penetrated the thin partitions of the Denver House night and day. On the third night after Greeley's arrival, Villard was attending the suffering editor in his room when the ambient racket grew particularly acute. Although haggard from sleeplessness and barely able to walk, the older man insisted that Villard help him into the saloon. There he dragged himself to a chair, somehow succeeded in distracting the crowd from the pursuit of its vices, and delivered a temperance lecture that Villard called "one of the most pathetic appeals I ever heard." Interestingly enough (these were the old days), it worked; Greeley's formerly raucous audience sheepishly withdrew, gambling operations were suspended, and the bar closed at eleven for the remainder of the editor's stay.

Several days later, after Greeley's recovery from his injuries, Villard escorted him and Richardson to Gregory Gulch so they could witness the mining operations firsthand. While crossing Clear Creek, Greeley—still at odds with the animal world—lost control of his mule, who thrashed and swam rapidly downstream for some distance, striving to dislodge the annoying burden that clung so desperately to his neck. Villard galloped down the bank and finally succeeded in pulling mule and man from the water. Greeley refused to mount this mule for the return crossing, but lost his belongings nonetheless when the animal's saddle girth broke.

Despite these contretemps, Greeley was impressed by what he saw and issued a statement in conjunction with Richardson and Villard. This document, known as "Greeley's Report" and published in newspapers all over the country, described the state of the mining activity along Clear Creek and attested to the findings there. Satisfied at having done his journalistic duty and enhanced the allure of the West, the editor of the *New York Tribune,* no longer a young man, hightailed it eastward, away from the gold and the mountains and back to civilized Manhattan.

Villard remained in Denver, where throngs of new arrivals provided daily proof that his and his colleagues' glowing reports had found an appreciative, responsive audience. In recognition of his public relations efforts, the newly organized city fathers (the Denver Company) voted Villard a one-forty-eighth share in the town properties. By September there were close to sixty thousand people seeking riches in the nearby mountains, and hundreds of newsmen were on hand to chronicle the vicissitudes of the quest; Villard had been one of the first, but now he was one of a crowd.

This meant that he had to work all the harder. He spent much of his time in the mountains, investigating every new claim and visiting all the camps and settlements that were springing up near the mines. At regular intervals he returned to Denver to write and file his accounts. His journalistic duties left him sufficient leisure, however, to enjoy the pleasures of the mountain man's life: hunting, fishing, observing and admiring nature. Though by background and temperament a most civilized man, Villard was always fascinated by the freedom and challenges of life at the edge of civilization. His sojourn in the Pikes Peak country showed him that he could combine an active and adventurous life with important, productive work. The experience he gained in the Rockies was a crucial part of his development and an essential prelude to his future Western successes.

With the approach of fall came sobering thoughts of a mountain winter. Gold activity was slowing down, fewer people were arriving, more were departing. Rich strikes were still being made, but many older ones were petering out, and the vast majority of hopefuls made no strikes at all. Others managed to eke out a living by dint of constant labor, and many were beginning to realize that most auriferous veins lay buried deep inside the mountain rock, where it would take more capital than the average miner could put up—and more advanced technology than picks and prospecting pans—to tap them.

As gold fever surged and subsided around him, Villard remained comparatively immune. He had never pursued very intensely his dreams of establishing a claim and striking it rich himself, but now he conceived of a way to mine his experience. News, he saw, would be scarce until the spring brought renewed mining activity and fresh waves of fortune hunters, who would form a large, ready-made market for a guidebook to the Pikes Peak regions. Villard decided to travel back east, write such a book, and have it printed in time for the spring rush. Several Denver businessmen encouraged his scheme and pledged to buy many copies for resale to their customers. By the middle of October, Villard was preparing to return to the States.

At the same time—October 16–17, 1859—there occurred in far-off Virginia an event that would refocus the nation's attention upon more serious matters, namely the cancer in its vitals. John Brown and twenty-one of his followers, including a couple of his sons, staged their monumentally ill-conceived raid on the United States armory at Harpers Ferry. Unless its deep purpose was to move the country much closer to civil war, the raid was a dismal failure; several men died, including Brown's sons and a totally innocent free man of color, but there was no sign at all of the general slave insurrection that Brown evidently hoped to instigate. In the aftermath of the raid, however, Southern and Northern views of the matter diverged with such vehemence that mutual butchery could not be far behind. For most Southerners, John Brown was a madman and a murderous villain; for many Northerners, and they the loudest, he was a crusader against a great evil who would soon achieve a martyr's crown.

Toward the end of October, to the detriment of his future heirs, Henry Villard sold the interest in the town properties that he had been granted by the Denver Company. For this interest (slightly more than 2 percent of downtown Denver), he received $1,200, a gold watch, a good-sized wagon, two horses to pull it, and a rifle. Having found a couple of paying passengers (at $30 each), he left Denver with them in his new wagon on October 29, traveling back by the same way he came.

The trip across the prairie, though arduous, was largely uneventful. Villard and his companions traveled twenty to thirty miles a day. The trail was well trodden by now, easier to follow, but still surrounded by the big sky and a lot of empty space, made emptier by the buffaloes' recent passage. At night the three men picketed their horses, cooked their meals over burning buffalo chips, and slept in and under the wagon, wrapped in their luxurious buffalo robes. Eventually the trail turned into a military road; the signs of civilization became more frequent; they reached forts, then settlements, and then—finally—roadside inns.

After more than three weeks they were on the last leg of their journey, driving through northeastern Kansas about thirty miles from St. Joseph, Missouri. It was a bright, cold morning in late November, and Villard's wagon was rolling across the open prairie. A speck on the horizon approached, grew larger, and became a buggy, one of whose occupants bore the melancholy, unmistakable features of Abraham Lincoln.

Villard stopped his horses, shouting Lincoln's name, and climbed down from the wagon to shake hands. He was in total pioneer mode, all buckskin and thongs and bandannas and mountain boots, with a full and flowing beard to match; no wonder Lincoln didn't recognize him. When Villard identified himself, Lincoln, amazed, burst out laughing. "Good gracious," he said, or words to that effect. "You look like a real Pikes Peaker!"

Continuing his assault upon his great rival, Douglas, Lincoln made speeches in several Northern states during the latter half of 1859. He had already addressed appreciative audiences in Ohio, Indiana, Iowa, and Wisconsin, and now he was in Kansas, he told Villard, as part of his speaking tour. Lincoln shivered as he talked, sitting in his open buggy with neither a proper coat nor any covering for his legs. Villard offered him a precious object, one of his buffalo robes, and Lincoln accepted it eagerly, promising to return it at the earliest opportunity. The next time Villard saw Lincoln, he was the Republican candidate for president, and he would see much of him thereafter. But Lincoln never gave him his robe back, nor (worse) ever alluded to it again, thus earning himself yet another entry in Villard's catalogue of his offenses.

Villard's little group reached St. Joseph the next day, after a "very quick trip" of twenty-four days. Within a few days he was in Cincinnati, and he spent an agreeable few weeks there and in St. Louis. In both cities he "received a good deal of attention, especially in business and newspaper circles."

Villard obtained many new subscriptions for his book from businessmen in St. Louis, and then made a quick, successful canvass in Chicago and the Missouri River towns, bringing the total number of subscriptions to some ten thousand. He was rising in his profession, he had in hand a project guaranteed to bring him a handsome profit, and as he sat down to write his book in a St. Louis rooming house at the beginning of February, he was well content.

By then, John Brown's body was a-moldering in his grave. His truth, however—that slavery was an abomination, that it must be abolished at any cost, that the cost must be measured in treasure and blood—was marching on.

ABRAHAM LINCOLN.

Photograph of the ambrotype made by
William Church in Springfield, Illinois, on May 20, 1860.

Courtesy of the Library of Congress.

8

The Eve of '61

. . . a new sun has risen on the political horizon.

HENRY VILLARD
(November 1860)

he Past and Present of the Pike's Peak Gold Regions, with Maps and Illustrations, by Henry Villard, "Special Correspondent of the Cincinnati Daily Commercial," is in many ways an exceptional work. First of all, there's the language: clear, vivid, serious, straightforward, precise. It exhibits the stylistic equivalent of a German accent—

> During the mining season outrages upon persons were more numerous in the towns than depredations upon property. During the winter, however, when the many that had been idle during the summer commenced being reduced to straights, thieving commenced to be very common, and called for the interference of the committees. Shooting affrays also occurred frequently. Of murders, four were committed since the first settling of the country. . . . Anomalous as it may seem, the sensitiveness of the feelings of honor is very great among a certain class.

—and very little intentional humor, but it represents a remarkable feat for an author who six years previously could neither speak nor read simple English. Moreover, the book shows a high level of expository talent, admirable descriptive powers, a gift for being both thorough and concise, and an instantly credible frankness. It was an honest, complete, professional guidebook, and it deserved the lucrative success its author was counting on.

Through no fault of his own, however, such success eluded him. Writing with commendable discipline and mastery of his material, he finished his manuscript by mid-March and delivered it to his publisher. Midway through printing, the publishing firm failed. Its assets were seized (including Villard's manuscript and the plates for his book), and it took him weeks of the most dogged effort before he was finally able to wrest his manuscript and the finished plates from the fell clutches of the legal profession.

Seven weeks after the delivery date that he had promised his advertisers and subscribers, the book was finally ready. But by then Villard's target audience, the springtime gold seekers, had set out on their arduous journey without the benefit of his carefully organized advice, and many subscribers refused to accept merchandise they had little hope of selling. Instead of the projected minimum of ten thousand copies, Villard sold twenty-five hundred, barely enough to break even.

Like the prospectors he wrote about, he had confidently expected the Pikes Peak gold regions to bring him nothing less than financial independence. In this blissful state, he thought, he would be able to take up only such literary work as he found congenial. Gradually, however, the bitter truth dawned on him: instead of enriching him, his book was going to cost him money; he was going to wind up in all-too-familiar economic straits; and he was going to need a paying job.

With his journalistic credentials, and with the country passing from one critical stage to the next, Villard had no trouble finding work even before the final collapse of his hopes for the Pikes Peak book. The *Cincinnati Daily Commercial* hired him as a special correspondent and sent him to cover the Republican National Convention, held in Chicago from May 16 to May 18. Villard's growing professional reputation, abetted by his lucky star, once again put him in position to witness and report on one of the defining moments in American history.

The exact nature of his reporting on this event is not clear. Murat

Halstead, the news editor of the *Daily Commercial,* covered all the political conventions held in the United States during the turbulent spring of 1860, including the Republican meeting in Chicago. It was he who wrote the first-person articles published in his newspaper, and it was he who was chiefly responsible for their content and presentation. Villard's energetic inquisitiveness, impressive network of strategically placed acquaintances (among them the convention's eventual nominee), and knack for picking out essential facts no doubt enabled him to supply Halstead with much valuable material for his articles and helped produce "the best accounts that came out of the political gatherings," but the extent of the collaboration between the two cannot be determined. Neither of them seems to have mentioned it in print, though Halstead did refer to Villard as having been "among the 'historians' at the Chicago Republican Convention."

The Democratic Convention had been held less than a month previously, in Charleston, South Carolina. After a most contentious week, the delegates from several Southern states, miffed at their Northern colleagues for failing to advocate slavery with sufficient zest, had seceded from the convention. Several days later, the remaining delegates, unable to agree on a candidate, had adjourned the convention until June. This flagrant display of disunity among their chief rivals filled Republicans with confident expectations of victory in November, and forty thousand enthusiasts converged on Chicago, mostly by rail, fueling the fires of their Republican zeal with "ardent beverages" and "singing songs not found in hymn books."

The convention hall, a vast, hastily erected fire hazard known as the Wigwam, could accommodate only ten thousand people, and each session began with a fierce rush for seats or standing room. Every hotel in town was crammed to overflowing, and the very streets were alive with political activity day and night. A crowd of twenty-five thousand or more milled around outside the Wigwam, singing, chanting, arguing, caucusing, celebrating or deploring each bit of news that transpired from inside the building. The Republicans' wild revelry and certainty of success were tempered by deep political seriousness; everyone genuinely looked forward to hearing the speeches, and the thronged faithful outside even petitioned those inside to send out some good speakers for their edification.

Among the thousands of spectators, supporters, delegates, and party activists packed into the Wigwam, Villard encountered most of the important Republicans of the day, many of whom he already knew: the ex–Pikes Peaker Horace Greeley; the junior senator from Illinois, Lyman Trumbull; the editor from Albany, Thurlow Weed; the Palatinate native and former leader in the 1848–49 uprisings Carl Schurz. Schurz had already achieved prominence in the Republican Party and would go on to a brilliant political and military career. Like Villard's, his was a German-American success story, and the two countrymen would remain close friends until Villard's death.

Villard spent most of his time amid the fervid crush on the convention floor, speaking to delegates, listening to speeches, and scribbling notes. The air crackled with tension, anticipation, and urgency. Many Republicans, Villard included, had an inchoate sense of mission, believing that they and their party bore the grave responsibility of conducting the country through a fearful (none could know how fearful) but necessary period of transformation. The elevated level of the discourse, the sense of historical importance that permeated the atmosphere, the intelligence, passion, and character of the leading participants in the convention all made an indelible impression on the young reporter, and he always considered this thrilling spectacle as one of the greatest and most significant experiences of his life.

Mingled with all his exhilaration, however, was a large dose of disappointment. Like most Republicans, among them such expert pundits as Greeley and Halstead, Villard fully expected the nomination to go to his man, the front-running candidate, Senator William H. Seward of New York. Seward was vehemently antislavery and frankly anti-Southern. In 1858, in a widely publicized speech, he had referred with some relish to an imminent collision, "an irrepressible conflict between opposing and enduring forces" that would determine the future course of the United States as either a slaveholding nation or a free-labor nation. Seward's speech had made him famous in the North and infamous in the South, but many Republicans, whose party claimed few if any adherents south of the border states, saw no disadvantage in this open sectionalism. Other, more pragmatic Republicans disagreed. Abraham Lincoln opposed slavery no less sincerely than Seward and regularly denounced it as a moral and social evil; nevertheless, because he freely admitted that the Constitution protected the practice he deplored, Lincoln was perceived as a moderate. His supporters thought he could attract voters across the spectrum, including those in the crucial states of the conservative lower North, whereas there was a growing conviction that Seward was too much of an extremist to have a real chance of winning the election. The shrewd work of Lincoln's managers at the convention allowed the dark horse to overtake the favorite with surprising speed. On the dramatic third ballot, amid the deafening, uninterrupted din caused by thousands of Lincoln's supporters roaring and stamping in the galleries, the rustic Illinois Rail-splitter became the Republican Party's presidential nominee.

As had been the case with Douglas, Villard's support of Seward was probably as much a function of the antipathy he felt toward Lincoln as anything else. Villard's position on slavery and "the negro question" had indeed moved further to the left since the 1858 debates, but his reaction to Lincoln sprang from considerations that were more aesthetic, social, and emotional than political. It seemed to Villard outrageous that this "uncouth, common Illinois politician" should triumph over "the foremost figure . . . in the country." In 1858, Villard had praised Douglas in similarly extravagant terms; opposing Lincoln elevated a man in his eyes.

Nevertheless, Villard's loyalty to the Republican cause was strong enough to overcome his personal feelings, and he supported the Republican ticket, including its leader, in the pivotal election campaign of 1860. Lincoln had three opponents. The split in the Democratic Party resulted in the Northern Democrats' nomination of Stephen Douglas, while the Southern, or States' Rights, Democrats nominated John Breckinridge of Kentucky; the newly formed Constitutional Union Party offered a compromise candidate, John Bell of Tennessee. Lincoln was thus the only antislavery candidate, and as such, since the others would diffuse the proslavery and conservative vote, he seemed almost certain to win. That his election would precipitate some sort of crisis, probably involving violence, seemed equally certain to many observers, including Villard.

The young political reporter covered all these candidates in the months of intense activity that preceded the November election. In addition to sending dispatches to the *Daily Commercial,* he took on assignments for the *New York Tribune*—Horace Greeley was not a man to forget a favor—and the *Missouri Democrat,* whose editor Villard had met during his stay in St. Louis. Writing for a Democratic newspaper must have strained his political flexibility, but as usual he could count on editorial revisions to eliminate anything objectionable from his reports.

Villard labored long and hard, attending more than fifty important meetings and traveling nearly five thousand miles in four months. The Republicans campaigned with particular intensity, staging huge torchlight parades during which the party song—"Ain't You Glad You Joined the Republicans?"—was bellowed from thousands of throats. Villard was able to renew many old political acquaintances, make even more new ones, and hear all the leading figures of the day.

Villard was in Chicago on election day, and he was gratified, though perhaps not wholly enraptured, by Lincoln's victory. The Republican won over a third of the popular vote but secured a comfortable margin in the electoral college. Douglas, his closest rival in the popular vote (29 percent), received only 12 electoral votes; Breckinridge, a future general in the Confederate Army, got 18 percent of the popular vote and 72 electoral votes (all in the South) to Lincoln's 180.

As soon as the results were in, secessionist forces throughout the slave states redoubled their efforts. They wanted to dissolve the Union—they could not live under the presidency of Abraham Lincoln; Southern honor and the Southern way of life were at stake. Between the end of December 1860 and the first week of February 1861, seven Southern states seceded, with more expected to follow. The seceded states began to seize federal property lying within their borders, and on February 4 their representatives met in Montgomery, Alabama, to discuss the formation of a new country: the Confederate States of America.

In the meantime, while all this trouble was brewing, Henry Villard had received his most important journalistic assignment to date. After the election he had gone to New York, once again seeking a permanent position on one of the daily newspapers. Strangely enough, it was the *New York Herald,* a paper with distinctly racist leanings and a history of bitter opposition to Abraham Lincoln, that decided to take advantage of Villard's close personal acquaintance with the president-elect. The *Herald* assigned Villard to go to Springfield at once—it was the middle of November—and to remain with Lincoln until his inauguration the following March.

Villard traveled immediately to Springfield, arranged for lodging in the only decent hotel, and sought out Lincoln. The president-elect gave the reporter "a very friendly welcome." Lincoln must have known that Villard was working for a notably unfriendly newspaper, and probably had no trouble identifying a certain lack of warmth in the young man, but it was ever Honest Abe's way to disarm his enemies as gently as possible. Shortly he would name his four chief former rivals for the Republican presidential nomination to posts in his cabinet; as for Villard, Lincoln invited the *Herald*'s correspondent to call on him for whatever information he needed.

On November 16, 1860, Villard sent the first of his dispatches from Springfield to the *Herald,* which was bound by agreement to share them with all the other members of the Associated Press. In this way Villard settled into a remarkable situation, in which "hundreds of thousands of Americans learned of the words and actions of their President-elect only through the letters of this young foreign-born reporter," who was not even an American citizen.

Villard's vivid accounts of Lincoln's activities during the period when he was preparing to face the gravest crisis ever to afflict an American president provided his readers with verbal snapshots of great historical interest. Lincoln, true to his word, allowed the reporter nearly unlimited access. Villard saw the president-elect almost every day, and he saw him in the most varied circumstances: surrounded by strangers at large receptions, in conferences with his closest associates, in private conversations with Villard himself. The reporter and the politician were both men who naturally developed and maintained an extremely wide circle of acquaintance while remaining, in essence, loners. For such men the title of friend carried with it only the broadest implications of exclusiveness or intimacy, and thus we can say that Villard and Lincoln became friends.

At first Lincoln received visitors at his own modest home on one of Springfield's quiet, unpaved streets. When the crowds made such hospitality impracticable, he accepted the offer of the governor's room in the state capitol, where he made himself available to all who sought an audience with him from ten until twelve in the morning and from three until five-thirty in the afternoon, six days a week. In both settings Villard watched as visitors of every description presented themselves to Lincoln: politicians, farmers, journalists, preachers, long-lost friends, would-be advisers, elegant ladies, shabby backwoodsmen—some appraising, some starstruck, many merely curious, and many more seeking a favor, a handout, a place.

None of them needed an appointment; all of them were welcomed heartily, energetically, unceremoniously. Such a lack of formality in one called to high office at first shocked Lincoln's patrician observer, but he had to admire the way the president-elect dealt with his visitors. He rarely evaded a question, never avoided an argument, and gave each person who approached him some sort of special treatment, for Lincoln had the politician's protean gift of adapting himself to suit the personality of everyone he met.

He also had the gift of gab; talk poured from him unstintingly, resolving itself into ideas, questions, answers, opinions, observations, and—especially—stories. Villard, of course, already had some firsthand knowledge of Lincoln's fondness for the homely joke, the ludicrous tale, the illustrative parable; but daily, extended contact with Lincoln immersed the reporter, as it were, in an anecdotal sea. Lincoln's ready, inexhaustible store of anecdotes and jokes provoked a whole range of reactions in Villard. Sometimes, when Lincoln used

one of his funny stories to put people at ease or to deflect an incon-
venient question, Villard admired the president-elect's adroitness
and tact; sometimes Lincoln was being humorous for humor's sake,
and even Villard had to laugh. At other times, however, Lincoln's
"low talk" filled Villard with disgust and humiliation.

Lincoln was a countryman, with a countryman's forthright attitude toward matters considered indelicate by more sophisticated
men. It is recorded that the president-elect, speaking in public, characterized the secessionists' conception of the Union as "no regular
marriage, but rather a sort of free-love arrangement, to be maintained on passional attraction." We may imagine that evocative but
defiantly undignified metaphors of this sort grated harshly on Villard's upright ears, which were further offended by the inevitable se-
quel, the squealing laughter that denoted Lincoln's heartfelt
appreciation of his own jokes. Often this hilarity was accompanied by
a bizarre gesture that Villard remembered well from the railroad car:
Lincoln would clasp his knees tightly, draw them up to his forehead,
and rock with mirth.

Unlike his lewd jokes, Lincoln's intentions toward the secessionist movement in the South remained unspoken. When pressed on
the subject, either by Villard in one of their tête-à-têtes or by others
in Villard's presence, Lincoln talked in generalities, discoursing on
reasons why the Union ought to be preserved, stressing his duty to
maintain the Constitution, but never revealing anything specific
about how he planned to deal with the seceded states. In Villard's
view, Lincoln was clinging to the hope that peace could still be preserved, not imagining, or not yet imagining, how vast would be the
gulf between that hope and the actual event.

In one of his earliest dispatches from Springfield, dated November 19, 1860, Villard's remarks about the president-elect mingle
compassion and condescension:

> Mr. Lincoln's personal appearance is the subject of daily remark
> among those who have known him formerly. Always cadaverous,
> his aspect is now almost ghostly. His position is wearing him ter-
> ribly. . . . The present aspect of the country, I think, augurs one

of the most difficult terms which any President has yet been called to weather; and I doubt Mr. Lincoln's capacity for the task of bringing light and peace out of the chaos that will surround him. A man of good heart and good intention, he is not firm. The times demand a Jackson.

Villard makes this assertion with characteristic boldness, and the reader, who enjoys the benefit of hindsight, may speculate on what the headstrong, autocratic, slaveholding Andrew Jackson might have done in Lincoln's place. Jackson, after all, had been born in South Carolina, the state that began secession proceedings three days after Lincoln's election. In any case, despite Villard's foregone conclusions, his daily association with Lincoln would convince the young reporter that he had underestimated his eccentric and complicated subject, and that Lincoln indeed possessed the strength and vision that his job was going to require.

As Villard watched Lincoln dealing unflappably with the sycophants and place seekers who importuned him night and day, besieging both his home and his office, as he listened to Lincoln's rueful jokes about the hate mail that arrived by the bundle, as he contemplated daily proofs of Lincoln's moral earnestness, unfeigned compassion, inexhaustible humor, and fundamental melancholy, the observant young man gradually changed his tone. To his credit, he reported his shifting feelings honestly, and to the credit of his newspaper, his dispatches appeared in the *Herald* unaltered, despite the management's long-standing hostility toward Lincoln.

By December 7, Villard was writing about Lincoln's "conscientiousness and solicitous dutifulness" and predicting that Lincoln would be found "but little wanting" in "the innermost resources of the highest statesmanship." On December 16, Villard declared that the "most likely source of apprehension" in Lincoln's makeup was "his good nature," his "indiscriminating affability."

Villard's dispatch of January 19, 1861, showed that his empathy with Lincoln had deepened, while all trace of condescension had disappeared:

Few mortal beings ever carried a heavier load than that already and likely to rest hereafter, upon the shoulders of Abraham Lincoln. Nor can it be concealed that, although he stands up manfully under its weight, the burden is taxing at times his patience and power of endurance to the utmost. . . . He feels, in a measure, like one who, after groping in comparative dark, suddenly emerges upon scenes of intense brightness, and finds himself at first less at home amidst light than dimness, but gradually loses his bewilderment and realizes his position and surroundings.

Now Villard was defending Lincoln from malicious rumors, deploring the disrespectful behavior to which he was daily subjected, noting with approval the president-elect's increasing gravity as the number of secessions mounted, violence against federal authority in the South became an almost daily occurrence, and March 4, inauguration day, approached. On February 9, Villard observed that Lincoln fully realized "the solemnity of his mission" and was resolved "to fulfill it firmly, fearlessly and conscientiously."

While his admiration for Lincoln grew, Villard's feelings about Mrs. Lincoln moved in the opposite direction. Her family background of wealth and luxury, her excellent education, and her aristocratic manners at first dazzled the genteel young man, and he took exception to the rude visitors who crowded into her home and addressed her with insufficient deference. Eventually, however, he came to realize that she was, to put it mildly, unstable, and that her husband's infinite patience with her was a further proof of his magnanimity. Although never mentioned in his dispatches, Villard's awareness of Mrs. Lincoln's "inordinate greed, coupled with an utter lack of sense of propriety," began to dawn in Springfield. Her subsequent egregious behavior in Washington, where she foolishly accepted gifts in exchange for exercising her influence over her husband, would definitively revise Villard's opinion of her.

Lincoln's personal secretaries were much more congenial to Villard's taste. John G. Nicolay, a few years older than Villard, was like him a native of Bavaria and had begun his career as a journalist;

Nicolay's assistant, John Hay, a mere stripling of twenty-two, was a well-educated young man with literary leanings. Neither had been on the job very long, and—again like Villard—they were getting to know and appreciate Lincoln better every day. They made the reporter's job easier, occasionally giving him valuable tips, and their growing fondness for their boss probably had some influence on Villard's own evolving attitudes.

In the early months of 1861, as Lincoln was choosing his cabinet and preparing for his inauguration, the country that he had been elected to govern was falling apart. From what Lincoln said, both privately and publicly, Villard (among others) gathered that his ideas about what course of action he would take were clear only insofar as he knew what he was *not* going to do. He was not going to start hostilities against the seceded states, and he was not going to compromise or negotiate for his constitutional right to govern.

By way of introducing the new president to his fellow citizens and thereby (it was to be hoped) encouraging their loyalty and support in these troubled times, Lincoln and his advisers decided that he would take a special train on a roundabout, two-thousand-mile, twelve-day trip from Springfield to Washington. The presidential train would pass through several of the largest and most important Northern cities: Indianapolis, Cincinnati, Columbus, Pittsburgh, Cleveland, Buffalo, Albany, New York, and Philadelphia.

The gentleman in charge of these travel arrangements, one W. S. Wood, saw fit to exclude Villard's name from the restricted list (only about twenty people) of those who were to accompany the president-elect and his family on their journey to Washington. No journalists would be allowed to board in Springfield. This was quite the sort of slight that Villard was constitutionally incapable of standing for; he appealed directly to Lincoln, and the president-elect let it be known that his friend Henry Villard must have a place on his train. To crown Villard's triumph, he would be the only journalist on the train until it reached Cincinnati. Mr. Wood was also on board, but there is no record of any of the words or looks that he may have exchanged with Mr. Villard.

The train was to depart early in the cold and nasty morning of

February 11. Villard was in the station, watching closely when Lincoln arrived. The president-elect entered the waiting room, he reported, "and allowed his friends to pass by him and take his hand for the last time. His face was pale, and quivered with emotion so deep as to render him almost unable to utter a single word." Before leaving the station, Lincoln gave a brief speech, sad, nostalgic, apprehensive, humble, and almost obsessively religious. After it was over, Villard, who knew that Lincoln had spoken extemporaneously, asked him to write down what he had said. Lincoln obliged him, and Villard sent this hastily scribbled version of the speech to the *Herald* from the first telegraph station. Villard's text differs from the official stenographer's version so materially, and is so inferior to it, that one suspects Mr. Lincoln of having had less than total recall amid all the excitement. In any case, Villard now had something quite valuable, an autograph copy of a speech by Abraham Lincoln, but he lost it during the confusion of the war.

Along with Lincoln's speech, Villard telegraphed a vivid and ultimately waspish sketch:

> The train . . . moves at the rate of thirty miles an hour. It is driven by a powerful Rogers locomotive, and consists of baggage, smoking, and passenger cars. Refreshments for the thirsty are on board. The cheers are always for Lincoln and the Constitution. The President-elect continues reserved and thoughtful, and sits most of the time alone in the private saloon prepared for his special use. The Yankee Prince of Wales, Bob Lincoln, the heir apparent of the President-elect, adheres closely to the refreshment saloon, the gayest of the gay.

In his later dispatches from the trip, Villard took to calling seventeen-year-old Robert "Bob" Lincoln, the Rail-splitter's son, "the Prince of Rails" and fired more than one additional shot in the direction of the prince's youthful fondness for good times and good cheer.

Lincoln's preinauguration procession from Springfield to Washington, in the words of a biographer, "combined all the elements of a traveling circus, a political campaign, and a national holiday." The train meandered slowly through the countryside, making frequent stops along the way and stopping every night so that the passengers could put up in hotels (a few more years had to pass before Villard's future associate George Pullman would invent the railroad sleeping car). Everywhere there were crowds, not only in the big cities—twenty thousand in Indianapolis, a hundred thousand in Cincinnati, sixty thousand in Columbus—but also in the smaller towns. Even in the little places where the train stopped briefly and Lincoln did nothing but show his face and wave, there were bands, banners, artillery salutes, and cheering, excited throngs.

At most stops, large or small, Lincoln shook hands, kissed babies, politicked mightily, and talked, talked, talked, simultaneously shielding his deepest thoughts and fears from public scrutiny and preparing his fellow citizens for the difficult course he knew he would not flinch from taking. And all along the route Henry Villard was observing, taking notes, writing dispatches, and telegraphing them to the *Herald* every chance he got, sending them in in amazing profusion, sometimes several in the course of one day. He talked to Lincoln as often as he could, and when he couldn't, he talked to Lincoln's associates (several of whom were on board, including David Davis, his chief adviser), or to the members of the token military escort—Col. E. V. Sumner, Maj. David Hunter, and Capt. John Pope, all of whom became commanding generals during the Civil War—or to Lincoln's close friends, such as Ward Hill Lamon, his burly, banjo-playing, devoted aide and bodyguard, and Elmer Ellsworth, his dear young protégé and a beloved favorite of Lincoln's entire family.

On February 11, the day the journey began, Villard described for his readers the thirty-four-gun salute Lincoln received at the Illinois-Indiana state line and the crowds that lined the tracks for miles as the train approached Indianapolis, where even bigger crowds and more cannon were waiting. In Indianapolis the president-elect and his entourage got their first taste of the "merciless throngs," as Villard called them, that impeded their passage to every hotel they stayed in on the way to Washington. At the reception that evening, Villard declared, the president-elect shook three thousand hands.

On they went, from one scene of mass enthusiasm to another. Villard watched as Lincoln masterfully played the crowds that greeted him in his "march of triumph." Villard's dispatch from Pittsburgh, dated February 14, shows that he appreciated at least one aspect of Lincoln's skill: "The President's remarks had no particular significance. They were, however, always seasoned with his irrepressible wit and humor, and hence pleased his audiences hugely."

In his February 18 dispatch from Albany, Villard demonstrated his talent for memorable description when he depicted Lincoln conveyed through the streets and the cheering throngs while "standing upright in his carriage, bowing and swaying like a tall cedar in a storm, for the hill was steep and the carriage rocky."

Villard was impressed by the patience with which Lincoln endured the hordes that beset him, often rather roughly—the threatening mail he received and the rumors of assassination plots that swirled all around him seem to have provoked in him little thought for his personal security—and the reporter berated Buffalo and Albany, among other cities, for the disorderly conduct of their citizenry. In Buffalo Lincoln was charged and almost crushed by another merciless throng, and Major Hunter suffered a dislocated shoulder while trying to protect him; in Albany, Villard watched appalled as the police strove in vain to clear a path for the presidential party through the drunken crowd surrounding their hotel.

Although Villard did not note it, on February 18—the day on which Lincoln's train pulled into Albany amid cheers and celebratory explosions—about a thousand miles to the south, in Montgomery, Alabama, Jefferson Davis was sworn in as provisional president of the Confederate States of America. There, too, there were crowds and cheers and the festive smell of gunpowder.

After Albany the train traveled to Troy, then due south along the Hudson River to New York City, stopping at Hudson, Rhinebeck, Poughkeepsie, Fishkill, and Peekskill. As the train got closer to Washington, Lincoln became quieter, more solemn. He told fewer stories, and chose to sit alone in his private compartment for increasingly longer periods of time. By now, according to Villard's estimate, the president-elect had given some fifty extempore speeches; his voice was a hoarse whisper, his craggy countenance yet more deeply lined than usual, his unfailing good humor unable to mask his mental and physical exhaustion. For all that, and for all Villard's inability to overlook Lincoln's coarseness and awkwardness, on February 20 the reporter declared to his readers that

> no one can see Mr. Lincoln without recognizing in him a man of immense power and force of character and natural talent. He seems so sincere, so conscientious, so earnest, so simple-hearted, that one cannot help liking him and esteeming any disparagement of his abilities or desire to do right as a personal insult.

On the night of February 20, Lincoln and his wife went to a performance in New York City of Giuseppe Verdi's latest opera, *Un ballo in maschera,* a tragedy that ends with the assassination of a flawed but noble-minded head of state. The next morning the presidential train left for Philadelphia and the last leg of the journey, to Washington via Baltimore.

Like Lincoln, Villard was weary of the "travelling show," as he called it; unlike Lincoln, he didn't have to stay on the train. With his editor's permission, Villard remained a few days in New York after the departure of the presidential party. By the time he reached Washington on February 26, Lincoln had already arrived there, under most inauspicious circumstances.

Allan Pinkerton, head of the Pinkerton National Detective Agency, had uncovered a plot to assassinate Lincoln in Baltimore, a city noted for its pro-Southern sympathies. Lincoln was inclined to doubt the existence of the plot, but there was strong evidence for it. Colonel Sumner wanted to call out the cavalry and escort the president-elect, as forcefully as necessary, to Washington; others suggested an elaborate subterfuge, which would involve a stealthy switch of trains, a clandestine ride in the dead of night, and an unannounced arrival. Deeming it better to expose himself to ridicule than to precipitate violence, Lincoln agreed to this plan. And so the president-elect, disguised and under the protection of a single bodyguard, sneaked into the capital city of the troubled nation whose government would shortly pass into his hands.

CASSIUS M. CLAY BATTALION DEFENDING
THE WHITE HOUSE, APRIL, 1861.

President Lincoln may be standing in the center with cabinet members.

National Archives.

9

Look Away, Dixieland

War! an arm'd race is advancing! the welcome for
battle, no turning away;
War! be it weeks, months, or years, an arm'd race
is advancing to welcome it.

WALT WHITMAN,
"First O Songs for a Prelude"

While the president-elect was creeping into Washington, Henry Villard was sleeping in New York. There, in the few days before he followed Lincoln to the capital, Villard launched an undertaking that marked him as something of an innovator in American journalism, or as he himself less equivocally put it, "the pioneer in this business." Instead of corresponding with only one newspaper, he proposed to sell his news articles simultaneously to a number of different newspapers. They would purchase his work at a good price, which, since he was being paid several times for each piece, he could afford to give. Thus, combining his journalistic talents with the instincts of a businessman, Villard was creating a primitive syndicating service, one of the earliest news agencies. The *Cincinnati Commercial,* the *Chicago Tribune,* and the *New York Herald* (which warily agreed to print Villard's Republican-slanted articles unrevised) accepted his proposal; contracts were signed; and he arrived in Washington as the political correspondent for three important newspapers.

Villard had now arrived at a secure place in his chosen profession. Not only was he an experienced, resourceful, reliable reporter, but he enjoyed a special relationship with President Lincoln and had close ties to his innermost circle of friends and advisers. As a syndicated columnist, Villard was now earning a total of $55 a week, an eminently respectable income. He rented "a finely furnished suite of rooms" ($12 a month) and arranged to take his meals ($30 a month) at Willard's, the best hotel in the capital.

Washington itself, a city of some sixty thousand inhabitants (in addition to a transient population that hovered around ten thousand), appealed to Villard as little as it had during his brief visit there in 1856. The national capital was a pestilential, flyblown place, where pigs fed on the garbage and slops tossed into the fetid streets, mosquitoes bred prodigiously in stagnant pools, and rats and cockroaches flourished in every home, including the White House. Without even counting the deeds of politicians, the crime rate in Washington was unusually high. There were many hotels, almost all ill kept, a multitude of barrooms, and not a single decent restaurant.

As he had done four years previously, Villard looked disapprovingly at the plain, low buildings on unpaved streets and "the shabby public carriages with their ragged black drivers." In the negligent languor of the citizenry, in the generally slow pace of things, he identified certain undesirable regional characteristics—"a distinctly Southern air of indolence and sloth"—compounded by the disagreeable fact that slaves were legally kept and traded within the District of Columbia.

In the corridors of power, the months after Lincoln's election had been marked by a succession of more or less flailing efforts to ward off, or at least to mitigate, the approaching national disaster. Compromise measures, appeasement proposals, and a Peace Congress had come to nought, mostly because there was no abrogating the chief cause of Southern secession, the election of Abraham Lincoln. The South wanted no part of a Union that had passed out of its control, and many leading Republicans, including Seward, Greeley, and Thurlow Weed, thought that it would be better to let the seceded states go in peace, and good riddance, than to bring them back by violent means. Lincoln, however, saw the maintenance of the Union, by force if necessary, as his highest duty. As to compromises, he was no more willing to countenance the extension of slavery than Southerners were willing to renounce it. Some wishful thinkers (Lincoln may have been among them) believed that the secessionists would relent, or that some last-minute agreement would be struck, or that both sides were bluffing and would stop short of war; but Villard and others saw that the reciprocal intransigence of North and South made a bloody civil conflict inevitable.

As Lincoln's inauguration approached, the pressure upon him grew to immense proportions. Not only must he ponder how to cope with the gravest crisis in the history of the country, what to say in his inaugural address, and similar overwhelming preoccupations, but he also had to contend with an onslaught of increasingly determined place seekers, who literally gave him no rest. Lincoln found this consequence of elevation to high office particularly vexing. On one of the occasions when Villard saw the president-elect in the week preceding his inauguration, Lincoln complained bitterly about his importuners. "Yes, it was bad enough in Springfield," he told the reporter, "but it was child's play compared to this tussle here. I hardly have a chance to eat or sleep. I'm fair game for everybody of that hungry lot."

The activities of Mrs. Lincoln increased Villard's sympathy for her husband. She meddled with everything, from the distribution of minor offices to the assignment of cabinet posts, and she began to surround herself with a set of sycophants and flatterers, including one who especially appalled Villard. This was "Chevalier" Wikoff, vaguely European, a smooth talker in several languages, a man of the world whose elegant manners, genteel bearing, and winning ways helped him to insinuate himself into the very highest social and political circles in Washington. To Villard's disgust, Mrs. Lincoln accepted Wikoff's fulsome and impertinent compliments with nary a blush and made the chevalier one of her most trusted advisers.

The intensity of the revulsion Villard felt for Wikoff was caused in part by the former's recognition that he and this adventurer shared certain similarities of background and style. Even more ironic was a fact unknown to Villard at the time: the *New York Herald*, his own principal employer, had planted Wikoff in Washington as its undercover reporter and source of news, much of which he gleaned from the first lady's indiscreet chattering. Villard and this man he despised were colleagues, working the same beat, each focused on one of the first couple.

Although inauguration day, March 4, 1861, was raw and cold, masses of people lined the presidential route down Pennsylvania Avenue, and a crowd of some thirty thousand, including Henry Villard, pressed around the wooden platform erected in front of the east portico of the Capitol. After witnessing Lincoln's swearing-in by the ancient chief justice, Roger Taney—in Lincoln's view one of the persons chiefly responsible for propelling the country into its present disastrous predicament—the assembled multitude heard the first official words of their new president.

His speech, Villard thought, was "a heterogeneous compound," a mixture of veiled threats, conciliatory reassurances, and obscure qualifications. In point of fact, however, just before ending his address with his hopeful image of "the better angels of our nature" strumming "the mystic chords of memory" and reestablishing national harmony, Lincoln had issued a grave and unequivocal warning to the secessionist states of the South:

> In *your* hands, my dissatisfied fellow countrymen, and not in *mine*, is the momentous issue of civil war. The government will not assail *you*. You can have no conflict, without being yourselves the aggressors. *You* have no oath registered in Heaven to destroy the government, while *I* shall have the most solemn one to "preserve, protect, and defend" it.

Villard was not alone in underestimating the degree of Lincoln's determination and his capacity for resolute action. On April 12, 1861, Confederate artillery under the command of Brig. Gen. Pierre Gustave Toutant Beauregard began bombarding Fort Sumter, a Federal stronghold built on an island in the harbor off Charleston, South Carolina. Thirty-four hours later, on April 13, the commander of the Fort Sumter garrison surrendered. No one had been killed; the attack's only significance was symbolic; but four thousand shells make a very powerful symbol. The guns that fired them signaled the beginning of the Civil War.

■   ■   ■

On April 15, 1861, President Lincoln issued a proclamation calling for seventy-five thousand men to be enlisted for a period of ninety days in the armed forces of the United States. By the next day war fever was raging everywhere, in the North as well as in the South. Villard received a wire from James Gordon Bennett, the *Herald*'s proprietor and editor in chief, summoning him to New York at once. That evening, Villard caught the night train.

Bennett, then in his mid-sixties, was one of the most innovative and influential men in the history of American journalism. As revealed in his editorials, he was also a rabble-rousing racist, a violent critic of antislavery advocates (particularly Republicans), and, Villard thought, a thinly veiled supporter of the South and the rebel cause. For all these reasons, chief among them Bennett's "sneaking sympathy" with the South, Villard had started thinking about severing his connection with the *Herald*. The knowledge that doing so would cause him little regret freed him from constraint as he set out to meet his formidable employer.

Villard had met Bennett on two previous occasions, both very brief, and was looking forward to learning more about so notorious a character. He had ample opportunity for close observation, as Bennett invited him to dine and spend the evening at his Washington Heights home. That afternoon Villard and his host left the offices of the *Herald* for the long drive up Broadway and Fifth Avenue and through Central Park.

Although Villard noted that Bennett's crossed eyes gave him a "sinister, forbidding look," the reporter was impressed by the older man's tall, slender figure, handsome features, and generally imposing appearance. Still, Villard required no extended acquaintance with his editor to perceive that Bennett was "hard, cold, utterly selfish," and invincibly ignoble. Throughout the drive and dinner (at which Bennett's twenty-year-old son was the only other person present), the editor plied his guest with questions about Lincoln, about the president's characteristics, habits, opinions, plans, movements, and about the circumstances of his acquaintance with Henry Villard. It was only after dinner that Bennett revealed the reasons for his summons.

First of all, the editor declared, he wanted Villard to carry a message to his special friend the president. The reporter was to assure Lincoln of Bennett's loyalty to the Union; the *Herald* would support all measures that the president and the Congress might deem necessary to put down the rebellion as thoroughly and speedily as possible.

This was a complete reversal of the newspaper's former Southern-friendly stance, which in the recent surge of patriotic feeling had provoked threats of mob violence against the *Herald*'s offices. Villard, of course, made no inquiry into his employer's motives. Instead he declared himself delighted to be the bearer of such glad tidings and promised at his earliest opportunity to deliver Bennett's welcome assurances to the president in person.

There was another thing. This was a message to Treasury Secretary Salmon Chase of Ohio, to whom Villard, as the Washington representative of Chase's strongest supporter, the *Cincinnati Commercial*, had ready access. Bennett proposed to offer Secretary Chase the younger Bennett's famous racing yacht, the *Rebecca*, as a gift from his family to the government revenue service. In return he wanted a lieutenant's commission for his son in that same service, which seemed a relatively safe assignment in time of civil war. Villard found the second message even more amusing than the first, but he agreed to present this tempting proposal to the secretary.

Bennett was apparently quite satisfied with his well-connected young employee. The next day, in the *Herald*'s offices, managing editor Frederic Hudson—a "courteous and obliging" man whom Villard greatly admired—informed him that he had been given a substantial raise, of $10 a week.

On balance, Villard could consider his New York trip, despite certain absurdities and a modicum of requisite tongue biting, a professional success. Now he was eager to return to Washington and the center of the critical events that were to decide the fate of the nation. Under the best of circumstances, the trip from New York City to the capital was a serious undertaking, requiring twelve hours' traveling time and included five train changes, three ferryboat crossings (over the Hudson, Delaware, and Susquehanna Rivers), and an hour-long streetcar ride across Philadelphia from one railroad station to another; in Baltimore, moreover, the railroad cars had to be pulled for some distance by horses.

Now, however, this nightmare of conveyance was intensified by the first stirrings of civil strife. The border state of Maryland was home to a large number of slaveholders and a great deal of pro-Southern feeling. On April 19, as Villard was preparing to leave New York City for the capital, troops of the Massachusetts Sixth Regiment, sent in immediate response to President Lincoln's call to arms, arrived in Baltimore. There many of them had to get off the train and walk while horses pulled the cars across town to the south station, where the soldiers would reboard for Washington. But the crowd of bystanders grew into a mob, insults were exchanged, stones were thrown, and then, inevitably, came the gunfire. Both soldiers and citizens died in this pitched battle in the streets of Baltimore, and the plight of the president and his capital city, barely forty miles away, risibly defended and encircled by hostile slave states, took on a parlous aspect. It was destined to grow worse.

At 3 A.M. on April 20, when Villard and his fellow passengers arrived at the hamlet of Perryville on the east bank of the Susquehanna River in northeastern Maryland, they discovered that the captain of the ferryboat scheduled to transport them across the river to Havre de Grace had received orders to remain where he was until further notice. Southern sympathizers, seeking to prevent the further reinforcement of Washington by Federal troops, had been busy that night, burning bridges and trestles between Havre de Grace and Baltimore, and all traffic was at a standstill.

Few things irked Henry Villard so much as enforced inaction, and here he was, stranded just out of reach of the news it was his job to gather and report. At first light, feeling the need of energy for the task ahead, he set out to talk his way into a breakfast at one of the few houses that constituted Perryville. He was successful, and a local farmer's wife served him "bacon, 'hoe-cakes,' and indescribable coffee." Next he sought out the owner of a small boat he'd noticed tied up at the riverbank, and for the bargain price of $1 he got himself rowed across the Susquehanna to Havre de Grace.

This village had a few hundred inhabitants, and most of them were in the street, discussing the interruption of the only railroad line between the North and Washington. It made Villard distinctly uneasy to hear how many of these Marylanders' hearts were gladdened by the reports of the burned railroad structures, and he realized how difficult it was going to be for Lincoln and the Union to hold on to the touchy border states. He kept his opinions to himself, however, and concentrated on making his way to Baltimore and thence to Washington.

Except for a generous selection of unsubstantiated rumors, no one in Havre de Grace had any idea what lay between their village and Baltimore, much less between Baltimore and Washington. Marauding guerrilla bands, swarming rebel cavalry, Union detachments bent on the total subjugation of Maryland—it was said that one or more of these could be encountered by traveling but a little way down the road. Unable to find anyone with a carriage who would risk driving him the thirty-eight miles to Baltimore, Villard decided to stop wasting time and set out on foot.

After six uneventful miles, he stopped at a large house by the roadside and requested a meal. The owner, a well-to-do planter who owned slaves but strongly opposed secession, chatted volubly with his young guest. When Villard offered him $25 for a ride to Baltimore, the planter accepted, called for a buggy, assigned the driving chores to one of his trusted slaves, and bade Villard farewell. The reporter and the slave drove together for more than thirty miles through the Maryland countryside—one can but wonder what sort of conversation passed between them—without meeting any belligerents, or for that matter any adventures at all. A little before dark, their buggy creaked into Baltimore, where everything seemed strangely calm.

Villard checked into a hotel and devoured the newspaper accounts of the previous day's street battle. He also learned, as he'd feared, that railroad communication both north and south of Washington had been completely interrupted. He slept hard and rose early the next morning, determined at all costs to reach the increasingly isolated capital.

No livery stable would rent him a horse and carriage at any price. At last he was able to rent a saddle horse ($100 down as a deposit, $5 a day plus feed until the return of the animal). On the byroads that he took, avoiding the main highway, Villard met only "harmless country folk," and he was in the capital before nightfall.

Life in Washington had changed completely during the few days of Villard's absence. Most noticeably, the place seemed deserted. Tens of thousands of residents had left town in all directions, chiefly south. The hotels, like the streets, were empty, and even Willard's, which had hosted a thousand guests for the inauguration, was closed indefinitely. Mail service had been suspended; the telegraph was out of order; the depopulated city lay cut off and nearly defenseless.

Villard daily expected the rebels to reach out and pluck this ripe fruit, but foresight, initiative, and decisive leadership were in short supply on both sides at the start of the Civil War. Meanwhile rumors persisted that the Confederate forces were gathering within striking distance of the capital. Winfield Scott, the aging general-in-chief of the United States Army, Virginia-born but loyal to the Union, used the few troops at his disposal to block the approaches to the city, patrol the Potomac, and guard the White House and other public buildings.

Washington seemed to be a city besieged, and the government was looking increasingly helpless and frightened. Villard saw Lincoln repeatedly during this period, recording the president's groans of impatience and frustration. Not only did he know nothing of the movements and intentions of the rebel forces, but, worse, he had no idea when or whether the Northern states would respond to his call and send troops to relieve Washington. While Lincoln was reviewing the men of the Sixth Massachusetts, Villard heard him exclaim to them, "I begin to believe there is no North. The Seventh New York

Regiment is a myth. The Rhode Island troops are another. You are the only real thing." The new president's dismay was beginning to show in public.

The tension in the capital began to subside on April 25, when the Seventh New York arrived, soon to be followed by regiments from Massachusetts, Rhode Island, and other loyal states. They came by an ingenious, though circuitous, route: by sea to Annapolis, on Chesapeake Bay; by forced march to Annapolis Junction; and by train to Washington, having first laid tracks and repaired bridges damaged by pro-Southern guerrillas. Villard stood amid the rejoicing crowd (secessionists had long since left the city) and watched exultantly as the New Yorkers, a crack parade unit nearly a thousand strong and gorgeously equipped, marched smartly up Pennsylvania Avenue to the strains of a "magnificent band."

Within a month the capital was teeming with upwards of eighty thousand soldiers, more than the seventy-five thousand militia President Lincoln had called for in his proclamation of April 15. Washington, now encircled by a nearly solid ring of military camps and safe (at least temporarily) from being overrun by the Southern hordes, cast off its downhearted air, quickened its sluggish pace, and became a scene of animated activity. There were military parades of every description—marching infantry columns, prancing cavalry troops, lumbering artillery batteries—and the participants in these exhibitions presented a most variegated appearance. The standard blue uniform that we know as the symbol of the Union soldier had not yet been manufactured in anything like the necessary quantities, and Villard saw infantry troops in the familiar (to him) uniform of the Bavarian army, others dressed like soldiers of Prussia, still others in the red blouses and jaunty *bersagliere* hats of the famous Garibaldi Guards or the baggy pants and embroidered vests of the Zouaves.

The daily spectacles put on by the soldiery attracted hundreds of curious visitors to Washington, and thousands of others came to visit relatives or friends in the camps. The public thoroughfares were thronged, all the old hotels (and several new ones) were open again, barrooms flourished, brothels throve; the city pulsed with the kind of untempered martial enthusiasm and belligerent confidence that is possible only for a people whose army has not yet fought its first battle.

Villard visited the White House and the various departments daily, conversing with the president as often as he could and getting to know the cabinet officers and their chief assistants. Soon he was on good terms with all of them, and he was able to supply his editors with news gathered from extremely authoritative sources. It did not take the shrewd young reporter long to realize, with the thrill of discovered power, that these great and influential men were "anything but impervious to newspaper flattery, and very sensitive under journalistic criticism." Seward, the secretary of state, seemed particularly concerned about his media image and was inclined to give favorable treatment to representatives of newspapers that eulogized him, the more fulsomely the better.

Although the *Herald*'s readers, like those of other Northern newspapers, were interested in the deeds and pronouncements of their political leaders, what they really wanted to see was news of the volunteer troops encamped around Washington and preparing themselves for war. The *Herald* wanted Villard to make the troops a special feature of his daily reports, and to that end he was authorized to buy a saddle horse. This excellent animal faithfully carried his new master on his daily rounds to the regimental camps. Villard loved this aspect of his assignment, spending several hours every afternoon riding in the delightful spring weather and conversing with the regimental officers, who included, as far as he was concerned, "the very flower of the youth of the land . . . remarkable for intelligence, patriotism, and devotion to duty." He took part in their off-duty frolics, shared their gaiety and mirth, and felt at home among them. There were, of course, some regiments, especially Irish-dominated ones from New York, that "consisted of a very low order of elements" and had "the worst types of local politicians as officers." Villard visited these contingents as rarely as his journalistic obligations allowed; the units that most interested him were those composed chiefly of non-Irish Europeans. Four New York regiments were exclusively German; others, like the Garibaldi Guards, included Italians, Frenchmen, Hungarians, Germans, and other nationalities.

Among the German regiments Villard found several officers who were old acquaintances. One was Col. Max Weber, owner of the Hotel Stadt Constanz, where the eighteen-year-old immigrant Heinrich Hilgard, fresh off the boat and barely able to pay for his room, had stayed almost eight years before. Another was the ex-revolutionary Col. Louis Blenker, late of the Palatinate, whom Villard had last seen in 1856, when Blenker was a disgruntled farmer, exchanging produce for meals and wine at the Prescott House in New York.

Mrs. Lincoln was a frequent visitor to the camps, but Villard doubted the purity of her motives. As far as he was concerned, Mary Todd Lincoln, like her husband a native of Kentucky, was "at heart a secessionist" and had no real sympathy for the cause of the troops she went among. What drew her to them, Villard thought, was the "adulation and hospitality" she received from the soldiers, especially from the officers of the Irish New York regiments, whom she therefore "favored especially" with her visits. Fraternizing with the Irish was not a fault that Henry Villard was likely to overlook.

In addition to cultivating the acquaintance of regimental officers, Villard got himself introduced to the men who occupied the very highest ranks in the army. General Winfield Scott, seventy-five years old, immense, infirm, practically immobile, had always liked seeing his name in the papers and proved most accessible to reporters. Villard, like the others, called on him daily. It took only a bit of cajoling before the stately, white-haired general began to grow garrulous, not to say indiscreet, discussing his plans openly and using a giant wall map and a long pointer to illustrate his strategical ideas.

Villard also met two high-ranking officers whose recent promotions and assignments had made them the most important soldiers in the U.S. Army. One was the quartermaster general, Brig. Gen. Montgomery Meigs, charged with the incalculable task—which he was to perform brilliantly throughout the course of the war—of keeping the Union forces supplied with whatever they required. The other officer was Brig. Gen. Irvin McDowell, whom President Lincoln placed in command of the troops defending the capital. His assignment was an impossible one: to turn his heterogeneous amateur forces, almost all of whom were volunteer militia enlisted for a period of three months, into an effective, battle-ready army. McDowell was an Ohio man who owed his advancement largely to the influence of Secretary Chase. Chase gave Villard a warm introduction to the general, and soon the two new acquaintances were on the best of terms. But although Villard admired McDowell's character and intelligence and sympathized with his predicament, he suspected that the commander was too lacking in self-confidence, too prone to be overwhelmed by difficulties to be capable of carrying out his great responsibilities successfully.

Before the Southern states began to secede, the United States Army, some sixteen thousand men mostly occupied with eliminating the Indian problem, was a small force with a correspondingly small number of commissioned officers. This rather restricted pool of professional military leaders was further reduced by the defections of the many Southerners who resigned their commissions and offered their services to the Confederacy. Only a tiny percentage of the loyal officers remaining had ever commanded any body of troops larger than a company.

As Villard noted, the government elected to redress this scarcity of high-ranking, qualified officers and to pay some political debts at the same time; it was thus "unavoidable that the largest number of officers should be taken from among civilians without the knowledge of even the manual of arms." The results included "the most extraordinary appointments," the commissioning of men with political connections but without any other qualifications.

Villard himself, had he been so inclined, might have received one of these extraordinary appointments. Secretary Chase, by way of demonstrating his gratitude to the *Cincinnati Commercial* for its loyal support, offered its Washington correspondent a captain's commission in the regular army. Though "sorely tempted," Villard refused, preferring the journalist's life to the soldier's.

His decision was consistent with his character and had nothing to do with personal courage. Henry Villard did not shrink from danger, he shrank from subordination. One of his reasons for emigrating to the United States in the first place had been to avoid being forced into the Bavarian army, and the Union Army, however much he supported its cause, presented the same opportunities for degradation, the same forfeit of independence, the same requirement not only to suffer fools but to obey them. Villard always, when he could, chose to stand both inside and outside events. He felt a great urge to participate in important doings, to mingle with the elite, to be at the heart of the action, but he also needed to remain aloof and apart from what was going on, to maintain his position as the solitary observer, able to withdraw at will. As an army officer he could meet only a few of these needs; as a war correspondent he could meet them all.

The Four Horsemen of the Apocalypse, so ardently summoned by both sides, were mounted and ready to ride down upon the country; everyone knew it was only a matter of time. Villard saw that a journalist who was going to report on a war would do well to know something about warfare, and so, exhibiting the best kind of German thoroughness, he gave himself a concise but meticulous course in the subject. He borrowed or bought books on war in German, English, and French, immersing himself in military theory, military strategy, military history. He read textbooks and commentaries on the campaigns of Frederick the Great, Napoleon, Wellington, and other great European strategists. When the Union Army finally began to march, Villard was better prepared than most of his colleagues to make some kind of sense of what he saw.

On May 20, the Congress of the Confederacy, meeting in Montgomery, Alabama, voted to move the capital of the new nation to Richmond, Virginia, only about a hundred miles south of Washington. To Northern war enthusiasts this seemed like a provocation, though the truth was that by this point each side considered the other's very existence a provocation. A number of newspapers, politicians, organizations, and private citizens had been clamoring since the bombardment of Fort Sumter for the government to invade the South at once and suppress the upstart rebels swiftly and violently. Now, with the secessionists' capital so tauntingly close, the clamor became a deafening roar. One of the leading hawks was Horace Greeley, whose *New York Tribune* printed the slogan "Forward to Richmond!" every day.

Virginia's secession, for weeks a foregone conclusion, became official on May 23. On May 24, wishing to establish a buffer zone between Washington and enemy territory, President Lincoln ordered Union forces to cross the Potomac into Virginia and occupy Alexandria. Among the troops that accomplished this mission was the flamboyant Eleventh New York Regiment, also known as the Fire Zouaves, a unit recruited and led by the president's former law clerk, the twenty-four-year-old Col. Elmer Ellsworth. Much beloved by the entire presidential family, Ellsworth had accompanied them on their train trip from Springfield to Washington and, like all the members of Lincoln's inner circle, was well acquainted with Henry Villard.

The Virginia troops evacuated Alexandria with hardly a shot fired. As the Fire Zouaves marched in, the impetuous Ellsworth saw a Confederate flag flying from the Marshall House, a hotel owned by one James Jackson. The colonel and a few followers rushed into the hotel, mounted the stairs, and removed the flag. As the little band was triumphantly descending the stairs, Jackson appeared with a shotgun, cut Ellsworth down at point-blank range, and was himself immediately shot to death by one of the young colonel's companions.

Hateful and nasty though it was, this incident was to pale nearly to insignificance in the transcendent nastiness of the next four years; at the time, however, it was seen as a terrible, unprecedented tragedy. For Lincoln, as for Villard, Ellsworth was the first close acquaintance to die in the war. As his body lay in state in the East Room of the White House, the North was convulsed with grief and rage, and the pressure on the government to punish the South grew unbearable. By the same token, James Jackson, outnumbered and gunned down on his own property while protecting his country's flag, became a martyr for the South. The murderous rage and mutual hatred so dramatically displayed on the stairs of the Marshall House reflected a level of national torment that only carnage could relieve.

On June 29, in the White House, the president, his cabinet, and the leading generals held a war council. Although several advisers, led by General Scott, counseled patience until better-trained troops were available, the government saw political necessity in the people's will and determined to strike the rebels before the three months' militiamen had to be discharged.

Confederate general P. G. T. Beauregard, the victor of Fort Sumter, had about twenty-two thousand troops concentrated around Manassas Junction, an important railroad hub some twenty-five miles from Washington. It was determined that McDowell and an army of some thirty-five thousand would move toward Manassas Junction and engage the enemy in what would be the first—and in the opinion of many, the last—battle of the Civil War.

General McDowell's headquarters had for some weeks been located in Arlington House (now in Arlington National Cemetery), the mansion that Robert E. Lee and his family had abandoned in the early days of the war. Villard rode every day to Arlington House, and McDowell talked freely to him about the impending fight. The general was far from sanguine; he thought his troops insufficiently trained and unprepared for a major offensive. Moreover, he blamed the politicians for the irrational haste that was being urged upon him, and he was certain that he would be the scapegoat if the attack should fail.

McDowell was right on all three counts, but Villard, who like many Northerners viewed the South with contempt, did not share the general's apprehension. On July 16, 1861, the Federal army began its ponderous movement southward. The reporter, having easily obtained permission to accompany McDowell's headquarters, expected a quick victory and was looking forward to "a very interesting and satisfactory experience," a sort of vacation from his Washington routine. Filled with adventurous expectations, pleased with his fine mount and the bright summer weather, Villard rode with the army in the general direction of Manassas Junction, which lay a few miles south of a little stream known as Bull Run.

COLONEL BURNSIDE'S BRIGADE, FIRST AND SECOND
RHODE ISLAND AND SEVENTY-FIRST NEW YORK REGIMENTS,
WITH THEIR ARTILLERY, ATTACKING THE
REBEL BATTERIES AT BULL RUN.

Sketched on the spot by Alfred R. Waud, July 21, 1861.

Gift of J. P. Morgan.

Courtesy of the Library of Congress.

10

First Blood

The scenes on the battlefield beggar description. The ground was strewn with the dead, the dying and the wounded. Here lay one man with his leg shot off, there another with a wound in the head, a third with an arm shot off, and hundreds wounded in nearly all the various portions of the body. . . . The barbarity practiced by the rebels towards wounded men in this encounter throws to the winds the boasted chivalry of the South. . . . Many Senators and Congressmen were present . . . also numerous New York gentlemen of the legal profession and mercantile community. . . . Some of these civilians ventured as far as the battlefield, and their presence contributed considerable to the panic which afterwards took possession of our soldiers.

NEW YORK HERALD
(July 24, 1861)

The War Correspondents' Memorial overlooks Antietam battlefield, scene of the bloodiest single day of combat in the entire four years of the Civil War. Erected by subscription in 1896, the memorial honors the reporters and artists (Henry Villard is among the many mentioned by name) who followed the sanguinary course of the conflict between 1861 and 1865 and "Whose Toils Cheered the Camps" and "Thrilled the Firesides" of the embattled nation. With a complimentary flourish that Villard must have appreciated, the inscription goes on to praise the correspondents for, among other things, educating "Provinces of Rustics into a Bright Nation of Readers."

Not the least of the war correspondents' accomplishments was the invention (it may be more accurate to say the improvisation) of the American form of their profession. There had been war correspondents (mostly English) before this, but the men who reported the American Civil War, particularly those who worked for Northern newspapers, produced a new and special kind of journalism. A combination of favorable circumstances—the unparalleled freedom of the press in America, the widespread telegraphic network, and the extensive and constantly growing railroad system, to name a few—made the war correspondents' job feasible, but it was the men themselves who made it valuable, essential, vivid, and even in some cases heroic. The correspondent, the "special" in the jargon of the day, traveled and camped with the troops, talked with officers and men, followed them into battle, and walked among the dead and wounded after the smoke had cleared. Like his subjects and companions, he went armed to his work.

The romance and adventure of covering the war at close range were tempered by the omnipresence of squalor, misery, suffering, and death, and the reporter's life was fraught with danger, lived at extremities of attention and drama. A shell decapitated a *Chicago Tribune* special named Carson as he stood not three yards from General Grant. The *New York Times* correspondent Samuel Wilkeson, who would become a longtime associate of Villard's in his railroad career, wrote his dispatch from the battlefield at Gettysburg while contemplating the corpse of Lt. Bayard Wilkeson, his eldest son. The anonymous correspondent who wrote a dispatch to the *New York Herald* after the battle of Bull Run (possibly Villard himself) described how a badly wounded Confederate officer lying on the battlefield had aimed his rifle at the reporter, whereupon, "acting on the maxim that 'self preservation is the first law of nature,' your correspondent put a bullet through his head."

The Union armies were shadowed by "a small army of Northern correspondents," perhaps as many as five hundred, who made the Civil War the most thoroughly covered and widely reported conflict in history up to that time. As General McDowell's columns marched toward the first significant battle of the war, some twenty-five or thirty newspapermen rode or walked with them. So did the photographer Mathew Brady and the artist Alfred Waud, two of the pictorial journalists who would provide the public with unprecedentedly graphic and accurate images of mortal combat.

Always keen to be on the spot for what is now called breaking news, Henry Villard joined the First Division, commanded by Brig. Gen. Daniel Tyler. Starting at the rear of the march, the correspondent gradually made his way to the leading elements, reining in his mount from time to time in order to chat with the brigade commanders and their staffs. One of these commanders was Col. William Tecumseh Sherman, a soldier whom Villard knew and admired despite the fact that Sherman was at the head of "the so-called Irish brigade," whose regiments were drawn almost exclusively from the Irish population of New York City. Villard noticed with some distaste that certain Irish officers attached to this and other units "had braced [themselves] up internally for the fight."

Their festive behavior, however, was not out of keeping with the aura of pageantry and procession that surrounded the early stages of the stately march. The soldiers' multifarious uniforms were fresh and unsullied and bright, the variegated silk of the new regimental flags shone brilliantly in the July sun. There was a cheerful lack of military discipline: men broke ranks at will to go blackberrying in the fields, to relieve themselves, to rest from their exertions. "No more informal, individualistic collection of men in uniform," writes a distinguished historian, "ever tried to make a cross-country march." Carriages filled with congressmen, important personages, society ladies, relatives and friends of the soldiers, and curiosity seekers accompanied the troops; almost everyone was looking forward to a lively spectacle, a few frissons, and a crushing victory.

On the night of the second day's march, the Union Army, having advanced as far as Centreville, Virginia, twenty miles from Washington, made camp on the outskirts of the village. Villard's Colorado adventures had provided him with a good deal of experience in bedding down on the ground; he saw to his horse, turned in, and slept soundly.

The next day, July 18, began early; reveille sounded before sunrise. General Tyler, ordered by General McDowell to observe the roads, deemed himself authorized to make a reconnaissance in force and set out for Bull Run with three companies, which were later joined by a brigade and an artillery battery. Planning to do some observing of his own, Villard rode out with the troops.

From the high ground overlooking Blackburn's Ford, which crossed the sluggish waters of Bull Run about three miles south of Centreville, the Union soldiers and the war correspondent, all of whom were about to receive their baptism of fire, looked down upon the thickly wooded banks of the stream. Apparently operating on the principle that game must be flushed before it can be observed, General Tyler ordered his artillery to shell the woods on the southern bank of Bull Run. Villard thus witnessed "the first cannon-shots fired against the rebels in front of Washington," and he grew more excited with each barrage. When there was no response, Tyler ordered skirmishers to advance down the slope to the river, several hundred yards away.

By now, Villard had been joined by two of his colleagues: Edmund Stedman, a young poet who corresponded with the *New York World,* and Edward House, who worked for Horace Greeley's paper, the *Tribune.* The three specials followed the skirmishers on foot, but hunger overcame their sense of reportorial duty and they stopped at a farmhouse not far from the riverbank to ask for something to eat. Not surprisingly, the tenants of the house had locked it and left, but a cherry tree laden with fruit promised at least a refreshing snack. Tall, lean, and agile, Villard volunteered to climb into the tree and pick enough cherries for the three of them, so he was literally out on a limb when the rebel forces hidden in the woods finally announced their presence by firing a tremendous volley at the skirmishers. Because of a bend in the river, Villard and his two friends found themselves directly in the line of fire of what turned out to be an entire Confederate brigade. The deafening roar froze the cherry pickers, and it took a few seconds for them to realize that the whistling, pattering, spattering sounds all around them were being made by bullets striking branches, twigs, farm buildings, tree trunks, and fences. They had scant opportunity to consider the implications of this circumstance, however, for a second volley, following hard upon the first and underlined this time by the thunder of artillery fire, sent Stedman and House scurrying around the farmhouse and blasted Villard out of the tree. As he lay full length upon the ground, stunned by the explosion and pelted by cherries, his terrified colleagues called to him from behind the house. Was he hurt? they wanted to know, but he wasn't sure himself. Only after a headlong dash to the sheltering farmhouse could he be certain that he had escaped unscathed.

The correspondents kept their heads down as the reconnaissance that had turned into a skirmish turned into a full-scale fight. Union troops penetrated the woods along the opposite riverbank several times, but each time they were driven back by the Confederates, who fired on them from concealed and well-defended positions. Finally the engagement at Blackburn's Ford was over; the Union forces withdrew to their encampment near Centreville; and the reporters, having spent some three hours pinned down under a blistering fire, gratefully joined them. On this first day of combat, Villard wrote, he had undergone "a fire as hot as I was ever under in my varied adventures as a war correspondent." Henceforward he considered himself a veteran and declared that, after so violent an overture, "the music of bullet, ball, and grapeshot never had much terror for me."

It was well for Villard that he was able to achieve such a state of soldierly calm under fire, for he, like every combatant and every correspondent at Bull Run, was about to form an unmediated acquaintance with the gruesome realities of war and the awful consequences of all that firing. Casualties at Blackburn's Ford, a preliminary to the main event, included at least thirty-five killed and nearly a hundred wounded, North and South. Both sides now prepared for bloodletting on a grander and better-organized scale.

During the next two days (July 19 and 20), McDowell and his staff gathered as much information as they could about the terrain, the roads, and the Confederate defenses, planned their strategy, and prepared their forces for the great battle. One important piece of information escaped them: Confederate troops under the command of Gen. Joseph E. Johnston had begun to arrive in the vicinity of

Manassas. By the day of the battle, these reinforcements had nearly wiped out the disparity between the two armies. McDowell and his commanders laid their plans in the belief that the Union's numerical superiority was far greater than it actually was.

Ears cocked, eyes narrowed, Villard and other newspapermen sought to learn the nature of those plans. They haunted the commanders' quarters, making inquiries both discreet and indiscreet, but the only information they were able to gather was general. The army would advance early on Sunday, July 21; it would attack the waiting rebels at various points along their line, roll them up, and drive them from the field.

Villard got little sleep the night before the battle. Kept awake by his excitement at the prospect of a big fight and his fear of missing some important piece of news, he wrote a dispatch at midnight, not long before the army was aroused and set in motion. In the ominous stillness, fraught with anticipation, he contemplated the possibility of an apocalyptic struggle:

> Not a sound is heard except the measured tread of the sentinels and the occasional snort of a horse. For we are on the eve of a great battle—perhaps the battle that is to make the bloodiest picture in the Book of Time. . . . The whole army is to move out from two to half past two o'clock. The battle is expected to begin at daybreak.

McDowell's plan was a complicated and ambitious one, especially considering that the vast majority of his fighters were three-month volunteers with little training. One brigade was to hold the attention of the right flank of the rebel army at Blackburn's Ford; some five miles upstream, three brigades (under the command of General Tyler) were to attack the Confederate left near a stone bridge over Bull Run; and two full divisions were to execute a giant flanking movement, a long, looping march designed to take the rebel left flank by surprise. Knowing none of these details and forced to guess where the thick of the battle would be, Villard considered Tyler's demonstrated pugnacity, plus the fact that his brigades were moving out first, and decided to stick with them.

The hilly ground south of Centreville commanded an overview of Bull Run and its environs, and on the morning of July 21 crowds of onlookers gathered on the grassy slopes, dressed in their Sunday best and spoiling for a spectacle. The day had dawned clear and bright; confidence was high, and so was visibility. In order to enhance their viewing pleasure, many members of the audience at this theater *en plein air* had brought along spyglasses, opera glasses, or even field glasses. Picnic baskets held refreshments to slake the thirst and quell the hunger of the vicarious warriors—many of whom had accessorized their Sabbath finery with firearms—and their fashionably dressed companions. Eagerly looking forward to the performance (even though they thought they knew how it was going to end), the ladies and gentlemen chatted and waited for the show to start.

They had not long to wait. Tyler's vanguard had moved out in the dead of night, leaving behind them their smoldering campfires and the mingled aromas of coffee and bacon. Just after sunrise the troops came within sight of the stone bridge. Two newspapermen accompanied them: Charlie Coffin, who worked for the *Boston Journal,* and Henry Villard.

Tyler's division formed ragged lines in a gently sloping field a few hundred yards from the little river, the bridge that spanned it, and the sinister woods on the opposite bank. Curious about those woods, Villard and Coffin tethered their horses behind the Union lines and set out on foot for a closer look. From a cornfield near the stream, they could make out the rebel defenses—mounded earth, felled trees—and behind them, the occasional glint of metal in the slanting rays of the early-morning sun.

As the two correspondents watched and listened, the singing of the dawn birds and the gurgling of the water under the arches of the bridge were drowned out by the roar of artillery; Tyler's batteries had opened fire, announcing the beginning of the battle. When these guns fell silent, however, Tyler's troops made no move. Other Union artillery was still engaged; moreover, the reporters could hear the crack and rattle of small arms fire. They confronted the awful truth: news was being made somewhere else. Coffin, guessing badly, sprinted for his horse and galloped off in the direction of Blackburn's Ford; Villard stubbornly clung to his confidence in Tyler's belligerence.

Eventually Tyler did order an attack, sending two brigades wading across Bull Run about half a mile upstream on the theory that the stone bridge was thoroughly covered, and probably mined, by the rebels. Villard was faced with another choice: should he accompany Colonel Sherman's brigade, or Col. Erasmus Keyes's? The preponderance of Irishmen among Sherman's forces no doubt influenced Villard's decision to follow Keyes; however, this ethnic intolerance doomed the reporter to purposeless meandering. Colonel Keyes's brigade, along with General Tyler and his staff, became isolated from the attacking forces and lost contact with both Sherman and McDowell. The battle was being fought (and fought heavily) elsewhere, but Villard could neither see it nor find out anything about it.

"Elsewhere" was the Confederate left flank. Engaging the enemy after a march of more than seven hours, McDowell's two divisions gained ground steadily until rebel troops under Gen. Thomas J. Jackson stood firm on Henry House Hill and halted the Union advance. (It was here that Jackson earned his sobriquet, "Stonewall," though surely no one ever dared address the dour general in this fashion.) Thus stymied after having marched all night and fought all day, the weary Union soldiers were unable to withstand the Confederate counterattack that began at four o'clock in the afternoon. The Federals fell back, at first, in fairly good order, but eventually confusion and fear would turn the bulk of the Union troops into a mob of defeated, panicked individuals dedicated exclusively to self-preservation.

While the Confederates were making their successful counterattack about three quarters of a mile away, Colonel Keyes and his brigade, General Tyler and his staff, and Henry Villard were all more or less immobile in the little limbo the unit had stumbled into, the triangle formed by Bull Run, the road that crossed the stone bridge (the Warrenton Turnpike), and a small tributary of Bull Run called Young's Branch. After four o'clock the gunfire that had been in their ears all day long gradually began to fade into silence, pierced now and then by a few random shots. This bad omen was confirmed by the appearance of one of General Tyler's aides, returning after two hours from another fruitless effort to contact General McDowell and bringing the news that the Union forces were in retreat.

Villard leaped to his horse and made for the Warrenton Turnpike. He found the road and the stone bridge "already swarming with fugitives from the battle-field," not one of whom could tell him how to find General McDowell's headquarters. Villard stood at the bridge for twenty minutes as the retreating troops grew more numerous and disorderly. Finally a passing staff officer reined in his mount long enough to shout a reply to the reporter's inquiry about McDowell. "You won't find him. All is chaos in front. Our troops are breaking and running. Get back to Centreville!" And having delivered this piece of advice, he spurred his horse and galloped away.

Villard stood his ground for a while, but the retreating army was starting to look more and more like a mob. Only a few fugitives had time to speak to him, and they all confirmed the staff officer's view of things. The war correspondent rode across the bridge and up the turnpike toward Centreville. He had not gone far, however, before he found that the road was at first blocked, then choked, by vehicles of every description—ammunition wagons, supply wagons, ambulances, artillery wagons, civilian coaches, hackney carriages, sutlers' carts. Horses neighed and shrieked, drivers cursed, retreating foot soldiers shouted as they shoved their way around and through the obstructions; some fugitives unhitched horses from the foundered wagons and trotted away; others took to the adjoining fields, pulling down fences to ease their passage.

The crowning touch to this unedifying scene was added by a rebel artillery battery, which unlimbered near the stone bridge and lobbed a few farewell shells in the direction of the fleeing Federals. One shell flew nearly two miles and came down on a supply wagon that was crossing the suspension bridge over Cub Run, a stream between Bull Run and Centreville. The result was a few severely wounded men and animals, total blockage of the turnpike, and mass panic. Privates and picknickers, congressmen and colonels, abandoned ladies and inconsiderate gentlemen fled for their lives.

Villard, luckily, had crossed the bridge over Cub Run a few minutes before the shell struck, but he continually met obstacles in the road, and many fugitives caught up with him. Several officers, their troops lost or left, rushed by; a famous newspaperman, mounted bareback on a badly bleeding artillery horse, urged the flagging beast mercilessly on; the hot air of late afternoon was filled with screams and heavy with dust. Villard rode into the fields, pulling down fences he couldn't jump, and reached Centreville by six o'clock.

The town was in complete confusion, which was destined to grow. McDowell arrived around nine, but he was hearing reports and had neither the time nor the inclination to talk to representatives of the press. By ten the general, shaken by his passage through his runaway army, had decided against making a stand at Centreville and opted to retreat all the way to Washington.

The Confederates, however, as inexperienced and nearly as disorganized as the Federals, had suffered nearly two thousand casualties (among them some four hundred dead) and were in no condition to pursue. The Union Army (three thousand casualties, about six hundred dead) was thus spared further destruction, and those civilians who had fancied a pitched battle for a Sunday entertainment managed to escape with their lives.

Whether the breathless rumors of a savage Confederate pursuit were true or not, Villard thought, his next move was obvious. "My newspaper instinct was fully aroused. I saw a chance of outstripping the rival correspondents with a report of the battle by reaching Washington as quickly as possible." The newspaperman's most coveted prize, the scoop, lay within his grasp. He saddled his horse again and set off for the capital by the light of the moon.

By one o'clock he had got past the last obstruction in the road and was moving at a brisk trot, flinching occasionally when waggish though defeated Union soldiers camping along the roadside gave their imitation of the wild rebel yell, which had helped them to such a good start on their way back to Washington. At one point a Union officer, minus both hat and sword, galloped down on him. Villard was able to recognize him in the moonlight by his great bald dome and his distinctive side-whiskers; he was Col. Ambrose Burnside, commander of the First Rhode Island Regiment, whom the reporter had interviewed in Washington a few weeks previously.

Colonel Burnside's response to Villard's greeting was to shout, over his shoulder, "I'm going ahead to get rations for my men!" before disappearing into the night. Villard didn't believe this for a minute—regimental commanders did not race away alone from battlefields, or make midnight rides in search of rations—and he marked down Burnside in his heart as a man whose abilities and courage were not to be trusted. Seventeen months later, at Fredericksburg, the reporter would remember this night.

Hungry, sleepy, but with a story to write, he reached his Washington rooms shortly before six o'clock. Cobbling his succinct dispatch together from the little he had seen and the much that he had heard, he wired it to the *Herald* shortly after the telegraph office opened. His account of the battle was printed at once in an extra morning edition, the first news the nation received of the disaster that had befallen its army, and the first of Henry Villard's several dramatic scoops.

The exhausted correspondent slept for several hours, then found and interviewed McDowell's aide-de-camp, Captain Fox, at Army Headquarters. That evening Villard, having requested and received from his editor permission to exceed the *Herald*'s limit of six hundred words per wire dispatch, telegraphed a longer, fuller story to the newspaper's New York offices in Printing House Square. Based on what he had learned during the retreat from Bull Run and on his interview with Captain Fox, Villard's dispatch presented a scathing account of the Union Army's performance; he criticized certain commanding officers for failing to follow McDowell's orders, leveled accusations of general incompetence, decried the troops' lack of courage and discipline, and condemned the Union general whose task it had been to keep Gen. Joseph Johnston's rebel army away from Manassas. Villard thought this story would make his mark as a perspicacious and sensational critic of things military, but to his disgust the decision makers at the *Herald,* fearful of offending the army, edited and softened his work beyond recognition. He had saved some of his harshest criticism for certain New York regiments and their officers, and his employers had no wish to arouse the wrath of their Irish readership. The editor's excuses and compliments failed to console the proud young reporter. For neither the first nor the last time, Villard had to bite his tongue and accept the mutilation of his prose; however, his frequent disappointments of this sort never caused him to be anything less than trenchant and forthright in his articles.

The first battle of Bull Run (known to the victorious Confederates as first Manassas) put an end to many things, among them the three-month militias, the word limits on journalists' wire dispatches, and the North's fond belief in a quick and effortless victory. Before many weeks passed, it was plain to Villard that no Union army anywhere near Washington was going on the offensive anytime soon. He persuaded the *Herald*'s editor to send him west, to Kentucky, the most likely scene of the next operations. Near the end of August 1861, he checked into Galt House, the best hotel in Louisville.

GEN. WILLIAM TECUMSEH SHERMAN
ON HORSEBACK AT FEDERAL FORT NO. 7,
ATLANTA, GEORGIA.

Photograph by George N. Barnard.

Courtesy of the Library of Congress.

11

The Slaughter
of the Innocents

Skimming lightly, wheeling still,
  The swallows fly low
Over the field in clouded days,
  The forest-field of Shiloh—
Over the field where April rain
Solaced the parched ones stretched in pain
Through the pause of night
That followed the Sunday fight
  Around the church of Shiloh—
The church so lone, the log-built one,
That echoed to many a parting groan
  And natural prayer
  Of dying foemen mingled there—
Foemen at morn, but friends at eve—
  Fame or country least their care;
(What like a bullet can undeceive!)
  But now they lie low,
While over them the swallows skim,
  And all is hushed at Shiloh.

HERMAN MELVILLE,
"Shiloh: A Requiem"

The ambiguous loyalties of the citizens of Kentucky, which counted among its native sons both Abraham Lincoln and Jefferson Davis, illustrated the dilemma of the border states. An extreme example of the deep divisions that characterized Kentucky was offered by the distinguished and unhappy Crittenden family.

John J. Crittenden, the father, was a United States senator and the leader of the failed last-minute compromise effort in the weeks before the war began. One of his sons, Maj. Gen. Thomas Crittenden, served in the Union Army; another son, Maj. Gen. George Crittenden, fought on the side of the Confederacy. Kentucky was officially neutral, though both North and South diligently recruited troops within its borders during the first months of the war.

This uneasy situation began to actualize its potential for violence in September 1861, when both sides started moving troops into the state and occupying strategic positions. There followed a wary period of probing and thrusting, and Villard made regular forays from his base in Galt House, seeking out the places where action was most likely to occur and trying as always to acquaint himself with the men who would command it. Two of these particularly impressed him. One was Brig. Gen. William "Bull" Nelson, a Kentucky native who had transferred into the army from the navy and was mightily engaged in recruiting and training Kentuckians loyal to the Union cause. Nelson was an imposing figure, "thirty-six years old, over six feet high, with a mighty frame, a Jove-like head, of tireless, infectious energy, and altogether a remarkable personality." His boisterous good nature, however, frequently gave way to the violent and brutal temper that was to prove his undoing.

Villard had already met the no less remarkable William Tecumseh Sherman as a colonel on the way to Bull Run. Now a brigadier general, Sherman arrived in Louisville on October 8 to take command of the entire Union Department of the Cumberland. Neither Villard nor any other correspondent rejoiced at Sherman's appointment, for he was already notorious among newspapermen for considering them "a nuisance and a danger at headquarters and in the field, and [he] acted toward them accordingly." Sherman was not the last American general who believed that freedom of the press should be suspended during wartime, but none has ever expressed himself on the matter more forcefully: "I say with the press unfettered as now we are defeated to the end of time."

In his mature years, Villard came to share Sherman's opinion of the harm caused by war correspondents—"If I were a commanding general," the ex-reporter wrote, "I would not tolerate any of the tribe within my army lines"—but in 1861, of course, he failed to appreciate Sherman's point. Nevertheless, with his genius for befriending historically significant people, Villard managed to find ways of approaching the gruff, volatile, intense general. They met frequently at Galt House, where Sherman also lodged when not in the field, and at the Louisville telegraph office, where they went to learn the news from the Associated Press report at nine o'clock every evening.

By studiously refraining from asking Sherman questions, Villard gained the general's trust, and soon he was relaxed and chatting as volubly as any reporter could desire. Sherman seemed particularly expansive at the telegraph office, where he would regale his audience (Villard and the telegraph operator) with opinions and comments on the incoming news, assessments of military and political leaders, and speculations about the future course of the war. Most of what he had to say proved to be accurate and insightful, and Villard came to feel a great deal of respect for him.

Sherman had spent much of his army career stationed at posts in South Carolina and other Southern states, and when the war broke out he was superintendent of the state military academy in Louisiana. More than any other Union general, he knew the South, its passions and its hatreds, its attachment to tradition and abhorrence of change, and he knew it would not be easily subdued. When Secretary of War Simon Cameron, accompanied by the reporter Samuel Wilkeson, came to see what Sherman was up to, the general, who was unaware of Wilkeson's profession, spoke his mind: he told Cameron that the Union would need at least two hundred thousand troops to put down the rebellion.

Cameron was one of many Northerners who still clung to the wistful belief that the backward, agricultural South could, like some ignorant bully, be made to see reason after a couple of stern drubbings. He thought Sherman's talk of total war was dangerous and crazy; he was determined to replace him, and he said as much to Wilkeson, who repeated the secretary's views to his colleague Villard.

The latter had often seen Sherman pacing the corridors of his hotel, muttering to himself, had heard the general's anguished complaints about the rawness of his troops and the "fanatical, bloodthirsty hostility" of the South, and he thought that perhaps Sherman's nervous excitement and deepening gloom might indeed be signs of mental instability. In a confidential note to his old friend at the *Cincinnati Daily Commercial,* Murat Halstead, who was very close to the Sherman family, Villard expressed his concern for the general's mental health.

The resulting furor taught Villard a lasting lesson about trusting the powerful and must have confirmed Sherman's opinion of the press, in his words, "to the end of time." The day after receiving Villard's private note, Halstead published an editorial in the *Commercial* saying that "the country would learn with surprise and regret that Brigadier-General Sherman had become insane." Shortly thereafter, Cameron allowed Wilkeson to publish in the *New York Tribune* a full account of the conversation with Sherman (in which Wilkeson had participated, as it were, incognito), complete with "sarcastic criticisms" of Sherman's "timorousness" and his "absurd demands for troops." Villard called this an "abominable outrage"; Halstead later claimed, somewhat improbably, that Villard had known what he was doing and had acted on behalf of certain Louisville citizens who wanted to be rid of Sherman. In any case, the upshot was that Sherman ceded his command in November to Brig. Gen. Don Carlos Buell and was transferred to an obscure post in the Department of the Missouri. His troubles, however, were not yet over; the commander of his new department, Maj. Gen. Henry W. Halleck, either because he believed what he read in the newspapers or because he saw that there was some truth to the rumors of a nervous breakdown that were swirling around his eccentric officer, detached Sherman and sent him home on leave to Ohio early in December. Inevitably, Halstead learned of Halleck's decision and recalled Villard's note. On December 11, 1861, the headline in the *Commercial* read, GENERAL WILLIAM T. SHERMAN INSANE, and the accompanying article included such phrases as "stark mad."

It is an indication of Villard's considerable personal charm that the press-hating Sherman never held him in any way responsible for his part in causing this blight on the general's brilliant career. When he described these events in his autobiography, Sherman made no mention of Villard and laid the blame for his trouble on Halstead; moreover, after the Civil War the friendship between Villard and Sherman prospered, and members of Villard's family remembered that until the general's death in 1891 he was a frequent guest in their home.

General Buell, Sherman's replacement in Kentucky, detested the press as much as his predecessor but had none of his bizarre charisma, nor was he susceptible to the charm of Henry Villard. Buell moved cautiously, reacted slowly, and gave no interviews. As the year 1861 came to a close—"in sorrow, consternation, and doubt," as two historians memorably put it—there was little action along any front of the war, including Kentucky, though doom impended every-where.

Villard's determination to provide the *Herald*'s readers with news, despite these hindrances, led him to conceive another jour-nalistic coup. Since so many citizens of Louisville had gone south to serve the cause, he reasoned, they must have some organized means of maintaining contact with loved ones left behind at home. After some discreet investigation, he discovered that secret couriers of both sexes were continually traveling between Louisville and Nashville, carrying letters, documents, and the like. By the judicious distribution of some hard Yankee cash, he became a client of the un-derground courier service, which gave him regular access to all the leading Southern newspapers. Creatively and resourcefully, he had devised a way to satisfy the Northern public's great curiosity about goings-on in the sealed, mysterious South; excerpts from the smug-gled papers, complemented by Villard's own commentaries, became a prized feature of his dispatches to the *Herald*.

Early in February, the news that Lincoln and the North had been waiting for began to come in, not from Kentucky but from Ten-nessee. The Union Army, it seemed, included among its general of-ficers a soldier both eager to fight and capable of winning when he did. He was Ulysses Simpson Grant, a West Point graduate and Mexican War veteran who had left the army in 1854 and spent the intervening years failing at various businesses and clerking in his father's leather store in Galena, Illinois. By September 1861, he was a brigadier general of volunteers, with his headquarters in the southern Illinois town of Cairo.

At the end of January 1862, Grant succeeded in extracting permission from his commander, General Halleck, to attack two Confederate forts in western Tennessee, just south of the border with Kentucky. The smaller of the two was Fort Henry, near the mouth of the Tennessee River; the other, not far away, was the large and powerful Fort Donelson, which guarded the Cumberland River.

Working in conjunction with Union gunboats—including some new, custom-built ironclads—Grant's fifteen thousand troops easily took Fort Henry on February 6, then marched overland to besiege Fort Donelson. The announcement of Grant's victory at Fort Henry bestirred the other Union commanders in the West, including the sluggish Buell, and excited correspondent Villard with the prospect of imminent action. While he was trying to decide whether to accompany Buell's army on its southward march or to travel by riverboat to observe the siege of Fort Donelson, the country was electrified by the news that Grant, after several days of sharp fighting, had captured the fort and its reinforced garrison of at least twelve thousand rebel soldiers. Grant's reply to the Confederate commander's request for an armistice to discuss terms became famous throughout the North: "No terms except an unconditional and immediate surrender can be accepted. I propose to move immediately upon your works." Grant's initials, it was said, stood for "Unconditional Surrender," and with this, the first significant Union victory of the war, his dramatic rise from obscurity had begun.

On February 17, the day after the surrender of Fort Donelson, Villard left Louisville by riverboat and arrived at the newly captured stronghold the next morning. There he contacted his friend General Nelson and spent the next several days inspecting the fort, talking with the Confederate prisoners, and contemplating the grisly aftermath of the battle. "Mournful was the sight of long rows of fresh graves containing the killed on both sides," he wrote, "and of the field hospitals crowded with Federal and Confederate wounded."

A few days later, Villard sailed with General Nelson's division up the Cumberland River to Nashville. The Confederate commander in the West, Gen. Albert Sidney Johnston, realizing that the Union victories at Henry and Donelson had driven a wedge between his forces and at least temporarily rendered both Kentucky and Tennessee untenable, had elected to fall back all the way to Corinth, a railway hub in northern Mississippi, close to the Tennessee border. Thus left defenseless, Nashville, the first Confederate state capital to fall to the Union, was occupied by troops under General Buell, Nelson's commander, a few days after Villard's arrival.

In Nashville Villard followed his standard routine: he inspected the city, secured board and lodging at the leading hotel, and introduced himself in the offices of the principal newspaper, the *Daily American*. Understandably enough, the gentlemen he found there were nervous about their future and that of their paper, but Villard, presuming to speak for the military authorities, declared that his Southern colleagues would be allowed to continue publishing so long as they concentrated on objectively reporting the news and avoided any editorial comment that could be construed as sympathetic to the Southern cause. This was, as it turned out, good advice, and the *Daily American* remained in print.

Shortly thereafter General Grant arrived in Nashville, and Villard was able to catch a glimpse of him as he and his staff rode to General Buell's headquarters. Ever prone to judge by appearances, Villard was disappointed in Grant's, which he found "commonplace." In part because of his idealizing, romanticizing temperament and in part because the forms and ceremonies of his European youth had permanently colored his outlook, Villard always expected leaders to look superior, heroes to look heroic; and the unprepossessing Grant, like the unlovely Lincoln, fell far short of his ideal. Grant was small, inward, laconic; his idea of dressing like a commanding general was to pin the straps that bore the stars of his rank to an ordinary private's coat; he seemed positively to favor battered slouch hats and muddy boots; he detested and avoided all publicity and all panoply, military or otherwise. Villard's Americanization was well advanced, but the modest, inconspicuous Grant was beyond his comprehension.

Grant was not the only future president who was in Nashville around this time. The United States senator from Tennessee, Andrew Johnson, a committed Unionist whom Lincoln made military governor of the occupied state after the fall of Nashville, also came under the gaze of Villard's fastidious and appraising eye: "I saw Johnson almost daily, and watched him closely, in his official and private relations. My judgment of him was that, while he was doubtless a man of unusual natural parts, he had too violent a temper and was too much addicted to the common Southern habit of free indulgence in strong drink." Whatever may have been the nature of his weaknesses, Johnson adopted "very vigorous measures" in Nashville. When the mayor and the city council refused to take an oath of loyalty to the Federal government, Johnson summarily dismissed them, appointed a more biddable mayor, and otherwise made it quite clear that he intended to have no truck with the rebellion he deplored.

By the middle of March, General Buell was ready to continue his leisurely pursuit of the retreating Confederates. His Army of the Ohio was to march southwest to join Grant's Army of the Tennessee, which was advancing due south, or upstream, along the Tennessee River to the rendezvous point at Savannah, Tennessee, some thirty miles northeast of Corinth, Mississippi, where the rebel forces were gathering. The news from Nashville had by this time grown fairly routine, and Villard was glad to saddle up his big black horse, a recent purchase, and set out with the leading division of Buell's army. The commander of this division was Gen. Alexander McDowell McCook, one of the famous Fighting McCooks, an Ohio clan that sent no fewer than fifteen of its members to fight for the Union and mourned a disproportionate number of deaths in battle.

Sometime before his departure from Nashville, Villard had severed his connection with James Gordon Bennett's *New York Herald*. The reporter had distrusted the turbulent, tyrannical Bennett from the moment he set eyes on him and had several times been on the point of ending their association. This underlying tension was evident in the *Herald*'s pages. After Bennett had got over his early fear that his semitraitorous effusions would provoke mob violence against the *Herald*, the paper had continued to run editorials that were at least anti-Lincoln, if no longer blatantly pro-Southern, alongside the comparatively objective and evenhanded news accounts submitted by Villard and others. Moreover, the major emphasis in Villard's pieces was accuracy, which he was unwilling to sacrifice for speed, the chief concern that Bennett inculcated upon the large crew of war correspondents who worked for him. Villard was as interested as anyone else in scoops—they were called "beats" in the jargon of his day—but he had too much integrity to pad them with unverified facts or generic purple passages celebrating the triumph and tragedy of military enterprise.

We do not know the specific reason or incident, if any, that provoked Villard's decision to leave the *Herald* during this period. In any case, by the time he set out from Nashville with General McCook's division, Villard was corresponding with the *New York Tribune*, whose editor, Horace Greeley, an old friend from the gold rush days, was for all his eccentricities a much more congenial employer with much higher journalistic standards. The *Tribune*

produced, man for man, the best reporting of the war. Better equipped, better mannered, treated as individuals and not merely as interchangeable parts in an implacably grinding news machine like Bennett's, the *Tribune* "specials" were far less concerned with scoring beats than getting it right. . . . Villard . . . found the Republican air more congenial and his plain, factual reports, stressing policy and strategy over color and emotion, more highly prized. The difference between the *Herald*'s coverage, with its field men strongly dictated to by its editors in New York, and the *Tribune*'s, far more reliant on the judgment and integrity of correspondents on the scene, was well illustrated by Villard's reaction to a letter from the *Tribune* managing editor, Sidney Howard Gay, urging him to ingratiate himself with the commanding general by showing him dispatches and inviting his comment and amplification. Such a step could not be taken,

Villard replied, "without degrading me to a mere mouthpiece of him, as which my self-respect and conception of professional dignity will never allow me to serve."

The unhurried progress of McCook's division came to a complete halt thirty-five miles from Nashville, on the northern bank of the Duck River. Detachments of rebel cavalry under the command of the redoubtable Nathan Bedford Forrest had destroyed the bridge over the swollen Duck after the passage of the retreating Confederate Army. Since no pontoons were available, it was necessary for the Union troops to build their own bridge, and this task devolved upon the mechanics of one of the many Federal units composed entirely of Germans, the Thirty-second Indiana Regiment. It was in these circumstances that Villard made the acquaintance of the regimental commander, Col. August von Willich, the scion of an old Prussian military family and yet another of the many veterans of the 1848–49 German revolutions who fled to the United States and played prominent roles in the history of their adopted country. Von Willich, according to Villard, held "astonishingly radical political views for one of his antecedents"; these views seem to have done nothing to hinder the friendship here begun, which endured until von Willich's death, long after the war.

The bridge over the Duck was ten days in the building. Confederate general Johnston, with about forty thousand troops gathered in the vicinity of Corinth, knew that Buell was marching to join Grant, but he thought he saw a chance to defeat the Federals before their two armies could unite. His plans centered around the Union encampment recently established at Pittsburg Landing, on the left, or western, bank of the Tennessee River. The key point of the Federal position, on a ridge almost three miles from Pittsburg Landing, was a meetinghouse built of logs and known as Shiloh Church. In this huge encampment—it covered more than ten square miles—General Sherman, back on active duty and with his nerves apparently intact, was organizing his and other divisions of Grant's Army of the Tennessee. Grant himself was at Savannah, several miles downstream, awaiting the arrival of Buell and his Army of the Ohio. The combined Union armies would then move south to seek and destroy Johnston's forces.

If they hesitated too long, the rebels reasoned, they would be badly outnumbered; if, on the other hand, they attacked before Buell's arrival, they would be fighting a force the size of their own—Grant's army numbered a little over forty thousand men—and they would have the advantage of surprise. Johnston and his second in command, General Beauregard, consolidated the Confederate forces on March 29 and determined to start their move against the Federals five days later, on April 3.

While all these plans and preparations were going forward, Villard was stalled with General McCook's division on the far side of the Duck. On the march he had been struck by the picturesque scenery of western Tennessee, rolling, fertile, well-cultivated country marked by great plantations and fine brick mansions, whose slaveholding owners had for the most part chosen discretion over valor and fled before the invaders. By the waters of the Duck, Villard spent his time speaking his native language to von Willich and his men or putting into writing his observations concerning things military, his descriptions of what he had seen on the march, and his many interviews with Union soldiers and members of the local civilian population. In a dispatch dated March 25 and composed upon the "North Bank of Duck River," Villard described some of these interviews:

> I conversed freely and frequently with both town and country people, and I must say that I failed to meet a single individual professing to be loyal. They did not show as much bitterness of feeling as the Rebels of Nashville, nor were they equally restive under the presence of the invaders; but it was nevertheless plain that their sympathies were all in one direction, and that the wrong one. The only smiling faces were those of the slaves I passed, and my military overcoat was saluted by them with a friendly deference, indicating plainly that, unlike their masters, they saw no enemies in the strangers from the North.

As the days slowly passed, Villard's friend the large and impetuous Gen. Bull Nelson, grew anxious. Like everyone else, he knew
about the rebel concentration at Corinth, but this intelligence seems
to have caused greater concern to him than to most Union officers,
including Grant himself. Grant, like Sherman, guessed that Johnston
would not forgo the security of his fortified base in Corinth; Nelson
apparently believed that Grant's army was in an exposed position
and must be reinforced as quickly as possible. To this end, he
pleaded with Buell to let him and his division attempt to ford the
river. Buell considered, then consented, and early in the morning of
March 29, accompanied by Henry Villard, General Nelson watched
the first of his troops approach the ford, hang their cartridge boxes
around their necks, strip off their trousers, roll them into small bun-
dles, affix these to the points of their bayonets, and step warily into
the cold waters of the Duck. It was, wrote Villard, a "very amusing
and exciting" scene. Fortunately, the heretofore swollen river had recently subsided a little, and the deepest section of the ford did not
exceed four feet. The entire division, including cavalry, artillery, and
wagons, made the sixty-yard crossing with but few mishaps and were
encamped on the south bank before nightfall. Villard, too, had made
it across, wearing his pants and mounted on his strapping black
horse.

The next morning, marching down narrow dirt roads that were
soon turned to mud by a steady, pelting spring rain, Nelson's division
moved toward Savannah. Astride his charger and dressed much like
a military officer, Villard rode with General Nelson and his staff and
at night was even afforded the privilege of sleeping on the bare
floors of the empty cabins that they commandeered along the way.
Villard must have thought of his vagabond days, only eight years ago,
as he stretched out on the floorboards. Outside, the men of Nelson's
division had to do the best they could in the muddy fields, under the
persistent rain.

The farms and houses that the correspondent and the soldiers
passed on this part of the march were low and shabby, and the fields
looked slovenly. Villard, with the little shudder that the lower classes
always provoked in him, recognized the signs of poor white folks,

people who, with nary a slave to help them, scrabbled a subsistence out of small parcels of land.

Early on April 5, Villard was riding alongside Nelson at the head of his division as it entered Savannah. Grant was already there; Buell arrived with the leading elements of his army late that night and retired without conferring with Grant. Meanwhile, about nine miles away, Johnston's Confederates, having suffered their own delays, foul-ups, and blunders, had arrived—two days later than planned, but for the most part undetected and unsuspected—within striking distance of the Federal encampment around Pittsburg Landing.

The troops, both Union and Confederate, that fought the battle of Shiloh (or Pittsburg Landing) were for the most part raw recruits, boys and young men with little training and less experience, carrying recently issued muskets onto their first battlefield. Shiloh was, in fact, the first of the terrible slaughters that came to characterize the Civil War (Antietam, Fredericksburg, Gettysburg, and the Wilderness are a few of their familiar and still chilling names), and the grim lessons it taught represented a final loss of innocence for the soldiers, commanding officers, political leaders, and citizens of both the North and the South. The thousands of casualties at Shiloh included an entire contingent of grand illusions.

At six o'clock on Sunday, April 6, 1862, a soft morning full of the promise of spring, General Johnston sent his troops against the Union camps along a three-mile front, the men surging forward in great waves and howling as they charged across the rolling countryside. Though ignorant of the rebels' proximity in such numbers and surprised when they burst out of the woods, the Federal army was not wholly unprepared for such an assault, and from its opening moments the struggle was massive, savage, and intense.

When the guns began to roar around Shiloh Church, Gen. U. S. Grant was sitting down to an early breakfast in his quarters at Savannah, eight miles downriver, and Henry Villard was asleep in the riverboat berth he had hired for the night. Even at this distance, the sound of the firing was so loud that it sent the general rushing away from his table and awakened the deeply slumbering correspondent.

Before dashing off to join his army, Grant sent General Buell a hurried note, explaining his reason for skipping their scheduled meeting. Buell, taking this broad hint, ordered his troops to march overland down the east bank of the Tennessee to a point across from Pittsburg Landing and decided that he and his staff would travel upriver by boat to the battlefield. As was his wont, however, Don Carlos Buell moved with all deliberate speed, no faster. The leading elements of his army, with General Nelson's division in the van, did not set off on their march until one o'clock in the afternoon. The steamboat that Buell chose among the many such vessels available in Savannah—it was Villard's, and he was already on it—failed to get under way until well past three, and by the time it reached Pittsburg Landing the battle had been raging for some nine hours.

As the boat approached the landing, the din of the fighting grew louder, and sulfurous smoke thickened the air. The riverbank ran under high bluffs, and Villard could see that it was crowded with thousands of soldiers, "of all arms and of all ranks, from field officers down, all apparently entirely bereft of soldierly spirit." Many of these men were wounded, a great many others were skulking, and all pressed as close to the wall of the overhang as they could. Shocked by so familiar an image of disorder and defeat, Villard exclaimed to Buell's chief of staff, who was standing next to him on the steamboat's top deck, "Oh, heavens! Captain, here is Bull Run all over again!" The high ground above shimmered in the smoke and trembled under the force of thousands of large and small explosions, muskets and artillery combining in one unmodulated interminable detonation. When two Union gunboats in the middle of the river began to shell the Confederate positions, the cacophony was complete.

Disembarking on the landing with his horse, Villard watched General Buell add his measured exhortations to those of the officers who were trying to rally the cowering soldiers, but none of them had any success. Soon General Nelson arrived from the opposite bank with one of his brigades and attempted, in his own style, to recall the shirkers to their duty. Villard remembered Nelson's escalating fury:

With that Jupiter head on his herculean figure, mounted on a heavy charger, he looked the personification of Orlando Furioso, as he rode up through the packed crowds, waving his hat and shouting: "Fall in, boys, fall in and follow me! We shall whip them yet!" Finding this did no good, he drew his sword and commenced belaboring the poltroons, berating them at the same time with his stentorian voice, in language more forcible than polished. His extraordinary swearing indicated plainly that he had had great practice in that sort of admonition on the quarterdeck.

Nelson's profane eloquence, however, elicited no volunteers, and Buell rejected his overwrought request for permission to bayonet the frightened soldiers back to the battlefield and to fire on them if that didn't work. Turning their thoughts to the enemy, the two frustrated generals led Nelson's brigade up the bluff and against an advanced battery of rebel artillery. Villard, too, urged his big horse up the bluff, where the music of bullet, ball, and grapeshot sang in his ears. Once the Yankee soldiers had reached the plain, the musket fire decreased—the rebel outposts were falling back—but the shelling continued as the reporter galloped from point to point in the hastily formed Federal line. Night fell soon, and the two battered armies paused in their work of destruction.

With night came rain, falling torrentially on the blasted battlefield, on the two thousand dead (among them Confederate general Johnston), on the ten thousand wounded (many of them still lying untended on the field), on the seventy thousand or so weary survivors, on the fifteen thousand fresh Union troops ferried across the river. Villard talked to a few soldiers, most of whom described how their units had been surprised and overrun, but the pouring rain curtailed his interviews and drove him back to the landing. After a long and miserable wait, he found that there was no longer room for his horse on the steamboat, which had been pressed into service as transport for Buell's troops. Too attached to his horse to leave it, Villard rode the beast into the wet dark and was lucky enough to stumble onto Nelson's bivouac in the woods, where he found a hearty welcome, a log fire, a makeshift shelter (a rubber blanket stretched between two trees), and a soldier's meal of hardtack and cold bacon washed down with brandy and water.

No one got much sleep on that "memorable, dismal night." The Yankee gunboats fired a salvo into the rebel positions every ten minutes, all night long; the rain drove down without interruption, accompanied by thunder and lightning; the helpless cries of the wounded still suffering on the battlefield came piercingly out of the darkness; and through it all there was the battle to meditate upon, both as it had been today and as it would be tomorrow. Basing their judgment on but little information, and that unreliable, Nelson's staff considered the day a Union disaster and awaited none too hopefully the inexorable dawn.

The day had indeed been a disaster, but it had equally afflicted both sides. Thousands of Federal soldiers broke and ran, but so did thousands of Confederates, who had much more room to run. As evidenced by the extraordinary number of casualties, however, the vast majority of soldiers, North and South, fought as hard as they could. After their initial big push, the increasingly uncoordinated Confederate attacks met with stiff resistance, yet slowly but surely the Yankees were forced to fall back toward the Tennessee River. By the time Villard and Buell arrived at Pittsburg Landing, Grant had stabilized a solid defensive perimeter, bristling with artillery, along a ridge above Pittsburg Landing. The Union forces had been driven nearly two miles behind their original positions, but at last their line had held. Although both armies were exhausted from twelve hours of vicious fighting, the Confederates, as Grant perceived, now were vulnerable, and he had fresh troops at hand. An early, strong offensive the next day, he knew, would carry the field.

Villard, who knew none of these things, stirred at 4 A.M. with the soldiers. An hour later the advance began, and the reporter followed in the rear of Nelson's division. At five-thirty the firing began in earnest—Villard could feel musket balls and artillery shells whistling and whizzing past him—and by eight o'clock the battle was roaring as loudly as it had the day before. His memory of the scene remained vivid:

> The battle was speedily raging with great violence. From one end of the line to the other, the combat lasted for hours, with hardly a lull in the deafening discharge of small arms and guns. Although but a short distance in the rear of the fighting and actually under fire, it was not possible for me to follow the course of the struggle from my position, owing to the character of the ground and the thickness of the atmosphere from the falling rain mixed with the dense powder-smoke that hung over the field. Nor could I expect to learn anything reliable by remaining in one spot. A sort of field-hospital was established near by, to which the wounded were being brought, in steadily increasing numbers, presenting sights that made me heart-sick.

The urge to learn something reliable drove him to ride all day around the fringes of the battlefield on his intrepid black horse, visiting all the division headquarters, trying to interview the commanders or their staffs. With projectiles humming all around him, he arrived at one headquarters in time to see Colonel von Willich's regiment fall back in confusion after an ardent but ill-fated bayonet charge. Villard trailed another division's steady advance and watched a coordinated flank and frontal attack that sent rebel units into full retreat. At around 4 P.M. the Federals had regained almost all the ground lost the previous day, and General Beauregard, who had succeeded to command on Sunday after the mortally wounded General Johnston bled to death in a peach orchard, broke off the battle and abandoned the field.

The rain had continued all day and was still coming down in torrents. Villard rode through the dripping thickets and muddy clearings of the battlefield and was shaken by the number of dead and wounded he saw and by the moans and cries for help he heard. Both he and his horse had eaten little and slept less for nearly thirty hours; he rode back to the landing, fortunately found a boat that would accommodate horse and rider, procured a stateroom and a hot supper, and slept for ten hours.

By eight o'clock the next morning—Tuesday, April 8—he was back among the Union camps, surveying the aftermath of the battle and seeking information about what exactly had taken place. With his usual luck, he managed to find General Sherman's headquarters just as the general was about to leave. Sherman's division of Ohio and Illinois volunteers had done some of the best and bravest fighting on Sunday. The commander himself had been slightly wounded twice, and three horses had been shot under him, yet he seemed to be in an expansive mood. Suspending for the nonce his hostility toward journalists and his memory of the Louisville fiasco, Sherman gave Villard a lucid, frank, and apparently honest account of his experiences in the battle.

Having noted Sherman's version, Villard then made the rounds of the other division commanders in Grant's Army of the Tennessee and Buell's Army of the Ohio. It was hard going, for the incredibly persistent rain had by now reduced the fought-over ground to mire a couple of feet deep. Mud-spattered and drenched, he and his long-suffering black horse thrashed around the battlefield, searching for the truth about what had happened. By three in the afternoon, Villard had talked to a wide range of soldiers, from generals to privates, and something like a coherent account of the battle seemed to be taking shape in his mind.

This, of course, was an illusion, as he himself confessed in a piece he wrote nearly three frustrating weeks later. In a tone of grudging despair, he asserted the impossibility of arriving at a unified, accurate, unambiguous view of past events, even recent past events, by sifting the accounts of those who had lived through them, including his own:

> In the camps, as in the newspapers, you find it difficult to winnow the truth from the bushel of falsehood. Here are the ordinary obstacles to learning the facts about a battle—the jealousies, the cliques, the inordinate ambitions, the untrustworthiness of eyes and ears during periods of great excite-

ment. . . . Every journalist who has spent the last two weeks in riding from camp to camp in the fathomless mud to question witnesses, verify assertions, and sift the truth out of contradictions . . . has concluded that the deepest of all wells in which the truth was ever sought is the Battle of Pittsburg Landing.

The validity of Villard's insight can be verified by anyone who compares the accounts that any two individuals, whether participants or historians, give of this particularly confused and confusing battle. In his memoirs, Villard himself, full of the certitudes of old age, forgot his healthy youthful skepticism and gave a version of Shiloh heavily influenced by his friend General Nelson, whose report Grant, writing a few months after the event, called "a tissue of unsupported romance from beginning to end."

What there could not be two opinions about was that Shiloh had been a huge, malignant battle. The total casualties for the two armies approached twenty-five thousand, a staggering 25 percent of those engaged, and at least thirty-five hundred young men had died outright. The North could claim victory, in that its forces had won back on Monday all the ground they had lost on Sunday; the South could claim victory, in that its forces had succeeded in killing a few dozen more Yankees than the number of rebels the Yankees had killed. As Villard contemplated the "grim, shocking, and sickening" spectacle of the battlefield, however, his thoughts turned aside for a while from questions of what had happened or who had won:

There was bloody evidence in every direction that the slaughter had been great. Neither the one side nor the other had removed its dead, and there they were, blue and gray, in their starkness, lying here singly and there literally in rows and heaps. I passed more than a thousand of them. It was morbid, perhaps, on my part, but I lingered to see the effect of sudden violent death on features and limbs. It surprised me that the faces of most of these victims of battle bore a peaceful, contented expression, and that many lay as though they had consciously stretched themselves out to sleep. But there were also many

ghastly exceptions, with features repulsively distorted by pain
and hatred.

Among the corpses there were still hundreds of severely
wounded men, many of them writhing and screaming in agony.
Their cries penetrated Villard's ears as his eyes contemplated the
piles of amputated limbs outside the field hospitals he passed. But
"the most woeful scene in all this sadness," the one whose horror
fixed itself in his memory for life, confronted him when he visited
Shiloh itself, the little meetinghouse (named after a religious center
and sanctuary in ancient Israel) that gave its name to the battle: "The
seats for the worshippers had been removed, and on the floor were
extended, in two rows, on the bare planks and without any cover over
them, twenty-seven dead and dying rebels, officers and men. Not a
human being was about to offer them tender mercies. They had
been left to their fate, all being obviously beyond relief." It was on
Shiloh battlefield that Villard felt the first overwhelming impulses of
his later commitment to pacifism.

Shocked and sickened by what he had seen, and convinced that
both sides had had their fill of fighting for a while, Villard left his
horse in charge of a quartermaster friend and boarded a side-
wheeler bound for Cairo, Illinois, where he would post the battle report he planned to write under way. The steamer, loaded with
wounded men, was transporting a couple of other newsmen, including the tall, elegant, twenty-four-year-old Whitelaw Reid, a special
who reported the war for the *Cincinnati Gazette* under the pseudonym
"Agate." The journalists interviewed the wounded, exchanged notes
and stories with one another, chatted, scribbled, sought to make a
whole out of many fragmented parts.

A few days after Reid reached Cincinnati, the *Gazette* printed his
story, a "powerful, gloomy narrative" 19,500 words long that covered
the entire front page of the newspaper plus twelve more columns inside. This, "one of the most celebrated and controversial dispatches
of the war" in the words of one historian, attracted national attention
and was reprinted by many other newspapers, including the *New York
Herald*. Eventually, having waited in vain for Villard's report—like 35

percent of all dispatches, it was lost in the mail—Sydney Howard Gay, the managing editor at the *Tribune,* reprinted Reid's story too. According to Gay, Greeley never forgave his young reporter for losing this scoop to the *Herald,* but this was not the last time that Whitelaw Reid would profit from the misfortunes of Henry Villard.

GEN. AMBROSE E. BURNSIDE.

Photograph by Mathew Brady. The Brady Collection.

National Archives.

12

Trampling Out
the Vintage

*It can hardly be in human nature for men to show more
valor, or generals to manifest less judgment, than were
perceptible on our side that day.*

CINCINNATI COMMERCIAL
report on the battle of Fredericksburg

Villard's stay in Cairo was extremely brief. Learning that the
Union forces gathered at Pittsburg Landing would soon be on
the move, he hastened away from Cairo on April 10 (his
twenty-seventh birthday, celebrated "only in thought") and the next
day was back with General McCook's division.

Another arrival at Pittsburg Landing on April 11 was Maj. Gen.
Henry W. Halleck, Federal commander in the West, come to take
over field command of Grant's and Buell's armies. Halleck was a fine
administrator and military theorist, but (in one Civil War scholar's
tart evaluation) "at heart he was a shuffler of papers," unfit for a
combat command. It did not take him long to develop an acute case
of the multiplication disorder that afflicted nearly all the commanding generals in the Yankee army, who consistently overestimated by a
factor of two or three the size of the rebel armies they faced. When
Gen. John Pope's Army of the Mississippi disembarked at the landing, Halleck's concentration of his forces was complete, and a mighty
host, more than a hundred thousand men, started marching toward
the Confederate stronghold at Corinth on May 2, 1862.

Villard had spent the intervening weeks in bivouac with the

troops, under the unending rain, yet he regularly visited all the camps and must have conducted many a sodden interview. Grant, whom Halleck had seen fit to appoint to the largely decorative post of second in command, proved to be much more accessible to the press, with nothing to do and time on his hands. Villard conversed with him at length on several occasions, finding him approachable, unpretentious, not always reticent, and "very plain." In fact, Villard noted, Grant's "ordinary exterior . . . made it as difficult for me as in the case of Abraham Lincoln to persuade myself that he was destined to be one of the greatest arbiters of human fortunes." Writing nearly thirty-five years after the fact, Villard still couldn't get over this discrepancy between the ideal and the real. Nevertheless, as with Lincoln, increased contact with Grant and exposure to the conversation of his devoted staff enabled Villard to recognize the general's merits, however unsatisfactory the vessel that contained them.

General Halleck's grand army moved like a glacier over the twenty-odd miles that lay between Pittsburg Landing and the rebel fortifications around Corinth, and by May 29 was within half a mile of them. The last two days of this cautious march had been marked by heavy skirmishing, and the Yankee brass was certain that the rebels were preparing a mighty blow. What they were really preparing, however, was a practical joke. Throughout the night of May 29, Villard kept a vigil with General McCook and his staff—the other Union generals and their staffs were equally sleepless—listening to what sounded like a continuous stream of trains running between Corinth station and the rebel front lines; a large and growing body of rebel troops seemed to greet each arrival of what was plainly reinforcements with the bloodthirsty whooping that had such a marked effect on Northern imaginations. In fact, the anxious Federals, ears straining and minds on fire, were General Beauregard's dupes: the stream of packed trains was actually one empty train, sedulously shuttling back and forth, and the raucous greeters belonged to a single, specially assigned cheering detachment. Convinced that a screaming rebel army at least two hundred thousand strong was going to fall upon them in the morning, the Yankees hunkered down.

By the time Halleck and his generals realized the truth, Beauregard's seventy thousand men, carrying with them their munitions and heavy guns, had skillfully and stealthily evacuated Corinth. Early the next morning, Henry Villard rode his black horse into the abandoned city, which, he thought, "badly belied its classic name." Shortly thereafter Corinth was occupied by the victorious if somewhat shamefaced Federals. After a few days, Halleck called off the pursuit of the rebels, who had made a clean getaway and soon took up a much stronger defensive position around Tupelo, fifty miles to the south.

For Villard as for the Union troops, there followed a period of idleness. Into this almost total dearth of news came word that on June 6, on the Mississippi River at Memphis, Union ironclads and rams had won a lopsided victory over an inferior fleet of Confederate gunboats. With the ostensible purpose of interviewing witnesses to this "terrible spectacle" (people had thronged the bluffs overlooking the river to watch the short, savage fight), but equally motivated by the prospect of breaking the routine of camp life, enjoying a few decent meals, and sleeping in a bed, Villard made a quick trip by rail to occupied Memphis on June 9.

There, in "the principal hostelry of the city," he met several colleagues whom he had last seen at Cairo and spent an enjoyable couple of days. However, his brief respite was cut short when he learned that General Buell's Army of the Ohio had received its marching orders. Villard filed his report on the battle of Memphis and took the next train back to Corinth.

Buell had been ordered to march on Chattanooga, about two hundred miles away, and as his troops, some forty thousand strong, moved through this wide expanse of enemy territory, they were to repair whatever wrecked railroads and rebuild whatever demolished bridges they might come across. The spring deluge had by now given way to a summer drought; the parched soldiers tramped along in the wilting heat, choking on dust and slapping at mosquitoes. Their assigned task necessitated slow movement and frequent, often lengthy, stops, and they were under the constant threat of harassment by rebel guerrillas and mounted marauders.

Like the soldiers, Villard soon grew weary of the interminable routine of trudging, camping, and waiting. The continuing drought caused streams to run dry, and locating water became a major priority of General Buell's army. Meanwhile, as the long, hot summer of 1862 dragged on, the Confederates decided to change the pace of events.

In June, Jefferson Davis had replaced the ailing Beauregard with Maj. Gen. Braxton Bragg, an officer whose disciplinarian enthusiasms and organizational skills served to conceal his essential mediocrity. He was talented enough, however, to do a fair job of outmaneuvering Buell. At the end of July, Bragg moved about thirty-five thousand of his men south to Mobile and then shipped them north, by rail, to Chattanooga. This innovative end run, the first strategic use of the railway system to transport a large number of troops over a long distance, took Buell completely by surprise, but he continued his dogged, intermittent progress across northern Alabama and into Tennessee.

In August it became clear that Bragg's army was marching northward from Chattanooga and that he planned to link up with Gen. Kirby Smith's smaller force, which was moving north out of Knoxville. Buell suddenly found himself on the defensive, faced with the prospect of a Confederate invasion of Kentucky. He deflected the direction of his march from Chattanooga and headed for Louisville by way of Nashville and Bowling Green. For weeks the two armies, Buell's and Bragg's, marched on gradually converging lines, both racing for the Ohio River.

From the beginning Villard had chafed under the discomforts and monotony of the march. To add to his distress, he had, along with other correspondents, taken a pledge (religiously kept) not to report on the movements or plans of the army he accompanied, and his chances of writing meaningful dispatches were thus severely limited. Although he rather grimly enjoyed the irony of such place-names as Florence and Athens, Alabama, for the most part he was bored to death by the dusty country, the daily routine, the snail's pace, the dreadful food.

Near the end of August he leapt at the chance to accompany a daredevil cavalry regiment (commanded by another fighting Mc-

Cook, Col. Edward M., first cousin of the general) engaged in "scouting, hunting, and fighting guerrillas." For a week Villard followed this search-and-destroy mission, rejoicing in the hard riding, the open air, and the excitement of the chase, constantly reminded of a song from Schiller's play *Die Räuber* (The Robbers): "Ein freies Leben führen wir" (Free Is the Life We Lead). Colonel McCook's men covered as many as forty miles a day, bivouacked under the stars, and lived off the country, picking it clean "like a swarm of locusts." Often reminded of his Colorado adventures, Villard was well content, quite willing to trade exposure to danger for the possibility of observing something that he could fashion into news.

Villard always rode in the van with the colonel, witnessed some "lively bush-fighting," and participated in several wild chases, but the most memorable incident was wholly without romantic overtones and served to underline the everyday brutality and misery integral to the enterprise his subjects were engaged in. A private, having asked leave to fall out "for a certain purpose," climbed a fence into a cornfield; a few minutes later Villard and the other soldiers heard the crack of a gunshot; after a brief search, the trooper's comrades found his body. Villard galloped with the colonel and a small detachment to the farmhouse, where they found only women, children, and slaves, one of whom they threatened into confessing that "young Massa" had fired the shot. Unable to find young Massa, the colonel ordered everyone out of the farmhouse and the surrounding buildings, which his soldiers then burned to the ground. After scattering the livestock, the Union troops rode away, leaving the stealthy hero's family and slaves to do the best they could without food or shelter. Sterner retribution, including hanging, was meted out in other cases, among them one that involved yet another McCook, Brig. Gen. Robert L., who became ill on the march and was murdered by rebel guerrillas as he rode in an ambulance. The life that the soldiers led, and that Villard shared and reported on, may sometimes have seemed dashing and free, but its reality was irredeemably nasty.

On September 7, Colonel McCook's regiment was ordered to rejoin the march, and Villard's cavalry adventures came to an end. On the way to "liberating" Kentucky, Bragg's Confederates were causing plenty of havoc and destruction in Tennessee, tearing up railroad tracks, burning bridges, and capturing entire Yankee garrisons, and General Buell was determined to get ahead of them.

In Virginia, too, the rebels were on the offensive. Early in September, Gen. Robert E. Lee's Army of Northern Virginia invaded Maryland. By the middle of the month, the Confederates had occupied positions around the town of Sharpsburg, near the banks of Antietam Creek, and Federal troops under Gen. George McClellan were advancing to meet them. On September 17, when the great and bloody battle of Antietam was fought—the single day of combat produced a combined total of more than twenty-six thousand casualties—General McCook's division of Buell's army, faithfully accompanied by an increasingly travel-worn Henry Villard, was past Bowling Green and bound for Louisville.

Thirty-five miles from Louisville, when the Union and Confederate Armies were no more than twenty miles apart and skirmishing between them was occurring with increasing frequency, Bragg suddenly turned east. Whatever this might mean, Buell was determined to reach Louisville—his starting point back in March—and his army tramped steadily on.

By September 27 they were ten miles from Louisville, and Henry Villard could stand it no longer. Irresistibly drawn by the thought of a real bath, fresh underwear, and a change of clothes, he urged his horse ahead of the army and arrived at Galt House at 10 P.M. He was wildly bearded, his face black with sweat and dust, his clothing stiff with dirt, and he made his request for a room with a certain pungency. The night clerk, failing to recognize him, announced that there was no vacancy, but Villard mentioned his name and was immediately escorted to a good room on the third floor. His trunk, stored since February, was sent up; he gazed joyously upon the selection of clean underwear it contained; he bathed, shaved, dressed in fresh clothes, ate a large, hot meal, went to bed, and slept for eleven hours. He was off the march.

But not for long. The next day Villard learned that Buell's superiors, including Abraham Lincoln, their patience worn out by what they perceived as the general's intolerable slowness, had ordered him, under the threat of losing his command, to find Bragg's army and bring it to battle. Faced with disgrace, Buell threw himself with unwonted zeal into the task of preparing his army for an immediate offensive. The presence of additional troops in Louisville brought the Union strength up to nearly sixty thousand effectives, whom Buell organized into three corps.

The pace of events now quickened. Villard's friend and fellow guest at Galt House, Gen. Bull Nelson, had been in Louisville for some weeks, ordering its defenses against the threat of a Southern invasion. During these preparations, after a "violent scene," Nelson had rudely dismissed one of his subordinates, Brig. Gen. Jefferson C. Davis, who must have thought his name abuse enough. Superior authority restored Davis to his command, and he returned to Louisville on September 28. The next morning, while Villard was enjoying a leisurely breakfast in the dining room at Galt House, General Davis approached General Nelson in the lobby and demanded from him an apology for his rude behavior. Nelson refused; Davis insisted; Nelson, who towered over him, called him an "insolent puppy" and slapped his face; Davis ran from the hotel and returned at once with a pistol. This time he positively *required* an apology, but Nelson expressed his profound contempt for the little general, for his demand, and for his gun; whereupon Davis fired it at his chest.

At the sound of the shot, Villard leaped to his feet and ran to the lobby. He watched Nelson being helped to his room and sadly contemplated his rash friend as he lay bleeding on his bed. The giant general reminded Villard of "a dying lion." Ten minutes later he was dead indeed, the victim not only of his fellow officer but also, as Villard honestly reported, of his own brutal temper. Before General Davis was placed under arrest, Villard talked with him and noted his view of the matter: "I gave him a chance to apologize." The public murder of one Union general by another, thoroughly reported by Villard, caused an immense sensation in the North, but it was apparently too unprecedented, too unimaginable, too unspeakable—too awful, in short—to admit of any official reaction. Davis's arrest was brief, he was never brought to trial, and he commanded troops honorably until the end of the war. Villard grieved for his friend, whom he had genuinely liked, but he never tried to justify Nelson's egregious conduct.

Two days later, on October 1, Buell's army marched out of Louisville and set about locating General Bragg and his Confederates. General McCook was now in command of an army corps of three divisions, and once again Villard accompanied him and his staff, riding in the summer sun over rolling hills covered with bluegrass. After a week and sixty miles of searching, a portion of the Union Army found the fight it was looking for. This was the battle of Perryville, which, it is said, "set a new record for confusion among top brass on both sides." The encounter might have seemed farcical had the young men who participated in it not managed, despite their bewildered commanders, to shoot and cannonade one another so effectively; more than fifty-five hundred of them were wounded, and more than thirteen hundred killed outright.

The battle began when elements of both armies, including McCook's corps, tried to seize access to a half-desiccated creek whose standing pools of water had been rendered precious by the disastrously long drought. In the ensuing collision, around sixteen thousand Confederates engaged more than twice as many Union troops, but since the rebels grossly underestimated the size of the Federal force they were attacking and the Federals, in accordance with their standard practice, exaggerated the number of their opponents, the battle was fought on even terms. Neither commander managed to commit anything near his full resources to the fight. Bragg's Confederates were spread out over the fifty-odd miles between Perryville and Frankfort—Bragg himself was in Frankfort when the battle began—and a rare phenomenon known as acoustic shadow prevented the hapless Buell, whose much larger army occupied a much more compact area, from hearing the combat that was raging less than two miles from his field headquarters.

The battle, for all its confusion, followed a familiar general pattern: massed and howling Confederate units mounted a spirited attack, throwing the Union forces back and causing thousands of raw troops to flee in disorder; the Federals stiffened, halted the rebel advance, and counterattacked in force, driving the outnumbered enemy from the field. Union general Philip Sheridan, heretofore little known, distinguished himself at Perryville, for it was his troops whose firm stand stalled the Confederate surge, and it was he who led the successful Federal counterattack.

As for Henry Villard, Perryville gave him a far better opportunity to observe a pitched battle than either Bull Run, where the division he accompanied did very little fighting, or Shiloh, where he arrived after much of the fighting had been done. Moreover, the weather and the topography of the battlefield were in his favor; the hilly, lightly timbered ground and the bright sun afforded clear views of the two armies at their work. Finally, it was McCook's corps that took the brunt of the rebel attack, and Villard found himself in the midst of a huge swirl of excitement and danger. Shells exploded over and around him, bullets hissed about his ears, hundreds of men were cut down before his eyes as he raced from one vantage point to the next. He was able to include in the dispatches he sent to the *Tribune* a great deal of firsthand, frontline reporting.

On the night of October 8, the scene of this incoherent struggle, illuminated by a brilliant moon, was littered with the intermingled wreckage of war—human and animal, Confederate and Union, wounded, dying, and dead. Buell, finally in touch with all his commanders, ordered a counterattack at daybreak. But Bragg, disheartened by the casualties his men had suffered in so inconclusive a fight and at last aware of how heavily Buell's army outnumbered his own, pulled his troops out during the night. His efforts to liberate Kentucky had brought no bellicose Kentuckians rallying to his standard, and now he had lost thousands of men in a clumsy and misdirected melee. A few weeks later his army would evacuate Kentucky altogether and return to eastern Tennessee, its starting point, with little to show for its exertions. Rebuffed at Perryville and battered at Antietam, the Confederates had suffered no clear-cut defeat, but their two-pronged invasion of the North was at an end.

In the field, Perryville seemed like anything but a Union success. The Federal troops who moved out to the attack at dawn discovered that their foe had given them the slip, and Buell, trying his superiors' patience for the last time, failed to pursue the retreating enemy. The officers whom Villard interviewed made little attempt to disguise their frustration and chagrin, and in the dispatch he wrote that very day he called the battle a Southern victory.

Later that afternoon, his sense of journalistic duty and his unabashedly morbid curiosity once more drew Villard to take a long, contemplative horseback ride past scenes of shocking carnage—"as horrifying a spectacle," he thought, "as those on the field of Shiloh." He saw the corpses lying in swaths where the cannonballs had passed, followed the long trails of blood, carefully observed the mutilations, gloomily listened to the last agonies of the doubly unlucky. The Confederate dead provided "awful proof of the blind heroism, born of fanatical devotion to their bad cause, with which the rebels faced—yea, courted—death," and as he roamed the battlefield he became more powerfully convinced than ever before that the struggle was going to be long and desperate.

In keeping with his professional habits, Villard interviewed as many soldiers as he could, officers and men. One of the McCooks introduced him to General Sheridan, with whom the reporter had a long talk, thus forming an acquaintance with yet another future commanding general of the United States Army. Sheridan failed to impress Villard "as a man of more than ordinary intellectual ability," but this stricture may actually have been based on considerations of height and ethnicity: "His exterior was anything but prepossessing. Of hardly middle height, with a round head, low brow, and decidedly coarse Irish features, a disproportionately broad and long body on short legs, he did not make a very imposing personality. He looked like a bold *sabreur,* but nothing more." Villard was an observant man, but as we have seen, he often had to peer through distorting lenses of his own devising.

With no enemy and no pursuit, Buell's army offered slim pickings to the reporter hungry for news. A week after the battle, Villard decided to return to Louisville and set out on horseback for the nearest railroad station. At the beginning of his journey he had to cross a portion of the battlefield. Drawn by "a sickening stench," he came upon a scene that would take second place to none of the memories of atrocious horror that he acquired during the Civil War:

> In a clear space of not over an acre, there were more than fifty dead rebels, off whom at least a hundred hogs were making a sickening feast. The fallen Confederates had evidently been overlooked by our burying parties. Decomposition had swelled the bodies into awful monstrosities, and the nasty beasts were hard at work disembowelling them and gnawing into the skulls for their brains. Such is war!

Back in Louisville, Villard wired the *Tribune* for instructions now that the campaign was over. The wire he received the next morning directed him to report to the *Tribune* offices in person. More than ready to take a break from the military life, to say nothing of the killing fields, Villard left Louisville for New York on October 20.

▦   ▦   ▦

A few days later, looking a bit nattier than he'd looked for most of the past eight months, Henry Villard climbed the iron stairs to the *New York Tribune*'s offices at the corner of Nassau and Spruce. Entering the headquarters of the "most influential paper in the land," he proceeded to a meeting with Horace Greeley and his managing editor, Sydney Howard Gay, who gave their Kentucky correspondent a warm and friendly welcome.

Gay, a Massachusetts native, was a committed abolitionist; he had abandoned the study of law after realizing that lawyers must swear an oath to uphold the Constitution, which condoned slavery, and in Boston he had been a member of William Lloyd Garrison's circle. In 1857, after a successful career as the crusading editor of an abolitionist newspaper, Gay, swayed by Greeley's persuasive powers and impressed by the prestige and circulation of the *Tribune*, had accepted the post of managing editor. His intellectual fervor and moral integrity had helped to make the *Tribune* the polar opposite of Villard's former newspaper, James Gordon Bennett's *Herald*. Gay's connection with Garrison, the veteran leader of the radical antislavery movement, was to prove fateful for Henry Villard.

Seeing, or guessing, how much of himself Villard had used up in his pursuit of news from Kentucky to Mississippi and back again, Greeley and Gay, after a little light but encouraging conversation, told their reporter to take a week off. When Villard returned at the end of his leave, the three men got down to the business of his future.

George Smalley, formerly the *Tribune's* correspondent with the Army of the Potomac—Villard called his dispatch on the battle of Antietam "the best piece of work of the kind produced during the Civil War"—had returned from the field, suffering from the burnout that sooner or later afflicted most Civil War correspondents, and had been reassigned to the relatively serene task of writing editorials on military affairs. Gay had been obliged to overcome Greeley's objections to appointing Villard in Smalley's place—the *Herald's* Shiloh scoop still rankled—but now the two editors concurred in offering Villard the job of the *Tribune's* chief correspondent with the Army of the Potomac. This meant more pay, more prestige, more access, and more responsibilities, among them a crew of three assistants, and Villard naturally leapt at the chance.

Early in November, Villard arrived in Washington, his new base of operations. The *Tribune's* Washington bureau chief was Sam Wilkeson, whom Villard had last seen in Louisville, when Wilkeson had passed along some conjectures regarding the sanity of William Tecumseh Sherman. Now Wilkeson was covering the Washington political scene, and like Villard, he reported directly to Sydney Gay. Villard also had a colleague's nodding acquaintance with Wilkeson's chief assistant, Adams S. Hill.

Since it was obvious that the Army of the Potomac, despite incessant prodding from President Lincoln, would not be fighting any battles in the immediate future, Villard stayed in Washington for several weeks before joining the army in the field. He spent part of this time submerged in the records of the War Department, reading the official reports of the Tennessee and Kentucky campaigns. In the evenings, using the fruits of his research and his own field notes, he drafted a "full review of the operations of the Army of the Ohio under Buell." This military critique filled an entire page in the *Tribune*'s issue of November 12, 1862. It was characteristic of Villard that he wished to complete his understanding of every battle he witnessed by reading everything written about it and then writing his own thorough overview, but it was likewise characteristic that the methodical, heavy-handed, and sometimes overbearing pieces he proudly produced after all this slogging were far inferior to the vivid, keenly observed dispatches he wrote when events still burned hot in his mind.

The Army of the Potomac wasn't fighting, but it was constantly in the news. Its controversial commander, Maj. Gen. George B. McClellan, dilatory, pettifogging, overcautious, and overweening, finally tested President Lincoln's patience beyond his enduring, and on November 5, to McClellan's astonishment, Lincoln relieved him of his command. Although the main reasons for Lincoln's decision revolved around the general's incorrigible reluctance to move his huge, well-supplied army and engage the comparatively ill-shod, hungry, poorly equipped, and far less numerous Confederate forces under Gen. Robert E. Lee, several additional considerations came into play. For one thing, there was McClellan's overt opposition to the preliminary Emancipation Proclamation that Lincoln had presented to his cabinet at the end of September; for another, there was the fact that Little Mac gave his commander in chief a profound and abiding pain.

As McClellan's replacement, Lincoln chose Gen. Ambrose E. Burnside, the officer who, citing his troops' need of rations, had galloped past Henry Villard on the dark turnpike north of Manassas battlefield. Villard, who doubted Burnside's ability to command as well as his courage, viewed his appointment as an invitation to disaster. Events would prove him right.

Having brought his essay in military criticism to a satisfactory close, Villard employed his remaining time in Washington preparing himself for his new assignment. He talked to cabinet members, army officers, and government officials, and he read newspaper accounts and army reports, learning what he could about the Union war effort in general and the Army of the Potomac in particular, and incidentally picking up along the way plenty of fresh-ground meal from the Washington gossip and rumor mills. Among the juicier items were predictions of an imminent coup, to be led by the wronged and indignant McClellan, and lurid speculations about the effects of the proposed Emancipation Proclamation. As he moved about the city, Villard was struck by the amount of new building that was going on, an impressive sign of faith, he thought, in the government's ultimate triumph. It seemed unlikely that contractors were equally hard at work in Richmond or Charleston or Atlanta.

Before leaving the capital, Villard called on the president at the White House and was more than happy to give exhaustive answers to Lincoln's questions about General Buell, his officers, and his campaign. Lincoln had realized early on that the Union war correspondents were the most knowledgeable, accurate, and objective sources of the information he constantly craved. As a historian notes, "The President particularly liked to sound out army reporters about officers, for . . . [the reporters] enjoyed better opportunities for observation than most of his informants, and they were less likely to have axes to grind." Villard was pleased and flattered by this meeting; Lincoln listened closely to what he had to say, complimented him on his printed review of Buell's campaign, and looked forward to his opinions concerning the Army of the Potomac. This evidence of the president's discernment raised him higher in Villard's esteem than ever before, and as he left the White House he was filled with confidence in the success of Lincoln's policies and the Union cause.

In the afternoon of November 29, Villard took a steamer down the Potomac to Aquia Creek, Virginia. The next day he traveled on horseback the twelve miles between Aquia Creek and the Army of the Potomac's encampment around Falmouth, on the north bank of the Rappahannock River near Fredericksburg, which lay on the south bank a few miles away. This area included some of the most fought-over ground of the Civil War; sometimes riding his horse, sometimes dismounting and walking, the reporter passed through a burned, ravaged landscape, traversed by a road that thousands of heavy army wagons had rutted and scarred.

Except for his slight acquaintance with Burnside himself, Villard had met none of the ranking officers in Burnside's army. The reporter spent his first few days in camp conscientiously getting to know the commanding generals of the three "Grand Divisions" (each with two corps, about forty thousand men) into which Burnside had reorganized his forces. Of the three commanders (Generals Sumner, Hooker, and Franklin), Villard was most impressed by the tall, handsome Hooker—"fully six feet high, finely proportioned, with a soldierly, erect carriage"—who looked "like the ideal soldier and captain, fit for a model of a war-god."

As for Burnside, Villard recognized his "prepossessing *bonhomie*" and his "genial, frank, honest, sincere nature." Despite these attractive qualities, however, the reporter found nothing in the general's "exterior or in his conversation that indicated intellectual eminence or executive ability of a high order." No experienced or judicious person, Villard thought, would take Burnside for a great man.

As the days passed, Villard moved beyond the three Grand Division headquarters and interviewed all the corps and division commanders and many regimental and even brigade commanders. He observed them closely, gauging their strengths and their weaknesses, using his seriousness and his natural charm to prepare the ground for future contact. After two weeks, he felt "very much at home in the Army of the Potomac" and was pleased to discover that the competition was thin on the ground; many newspapers, thinking that Burnside was about to put his army into winter quarters, had sent no correspondents to Falmouth.

Burnside's ultimate objective was Richmond, fifty-five miles due south. Originally he had planned to send his entire army, 120,000 men, across the Rappahannock on pontoon bridges—the rebels had, of course, destroyed all the fixed bridges—in order to occupy Fredericksburg and the high ground south of it before General Lee's Army of Northern Virginia could arrive to contest the crossing. This was an unexceptionable plan, but through no fault of Burnside's, the promised pontoon bridges reached him a week late, and by that time Lee's army, more than seventy thousand strong, was dug in on the heights overlooking the town and awaiting the Yankees' next move.

These new developments—the tardy bridging material, the rebels already in the positions he had wished to occupy—gave Burnside pause. Days later, after much dithering, he had excogitated a new, undaunted scheme: he would order his engineers to lay six bridges, three directly to Fredericksburg, in the face of the enemy, and three more a couple of miles downstream, near where the Confederate right wing, commanded by Stonewall Jackson, was encamped among the tree-clad hills; the Union troops would cross the river on the newly laid bridges and fall upon the foe.

When Villard reached the Union camps at the end of November, Burnside was in the midst of working out the details of his offensive, and the engineers, like the rest of the army, were awaiting his orders. The enemy's distinct positional advantage, along with bad weather, uncertain reconnaissance, further logistic muddles, and the presence of a large body of rebel sharpshooters firing from riverfront buildings in Fredericksburg, were all factors that should have persuaded Burnside to rethink his attack. His mind, however, was made up. He was determined to prove his mettle and convince everyone, including himself, that he could do the job.

Villard's position as chief correspondent of a major newspaper entitled him to request a private interview with the general, and the two met in early December, not long after the reporter's arrival. Burnside spoke with eager pride of his recent conference with Lincoln. The president, he confided to the reporter, had suggested a craftier, three-pronged advance against the rebels, but he, Burnside, had expressed his preference for a direct attack designed to "defeat Lee where he was," and Lincoln had bowed to his general's judgment.

As it turned out, that was but a small thing to bow to. On December 11, Burnside ordered his engineers to throw the bridges across the river. They began their work several times, and each time rebel snipers took a heavy toll of them. A violent artillery barrage, a dash across the river by a few regiments in assault boats, and hand-to-hand fighting in streets and buildings were required to dislodge the sharpshooting Confederates. Late in the afternoon the Army of the Potomac finally began to move across the new bridges to the old colonial town, once home to George Washington's mother, now partly in ruins and abandoned.

By the evening of the following day, Burnside's Right and Center Grand Divisions, nearly eighty thousand men, were occupying Fredericksburg; many of them distracted their thoughts from the imminent battle by pillaging and vandalizing the defenseless town. Downstream General Franklin's Left Grand Division made an uncontested crossing. Secure in their strong defensive positions, the rebels watched and waited all along the line.

The defeat suffered by the Union Army on the next day, December 13, 1862, was one of the most disastrous of the war. In the morning General Franklin, confused by Burnside's fatally vague orders, mounted an incoherent attack on the Confederate right; after some initial success, this attack was repulsed, nor was it ever renewed, despite an explicit order from Burnside to renew it. Seeing that the first part of the battle plan was doomed to failure, several of Burnside's officers tried to dissuade him from implementing the second part, but he resolved to sweep Lee's army from the heights by a direct frontal assault, even without support from Franklin. At Burnside's command, General Sumner's troops moved through the streets of Fredericksburg and stepped into the open fields on the outskirts of the town. General W. H. French's division was in the van, and riding with French and his staff was the intrepid Henry Villard. As the Federal vanguard formed battle lines and began to advance across the field, Villard dismounted, walked up to the crest of a small rise in the ground, and stretched out on his belly to watch the fight. What he watched instead was a butchery, a colossally sanguinary blunder prolonged beyond all reason.

The Union troops' impossible task—which they nevertheless attempted most valorously to perform—was to advance about half a mile across a gently sloping field and storm the rebel positions that commanded it. The topography of this open area—which included on one side a creek, on the other a brimming canal and a marshy slough, the whole traversed by a wide drainage ditch and hemmed in by ravines—constricted the Federal attack, kept Burnside's soldiers in the open, where they were exposed to blanketing artillery and rifle fire, and funneled them toward the most impregnable portion of Lee's entire defensive line. This was a stone wall, about four feet high and six hundred yards long, running along a sunken road at the foot of the heights from which Lee and the commander of the Confederate left wing, Gen. James Longstreet, directed the battle.

"The Army of the Potomac," its historian writes, "was up against its old, old difficulty: visibly outnumbering its enemy, it nevertheless was put into action in such a way that where the actual fighting was going on there were more rebels present than Yankees." All afternoon long, wave after wave of Federal soldiers formed up on the outskirts of Fredericksburg and advanced toward the stone wall while shells exploded among them and canister tore great gaps in their lines. Behind the wall, the rebel infantry, whose marksmanship was not affected by their incredulity, stood in ranks up to six men deep and fired their weapons as fast as they could load them. No Yankee came within thirty yards of that wall, all afternoon long. Late in the battle, as the Union soldiers advanced over the corpses of their comrades, they were hindered by the survivors, most of them wounded, who littered the ground and caught at their legs as they passed and implored them not to go any farther.

Their commanding general, however, had a different view of the matter, for only nightfall, and no order of his, put an end to the mindless sacrifice. A few years before, at Balaklava in the Crimea, the French marshal Pierre Bosquet, observing the charge of the Light Brigade, had remarked, *"C'est magnifique, mais ce n'est pas la guerre."* He might have felt the same about the battle of Fredericksburg. When it was over, ten thousand dead and wounded Union soldiers, theirs not to reason why, lay on the battlefield as the cold December dark came down.

Before that happened, however, Henry Villard had had enough. Nauseated by what he had seen and enraged at the idiocy that had first set it in motion and then failed to stop it, the reporter left the battleground late in the afternoon and reentered the town. The streets were filled with soldiers, some moving to the front, others returning; of these latter, many were walking wounded, some were skulkers and stragglers—very few, considering the provocation—and

Erasmus Theodor Engelmann (1730–1802), Henry Villard's great-great-grandfather. He matriculated from Heidelberg University at the age of fourteen. In 1761 he became rector of the Reformed Protestant church in Bacharach.

Alexandra Villard de Borchgrave Private Collection

Bacharach, c. 1761, with the Reformed Protestant church in which Henry Villard's ancestor Erasmus Theodor Engelmann served as rector.

Alexandra Villard de Borchgrave Private Collection

Anna Margarethe Engelmann, née Hartmann (1742–1825), Henry Villard's great-great-grandmother. She married Erasmus Theodor Engelmann in 1756 at the age of fourteen, and gave birth to thirteen children.

Alexandra Villard de Borchgrave Private Collection

Friedrich Theodor Engelmann (1779–1854), son of Erasmus Theodor and great-granduncle of Henry Villard. He emigrated to America in 1833. His farm in St. Clair County, Illinois, became the gathering place for the Latin farmers from the Palatinate.

Courtesy of Mary E. Armstrong

Gustav Leonhard Hilgard (1807–67), Henry Villard's father. Appointed justice of the Supreme Court in Munich in 1856, he was the only Hilgard of conservative political leaning.

Alexandra Villard de Borchgrave Private Collection

Katharina Antonia Elisabeth "Lisette" Hilgard, née Pfeiffer (1811–59), Henry Villard's mother. Her father was the administrator of the Palatinate saltworks.

Alexandra Villard de Borchgrave Private Collection

Henry Villard just before his wedding to Fanny Garrison on January 3, 1866, at Rockledge, the Garrison family home in Roxbury. His eyes reflect the wisdom gained from covering the horrific battles of the Civil War.

Alexandra Villard de Borchgrave Private Collection

Henry Villard in 1877, photographed by Rockwood, after his appointment as receiver of the Kansas Pacific Railroad and the beginning of his contest with Jay Gould.

Sophia Smith Collection, Smith College

Henry Villard with his mother, his sister Emma, and his half uncle Robert Hilgard, c. 1848, prior to his first trip to the Frankfurt Parliament.

Alexandra Villard de Borchgrave Private Collection

The Villard children Harold, Helen, and Oswald in 1876, when the family lived at the Westminster Hotel. Photographed by Rockwood.

Sophia Smith Collection, Smith College

The Villard last-spike excursion in September 1883 to open the Northern Pacific Railroad, famously photographed by F. Jay Haynes. Four special trains transported hundreds of American and European guests—including Ulysses S. Grant, Lord Chief Justice Charles Russell, members of the diplomatic corps and the U.S. Congress, governors, mayors, and the press—from Chicago to Portland. President Arthur joined the celebration in Minneapolis.

Alexandra Villard de Borchgrave
Private Collection

Gold Creek, Montana, September 8, 1883. A gaily decked pavilion had been erected to seat a thousand spectators. Henry Villard can be seen standing (wearing a hat, next to the second post on the left) as he addresses the crowd before the driving of the last spike to mark the completion of the Northern Pacific line.

Alexandra Villard de Borchgrave Private Collection

The Northern Pacific
Special stopped outside
St. Paul, Minnesota, in front
of a splendid waterfall,
where the guests gathered
to be photographed by
F. Jay Haynes.

Alexandra Villard de Borchgrave
Private Collection

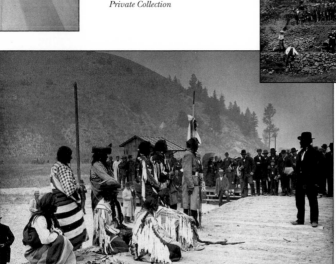

A group from the two
thousand Crow Indians
who performed war
dances for Henry Villard's
Northern Pacific guests in
eastern Montana gather
by the newly laid tracks.

Alexandra Villard de Borchgrave
Private Collection

Gold Creek, Montana, September 8, 1883. A thousand
feet of track was left unfinished prior to the last-spike
ceremony so that Henry Villard's guests could witness
the speed at which rails were laid down.

Alexandra Villard de Borchgrave Private Collection

Villard House, detail of mantel frieze, 1885, by an unidentified photographer (McKim, Mead and White Collection). Sculpted by Augustus Saint-Gaudens above the stunning fireplace he created for the entrance hall, the detail shows a graceful woman in a flowing translucent robe, a naked child on each side, and the word PAX inlaid in the mosaic pattern on the wall.
Collection of the New-York Historical Society

Villard House, music room, 1885, by an un-identified photographer (McKim, Mead and White Collection). This golden room was dominated by plaster casts from Luca Della Robbia's fifteenth-century *cantoria* (singing gallery) in the cathedral of Florence and reflected the Villard family's love of music.
Collection of the New-York Historical Society

Fanny Garrison Villard holding baby Hilgard, age two, in Berlin. The Villards moved to Germany for two years in August 1884, after the financial disaster of 1883.
Alexandra Villard de Borchgrave Private Collection

Villard House, triple drawing room, some time after 1884, by an unidentified photographer, was designed in an Italian Renaissance style using intricate mahogany marquetry highlighted with mother-of-pearl.
Alexandra Villard de Borchgrave Private Collection

Werner von Siemens, German electrical inventor, head of Siemens & Halske in Berlin. Following Thomas Edison's advice, Henry Villard proposed a joint venture with German and American interests in the Edison light and manufacturing companies, out of which grew the Edison General Electric Company.

Courtesy of the Landes Archive

Prince Otto von Bismarck, the former chancellor of Germany, was visited by Henry Villard at Friedrichsruhe, his country estate, in the summer of 1890.

Courtesy of the Landes Archive

Fanny Garrison Villard and Oswald, photographed by Hof Photograph, G. Th. Hase & Sohn, in Freiburg during the family trip abroad after Hilgard Villard's death, in 1890. The sorrow is evident in Fanny's eyes.

Sophia Smith Collection, Smith College

Henry Villard holding his first grandson, Henry Serrano Villard, born March 30, 1900, in a rare photograph of him smiling, with his beaming son Harold standing next to him.

Alexandra Villard de Borchgrave Private Collection

Fanny Garrison Villard surrounded by her grandchildren at Thorwood, Dobbs Ferry. Clockwise from left: Marquita, Vincent, and Henry Serrano Villard; Dorothea and Hilgard (later renamed Henry) Villard.

Alexandra Villard de Borchgrave Private Collection

Birthplace of Henry Villard in Speyer, Rhenish Bavaria. This was the home of his maternal grandparents, Franz and Marie Anna Pfeiffer.

Alexandra Villard de Borchgrave Private Collection

Thorwood, Henry Villard's mid-nineteenth-century house in Dobbs Ferry, purchased in 1879 in Fanny Villard's name. Henry Villard loved the vast park of chestnut trees. He died there on November 12, 1900, and Fanny followed him twenty-eight years later. It was torn down in 1929.

By permission of the Houghton Library, Harvard University

Henry Villard's firstborn son Harold Garrison Villard, photographed by Pach Brothers in Cambridge, Massachusetts, while he was a student at Harvard

Sophia Smith Collection, Smith College

Monument by the renowned architectural sculptor Karl Bitter presides over Henry Villard's final resting place at Sleepy Hollow Cemetery, Tarrytown, New York.

Courtesy of Katharine N. Villard

some were shocked and disoriented. Ambulances rattled past, jostling their moaning human contents and leaving bright trails of blood behind them in the muddy streets.

At some point the accumulated horrors of the day overcame Villard. Utterly fatigued, drained of his wonted energy, he took refuge in a fine brick home that had been abandoned by all its inhabitants except a few slaves, one of whom the desperate reporter bullied into letting him stay for a while. The firing outside was dying down as he lowered himself into a plush armchair and sought a few minutes of sweet oblivion, only to be slammed back into consciousness by an artillery shell that blew off part of the top floor of the house. Taking this as a summons back to his journalistic duties, he remounted his horse, made his way across one of Burnside's pontoon bridges, and rode up the slope that led to his headquarters.

There he found that the general and some members of his staff had apparently entered an alternate reality; intent on finishing the job so auspiciously begun, the perfervid Burnside planned to renew the attack in the morning, place himself at the head of his troops, and lead them, thus inspired, to victory. Other staff officers were not so confident, and Villard learned that General Sumner hoped to dissuade his commanding officer from this culminating folly.

Soon Villard's assistants, who had covered the other two Grand Divisions, arrived with their reports; they turned out, however, to be thoroughly unsatisfactory. We may imagine that Villard was a demanding and punctilious taskmaster, but in this tense situation he had good cause for complaint. One of his assistants had managed to gather only scanty material and was "mulish and intractable" to boot, while the other was drunk to the point of stupefaction. It was clear to Villard that he would have to acquire information about the rest of the battle for himself.

As the officers of divisions that Villard had not observed reported to Burnside's headquarters, the reporter asked them as many questions as they would stand, both about the day's events and about those proposed for the morrow. Among these men Villard found a great deal of gloom. Unlike Burnside, most Union officers seemed to realize that their side had suffered a ferocious, disabling calamity.

Some of them assured Villard that there would be no further assault on the rebel defenses, while others, more zealous than wise, claimed that the day's battle had been only a temporary setback.

The reporter, however, had the evidence of his eyes to rely on, and he felt

> fully persuaded that our defeat was irretrievable, and that nothing remained to the Commander-in-chief but to solve the seemingly desperate problem of getting the army again over the river without further harm. I was sure . . . that . . . a resumption of the offensive . . . would be vehemently opposed by Generals Sumner and Hooker, and by their corps and division commanders. Nor was my conviction shaken by the sneering and contemptuous rebuffs my corresponding expressions met with from certain members of Burnside's staff. . . . Their swagger was so confident that, stirred up as I was by the great peril of the army, I came near yielding to an impulse to approach Burnside and tell him the dire truth, which I feared he did not know.

Now certain that the fighting around Fredericksburg would not be renewed on the following day, Villard made up his mind to take the news of this latest Union fiasco to Washington in person. His resolve was strengthened when he learned that Burnside had interdicted all postal and telegraphic messages concerning the battle. Such a move, Villard thought, indicated a certain amount of desperation and corroborated his own opinion of the catastrophe that had befallen the army; in addition, and more important, the clampdown on wire reports opened up for him "the possibility of achieving a great 'beat' for the *Tribune* by exclusive first news." All he had to do was to stay a few steps ahead of the competition.

By the time he had conducted his last interview, arranged his notes, and sketched out a few paragraphs, it was past midnight. He slept for only a few hours—the prospect of a scoop gave him new energy—saddled his horse, and set out at three in the morning for the quay at Aquia Creek.

Thus began the most terrible ride of his life. The sky, moonless and overcast, rendered the darkness absolute; heavy rains and endless wagon traffic had churned the road into a quagmire; Villard's horse, feeling his way in the dark, took a roundabout and sometimes circular route, stumbled often, fell a couple of times, and threw his hapless rider once. Covered with liquid mud, Villard rose from where he had landed, remounted, and plunged again into the dark. Daylight helped both horse and rider get their bearings, and around 9 A.M. the mud-bespattered pair, having traveled twelve miles in six hours, rode into the army checkpoint at Aquia Creek.

There the pleasure of sharing the quartermaster's hot breakfast (hominy, ham, coffee) was overshadowed by the displeasure of hearing what the quartermaster had to say. Burnside had wired orders stating that no soldiers, no civilians, and especially no war correspondents were to be allowed beyond Aquia Creek without a special permit signed by General Burnside himself. The general seemed to have recovered from his postbattle fantasies and to have decided to withhold the news of the great Union defeat as long as possible. Villard invoked his name, his employer, his position, and the First Amendment to the Constitution, but to no avail. As far as the quartermaster was concerned, Mr. Villard of the *Tribune* was as close to Washington as he was going to get until General Burnside rescinded or changed his orders.

To complete Villard's disgust, while he was pleading with the quartermaster one of his press colleagues, as muddy as himself, arrived at the checkpoint. This was Charles Coffin of the *Boston Journal,* who had stood beside Villard and peered through the cornstalks at Bull Run. Villard liked Coffin and knew him to be a conscientious and resourceful reporter, but at this moment the sight of him brought no joy. "One never likes to discover that other people are as smart as one's self," Villard reflected.

Coffin received the news about Burnside's orders with equanimity; the thought of a scoop had not filled his veins with adrenaline as it had Villard's. Famished and exhausted, the *Journal*'s special ate one of the quartermaster's hearty breakfasts, stretched out on a cot, and fell fast asleep.

His rival's instant descent into oblivion gave Villard new hope.

After stabling his horse, he shouldered his saddlebags and ambled casually toward the quay. The quartermaster, who knew that armed guards were stationed at the landing, made no objection and turned to his own affairs. The reporter, having observed the guards on the wharf, proceeded to take a nonchalant stroll down the riverbank. He had noticed a pair of black fishermen pushing their rowboat into the Potomac, and a plan had formed in his mind.

After a few minutes a bend in the river and a conveniently placed warehouse made him invisible from the wharf and the quartermaster's shed. Soon he came upon the two anglers, placidly watching their lines not far from shore. The reporter hailed them, offering them $1 apiece if they would make room for him.

The fishermen had spent their lives catering to the whims of white folks, usually without reward, and they were poor enough to think $2 more than adequate compensation for taking a muddy white man with a strange accent aboard their little boat and rowing him about the Potomac River. They assented, the reporter boarded. Out on the river they fished for a while, warily eyeing Villard as he stared intently downstream. At last, having spotted what he'd been looking for, he astonished his companions with a new offer: $5 apiece to row him into the steamship channel.

This was a proposition too lucrative to turn down, and the two fishermen, delighted with their catch, rowed him into the path of the approaching transport ship, a government steamer, or "freight-propeller," obviously bound for the capital. Rocking the boat, Villard shouted and waved; the captain slowed his vessel, and Villard urged his companions, who were beginning to get a little nervous, to draw their small craft alongside the big steamer. Villard brandished documents and asked the captain for permission to board, which was firmly denied; but the reporter would brook no refusal. He tossed the fishermen their money, grasped a stanchion, and hauled himself aboard the freighter.

The captain, Villard wrote dryly, was "at first disposed to be wrathy at my summary proceeding," but he eventually succumbed to Villard's ardent self-advocacy, his air of importance, and his promise of a handsome reward. This took the form of a fifty-dollar bill, presented when the freighter docked in Washington shortly after eight o'clock in the evening.

By this time Villard had slept for three hours in the past forty, but with the goal in sight he showed no signs of slowing down. In the *Tribune*'s bureau on F Street he finished the dispatch he had begun on the freighter. His report on the battle was detailed, angry, ominous, accusatory. It stated "as strongly as possible that the Army of the Potomac had suffered another great, general defeat; that an inexcusable, murderous blunder had been made . . . and that the Union cause was threatened by the greatest disaster yet suffered."

Wilkeson was at his desk, and when he read Villard's account he knew it would never get past the army censors in the telegraph office. The two reporters sent it by messenger to Printing House Square on the night train, and Villard, by a wide margin the first correspondent to return to Washington from Fredericksburg, had his scoop.

Ironically, however, although Villard had circumvented the censor, he couldn't circumvent Greeley and Gay. They found his report too shocking, too demoralizing, to print as it stood, and it appeared in the *Tribune* in a much modified and softened version. It was, nevertheless, the first authentic news about the battle to reach the North, and its publication loosed a storm in the metropolitan papers.

The senseless waste of life at the battle of Fredericksburg and his frustrated attempt to report the whole harsh truth about it exercised Villard all his life. Three decades later, ending his description of the battle in his *Memoirs*, he indulged in a little sententious thundering to assuage his pent-up rage: "With this I gladly close the sickening story of the appalling disaster for which Ambrose E. Burnside will, to the end of time, stand charged with the responsibility."

For the moment the newspaperman's work was done, and now he was hungry. In the dining room of Willard's Hotel, Senator Henry Wilson of Massachusetts, "the most persistent news-hunter in Washington," observed the mud that still clung to Villard's clothing, guessed where he'd come from, and asked him for news of the battle. The disgusted reporter spoke bluntly, and Wilson hastened away.

Half an hour later, Villard was back in the *Tribune*'s offices, making out his expense account, when Senator Wilson appeared before him. Lincoln, Wilson explained with some urgency, wished to speak to the reporter, in person, now; and shortly after ten o'clock the hardly presentable Villard found himself in the White House, being debriefed by the president of the United States. What had been the disposition of the battle? What was the extent of the casualties, the strength of the rebel defenses, the morale of the Union troops? Could a renewed attack succeed? Unawed—Lincoln was, after all, an old acquaintance—and never one to mince words anyway, Villard told the president that the battle had been a crippling defeat for the Union (it was, in fact, the worst defeat in the history of the American army) and that every general officer he had spoken to believed that a second attack would fail as utterly as the first. The army, Villard declared, must fall back to the north bank of the Rappahannock or risk destruction. The president smiled sadly. "I hope it's not so bad as all that, Henry," he demurred.

But it was, and apparently Burnside was brought to a more accurate assessment of his plight, for even as Villard and Lincoln spoke, the general had begun a skillful and efficient withdrawal of his troops across the river; Lee was criticized in the South for letting him get away. The Union Army, encountering a foe it outnumbered by more than 50 percent, had suffered more than twice as many casualties as it had inflicted, a ratio that rises to four to one if the fight in front of the stone wall is considered alone.

Villard walked away from his presidential interview "with a sense of having discharged a patriotic duty." If we ignore, as he did, the fact that he was still a citizen of the kingdom of Bavaria, we can agree with him. He took his role as a journalist very seriously. His analysis of events was accurate, it concerned the welfare of the country, and he had done his best to spread the truth. Now, at the end of a day that had included a trip in a rowboat with two poor black fishermen and a consultation on military matters with the president of the country, Villard was just about ready for bed; but first he had to finish that expense account. A war correspondent's salary, far from princely, provided a limited amount of ready cash; for a special so given to lordly expenditure as Villard, filing for his expenses was very nearly as important as filing his copy.

As he was completing his expense account, Wilkeson, whose journalistic pursuits that evening had included several hours at the bar in Willard's, clattered back into the office. This, Villard thought, was as good a time as any to present his account, and he handed it to his bureau chief, who focused, read, and began to sputter. Twelve dollars to Negroes in a rowboat? *Fifty* dollars for a passage on a freighter? This account was falsified, Wilkeson declared, and flagrantly false at that.

Villard prided himself on his integrity and could not bear to have it impugned. His response to the bureau chief was harsh and acidic, and when the acid combined with the alcohol in Wilkeson's brain he could think of no better response than to strike "the big Bavarian" in the chest. Wearily and methodically, Villard knocked his opponent down, let him get up, and knocked him down again. After repeating this a few times, Villard decided to call it a day—knocked off, as it were—and went back to his rooms. His heartbreaking, maddening adventures with the Army of the Potomac had found an appropriate epilogue in this sordid brawl. All over the North nerves were clenched, and the worst was yet to come.

THE SINKING OF THE *CUMBERLAND* BY THE IRONCLAD
MERRIMAC OFF NEWPORT NEWS, VIRGINIA, MARCH 8, 1862.

War and Conflict, no. 184.

National Archives.

13

Free at Last

No more auction block for me,
No more, no more,
No more auction block for me,
Many thousands gone.

AMERICAN SLAVE SONG

For a few days, Henry Villard was the only person in the District of Columbia who had witnessed the battle of Fredericksburg. As such, he was the object of considerable attention—"quite a lion," as he put it—and his new celebrity status did nothing to discourage his natural inclination to speak his mind. To the army officers, congressmen, businessmen, and others who crowded the *Tribune*'s Washington bureau night and day, to the "eager inquirers" who accosted him at Willard's and on the street, to the grave gentlemen and fascinated ladies he met in private homes, he told the story of the fighting as he had witnessed it, pulling no punches and allaying no fears. His tale of gross incompetence, futile heroism, and tragic waste contributed much to the gloom that settled over the nation's capital and to the ensuing congressional inquiry into the conduct of the battle.

Villard was now in the front rank of the "Bohemian Brigade," as the Union war correspondents were called. His fearlessness and uncompromising accuracy, to say nothing of his fierce competitiveness, had won him the respect of his colleagues and enhanced the standing of his newspaper. Even though he was at the top of his profession, however, he had little to show for it. Glamor and prestige, but not much in the way of cash, rewarded the efforts of even the best Civil

War reporters, most of whom (including Henry Villard) earned about $25 a week. The temptation, therefore, was to submit "remarkable expense accounts," and padding was commonplace. Viewed in this context, Wilkeson's reaction to the costs involved in Villard's Fredericksburg scoop was understandable, though inappropriate; Villard was too meticulously, haughtily conscientious to pad expense accounts.

The statement of his Fredericksburg expenses has not been preserved, but we do have a record of the account he submitted a few months later, covering fourteen weeks from April to July 1863. It's reasonable and unremarkable: $5.75 for stationery, $105 for a horse, $42 for accoutrements (saddle, bridle, etc.) and forage, $74 for meals in the army mess. The only surprise is an expenditure of $20 for a servant. It has not been possible to determine what this servant's duties were or how long he was in Villard's employ, but we can assume that the *Tribune*, which paid its chief correspondent less than a good compositor or copyist could make, would not have subsidized a servant of his, however meanly paid, for any extended period of time.

Money, however, was not the point; the point was the news. Faced with the prospect of inactivity while the Army of the Potomac recovered from its discomfiture and winter made a new campaign unfeasible, Villard cast about for a more promising scene of action. He had experienced the war in the West and in the East; now, he thought, he would investigate the war at sea. Believing (mistakenly, as it turned out) that the Federal forces and some of their new ironclad ships were about to launch a combined land and naval assault on Charleston, he persuaded Gay to send him to South Carolina. On January 4, 1863, Villard boarded a government steamer bound for Hilton Head Island.

Four days earlier, on January 1, President Lincoln had at last officially recognized the true character of the war. He had signed "the most execrable measure," according to Jefferson Davis, "in the history of guilty man": the Emancipation Proclamation.

Most Northerners justifiably considered South Carolina the chief instigator of the Civil War, and from the beginning there was a great deal of public pressure to give the state the punishment it deserved. In 1865, this demand would at last be thoroughly answered by General Sherman's troops, who marched through South Carolina even more vindictively and more destructively, though less famously, than they had marched through Georgia; but the North's attempt to mete out specific punishment to South Carolina had already begun in the first year of the war.

On November 7, 1861, a powerful Federal squadron, steaming into Port Royal Sound ahead of a fleet of transports carrying some twelve thousand Union soldiers, systematically pounded the two forts that guarded the entrance to Port Royal harbor with a series of withering broadsides. First the rebels abandoned Fort Walker, on Hilton Head Island south of the harbor entrance, and shortly thereafter they fled from the stronghold that guarded the north side of the harbor and bore the symbolically satisfying name of Fort Beauregard. While rebel troops and civilians precipitously evacuated all the Sea Islands off the coasts of South Carolina and Georgia, Federal forces landed on Hilton Head and set up their camps. This Union enclave, with its center in the Port Royal–Hilton Head area, would gall the flank of the Confederacy until the end of the war. Federal control of the Sea Islands contributed to the effective blockade of such ports as Savannah and Charleston, and the presence of a large body of Federal troops on the islands threatened the rebels' Atlantic coast all the way down to Florida.

The great plantations on the Sea Islands were home to thousands of the most backward and imbruted slaves in the South, the victims of generations of isolation, severe treatment, and primitive conditions. As elsewhere, when the planters and their dependents fled before the Yankee invader, they deserted their property, including the slaves whose thralldom they had gone to war to perpetuate. These abandoned slaves were soon joined by a steadily increasing number of their fellows, fugitives who made their way to the Hilton Head area and besought the protection of the liberators.

The army commander of this area, designated the Federal Department of the South, was Maj. Gen. David Hunter. One of the few military men to accompany Lincoln on his inaugural train journey in 1861 (Hunter dislocated his shoulder protecting the president-elect from a mob in Buffalo) and a veteran of the first battle of Bull Run, where he served with some distinction, General Hunter was no stranger to Henry Villard. As it happened, Hunter had been away from his command and was now (January 4, 1863) returning to it on the same steamer that carried his young acquaintance. The general and the reporter had often met at Willard's in the ominous weeks between the fall of Sumter and the preparations for Bull Run, but after that battle their paths had diverged, and so they had much in the way of divergent experiences to recount to each other, and many grounds for speculation and discussion. The voyage passed quickly for Villard, but he had time enough before the ship reached Port Royal to receive from the old general, who knew his young friend's discretion could be trusted, an expert overview of conditions in the Department of the South. Villard also gained some insights into the government's plans for the occupying troops and for the people of the islands, almost all of whom were former slaves.

General Hunter's passionate opposition to slavery had earned him a certain amount of national notoriety. In May 1862, four months before Lincoln submitted the preliminary version of his Emancipation Proclamation and nearly eight months before it was promulgated in its final form, Hunter had issued a famous order emancipating the slaves of South Carolina, Georgia, and Florida. When the president, deeming that Hunter had overstepped his authority, revoked this edict, the general tried another way of bettering the lot of the African-Americans within his jurisdiction. He set about turning the uprooted, tatterdemalion ex-slaves on the Sea Islands into soldiers of the United States Army.

Hunter was not alone in his concern for the former slaves. In the Federal enclave, more than fifty volunteers from Massachusetts and other Northern states were busy as teachers and overseers, trying to bring the blacks a little of the education that had been denied them in servitude, helping them work (for wages) some of the land abandoned by the planters, assisting their adjustment to freedom, and preparing them for citizenship. As the number of fugitives grew, the War Department felt constrained to take a hand. Brig. Gen. Rufus Saxton, whom Villard called "one of the few outright abolitionists in the army," was sent to South Carolina to take charge of the Freedmen's Aid movement, and as military governor of the islands he assisted General Hunter in enlisting volunteer soldiers.

Command of the regiment thus formed, the First South Carolina Volunteers, was given to Col. Thomas Wentworth Higginson of Massachusetts, a Unitarian minister, antislavery activist, and man of letters, who arrived in Hilton Head in November 1862. Best known today for his long and occasionally bewildering correspondence, begun the same year, with Emily Dickinson ("Perhaps you smile at me," she wrote to him in July. "I could not stop for that—My Business is Circumference"), Higginson must sometimes have found Gulla, the Sea Island Creole spoken by many of his new soldiers, more comprehensible than the gemlike, pressurized language of the Belle of Amherst.

Thus the world that Henry Villard entered when he "stepped for the first time upon the sacred soil of the Palmetto State" (as he sardonically put it) was a hotbed of progressivism and abolitionist fervor, where military practicality, intellectual idealism, social experimentation, and racial interaction combined in a way that was unique in the United States at that time. Sydney Howard Gay, as we have seen, was a committed abolitionist, and one of the reasons why he sent Villard to the Department of the South was his confidence that the reporter shared his political beliefs and would be sympathetic to the undertaking that was going forward there.

Gay's faith was not misplaced. Since the fleet of ironclads was not yet assembled and the attack on Charleston was indefinitely postponed, Villard took the opportunity to tour several of the islands and gauge the considerable efforts being made on behalf of, and by, the former slaves. He met the Northern military and civilian leaders, visited the schools and farms, and carefully observed the training of the First South Carolina Volunteers. This was for him "the most interesting feature of South Carolina," and on January 22, 1863, he sent the *Tribune* the most optimistic dispatch he had filed in some time, an

enthusiastic account of the freedmen's progress: "I have no hesitation, with my extensive observations of the capacities and acquire-
ments of white volunteers in both the Western and Eastern armies,
to say that no body of men in the service has done better in seven
weeks, the period during which the dark-skinned South Carolinians
have served upon the drilling-ground." Villard went on to praise the
volunteers' enthusiasm and spirit, their "unmistakable intelligence"
and "firmness of resolution," and to quote approvingly General
Hunter's declaration that they would make "as good soldiers as any
in the world."

Shortly after Villard wrote this dispatch, Colonel Higginson led
the First South Carolina on a raid along the St. Marys River, which
runs between Georgia and Florida. The several purposes of this expedition—to circulate the Emancipation Proclamation among the
slaves, to motivate them to join the Union cause by the sight of black
men in Federal uniforms, to secure various kinds of military necessi-
ties, to harass the enemy—were admirably fulfilled; the soldiers performed well under fire, and Higginson praised them highly in his
official report. The discipline, bravery, and skill of his troops led him
to some forceful conclusions that must have startled many of his superiors:

> No officer in this regiment now doubts that the key to the suc-
> cessful prosecution of this war lies in the unlimited employment
> of black troops. Their superiority lies simply in the fact that they
> know the country, while white troops do not, and, moreover,
> that they have peculiarities of temperament, position, and mo-
> tive which belong to them alone. Instead of leaving their homes
> and families to fight they are fighting for their homes and fam-
> ilies, and they show the resolution and the sagacity which a per-
> sonal purpose gives. It would have been madness to attempt,
> with the bravest white troops, what I have successfully accom-
> plished with black ones.

Villard, meanwhile, was filing dispatches that echoed these enlightened sentiments. In the middle of February, he announced in

the pages of the *Tribune* that another expedition of colored troops would be sent into the interior of South Carolina and Georgia to recruit more black soldiers for the Union. The conservative Republican and Copperhead press (Copperheads were Northerners sympathetic to slavery and the Southern cause) denounced his report as a malicious fabrication and an incitement to "servile insurrection," but a week later Higginson led more than a thousand black troops on just such an expedition, and the accuracy of Villard's reporting was reconfirmed. The success of the First South Carolina Regiment led to the organization of a second, Col. James Montgomery commanding, and he and Higginson subsequently led their African-American fighting men on a series of raids into the interior of Georgia and Florida, even capturing and occupying Jacksonville in March.

Many *Tribune* readers looked with amazement, disgust, or simple disbelief on Villard's reports from South Carolina, where military successes were being achieved by former slaves; racial prejudice was by no means an exclusively Southern affliction, and even "friends of the Negro" feared that generations of humiliation and degradation had rendered him unfit for soldiering. Villard's employers, however, stimulated by the news he sent, drew the conclusions that to us seem obvious but were not apparent, or not yet apparent, to most of the country's military and political leaders, including Lincoln, Grant, and Sherman. On March 28, a *Tribune* editorial not written by Villard but clearly based on his reports stated:

> Enemies of the negro race, who have persistently denied the capacity and doubted the courage of the Blacks, are unanswerably confuted by the good conduct and gallant deeds of the men whom they persecute and slander. From many quarters comes evidence of the swiftly approaching success which is to crown what is still by some persons deemed to be the experiment of arming whom the Proclamation of Freedom liberates.

Insofar as he sympathized with the abolitionists, Henry Villard had again, in a way, put on his Hecker hat, defying conventional beliefs, opposing authority, and demanding freedom. He was in the vanguard of those "radicals"—the word looks sad and ludicrous from our somewhat advanced vantage point—who saw that a slave was less than human only insofar as he was a slave, and that no soldiers would fight harder to end slavery than those who had recently been slaves themselves. At least on this issue, the child of the German revolutions had aligned himself, fifteen years later, with the American version of the extreme left.

Villard's sojourn on the Sea Islands, a comparatively inactive period for him, came to an end early in April, when the Union land and sea forces were at last ready to make their often-delayed attack on Charleston. Villard had much cultivated the acquaintance of the fleet commander, Rear Adm. Samuel Francis Du Pont, during the foregoing months. The reporter found the admiral to be "one of the stateliest, handsomest, and most polished gentlemen I ever met. He looked the ideal naval commander." For his part, the stately admiral responded positively to the admiring young newspaperman with the formal European manners. He took Villard on a tour of his flagship, discussed his attack plans with him, and gave him permission to be on board one of the Union ironclads, the *New Ironsides,* during the action in Charleston harbor.

Early in the morning of April 4, 1863, the Union fleet, a heterogeneous assortment of fast steamers, beautifully proportioned sailing ships, and unsightly ironclad monsters, set out for what Villard called "arch-rebellious Charleston." Shortly after dawn on the sixth, the fleet lay just outside Charleston harbor. Shore batteries lined this haven on both sides; overlooking its entrance, on the northern shore, loomed the massive bulk of Fort Moultrie, and in the very middle of the channel stood the menacing emblem of Southern belligerence, Fort Sumter itself. The long-awaited hour of Northern vengeance was at hand.

Hot on the trail of another scoop, Villard chose this moment to make his move. With the thirteen other correspondents who accompanied the Union expedition, he had been assigned to a transport ship that would ride at anchor outside the harbor, a couple of miles away from the scene of the action. Now, brandishing Admiral Du

Pont's written permission, Villard had himself rowed to the *New Iron-sides,* "a metal fortress with slatted sides and bristling rows of guns." While the other specials stood on the decks of their transport, well out of danger, and peered at the battle through field glasses, Villard would be in the thick of it, riding inside the great belly of the *New Ironsides,* which Du Pont had chosen as his flagship.

For a long hour on April 7, this behemoth and its eight smaller companions, all of them floating arrangements of huge metal plates bolted and welded together, provided targets for the Confederate forts and shore batteries in Charleston harbor. In the course of the fight, the ironclads' guns managed to fire just 150 times; the rebel cannon, on the other hand, threw more than twenty-two hundred shells, repeatedly striking the ships in the Union flotilla like so many gongs.

In the *Ironsides*'s murky interior, where the air was thick with the smell of gunpowder and the laboring sailors' sweat, Villard squinted through what openings in the armor he could find—the pilothouse, the cannon ports—and marked his notebook every time a shot clanged or a shell burst against the ship's thick metal hide. He made sixty-eight marks, each one representing a bone-rattling crash and its attendant reverberations. "As the forts and batteries," he wrote, "sent forth one torrent of destruction after another, my heart failed and panged with the fear of seeing these little monitors shivered into atoms." The monster proved extremely difficult to steer in the tricky tidal waters of the harbor, which was, moreover, crisscrossed by thick cables, mined by sunken torpedoes, obstructed by deep-driven piles and other barriers. Soon after the firing had begun and the tumult of the enemy guns had quickly grown into one continuous roar, the heavy-draft *Ironsides* ran upon a huge boiler, placed vertically in the channel several feet below the surface, packed with explosives, and connected by wires to an onshore galvanic battery. This, the latest product of American ingenuity to be devoted to the cause of mass de-struction, was calculated to detonate the massive charge at an op-portune moment. Now the opportunity had come; the great, unwieldy, underengined vessel hung on the deadly boiler for half an hour, vibrating like an anvil from one well-aimed rebel shot after another; but the Confederate officers in Fort Moultrie kept pressing the key of their newfangled device in vain. Henry Villard's son Oswald Garrison Villard later wrote that a rebel teamster had "in all likelihood" inadvertently saved his father's life by driving his wagon over, and severing, the crucial wires that were supposed to carry the detonating current from the battery to the boiler.

Henry Villard, the flagship, its officers, and its crew were thus spared, but the Federals nonetheless suffered "a bitter repulse." Although casualties were light on both sides, all of the ironclads had been struck dozens of times; all were heavily damaged, five were disabled, and one, the USS *Keokuk,* having taken ninety hits, sank the following day. The Union nemesis, Fort Sumter, had suffered no damage that was not easily reparable, and its guns had blazed undaunted throughout the brief but intense battle. The Union defeat would have been more ignominious had Admiral Du Pont not given the signal to withdraw from the harbor as quickly as he did; his ringing ears, the floundering clumsiness of his untried ships, and the fury of the Confederate defense had convinced him that Charleston could not be taken by naval force alone.

As the only correspondent to witness the abortive Union effort from one of the attacking ironclads, and the flagship at that, Villard had his scoop, a batch of reports that he delivered to the *Tribune* in person and had the satisfaction of seeing printed in full in an extra edition on April 13. To his monumental annoyance, however, the *New York Times* ran, on the same day, a vividly written piece describing the battle in Charleston harbor and bearing the dateline "U.S.S. *New Ironsides.*" The crafty *Times* correspondent, William Swinton, one of those less adventurous souls who had viewed the fighting from the safety of the survey steamer, was claiming credit for exposing himself to the same dangers and making the same heroic efforts as the valiant Villard!

Villard's profound and thoroughly Teutonic indignation at this failure to play the game by the rules was mollified somewhat when Greeley and his editorial staff denounced the *Times* and its reporter and exposed "the impudent fraud." Such chicanery was, in truth, no worse than the machinations that the *Tribune* occasionally saw fit to employ; nevertheless, the unique status of its star correspondent's eyewitness report was vindicated.

Villard's competitive dudgeon was further soothed by the acclaim his journalistic exploit received. Greeley and the *Tribune*'s editorial staff complimented their reporter warmly in private and praised him considerably in print, and this praise was echoed in other newspapers. In addition to Villard's various professional garlands, Capt. C. R. P. Rodgers, commander of the *New Ironsides,* wrote two letters on April 25. In the first of these, addressed to Villard himself, Rodgers lauded the reporter's "graphic and powerful account of the attack" and his "personal gallantry and unhesitating devotion in the exercise of [his] professional duty." In the second letter, directed to George Smalley, the *Tribune*'s military and naval editor, Rodgers gave his view of the reasons for the navy's setback, thanked Smalley for his newspaper's support of Admiral Du Pont, and added this postscript: "I had occasion to observe and admire the nerve and courage of Mr. Villard, and to witness the untiring fidelity with which he sought to perform his duties as an observer and recorder of all that was occurring." A few weeks later, a magazine called Villard's account of the battle "the only one worth reading. . . . It has the smoke of battle about it."

Immediate and palpable recognition, however, came to Villard from the management of the *Tribune* in the form of a hundred-dollar bonus and the offer of a two weeks' leave of absence. "I'm much obliged," he told Gay, "but where shall I spend it?"

Gay had close connections, both personal and political, with people in Boston who, he was sure, would find his reporter's experiences fascinating and his views congenial. "Have you ever been to Boston?" he asked, and when Villard replied in the negative, Gay advised him to "go to the 'Hub,' by all means." A few days later, fresh, rested, and armed with some impressive letters of introduction, Henry Villard took a train to Boston and the most important meeting of his life.

WILLIAM LLOYD GARRISON AND
HELEN FRANCES "FANNY" GARRISON.
Photograph of the famous abolitionist and editor of
the *Liberator* with his only daughter, c. 1865.
Sophia Smith Collection, Smith College.

14

Come In and
Shut the Door

Oh, do not stand so long outside, why need you be so shy?
The people's ears are open, John, as they are passing by!
You cannot tell what they may think, they've said strange things before;
And if you wish to talk a while, come in and shut the door.

Nay, do not say, "No, thank you, Jane," with such a bashful smile;
You said when ladies whispered "No," they meant "Yes" all the while!
My father too will welcome you, I told you that before;
It don't look well to stand out here, come in and shut the door.

AMERICAN POPULAR SONG
(published 1863)

Although Henry Villard was now barely twenty-eight, the lines around his deep-set, serious eyes and his prematurely thinning brown hair added several years to his appearance. His tall physique, lean but solid; a certain piercing quality in his gaze; his cleft chin; and his thick mustache—allied with the great self-confidence of his bearing, his general air of entitlement, and his attachment to forms and ceremonies—made him a handsome, imposing, unignorable presence. He was at this time enjoying one of his longest periods of untroubled health, but it would be his last, and it was about to come to an end. Like oversized engines, his energy and will were too powerful for his body, and they frequently drove it to exhaustion. Moreover, the soldier's life—the life he led—was hardly conducive to thriving; disease killed twice as many men as deadly weapons did in the American Civil War.

For the moment, however, he felt fine, and he looked forward to a period of leisure in a new and interesting place. The scenes of war had fascinated, horrified, and aged him; now he was glad of a respite, however temporary, and ready to indulge in more civilized pursuits. Many months passed in exclusively male company had not dulled his taste for refinement and an active, well-rounded social life, and Boston could offer him plenty of both. He arrived there on Thursday, April 23, and spent the next day carrying out the solitary reconnaissance that he preferred whenever he came to an unfamiliar city—he liked to get his bearings and gather his first impressions alone. By Saturday he was ready for society, and he began to wield his letters of introduction.

The first person he called on, Mrs. Severance, the wife of an official at Port Royal, was not at home, but her daughter Julia received Villard and invited him to accompany her to—of all things—an exercise class. The prospect of watching nubile young ladies wearing (it was to be hoped) bloomers and performing calisthenics must have had a strong appeal for our bachelor correspondent, who was accustomed to watching exercises of a less genteel sort, involving large groups of distinctly unpolished men training for proficiency in the intricacies of drill or the manipulation of firearms. Declaring his interest in physical fitness, Villard escorted Julia Severance to the gymnasium run by the resoundingly named Dr. Diocletian Lewis, personal trainer to the progressive and modern-minded youth of Boston.

The sight of such dedication to the principle of a sound mind in a sound body so enchanted Miss Severance's guest that he stayed for the entire class. Among the people he met were Dr. Lewis himself, who was always glad to receive visitors (potential witnesses to the efficacy of his methods), and a fellow onlooker whose identity Villard was doubly pleased to learn. This young man's name was William Lloyd Garrison Jr., and he was the twenty-five-year-old son of the most famous (and most notorious) abolitionist in the country. Villard's disgust for the national disgrace of slavery had always been coupled, he wrote, with "the deepest sympathy and admiration" for "the inspired patriots who demanded the abolition of the horrible institution," and he was therefore delighted to make the acquaintance of someone so intimately related to the most inspired patriot of all.

This chance meeting might have been serendipity enough, but there was more to come. In the course of the conversation, young Will casually mentioned that he was also the brother of one of the strenuous damsels they were watching; perhaps Villard had noticed her, the particularly intent one over there. As it happened, the observant reporter had indeed noticed the girl in question; in fact, her pretty face, lustrous hair, dark, intelligent eyes, and flourishing young body had struck him almost from the moment he entered the gym. Now he was thrilled to discover that the object of his attention was Helen Frances Garrison, known as Fanny, William Lloyd Garrison's only daughter, a blooming maiden of eighteen years. Villard was chatting with the affable son, and admiring the attractive daughter, of the man who stood at the very center of the antislavery movement in the United States.

Impressed by the reporter's exploits, Will invited him to church the following day; they would hear a well-known liberal preacher and then dine at the Garrison family home on Dix Street, a few blocks south of Boston Common. The prospect of sitting in a church and listening to a sermon held no appeal for Villard, but things promised to get better after that, and he readily assented.

The next day, as Villard, Will, and his fourteen-year-old brother, Frank, were leaving the church, Fanny joined them. The correspondent's delight, however, turned to mortification as he realized that his distracted companions were not going to present him to their sister. This was nothing more than a casual oversight, but Villard, hardly a casual man, felt compelled to abide by the rules of good society and to refrain from addressing a young woman, no matter how fetching, to whom he had not been properly introduced. Fanny's impassive face, glimpsed on the sly as they trudged along, increased his embarrassment and chagrin.

Villard's ordeal ended as soon as the group reached the Garrison home. The gracious Mrs. Garrison made him welcome at once; yet another of her sons, Wendell, echoed his brothers' patent delight in their gallant visitor; Fanny, duly presented, spoke little, but even her silences ravished him; and the head of this agreeable family proved to be a most pleasant surprise.

⬛   ⬛   ⬛

William Lloyd Garrison (1805–1879), newspaper editor, antislavery agitator, and radical reformer, was (in the words of his biographer) "an authentic American hero," a champion of human rights worthy of a place of honor alongside Thomas Paine, Henry David Thoreau, and Martin Luther King in the distinguished American tradition of principled and eloquent dissent. His beginnings (in the small coastal town of Newburyport, Massachusetts) were classically humble. His maternal grandparents had come to America as indentured servants; his father was a frequently absent sailor who sailed away for good when his three children were still small. Raised in poverty by a hardworking single mother, Lloyd—as the boy was called—received almost no formal education. But he read widely and constantly, and dreamed of becoming a writer himself. From the age of thirteen until he was past twenty, Garrison worked as an apprentice in the shop of a local printer and newspaper editor, where he learned the trade he would follow for most of the rest of his life.

Garrison's moral fervor and sense of Christian justice, instilled in him by his pious mother, led him to embrace the abolitionist cause in 1828, thus casting his lot with those few courageous souls who constituted at that time this most marginalized and radical of American political movements. After two years of writing for an antislavery newspaper in Baltimore, where his ferocious diatribes had earned him a couple of weeks in the local jail, he resolved to dedicate his life to the definitive extinction of the institution of slavery in the United States.

On January 1, 1831, shortly after his twenty-fifth birthday, Garrison published in Boston the first issue of his newspaper, the *Liberator.*

His front-page editorial set the tone for all the hundreds and hundreds of issues to come:

> I am aware, that many object to the severity of my language; but
> is there not cause for severity? I *will be* as harsh as truth, and as
> uncompromising as justice. On this subject, I do not wish to
> think, or speak, or write, with moderation. No! no! Tell a man
> whose house is on fire, to give a moderate alarm; tell him to
> moderately rescue his wife from the hands of the ravisher . . .
> but urge me not to use moderation in a cause like the present.
> I am in earnest—I will not equivocate—I will not excuse—I will
> not retreat a single inch—AND I WILL BE HEARD.

What is most extraordinary about this string of extravagant promises and prophecies is that they were all fulfilled.

Every week for thirty-five years, until the ratification of the Thirteenth Amendment in December 1865 made slavery unconstitutional, Garrison produced a new installment of the *Liberator.* He started out with few, mostly black, subscribers; he persisted in the face of widespread hostility, constant ridicule, and personal threats, frequently in danger from mob violence and once, in 1835, narrowly escaping lynching; he weathered various equipment failures and financial crises, sometimes working at outside jobs to keep the paper running; and he had often to endure criticism even from his supporters when he seemed to them to go too far. But his principles remained inflexible and unequivocal, his opposition to slavery and to every accommodation with slavery absolute, and he never backed down. When a respected older friend advised him to temper his indignation, pointing out that Garrison seemed to be "all on fire," the younger man laid his hand on his counselor's shoulder and told him gravely, "I have need to be *all on fire,* for I have mountains of ice about me to melt."

In 1834 Garrison married Helen Benson, the serene and gentle daughter of a Connecticut family notable for its philanthropy and adherence to progressive causes, including abolitionism. Unlike her husband's, Helen Garrison's family was old and well established; in 1747 one of her great-grandfathers was a founding member of the Redwood Library in Newport, Rhode Island, the oldest surviving lending library in the country, still in daily use in its original building today. The Garrisons' marriage was a particularly loving one, and (in distinct contrast to Garrison's public life) their family life, however fraught and outwardly difficult, seems to have been unusually harmonious. Of their seven children, five—four boys and Fanny—survived childhood.

From the outset of his editorial career, Garrison occupied the most extreme reaches of the abolitionist movement. He heaped scorn upon those (for a long time Abraham Lincoln was among them) who favored the resettlement of African-Americans in Africa, calling their solution to the problem of slavery a fantasy and a racist sham. His own position, from which he never wavered, left no room for compromises, half measures, or schemes that involved any further injustices perpetrated upon the 4 million Americans of African descent: he demanded immediate, unrestricted, uncompensated, and irreversible abolition, together with complete equality and full citizenship for all black Americans, slave and free. In the 1840s he began to recommend that the free states secede from the Union, which was tainted by its toleration of slavery. NO UNION WITH SLAVEHOLDERS! became one of his rallying cries.

In Framingham, Massachusetts, at the 1854 recurrence of the annual Fourth of July picnic sponsored by the Massachusetts Anti-Slavery Society, several highly effective speakers, including Sojourner Truth, Wendell Phillips, and Henry David Thoreau, addressed the crowd of more than six hundred, but it was Garrison's literally fire-breathing discourse that highlighted and epitomized the occasion. As members of his family, including the nine-year-old Fanny, and the rest of the rapt crowd looked on, Garrison concluded his speech by burning a copy of the Fugitive Slave Law. Then, in a defining moment, "the pinnacle of his career in agitation," according to his biographer, Garrison set fire to what he considered "a covenant with death and an agreement with hell": the source, charter, and protector of the great national sin—the United States Constitution. This was an act of historical significance:

> No American before Garrison had so dramatically challenged his government's failure to realize and protect its ideals; no citizen before Garrison had staked the survival of the nation upon a spiritual revolution accomplished by a minority liberated from conventional politics and armed only with a righteous conviction of truth. . . . Garrison welcomed the growing polarization of the sections, insisted that the controversy turned upon a paramount issue of right and wrong, and labored steadily to bring the fundamental law into common contempt as the epitome of bondage. This confident absolutism remained his hallmark, and indeed his strategy, and he would not surrender it.

Garrison based his view of the matter on two quintessential documents, the Declaration of Independence and the Bible. While he served no church and belonged to no denomination, he was a completely convinced Christian, one of those pesky believers (St. Francis of Assisi is their historical prototype) who took the teachings of Jesus literally. He did the same with the Declaration, and the result was an unshakable belief in the sacrosanct justness of his cause. A committed pacifist, Garrison hoped to achieve abolition by moral suasion alone. It was therefore ironic, and perhaps inevitable, that his unyielding extremism, his endlessly reiterated insistence that Americans act according to the principles they claimed to believe in, helped push the national debate over slavery onto a moral level from which the only appeal was to arms.

Villard had half expected that the firebrand reformer, the master of unmitigated moral outrage, the symbol and epitome of American radicalism, would be a dour, disheveled patriarch with a prophet's beard and a fanatic's eyes; instead he was introduced to a slight, bald, bespectacled, clean-shaven, humorous, kindly man at peace with himself and serene in the reciprocated affection of his family. Garrison once explained his child-rearing methods to a friend: "I wish my children to know themselves." The placid atmosphere produced by such a parental attitude could not have failed to impress the son of Gustav Hilgard.

Garrison liked to say that he "loved all his children best, especially Fanny." It is still possible to appraise the tender bond that united father and daughter by studying a charming photograph of the two taken a couple of years after the memorable Sunday when Henry Villard came to dinner. Fanny sits sideways on her father's lap, her right arm across his shoulders, her cheek pressed against the side of his large bald head as both of them gaze calmly into the camera. The pose is natural, spontaneous, unforced; the two sitters take a frank physical delight in each other's presence, each other's nearness; their mutual affection lights up the old black-and-white picture. Hilgard family pictures, by contrast, show stiff, uncomfortable, unsmiling figures who turn away from one another as though from strangers. There is no physical contact, or if there is, it is reluctant and perfunctory, and the parties to it seem to be on the verge of flinching. Villard learned much from the Garrisons about radical politics, but he learned even more about the possibilities of familial love.

Around the time when Will and Fanny were watching their father burn the Constitution in Framingham, Henry Villard, an indigent monolingual immigrant with no identifiable skills, was spending his days loading lumber in a yard in Indianapolis. Now, less than nine years later, the heroic Garrison and his family were treating him like a hero newly returned from the battlefield. They all listened eagerly as their guest related some of his most remarkable wartime adventures—the dramatic dashes to Washington after Manassas and Fredericksburg, Grant's counterattack after the apparent defeat at Shiloh, the ironclad fiasco in Charleston harbor. It was the reporter's experiences on the Sea Islands, however, that proved to interest his audience most. They wanted to know all about how the former slaves were adjusting to freedom, and they were especially fascinated by Villard's positive report on the black soldiers of the First South Carolina Volunteers.

This was a theme close to the Garrison family's collective heart. A few months previously, Robert Gould Shaw, the son of a family of patrician abolitionists in Boston, had organized the Fifty-fourth Massachusetts, the first colored regiment in the state, and received a commission as its colonel. (In July 1863, this most famous of the Union's African-American regiments would lose half its number, including Colonel Shaw, as the Fifty-fourth Massachusetts led a valiant but doomed assault on Battery Wagner in Charleston harbor.) So many recruits responded to Shaw's appeal that a new black regiment, the Fifty-fifth Massachusetts, had to be formed, and its commander offered a second lieutenant's commission to the Garrisons' eldest son, George. The Emancipation Proclamation had made the fight for the preservation of the Union into a fight for the annihilation of slavery, and many young men who, like George Garrison, had been brought up as pacifist abolitionists now felt it their duty to join the struggle. Against his father's will, but ultimately with his blessing, George had accepted the commission, thus focusing his family's attention more closely than ever on the progress of the Union's black units. The Garrison men peppered their visitor with questions; his answers were elaborate and satisfying, and the whole family seemed impressed by his intelligence, his wide experience, his cultivated, European manners, and his advanced views, so compatible with their own.

The conversation continued long after dinner was over, giving Villard ample opportunity to observe the winsome Fanny. She was, he thought, "the very picture of a pretty, bright, emotional, yet guileless maiden"—it was important for a man like Villard to conclude that the object of his affection was without guile—and the few words she spoke expressed intelligence and understanding. Most expressive of all were "her lovely eyes, whose sweet spell" the smitten reporter "even then began to feel."

That night, April 26, Fanny Garrison wrote a letter to her dear friend and future sister-in-law Lucy McKim (later Mrs. Wendell Garrison) in Philadelphia. The first paragraph of this letter, could Villard have seen it, would have gladdened his heart: "Last night for a wonder Will & I went to the gymnasium & met there a gentleman from Port Royal, Mr. Henry Villard; he has been the Tribune's Correspondent for a long while. I like him ever so much. Today he dined with us . . . and a delightful time we had of it."

The following day young Frank Garrison, who was to become a sort of go-between in Henry Villard's romance with his sister, accompanied Villard to some of the sights of Boston, followed by a visit to the home of Wendell Phillips, probably the greatest of the abolitionist orators and at that time William Lloyd Garrison's closest collaborator. Villard was carrying a letter of introduction to Phillips from George Smalley, who had married Phillips's adopted daughter. Frank Garrison, of course, was well acquainted with Phillips, for whom his brother Wendell was named. The reporter, almost effortlessly, had moved into the abolitionists' innermost circle, a closed, tight, interrelated world where he seems to have found ready acceptance and welcome.

Villard was used to conducting interviews, and Frank was a willing subject. Throughout their time together, the reporter repeatedly led the boy to speak of his sister. Frank was exceedingly, gratifyingly fond of Fanny, and the only qualification he added to his praise of her was that she was "an awfully nice girl, but very green." This considered assessment, based on Frank's fourteen years and eight months' worth of worldly sophistication, greatly amused the green girl's incipient suitor.

The Fifty-fourth and Fifty-fifth Massachusetts Regiments were encamped in Readville, fifteen miles south of Boston, and that afternoon the reporter accompanied the Garrison family on a visit to George. Villard somehow contrived to travel to Readville and back in relative privacy, with Fanny at his side, and he confirmed his impressions of the night before. "She was very lovely," he reiterated, "and a good talker."

Evidence suggests, however, that the forceful Villard must have done something more than merely confirm his impressions, because Fanny remembered this outing all her life and frequently recorded its anniversaries in her diary. She got the date of the trip wrong—she consistently referred to it as having taken place on April 26, when in fact it was the following day, April 27—and as time passed she merged Readville into Dorchester, but she is clearly remembering that "Harry," as she and her family called Villard, made some sort of declaration. For example, on April 26, 1879, she writes, "16 years since Harry and I had that memorable ride." And four years later, on April 26, 1883: "Twenty years ago to-day, Harry took me to ride to Dorchester. A memorable day for me." As we have often seen, Henry Villard was a man whose preferred mode of action was the plunge, and it is not surprising that he would meet a girl, fall in love with her, secure an introduction to her family, and declare himself, all within about forty-eight hours.

When the reporter got back to his hotel room that evening, wrapped in the aromatic cloud of sudden love, he found a telegram, an intrusion of the real world into his idyll. The message was from Sydney Howard Gay. General William Rosecrans's Army of the Cumberland, encamped since the beginning of January near Murfreesboro, Tennessee, was at last ready to move. Gay requested that Villard cut his vacation short and prepare to return to central Tennessee and the war in the West. This request caused the correspondent to do some soul-searching, for he was uncharacteristically tempted to turn it down. Further and frank reflection brought him face-to-face with some hard truths: he was an adventurer, a wanderer in a dangerous, low-paying profession; he had no fixed domicile; he had no savings; he had no future prospects. He saw that it would make no sense to "yield to the impulse of the warmer feeling" and abandon his only source of income in order to remain in Boston and press a suit for the hand of Fanny Garrison. Sighing deeply, he wrote to his managing editor and promised to return to New York within forty-eight hours.

The following day, his last in Boston, Villard kept an appointment with Frank Garrison to go for a drive. This incongruous pair (Villard was twice the age, and nearly twice the size, of his beloved's brother) set off for suburban Boston together, but first they stopped in Dix Place to see if Miss Fanny would care to join them. Villard took upon himself the burden of presenting this offer. Inside, Fanny was playing the piano, and her eager suitor, alert to any hopeful sign that his affection was returned, was glad to see that his unexpected appearance put the girl into a state of some disarray. In her surprise she started instinctively to her feet, and Villard would always remember her flustered silence and the embarrassed way she thrust both her hands into her little white apron pockets as she rose. The drive was a huge success, despite the consciousness of imminent separation. Frank was the discreetest of chaperons, the Boston area abounded in points of interest, and Villard found an opportunity to convey to his fair companion, as expressively as he could, how very sorry he was to leave the city and how ardently he hoped to return to it soon. Her response was all, or almost all, he could have hoped: "My heart beat quicker when I saw her eye-lids droop and a slight red diffused over her face."

Courting the daughter of so progressive a family was not without difficulties. There was, for example, the matter of minor vices. At some point during the drive, both Fanny and Frank declared their opposition to tobacco, and more particularly to the little cigars that Villard was so fond of. With the air of a man sacrificing all for love, he handed Fanny his cigar case as a demonstration of his good intentions. On other points, however, he was able to stand firm. William Lloyd Garrison advocated temperance nearly as passionately as he advocated abolition, but as a European—as a German!—Villard could never give up, or discern any harm in, the moderate consumption of beer, wine, and spiritous liquors. More crucially, perhaps, Garrison was an early feminist, a vehement supporter of women's suffrage, and his wife and daughter felt at least as militantly about this issue as he did. As far as Villard was concerned, such notions were not as unacceptable as teetotalism, but persuasion would be necessary to move him any farther along the line. As his son explained, "it took some time to win one who was reared in Germany to woman suffrage."

Villard had no intention of letting such small differences as these stand in his way. Saddened as the moment of his departure approached, he found solace in Fanny's "speaking look, blushing," as she offered him her hand. A few hours later he was on the train to

New York, returning from the six-day trip that had altered the course of his existence. "It was to this chance visit to Boston," he later wrote, "that I owe the greatest happiness of my life—my marriage to Miss Fanny Garrison, the only daughter of the great abolitionist, to whose charms of mind and person I surrendered on first acquaintance."

Total surrender, however, must await the end of the war. After a few days in New York for instructions and other preparations, Villard traveled to Cincinnati to observe an important trial before moving on to Murfreesboro. Several days later, just before he left Cincinnati, writing in a careful, cramped, perfectly legible hand that bore little resemblance to his usual loose-wristed, ink-splattering approach to penmanship, he composed his first letter to his radical girl:

May 10th '63

Dear Miss Garrison,

I beg to enclose a vignette photograph of myself.

I venture to do this, inasmuch the promise the enclosure fulfils was made both to yourself & Frank & the latter hardly deserves any further token of good will at my hands until he has replied to the letter I wrote him previous to my departure from New York.

I cannot presume to ask an acknowledgment of the receipt of this by yourself, but will thank you very much for prevailing on Frank to "be a good Boy" & answer my letter.

Hoping that the likeness will at times recall to you the original, I remain

truly yours
Henry Villard

The following day, after posting this mixture of formality, boldness, and blatant contrivance, Villard turned away from the service of Eros and set out for Murfreesboro, where he would find the devotees of Mars.

GEN. ULYSSES S. GRANT AND (POSSIBLY) HENRY VILLARD.
Photograph of Grant (third from left) taken at his headquarters
at City Point, June 1864. The man seated second from left in the unidentified
group of men on the right bears a striking resemblance to Henry Villard.
National Archives.

15

War Fever

By the bivouac's fitful flame,
A procession winding around me, solemn and sweet and
  slow—but first I note
The tents of the sleeping army, the fields' and woods' dim
  outline,
The darkness lit by spots of kindled fire, the silence,
Like a phantom far or near an occasional figure moving,
The shrubs and trees, (as I lift my eyes they seem to be
  stealthily watching me,)
While wind in procession thoughts, O tender and
  wondrous thoughts,
Of life and death, of home and the past and loved, and of
  those that are far away;
A solemn and slow procession there as I sit on the ground,
By the bivouac's fitful flame.

WALT WHITMAN,
"By the Bivouac's Fitful Flame"

Early in May 1863, having obeyed his chief's urgent summons to join the Federal forces in the West, having departed suddenly from the newfound love of his life, Villard settled in for what turned out to be six weeks of a venerable army tradition: waiting. On December 31, 1862, and January 2, 1863, General Rosecrans's Union army and the Confederate forces under Gen. Braxton Bragg had fought each other to a bloody draw near Murfreesboro (the engagement is also known as the battle of Stones River). The efforts of the combatants resulted in close to twenty-five thousand casualties, about evenly distributed between the two sides, including at least three thousand killed. After this indecisive encounter—indecisive, that is, except for those who died in it—Bragg withdrew southward. Rosecrans did not pursue him, and the two armies had spent the intervening time binding up their wounds, replenishing their forces, and enduring the winter. Now, with the arrival of spring, they were almost, but not quite, ready to collide with each other again.

The dreadful bloodbath at Stones River had brought honor to neither Rosecrans nor Bragg, and the rattled Federal commander, at pains to rehabilitate his reputation, was only too glad to welcome so distinguished a member of the press as Henry Villard. Reporters' scuttlebutt had long ago marked Rosecrans as one who "tried to work the press systematically for his personal benefit." Unwilling to be worked, Villard tactfully declined the more extreme manifestations of the general's cordiality, such as his offer of sleeping quarters and a seat at his mess table. Instead the prudent reporter accepted a small but comfortable room in the brick mansion where his old friends General McCook and staff were quartered, and there he awaited the passage of the weeks in agreeable surroundings and amid convivial company.

It was also in the early days of May, back in the East, that Lee's Army of Northern Virginia, outnumbered two to one, inflicted a humiliating defeat on the much-abused Army of the Potomac at Chancellorsville. Union fortunes were at a low ebb that spring, and the voices calling for a compromise peace with the Confederacy were many and loud. According to Villard's friend and colleague Murat Halstead, it was shortly after Chancellorsville that the newly smitten correspondent was fortunate enough to receive a handsome inheritance in gold, which he promptly exchanged "for greenbacks within one point of the highest percentage of the premium for gold during the history of the country, and converted the fiat currency into United States bonds, so that by faith in our Government in the midst of disaster he multiplied his money by three within a few weeks." It is not clear whether this welcome bequest came to Villard from relatives in Germany or in Illinois. In any case, its successful investment was the first intimation of his future career as a financier, and its immediate effect was to help allay his fears that he might be unworthy to woo Fanny Garrison.

At first the tedium of waiting in the Federal encampment outside Murfreesboro was alleviated by campfires, singing, carousing, story-telling, and other delights of the soldier afield. Eventually, however, these too grew tedious. Visits to Rosecrans's headquarters were some-what more rewarding. Villard was always welcome, and he always re-ceived a full account of the wrongs inflicted upon the general by his superiors and of the grand design Rosecrans would carry out should he ever, by some wholly appropriate chance, take their place. The re-porter felt more comfortable talking to Rosecrans's chief of staff, Gen. James A. Garfield, who "looked like a distinguished personage." Once again, Villard had formed an acquaintance with a future pres-ident of the United States. (Garfield would become the second sit-ting president of the United States to die at the hands of an assassin, this one a disgruntled office seeker.)

Finally, after much prodding by those same criminally impatient superiors, General Rosecrans was ready to move. Villard was de-lighted, eager to exchange monotonous routine for unknown ad-venture, but his joy was short lived. At 3 A.M. on June 24, the army began to march southeastward, toward Georgia, and that night a tor-rential downpour that was to last the better part of two weeks began. Sleeping by a campfire and covered by a porous army overcoat, Vil-lard got thoroughly soaked, remained wet and cold even in the shel-ter of a hospitable general's fire-warmed tent, and was by morning unable to move. The chief surgeon diagnosed "malarial fever and in-flammatory rheumatism," and the *Tribune*'s chief correspondent in the West had to abandon the campaign within twenty-four hours of its beginning. After a night of "bilious nausea," weak, incapable of moving or eating, and partly out of his senses, Villard was trans-ported in an army ambulance through the driving rain to Murfrees-boro, put on a train to Louisville, and carried to Galt House, where he stayed nearly two months while his strength slowly began to re-turn. During the fateful first week of July, as Rosecrans was inching his cautious way south and other Union armies at Gettysburg and Vicksburg were putting an end to the Confederate string of victories, Villard was in a well-appointed hotel room, sipping clear liquids and taking an occasional tottering step.

Near the end of July, when he was finally able to move, Villard went to Ohio to gather material on the bold Confederate raider John Hunt Morgan, who was then terrorizing the Midwest. While in the neighborhood of Springfield, the reporter unhappily chose to spend two weeks at a place named Yellow Sulphur Springs, where he assiduously drank the "medicinal waters." These apparently contained the wrong medicine, for he suffered a violent relapse that featured "bilious intermittent fever" and threatened to turn into typhoid. This time his recovery (at Burnet House in Cincinnati) took three weeks. Toward the end of this period, on September 19 and 20, the armies of Generals Rosecrans and Bragg, together again at last, plowed into one another near Chickamauga Creek in northwest Georgia. An opportune Confederate charge drove nearly two-thirds of the Federals from the field in confusion, including in their number Rosecrans and two of his three corps commanders, who fled with their routed soldiers in the direction of the Tennessee border. The troops of the other corps commander, Gen. George Thomas, stood and fought all day before withdrawing, thus earning him (along with Rosecrans's job) lasting fame as "the Rock of Chickamauga." Although at dawn of the following day the rebels were masters of the field, each side had suffered nearly 30 percent casualties, a total of some thirty-five thousand men. Villard later wrote that missing this battle was the "greatest disappointment" he suffered during the entire Civil War.

Early in October, feeling fully recovered from an illness that had lasted more than three months, Villard made the difficult and circuitous journey to Chattanooga, where Bragg was laying siege to the Federal army. The rebels occupied the high ground south and east of the city, interdicting traffic on the Tennessee River and cutting off the Federals' supply line.

Rosecrans and Garfield gave the intrepid correspondent a warm welcome, Garfield because he had taken a genuine liking to Villard, and Rosecrans because he was desperately in need of some good press. Villard was wary, however, wisely perceiving that the days of a general who had participated in a panicked flight from his last battlefield must be numbered. Moreover, the reporter had never thought much of Rosecrans. Back in June, while the general was bid-ing his time at Murfreesboro, Villard had written a private letter to Sydney Howard Gay, advising him that the *Tribune* should not back Rosecrans too strongly: "There are flaws in his moral as well as intellectual composition and professional capacity, which the future will surely develop into prominent shortcomings."

The future that Villard had so astutely predicted was now at hand. In the middle of October, Rosecrans was relieved of his command of the Department of the Cumberland. He was replaced by General Thomas, who would, however, be subordinate to the newly promoted supreme commander of the Union armies in the West: Gen. Ulysses S. Grant.

On October 23, not many days after Villard bade farewell to the departing Rosecrans, Grant arrived in Chattanooga, having traveled over the barely passable mountain roads that led to the city from the north. He found the trapped Federal forces in a plight that was rapidly approaching desperation. Chattanooga, strongly defended, was in no danger from a rebel assault, but the supply situation had become critical. Horses were starving, men (down to quarter rations) were not doing much better, and there was some recourse to stray dogs or the occasional rodent. Grant immediately went into conference with Thomas on the subject of opening a secure route of supply.

By this time Villard had taken the measure of General Thomas and determined, among other things, that he resembled Grant both in his taciturnity and in his aversion to publicity, whether good or bad. Although the realities of this new situation caused a pang in his journalist's heart, Villard could see that there was little to be gained by importuning two such commanders as these for insights into their plans. His appearances at general headquarters became less frequent and less extended. Meanwhile he had accepted an invitation to share the "tent and table" of Gen. August von Willich, the former Prussian artillery officer whom Villard knew from his days with Buell's army.

Along with their mother tongue, von Willich and Villard had in common their upper-middle-class background. Furthermore, unlike most of the American general officers with whom Villard came in contact, the cultivated, well-informed von Willich was a man capable

of intelligent conversation on almost any subject. He and the reporter engaged in many a friendly debate about politics, for though
they agreed in detesting both monarchism and slavery, Villard was
otherwise far less radical than von Willich, who espoused "pronounced socialist views." Despite Villard's dislike of authority and his
fondness for the moral high ground, he shared most of the conventional beliefs, values, prejudices, and fears of the *haute bourgeoisie,*
and he could take no pleasure in envisioning a future society from
which class distinctions and private property had been eliminated.

One point on which Villard and von Willich were in full agreement was the value of Fritz, a private soldier who was von Willich's
servant and who extended his service to Villard when the latter became the general's guest. Fritz saw to their nourishment, waited on
them, cleaned their clothes, blacked their boots, and displayed,
when the army's supplies were nearly gone, a resourcefulness that
approached genius both in procuring rare items and in making improbably palatable meals out of what he had been able to obtain.
When the cold fall rains came down and the general's tent was neither warm nor dry, Fritz rose to the occasion with hot punch laced
with cognac from a stash he kept for just such emergencies. Despite
Fritz's ministrations, however, the reporter was slowly being forced to
the realization that his resistance to the damps and discomforts of
military life was not what it once had been.

During the darkest hours of a moonless night late in October,
Villard accompanied some three thousand Union troops on a daring
amphibious operation designed to bridge the Tennessee west of
Chattanooga (out of range of the rebel guns), to drive off the Con-
federate troops guarding Bragg's flank, and to open up the road between this new bridgehead and the Federal stores at Bridgeport,
Alabama. In a return to form, Villard was the first to gallop back to
Chattanooga with news of the complete success of this operation,
and within days the besieged town was being resupplied along the
new route, which the Yankees immediately began to call the "Cracker
Line." The benefits of the Cracker Line quickly became apparent to
Villard and von Willich, for Fritz, with ready access to a wide range
of ingredients, was able to give free rein to his artistic imagination.

It had taken Grant about a week to reinvigorate and reenergize the troops under his command, and now he set about preparing to lift the siege completely. Reinforced by a large contingent from the Army of the Potomac under General Hooker and by Sherman's Army of the Tennessee, which arrived in mid-November, the Federals enjoyed considerable numerical superiority and were ready and eager to break the rebels' grip.

On November 23, 1863, four days after Abraham Lincoln unforgettably dedicated the new military cemetery on the battlefield at Gettysburg, Grant moved to the offensive. Von Willich's brigade was ordered to join in General Thomas's assault on Orchard Knob, the high ground that lay between the Federal defenses and the even higher ground of Missionary Ridge, which overlooked Chattanooga on the east. Thomas's troops responded gallantly, swept away the rebel resistance, and by evening had secured Orchard Knob. Villard was back in the thick of things, exposed to enemy fire of all kinds, racing from one point to another to gather material for his battlefront dispatches. That evening, under a drizzling rain, the versatile Fritz constructed a makeshift hut out of scavenged planks, and there Villard slept, with only a rubber blanket between himself and the damp ground. Before morning the fever was on him again; by turns trembling violently and perspiring profusely, the correspondent witnessed the rest of the battle of Chattanooga in a state that bordered on delirium.

The next day Hooker's troops scaled the nearly perpendicular sides of Lookout Mountain, whose great bulk loomed southwest of the town. In the ensuing "Battle Above the Clouds," fighting in a thick fog, the Federals dislodged the rebel division stationed along the mountain crest and forced the Confederates to fall back on Missionary Ridge.

At dawn on the following day, November 25, Grant sent Sherman's men against the enemy positions at the north end of that ridge, but the Yankee advance was stymied throughout eight hours of hard fighting by a determined rebel defense. Fearing a counterattack that Sherman's weary soldiers would be unable to withstand, Grant decided to distract the Confederates by threatening their center. Late in the afternoon he ordered Thomas to send his troops forward from Orchard Knob and attack the first line of rebel rifle pits at the base of Missionary Ridge. Thomas's men, including von Willich's brigade, carried out their appointed task successfully, and then, in one of the Civil War's defining moments, they considerably exceeded the limits of what they had been ordered to do. While Grant and Thomas watched incredulously from behind the lines, the Union soldiers seemed to erupt spontaneously from the captured rifle pits and began ascending Missionary Ridge itself, first in smaller groups, then in entire regiments, colors and all, sweeping their officers along with them as they raced up the steep slope toward the frantically firing rebel defenders. Sometimes scrambling hand over hand, the Federal soldiers surged up and over the crest of the ridge, somehow penetrated the center of the Confederate line, and drove Bragg's army in disorder from the field. As the rebels broke and ran, above the battle din the Yankees' taunting screams—*"Chickamauga! Chickamauga!"*—were clearly audible.

The battle of Chattanooga, the third and last of the great Union victories achieved during the latter half of 1863, marked the beginning of the South's irreversible decline. At Gettysburg the Federals had repulsed Lee's final invasion of the North; at Vicksburg Grant had seized control of the Mississippi and split the South; now, after the temporary Union setback at Chickamauga, Grant's victory at Chattanooga paved his way to supreme command of the entire Union Army. Lincoln had at last found a general skillful, thorough, resolute, and relentless enough to win the war. (Bragg, by contrast, was relieved of his command.) The lifting of the siege at Chattanooga freed a large Federal army deep in enemy territory. Once again the Union was threatening to split the South, crosswise this time, and right across the heart.

Henry Villard was too sick to witness with his own eyes the uncommanded Union storming of Missionary Ridge. In a blur of high fever, raging headache, and disequilibrium, he had withdrawn from the field on the second day of the battle. As he slowly recovered behind the lines, he came to the painful conclusion that the recurring illnesses of the past six months had rendered him unfit to continue to work as a war correspondent. In December he returned to Washington for further recuperation, and while he was there he began to think about less debilitating ways of earning a living.

Although the privations and hardships Villard suffered as a Civil War correspondent seriously (and, it seems likely, permanently) undermined his health, there were other factors contributing to his decision to withdraw, at least for a time, from the dark and bloody battlegrounds. Like many, if not most, of his colleagues, he had simply seen and heard and smelled too much: too much mutilation, too much screaming, too much suffering, too much stupidity and waste, too much death. Another factor in his decision was the inconsiderateness of his boss, Horace Greeley, who got under the reporter's thin skin by complaining about deficiencies in his work at Chattanooga. Villard seems to have thought that the state of his health had no effect on the quality or acceptability of his dispatches, and so, "without bothering to explain that he had been ill," he resigned from the *Tribune* in December 1863. A few months later, in a letter to Frank Garrison, Villard justified the step he had taken: "I left the *Tribune* without regret. The crotchets of Mr. Greeley never suited me."

Despite his weakened condition, Villard was incapable of remaining idle. Early in 1864 he organized a Washington news bureau in direct competition with the well-established but complacent Associated Press. Villard's bureau would gather news, turn it into dispatches, and telegraph these to various newspapers. He was joined in this enterprise by his old friend Horace White, who was then the *Chicago Tribune*'s Washington representative as well as clerk of the Senate Committee on Military Affairs, and by his former *New York Tribune* colleague Adams S. Hill, who had also resigned his position in December, dissatisfied, as Villard had been, with what Hill called "Mr. Greeley's chameleon policy." The three partners named their bureau the Independent News Room (INR) and established an office on Pennsylvania Avenue, with the White House and the Treasury within easy reach.

Despite bitter attacks by the Associated Press, which objected to the disturbance of its monopoly, Villard succeeded in obtaining subscriptions from several important newspapers, including the *Chicago*

Tribune, the *Cincinnati Commercial,* and the *Boston Advertiser.* He was able to accomplish this by means of his considerable powers of persuasion, visiting the managers and editors of the various newspapers in person. It was while returning from one of these business trips that he was involved in a train wreck, sustaining painful injuries about which he was still complaining years later. Not yet fully recuperated from the terrible fever (typhoid? malaria?) that had struck him down at Chattanooga for the third time in five months, and now suffering from various sprains, cuts, and contusions, Villard spent the early months of 1864 feeling wretched.

Nevertheless, his news agency was "successful from the start." It provided him with independence, which he treasured above all things, and fully twice the amount of his former salary at the *Tribune.* At the end of January, as the Federal forces in east Tennessee were preparing a new offensive campaign, Gay tried to lure his star correspondent back to the *Tribune* in order to send him west again. After commiserating with Villard for his treatment at Greeley's hands and referring to the various "occasions when you have served us signally," Gay made a direct appeal: "You know the army & the country better than anybody else. Are you well enough to go at once?" But Villard, buoyed by the success of his new venture and plagued by various ills, had no intention of returning to the life of the military camps, especially not in the dead of winter.

In April, after a hiatus of nearly a year, he wrote a letter to Frank Garrison in Boston. Since Villard and Frank's sister were not yet sufficiently acquainted to conduct a private correspondence, Villard thus managed to adhere to the courtship conventions of the Victorian middle class while reopening an indirect line of communication with the young woman who stayed so immovably on his mind. Explaining to her brother that "a variety of circumstances—tribulations both physical and otherwise" had distracted him from all epistolary activity, Villard described his new situation and made crafty inquiries about Frank's family.

Early in May, feeling fully recovered and ready once again for the military life, Villard left Washington to join the Army of the Potomac as the INR's representative. The huge army, some 120,000 strong, was encamped north of the Rapidan River in Virginia, about fifty-five miles southwest of Washington. The commanding officer of the Army of the Potomac was Gen. George Meade, the victor of Gettysburg, but he was subject to Grant's orders, and Grant was accompanying the army.

In March, shortly after taking command as the Union's general in chief, Grant had appointed Sherman commander of the Federal armies in the West and himself joined Meade's command in the East. Now the two main Union armies were under the direct control of two men determined to make the war so intolerable to the South that it would have no recourse but to surrender, and no respite until it did. On May 4, the same day on which Sherman's men, a hundred thousand strong, left their base outside Chattanooga and started moving in the direction of Atlanta, Grant ordered the Army of the Potomac to cross the Rapidan and make its way through the Wilderness (a tangled, mazy region of dense second-growth forest, thick, brambly underbrush, and topographical surprises) before marching on to Richmond.

Villard reached the Union encampment shortly before the troops got their marching orders and the Rapidan crossing began. Grant's overall intention was to bring the Army of Northern Virginia to battle and to fight it, at whatever cost, either until it was destroyed or until what was left of it quit. His immediate objective, however, was to get through the Wilderness. After that he planned to march on Richmond, some sixty miles to the southeast, until Lee tried to stop him. But the Southern commander, who understood that the Yankees' numerical superiority would mean little in that wild woodland, attacked them before they could get out of it, the day after they crossed the river. Though this was not the ground he would have chosen, Grant characteristically counterattacked, and the battle was joined.

Lee's May 5 attack in the Wilderness south of the Rapidan began a series of savage combats that came to an end fifteen days later and twelve miles away, near a crossroads in the forest called Spotsylvania. For pure horror, the Wilderness campaign equaled any of the ghastly spectacles produced by the combatants of the Civil War. Men fought in dense underbrush, which hindered their movements and blocked their vision; smoke from a hundred thousand muskets hung, acrid and opaque, between the trees; in many places flashing weapons and bursting shells ignited the brush, starting small forest fires and burning to death many of the helpless wounded, whose shrieks pierced the incessant roar of gunfire. Against this hellish background, blindly struggling soldiers shot their comrades or stumbled into the midst of their enemies or fought them hand to hand.

Though often badly mauled, the Federals attacked again and again. By May 20, when Grant finally disengaged his troops for a few days, the Union Army had taken twice as many casualties as the Confederates. But the losses, considered proportionately, were about equal—30 percent of each army—and only one side had a manpower reserve sufficient to replace the numbers it had lost. From the campaign in the Wilderness until the end of the war, Grant never considered himself beaten; he constantly kept up the pressure on the Confederates, consistently sought new ways to exploit the Union's considerable advantages, and was always willing to fight again another day; now, unable to overrun Lee, he decided to outflank him.

As soon as it became clear, after two weeks of nearly constant battle, that Grant was going to pull his men out of their positions around Spotsylvania and march even deeper into Virginia, Villard began one of his patented dashes to the capital. Always proud to be the fleetest of messengers, whether the tidings he carried were good or bad, he was the first correspondent to reach Washington with a complete, firsthand report on the grisly doings in the Wilderness.

Two weeks later, Villard was back with the Army of the Potomac. On June 3, a furious and ill-advised charge against the impregnable Confederate defenses at Cold Harbor had cost Grant's troops seven thousand killed or wounded in a little over half an hour. Once again, however, Grant responded to a defeat with an advance, and the army marched grimly on. Having passed well to the east of Richmond, the Federals were now threatening to attack it from the south. Villard caught up with the army a couple of days before it crossed the James River and marched in the direction of the strong fortifications around the town of Petersburg, about twenty-five miles south of Richmond.

By the end of June, less than three weeks after Villard's arrival, the Federals had made several failed assaults on the Confederate works and then settled down to besiege the town. Lee's army was pinned inside Petersburg's defenses, and combat between the two sides had mutated into a static but bloody kind of trench warfare, a peculiarly squalid way of fighting that prefigured the murderous burrowing of World War I. As Grant slowly extended his lines to the west, closing in on the rebel supply route, a Pennsylvania regiment made up largely of coal miners dug a tunnel nearly two hundred yards long to a point under the Confederate fortifications. The Yankees packed the end of this tunnel with explosives and on July 30 set off an explosion that blasted a huge crater in the enemy line and hurled men, cannon, and earthworks fifty—some said a hundred—feet into the air.

This thunderous surprise should have given the Union troops a distinct advantage, but their follow-up attack was a disaster of ineptitude. Fifteen thousand confused, poorly led bluecoats moved slowly into the crater and stalled there so long that the rebels were able to regroup, artillery and all, and turn the great hole into a shooting pit. The ensuing massacre proved to be the last straw for Henry Villard, who left the Army of the Potomac for good two days later.

At around this same time, Villard received an urgent message from his family in Germany: the older of his two sisters, Anna, was slowly but inexorably wasting away with consumption. Their mother had died in 1859, without ever seeing him again. Now he felt that he must try to reach Anna's side before death took her as well. Before he sailed, however, he had certain stateside affairs to set in order, and this delay gave him time for a brief exchange with his much-neglected but still willing correspondent Frank Garrison.

In the letter that opened this exchange on August 10, Villard, still seething over what he had seen at Petersburg, launched into a tirade so heartfelt that one may imagine hearing in it the writer's authentic voice, complete with German accent:

I left the army on the 1st inst. utterly disheartened. The disaster of the 30th ult. took all hope—little though it had been for some time—of a creditable termination of the campaign. . . . It was the most shocking, most miserably managed affair of the war. I blame all that had anything to do with conducting it, from Grant down, for the disaster. It disclosed the most shameful neglect of duty and most disgusting incompetence. Such an incredible slaughter of men has never been heard of. I was so full of indignation at what I had seen—and I saw the whole of the performance from beginning to end, having accompanied Burnside's division commanders—that I could not win it over myself to stay in the Army any longer.

Villard went on to tell Frank about his imminent departure for Europe. Having recently learned of Wendell Garrison's betrothal, Villard wrote wistfully and transparently of the matrimonial state:

With my vagabond habits, I am bound to continue a batchelor all my life. Yet there is one being in this country, that could easily cure me of my restless, roving disposition. Unfortunately there is no hope that she will.

But I am saying too much. Let the above be "entre nous." For a man like me, love is weakness and I dislike to have others know, that I am as weak as they are.

After baring his soul in this extraordinary way to his fifteen-year-old correspondent, Villard perhaps feared that Frank would take him at his word and keep these passionate declarations to himself. By way of making sure that the messenger got the message, Villard in his closing paragraph practically begged Frank for reassurance: "As the Garrisons all seem to be doing finely in the matrimonial line, I suppose Miss Fanny is also under bonds. If she is, I hope she will find them easy to bear. Wendell is evidently very happy and she certainly deserves to be equally so."

The faithful Frank, quite aware of the game, responded provocatively to this cry for help, writing to Villard in New York on August

18: "You are somewhat mistaken in supposing that Fanny has entered into 'Matrimonial Bonds.' She is wonderfully destitute of beaus & has not got a single one, except—but I will tell you all when we meet."

These piquant revelations soothed Villard's greatest anxieties and made him long to wait upon the Garrisons before his departure. First, however, he was obliged to visit his German relatives in Illinois and Missouri, and then, back in New York, he finally obtained his certificate of naturalization. A few days later, hours before sailing for Le Havre, he scribbled a note to Frank in which he expressed regret for his failure to get to Boston before his departure and alluded to how "gratifying" it would have been to him to have "renewed my acquaintance with Miss Fanny." In fact, he plunged on, "I have been anxious for this ever since I first knew her." After promising to return in the spring, the suitor requested information on Fanny's "beau" (the existence of whom Villard had inferred from Frank's coy hint in his August 18 letter), hoped the maiden would not forget him, and declared that he would "deem it a very great privilege if she permitted me to write to her."

Frank's long reply, written on September 25, reached Villard in Europe. With a gravity beyond his years, the boy reported his sister's decision to deny Villard the privilege of an epistolary relationship. "I think that you will see," Frank solemnly pointed out, "the impropriety of a correspondence between you & Fanny after so slight an acquaintance." Then, his chaperon's duty properly discharged, the lad metamorphosed into an exuberantly candid Cupid: "But let me tell you, dear Villard, that Fanny loves you as much as you do her, & that from the first moment she met you, she felt interested in you. Her curiosity to see your letters &c. showed me that long ago. Now all you have to do, when you come back, is to go in & win."

Frank continued with a most gratifying description of Villard's erstwhile rival, a conceited and boring young man who, recently rejected by not one but two of her best friends, had turned his attentions upon Miss Fanny and received a curt dismissal for his pains. Frank filled the rest of his letter with a description of the new Garrison family home, in Roxbury, the latest war reports, chitchat about the upcoming presidential election, and so forth, and ended with a pert apology: "I hope the last two pages & a half of this letter have not been prosy. I have no fears about the first page & a half." He had, as he knew, told Villard exactly what he most wanted to hear.

The new American citizen left the United States on September 14, returning to Germany for the first time since his surreptitious departure eleven years before. He reached Speyer, his native city, a few days before Anna died there, in October. Villard spent the next five months in Germany, passing most of the winter in Munich with his younger sister, Emma—her husband, Robert von Xylander, was an army officer stationed at Nuremberg—and the ailing, considerably aged Gustav.

Back under his father's roof, Villard found that little in their relationship had changed. Although later he was pleased to suggest that he and his father had reached some sort of reconciliation before the latter's death, and even that Gustav had admitted having misjudged his only son, the similarity of their personalities and their lifelong incompatibility make it quite unlikely that such a reconciliation ever took place. It seems more probable that Gustav could never forgive his son for having defied his will and escaped his control, and that Villard could never forgive his father for failing to recognize his worth.

Even if there was an eventual reconciliation between the two before Gustav's death, in 1867, there is evidence to suggest that harmony and magnanimity did not characterize their relations during Villard's five-month visit in 1864–65. A German legal document dated November 15, 1864, and signed by Gustav Hilgard and "Heinrich Ferdinand Gustav Hilgard genannt [known as] Henry Villard," deals with their financial claims on each other. Among other things, this document reveals that Villard's share in his mother's estate, a handsome bequest of 5,000 florins, was reduced to the still-respectable but considerably smaller sum of 3,000 florins because of "various counterclaims that his father had against him." These counterclaims must have included the various debts that Villard contracted during his university years, including the borrowed sum that enabled him to leave Germany in 1853; the 500 florins that Gustav had paid in 1857 for a substitute to perform his son's obligatory service in the Bavarian army; the stipend that Gustav sent Villard during his financial struggles in the United States in 1855; and whatever later contributions, if any, Gustav made to his son's subsistence. This largesse had been bestowed, as a rule, most grudgingly, and here was Gustav's chance, despite his growing physical infirmities, to reassert his paternal power and reestablish the proper order of things by grabbing the purse strings and pulling them tight. When we read, elsewhere in the document, that Gustav gave Emma, Villard's younger sister, a dowry of 12,300 florins, we realize how little the forgiveness of his son's debts, many of them contracted while still a teenager, would have inconvenienced Gustav had he not been so strongly determined to make a point.

Villard's maternal inheritance (however sadly reduced) was sufficient to persuade him that now his social standing, boosted by the elevating power of inherited cash, was high enough, when combined with his achievements and professional prospects, to make him a worthy suitor of Fanny Garrison. He planned to return to the United States in time to witness and report the final campaigns of the war while simultaneously carrying out his own campaign to storm the citadel and win his beloved's hand.

The latter campaign took precedence, and Villard determined to visit his friends the Garrisons before returning to the life of a war correspondent. The charms of Miss Garrison and his augmented net worth made it seem less necessary for him to dash off at once to the nearest battlefield. Around the middle of March 1865, he bade farewell to his family in Munich; he made his way to Liverpool, booked a passage to Boston, and sailed on March 31. On April 15, when his ship entered Boston harbor, he had been at sea for nearly fifteen days. During that relatively brief period, however, three momentous events had occurred, and Villard was as stunned as any other passenger to learn of them: Richmond had fallen; Lee had surrendered the Army of Northern Virginia to Grant at Appomattox; and in a theater in Washington a deranged racist named John Wilkes Booth had murdered Abraham Lincoln.

ROCKLEDGE.

Photograph of the home of William Lloyd Garrison in Roxbury.

Photograph by Ronald Shelburne and Joseph Fisher.

Dudley Branch, Boston Public Library.

16

In Sickness
and in Health

As unto the bow the cord is,
So unto the man is woman,
Though she bends him, she obeys him,
Though she draws him, yet she follows,
Useless each without the other!

HENRY WADSWORTH LONGFELLOW,
The Song of Hiawatha, pt. X

Villard immediately called upon the Garrisons, but for once his impetuousness abashed him; he felt uncomfortable and unsure of himself, and he didn't stay long. Rightly viewing this loss of nerve as a momentary weakness, and believing with General Grant that the proper response to a setback was a renewed assault, Villard soon returned to the field. Before long Fanny found herself listening to his passionate declarations, delivered with a distinctly foreign blend of recklessness and formality, and culminating in a proposal of marriage. This turn of events could not have taken her by surprise; Villard had spoken to her with great ardor during their memorable carriage ride two years previously, and she surely knew that his letters to Frank were meant for her eyes. Nevertheless, she *was* surprised. She could not answer at once; she felt quite flattered; she hardly knew Mr. Villard.

Indeed, Mr. Villard and Miss Fanny had spent but little time together when he briefly visited Boston in 1863, and in the two intervening years she had not seen him again. It's a plausible conjecture that sometime during those few days of their first acquaintance, probably on the fateful carriage ride, Villard had declared his entire devotion to Miss Fanny and bemoaned his inability to offer her anything besides his heart. Now, modest inheritance in hand and visionary gleam in his eye, he felt authorized to promise her a life of material comfort. By the time he left Boston at the end of April, both he and Fanny knew that her capitulation was imminent.

Villard went to New York and exorcised a bit of his past by staying in the Astor Hotel, whose magnificence he had so wistfully admired as a poor immigrant boy twelve long years before. During his stay in New York, Horace White, now editor in chief at the *Chicago Tribune*, offered him a position as that newspaper's regular Washington correspondent. Villard accepted gladly, but before he reported for duty he betook himself once again to Boston, armed this time with proof of gainful employment to go along with his recent inheritance and his future prospects.

We don't know precisely when Villard won his beloved's blushing assent, but it was no later than May 15, for on May 20, a Monday, the future bride's astounded father wrote his son Wendell a letter that included an amusingly frank account of his paternal reaction to the happy news. This passage, which would not seem out of place in a Victorian novel, is worth quoting at length:

> Last Wednesday evening, I was called into the parlor by Fanny, and was taken by surprise by the announcement of Mr. Villard and herself that they had plighted their love to each other, and, as in duty bound, they wished me to give my fatherly sanction to the procedure! Of course, I had understood that, between them, there was a growing interest, which, on better acquaintance, and at some future day, might end in such an engagement; but this was so sudden as to be at least momentarily startling. My love for Fanny is so strong, and my estimate of her so high, that I have not been willing to entertain the thought of her cleaving to another in this manner. My acquaintance with Mr. Villard was next to nothing; he was of German birth, and I had no knowledge of or reference given me to his relatives

abroad; and though, relying upon your better acquaintance and positive appreciation of him, I had no doubt whatever as to his uprightness and manly honor, yet the whole affair was so sudden, and upon the face of it so hasty and impulsive, that I hardly knew what to say. However, what could I do but to tenderly acquiesce, with the hope that they fully understood and appreciated each other, and all would go well with them. They seem to be inexpressibly happy, and his whole behavior has been very honorable.

Garrison's words give us a glimpse of Henry Villard as seen through the eyes of the person with the very best motives for weighing him in the balance and finding him wanting. Though understandably anxious, the father of the bride-to-be is ready to accept the sudden Mr. Villard, whose conduct has been so exemplarily correct. In the course of a month, Villard had managed to take the daughter by storm while impressing the father with his honorable ways.

Shortly after he and Fanny announced their engagement, Villard also wrote a letter, the first of their acquaintance, to Wendell Garrison. Villard's only Garrison correspondent heretofore had been young Frank, but now he felt sure enough of his position to begin a correspondence with a significant older brother. He chose Wendell, the best educated (Harvard, 1861) and most intellectual of the Garrison children. Villard's letter is in one of his preferred modes, a mixture of sanctimonious canting and enthusiastic self-promotion. He asks for Wendell's friendship, assures him of his sincere love for Fanny, and expounds completely conventional attitudes concerning relationships between the sexes. He knows, he declares, that he can be made good by the love of a true woman, but soon it becomes apparent that he finds himself pretty good already: "I have no ignoble impulses. I aspire to ends, high and pure. I despise selfishness as heartily as yourself. My tastes and habits have never been vulgar. My aim of life is now identical with yours: the 'happiness of the woman I love' and 'intellectual distinction.' "

Obviously the two young men had engaged in some prior discussion of these matters, and Villard was not going to let anyone, not even a Garrison, outdo him in high-mindedness. Moreover, as Villard knew, Wendell himself was engaged to be married to one of Fanny's closest friends, Lucy McKim. Professing such noble sentiments to Wendell, Fanny's brother and her confidante's fiancé, was a kind of public relations effort for Villard, who was always eager to accumulate and display credentials. And like anyone who fancies himself a writer, he believed in the suasive power of words, especially his own. Often in his correspondence with the Garrisons, including Fanny, he would wax rhetorical, never seeming to realize that he wrote best when he gestured least.

Naturally Villard now began to spend as much time with Fanny and her family in Boston as his work in Washington allowed. During these visits he assiduously set about removing whatever doubts might have been troubling his future father-in-law in regard to Fanny's choice. The sensitive matters of Villard's family references (forthcoming) and Fanny's dowry (nonexistent) having been addressed in a more or less satisfactory manner, Garrison handed Villard a long letter (dated August 10, 1865) at the end of one of his visits to Boston.

To begin with, the conscientious father explains his initial hesitation to greet his daughter's engagement with unadulterated delight: Villard had been "an absolute stranger," the family had known nothing about his past, his antecedents, his qualifications; he had come to them on his own merits, "as they might be discovered on personal acquaintance." But now, Garrison continues,

> I am thoroughly satisfied that Fanny has made a wise and fortunate choice; that you possess an affectionate, generous and noble nature; that your intentions are in the highest degree honorable, and your aims pure and exalted; that you have an innate abhorrence of all hypocrisies and shams, and carry your heart in your hand, "like an open book"; that your love for Fanny is equalled only by her love for you; that you have alike a large brain and a large heart, and will be sure to employ both in the service of freedom and humanity; and that, as a family, we

may at all times safely rely upon your affectionate regard and friendly interest.

Garrison goes on to praise Fanny at length—she is "such as few parents have had the blessing to reckon among their children"—and attributes his inability to dower her to "a life consecrated to philanthropy," which has left him "without any pecuniary accumulation." Such an upbringing has made Fanny a girl with simple, quiet tastes, writes Fanny's frugal father, extolling the virtue of thrift for the edification of her future husband: "Be assured that you will best suit her wishes by avoiding whatever is extravagant or showy, and consulting only what is needed on the score of usefulness, beauty, and adaptation, all with a due regard to economical considerations."

For self-righteous rhetoric, for the urge to moralize, Villard had met his match. And indeed, one could scarcely expect Garrison, who for thirty-five years had preached morality to an entire nation, not to act a bit like Polonius. The above piece of paternal advice, however—namely, that Villard practice the virtue of penny-pinching—could hardly have been given to a man less likely to follow it. Villard's notion of what to do with money, when he had it, was to spend it hard and true. Garrison must have realized what he was dealing with before too long, but he never stopped making such recommendations; like Villard, he believed in the power of words to persuade. Both of them were, after all, journalists, both naturally gravitated to the critical and didactic modes, and each was delighted to publish his opinions.

A few days later, in his ceremonious reply to Garrison's letter, Villard gave as good as he got, describing to Garrison how his love for Fanny had exalted him: "It has filled me with the noblest ambition to do my whole duty to myself and fellow-man." This was enough; Garrison wrote back, saying that he and his wife "feel sure that you and Fanny were born for each other." Wedding plans began in earnest.

Meanwhile Villard had his job in Washington to attend to, and he was absent from Fanny for long periods of time, as he would be throughout their married life. In a letter dated October 30, he tells

Fanny of the extraordinary pleasure he takes in her letters, which he rereads regularly once a week and which are to him, "upon every perusal, sources of the holiest delight." So religious does he feel on this Sunday that he proposes to his betrothed a way for them, in their future united state, to keep holy the Lord's day without going to church: "This shall be our Sunday service: worship in the temple of pure love, comparison of our doings in each week to our standard of right and duty, and vows of improvement in case we find that we did not fully attain it."

The part about worshiping in the temple makes a promising beginning, but the rest sounds frankly intimidating. Less rigorous endearments followed, however, and the happy couple were joined in matrimony on January 3, 1866. About a month previously, Wendell had exchanged rings with Lucy McKim in Philadelphia; now Villard and Fanny plighted their troth in the parlor of the Garrison family home in Roxbury. Because it was built on a ledge of rock high above the street, the Garrisons called this large clapboard house Rockledge. The ceremony and reception at Rockledge were attended by the cream of abolitionist society, but none of Villard's relatives or old friends had made the trip to Boston. Such friends would have been in any case prevented from offering toasts; in the temperate Garrison home, no beverages containing alcohol might be consumed. The resulting enforced abstinence must have been a sore trial for a *Pfälzer* on his wedding day. As he would continue to do until he died, Villard showered Fanny with expensive presents, including a magnificent pearl brooch. The very next morning, from a room in Worcester, a joyous Fanny wrote her parents a letter bursting with gratitude and love.

Thus auspiciously united, Mr. and Mrs. Villard took up residence in Washington. The country was still quivering from the great trauma of the war, and the echo of Booth's derringer continued to reverberate in the air of the capital. President Johnson and the Congress had already begun their bitter struggle over Reconstruction and the treatment of the defeated South; there was no shortage of news. Harry (none of the Garrisons ever called him anything else) worked for the *Chicago Tribune,* Fanny busied herself with the requirements of her new home; they remained in close touch with Father and Mama, as they both called Fanny's parents. (Villard's family visit in 1864 had done little to soften his feelings toward his own father. When questioned by Garrison about his family, Fanny's suitor had answered in generalities, as though loath to dwell for long upon the thought of his parentage. Villard's readiness to bestow the paternal title elsewhere comes as no surprise.)

Villard was pounding the Washington political beat for the *Chicago Tribune,* but he had remained in friendly contact with the *New York Tribune* despite Horace Greeley's vexing capriciousness. Sydney Howard Gay, the *Tribune*'s managing editor, had tried more than once to lure his ace reporter back, and failing that had written him a radiant letter of recommendation, praising him to the skies as a professional journalist and as a person. In June, Gay sent Villard a wire, offering him a highly respectable salary and a generous expense allowance to cover for the *Tribune* the impending war between Prussia and Austria.

Villard was a natural choice for this assignment. He was an experienced war correspondent who spoke the language and knew the history and culture of the opposing states. And from his point of view, what could be better than a chance to travel (all expenses paid) with his new bride and introduce her to the civilization of old Europe, to the places and customs and influences that had formed him?

The Villards sailed early in July, but not before Garrison sent his daughter a farewell letter so like Polonius's admonitions to the departing Laertes that one expects at any moment to read that Fanny should neither a borrower nor a lender be.

Avoid the appearance of eccentricity, and learn to conform except in those cases where virtue is to be vindicated, a high morality exemplified, and principle adhered to, cost what it may. Consent to nothing that you conscientiously believe to be wrong. . . . Shun disputation. . . . Do not allow yourself to be drawn into any expensive, foolish, or unseemly custom as to dress.

The precepts march in serried ranks down the greater part of two pages. The ubiquitous European temptations of fashion, alcohol, nicotine, and other vulgar pleasures, the besetting dangers of lavish expenditure, are to be resolutely resisted. All Europe corrupts, as far as Garrison was concerned, and he was anxious lest Fanny acquire a taste for class distinctions and turn her back on radical politics. With better reason, he also feared that Harry would expose his wife to the unseemly influence and decadent tastes of European "gay society." Knowing nothing of his dour counterpart, Garrison enclosed a letter of joyful salutations to Gustav Hilgard and charged Villard with translating it for his father's benefit.

The Austro-Prussian War, also known as the Seven Weeks War, was deliberately provoked by Otto von Bismarck, minister president of Prussia. Playing a deep game whose ultimate goal was to unite Germany under Prussian domination, Bismarck had no intention of crushing Austria; indeed, he envisioned her as a future ally. His present purpose was simply to move her from his path and put her in her place, quickly and efficiently. By the time the Villards landed in Southampton, the war's major battle, a decisive Prussian victory known variously as Königgrätz, Hradec Králové, or Sadová, had been fought on July 3, the Prussians were nearing Vienna, and peace negotiations were already under way; Villard had sailed to Europe to cover a war that was virtually over.

The *Tribune*'s correspondent was not about to let such a detail as this end his assignment and abbreviate his European sojourn. He traveled by train with Fanny to Interlaken in central Switzerland, saw that she was safely settled in that lovely spot, and dashed off to Germany, determined to gather war news while it was still fresh. He was away from his new bride for a little more than a month, a separation that seemed long to them at the time but was in fact brief according to their later standards.

During this first prolonged separation of their married life, Villard—always a conscientious correspondent—wrote frequently to Fanny in Interlaken. These early examples of his correspondence with her, the first few of the many hundreds of letters that the roving, active husband wrote to his patiently waiting spouse down the years, exhibit characteristics that emerged consistently almost every time Harry took up his pen and addressed a few pages to his "Dearest darling," "Dearest love," "Dearest wife."

One immediately striking feature is his use of archaic second-person forms—"thou," "thy," and the like—a cloying Quakerish affectation no doubt picked up from the Garrisons, though Fanny was far less devoted to it than Harry. Equally noticeable is his tendency to address Fanny as though she were a child—"little wifey," "little bird," "my little girl"—and even to deliver the occasional sermon, instruction, or call to duty. His ailments and illnesses provide another constantly recurring theme, both because he indeed had wretched health and because he never wanted Fanny to think that he was enjoying himself very much without her. There is hardly a letter that does not express at some length, and sometimes with demure allusions to carnality, the pain he felt at their separation. Humor does not divert, nor wit distract, the no-nonsense forward stride of his prose.

Villard began his coverage of the Austro-Prussian War a few days after the signing of a preliminary treaty had put an end to hostilities. His plan was to talk to as many people, and to read as many reports, as he could find concerning the war; to visit the major battlefields, particularly Sadová; to find and interview combatants, eyewitnesses, and string pullers on both sides, high and low; and to distill this abundance of material, first, into informative articles for his newspaper, and then, possibly, into a book. His first stop was Munich, where he talked with various officials of the Bavarian government—Bavaria had unwisely thrown in its lot with Austria—and stayed in his father's house. After his first night there, he wrote Fanny a letter that set the tone for many more to come:

> And now my own, dearly beloved wife, I want to tell thee that I have thought of thee all the time and missed sadly the dear face, cheerful smile, and sweet kisses of the little girl—especially last night when I had to crawl alone under a mountain of feathers. Sweet one—I shall try to show my true love for thee by doing my whole duty and be back with you at the earliest possible moment. Ah, there is no one like thee.

This letter is signed, "Thy ardent lover, Harry."

Villard found his father "sadly changed to the worse." Gustav seemed physically weaker and intellectually diminished, interested only in trifling matters; his son tried and failed to engage him in conversation about the recent momentous events. In a rueful, revealing passage, Villard described to Fanny Gustav's response to her father's letter: "He told me, that to open communication with the relations of my wife would be a great embarrassment to him and he preferred to leave things as they are. This chilled me all over. Please don't write it home." Although not as agile as he once was, Gustav was still spry enough to pounce upon a fair opportunity to spite his son.

Villard moved on to Vienna, gloomy but still glittering, even in defeat, and stayed there for two weeks, conducting interviews, making forays into Moravia to retrace the path of the Prussian army, and attending operas and banquets, all the while longing to hug and kiss his little bird. He encourages her German studies; he knows, he says, that she will do her duty. At the formal dinner, he assures her, all the young ladies were ugly, and of the abundance of wine he took but one small glass. When he writes his book on the war, "the little girl will then have a chance to be very useful to me as a 'secretary.' "

Eventually Villard became ill—his usual symptoms: violent migraine, vomiting, leaping fever—and was confined for some days to his bed, pining for his little nurse, but well enough to observe to her that their separation was "good discipline" for both of them. Recovered, he set out for Moravia, where he got sick again, and then passed into Bohemia, whose towns and villages were "proverbial for squalor." Ill, weakened by bad food, wearied by bad lodging, at last he reached Sadová and the battlefield.

Although the battle was two months old, the witnesses he talked to, the terrain he examined, and the stinking field hospital he visited (where some of the casualties of the battle were still being cared for in conditions of unbearable squalor) confirmed the commitment to pacifism toward which he had been moving for several years. Now married into a family of pacifists, and having witnessed more than enough suffering to wring his heart, Villard remained opposed to war on principle for the rest of his life; two years before he died he joined his old friend Carl Schurz in a vehement protest against the United States' conflict with Spain.

In mid-September Fanny met Villard in Munich. Except for various forays to Austria, the Swiss Alps, and other parts of Germany, they made Munich their base through the winter of 1866–67. One of the attractions of the Bavarian capital must have been the nearness of Villard's family—father, aunt, sister, brothers-in-law—but Heinrich and his Frau seem to have taken separate lodgings of their own. Villard wrote articles for both *Tribune*s, Chicago and New York, giving a thorough, if belated, account of the recent war and then moving on to dispatches on Central European politics, especially those of the German states. His authoritative and insightful articles on this subject clearly reflected his liberal views.

Meanwhile he found plenty of time to act as Fanny's guide to the civilization of old Europe. They visited his birthplace and his Palatinate relatives; they admired the seasoned charms of Heidelberg and Salzburg; they went to castles and palaces, operas and theaters, gardens and parks, churches and museums. True to his promise, Villard was expanding his young wife's horizons, as well as those of his youngest brother-in-law, for Frank, taking advantage of the Villards' presence in Europe to spend a year abroad, had joined them there in October.

Ever hopeful of establishing some sort of contact with Gustav Hilgard, Frank's father prodded him by mail more than once, enjoining him to extend Garrison's compliments to Harry's father. This injunction went unfulfilled, for even at the Hilgard family's Christmas gathering Frank was unable to effect any sort of communication with Gustav, who sat as though on his judge's bench, remote from the company, and only occasionally turned his gaze outward. Garrison also wrote regularly to Fanny, sending her long, newsy, hortatory letters in which he deplored Harry's continuing headaches—caused, perhaps, by his tendency to gobble, rather than masticate, his food—and offered Fanny such tidbits of advice as, "Take care, darling, not to lose your native simplicity in regard to manners and dress, and vindicate your womanhood by high aims."

In March 1867 Horace White of the *Chicago Tribune* assigned Villard to cover the Paris Exhibition, one of the first world's fairs, and so Fanny, Frank, and Harry packed up and moved to the lively and fascinating capital of France, where the two native New Englanders, heirs to the Puritan tradition, must have encountered several examples of the insidious European evils against which their father kept warning them so strenuously.

For the liberator himself, 1867 was a year of vindication and triumph. In recognition of his long struggle and his lack of pecuniary accumulation, friends and supporters got together a subscription of $30,000, a sort of retirement fund that freed him from financial worries. He was selected as one of the three U.S. delegates to the International Anti-Slavery Conference scheduled for May in Paris, and plans for a triumphal tour of Great Britain were under way. On May 18, Garrison landed in Liverpool; two days later he arrived in Paris and was overjoyed when Fanny, Frank, and Villard met him at the train station. Several days later, in a letter to his wife, Garrison reported that "Harry and Fanny still appear to be in courtship rather than in a state of matrimony, by the admiration they feel and express for each other." He then went on to describe to Helen the splendors of Paris as seen through the exacting Garrisonian eye:

> It is the central point of the world for all that is splendid, fashionable, sensual, and frivolous. . . . It is "Vanity Fair," on a colossal scale . . . full of temptations and allurements to those who think only of present enjoyment, and forget all that relates to immortal life. . . . This must be Elysium to those who live in their animal nature.

Garrison's interpreter and guide through this maze of foreign decadence was, of course, his son-in-law, who lived somewhat in his animal nature, was not averse to present enjoyment, and viewed the great cities of Europe from an entirely different perspective. However, the two remained on the best of terms; until he died, Garrison's fascinated disapproval was never a match for Villard's enthusiasm, energy, and generosity.

On June 15 Fanny and Frank left Paris with their father, bound for England, and another, lengthier period of separation began for Mr. and Mrs. Villard. Harry had several good reasons for not accompanying the three Garrisons: his obligations as the Paris correspondent for Horace White's newspaper; the acute attacks of neuralgia that had been plaguing him for months; and his father's slow but steady decline. Villard's sister and other family members were keeping him closely apprised of Gustav's condition, and Gustav's only son, with profoundly mixed emotions, was awaiting an urgent summons to Munich.

William Lloyd Garrison was famous and popular in Great Britain, where it was widely believed that he and not Abraham Lincoln deserved the credit for striking off the slaves' fetters. His tour of England and Scotland with Fanny and Frank was a succession of victorious appearances, public and private, in the course of which he was thoroughly congratulated and admired. The high point in this crescendo of adulation was the breakfast held in his honor at St. James's Hall in London on June 29. Three hundred people attended, and several times as many had to be turned away. Many of Britain's principal reformers and leading intellectuals were on hand, including John Stuart Mill, Earl Russell, Herbert Spencer, and Thomas Henry Huxley; Charles Darwin, Gladstone, the Comte de Paris, United States ambassador Charles Francis Adams, and others sent laudatory messages and regrets at their inability to attend. Fanny and Frank, their eyes glowing with pride and love, listened as several speakers, among them Mill and the chairman of the breakfast, the duke of Argyll, heaped praise upon their noble father, who replied with an exuberant and thunderously applauded speech.

Meanwhile Villard languished in Paris. Though Fanny had asked him to cross over to London, attend the breakfast, and share the joy of her father's great moment, Villard had declined. In a letter written on June 27, two days before, he declared that he was "making a painful sacrifice" in denying himself this pleasure, but he cited the foulness of the weather, the expense of the trip, his bad cold, his diarrhea. After the fact, when it had become clear to him how important and meaningful the testimonial breakfast had been to Garrison and his family, Villard was overcome with guilt for not having bestirred himself, and in several abject, writhing letters to Fanny he was at pains to persuade her of the great distress his decision to stay away had cost him. Indeed, his sense of having failed Fanny seemed to exacerbate his ill health, and he began to suffer more than usual from racking headaches, sleepless nights, and general anxiety.

Part of Villard's problem was his dawning realization that a foreign correspondent's salary, even if combined with a generous expense account, was not going to allow him to live as he desired. There was certainly no dearth of news in Paris—the gigantic (it covered forty-one acres), impressive exhibition in the Champ de Mars, the endless cosmopolitan stream of famous visitors, the maneuvering of Napoleon III's government, the endemic French political unrest—but his career, after its meteoric rise in the Civil War, seemed now to have flattened out. Although he wrote long, authoritative articles for various American journals on subjects ranging from the wonders exhibited at the world's fair to the deep tangles of French and German politics, relatively few of his pieces were printed, and he was involved in disputes over compensation even with such old friends as George Smalley and Horace White. The simple truth was that his dispatches from Europe were not as immediate, vivid, or gripping—not, in short, as good—as those he produced during the Civil War. A good story was no longer of paramount importance to him, no longer worth any risk, and his current journalistic work went forward amid powerful distractions, both pleasant and unpleasant. Villard's focus had started to shift.

Already the previous year, in his correspondence with William Lloyd Garrison Jr. (a wool merchant, the only businessman among Garrison's sons), Villard had evinced his interest in such business matters as gold speculation and transatlantic money transfers. Now, living beyond his means and exercising a profession unlikely to make him much richer, Villard indulged his penchant for mixing fantasy and penetration and dreamed about a more lucrative career. He could not yet envision its precise shape, but he knew he would find it only in America. "I realize very well," he wrote to Fanny in July, "that there is no future for me in Europe, that all my hopes and aspirations for success in life are bound up with the United States and that hence all the time I remain abroad will be so much time wasted."

The summer of 1867 was a fairly low point in Villard's life. Physically beleaguered, financially strapped—his mother's inheritance had long since vanished, and his various creditors included Will Garrison—and separated from Fanny (their separations seemed worse when *she* was the one traveling), he alternated daydreams of future success with nightmares of anxiety and guilt. With his talent for projection, he imagined that it was Fanny's heart and not his own that was dead set on great material success and a life of genteel splendor, and next he brought himself to dread the prospect of disappointing her, of losing her good opinion through insufficient accumulation. His worst sufferings, however, revolved as they always had around his feelings for his father. Gustav was clearly dying, yet Heinrich hesitated to go to him in Munich, felt guilty about hesitating, felt he was not doing his duty, and still didn't go. He kept from Fanny, and probably from himself, the real reason why he was in no hurry to begin the final struggle with his lifelong adversary.

Early in August, however, Villard received a summons he could not ignore, gave up his Paris lodgings, and went to Munich. His letters to Fanny, who was still traveling with her father and brother, describe Gustav's descent into death in excruciating detail. Almost too weak to talk, Gustav nevertheless was capable of indicating when he wanted some unpleasant service or other performed—usually by Villard—and of dismissing his assistant with a sign when the service was completed. Otherwise he hardly spoke to his son or anybody else, and by means of gestures and glares he generally insisted on being left alone in his room.

Gustav lingered for a month as Villard grew more agitated and depressed. The old man was all but speechless during his last two weeks of life, and it seems probable that father and son never reconciled. Shortly after Gustav's death, Villard told Will Garrison with inadvertent candor that his father "was never nearer to my heart than during the last few weeks," that is, during the period when he was least alive.

On September 1, at the age of sixty, Gustav Hilgard died in his bed. Villard's letter to Fanny, written a few hours after his father's death, is a curious document. Although it purports to convey the heartbreak of a loving and dutiful son, it reads more like a florid rhetorical exercise, as though Villard, conscious of what Fanny would feel in his place, sought to reach a level of grief commensurate with Garrisonian standards. "Dearly loved wife," he begins, "The worst is come! My dear, dear father is no longer among the living." There follows a long, step-by-step description of Gustav's last hours, until finally

> his breath ceased as suddenly as the light of a snuffed out candle.
>
> Thus the sufferings of my dearly loved father came to an end. I closed his eyes and kissed his dear face for the last time.
>
> I am so absolutely overcome that I cannot give expression to my overwhelming grief. . . .
>
> I am so nervous that I can hardly hold a pen. The only solace I look to now is your love. . . .
>
> Thy grief-stricken Harry

In his next letter, written after the funeral, Villard prudently indicates that Fanny should consider his feelings of filial bereavement in terms of what her own would be: "What I felt when I paid the last tribute to the dear remains and cast the last glance at the coffin you can easily imagine."

One positive note amid all this grief was Villard's inheritance from his late father. Though he never talked about any family fortune, preferring to present himself as a self-made man, Villard's share in his father's estate was obviously large enough to enable him to pay his debts and feel free from financial worries for some time. His father's death, he said, released him from any obligation to remain in Europe, yet eight more months were to pass before the Villards returned to America. In the fall of 1867 they toured Switzerland with Garrison and Frank, parting from them in early October in Zurich, whence father and son began a slow journey back to Boston and the Villards made their way to Paris once again.

Villard continued to write dispatches as he and Fanny decided what to do. Genteel living cost considerably less in Europe than in America, and Villard's inheritance from Gustav would last longer if they remained abroad. In February 1868, after Harry filed one last world's fair story, the Villards left Paris and traveled to Italy. On the way they stopped at Avignon and visited John Stuart Mill, who was living there in retirement. The great philosopher and champion of women's rights knew Fanny from the Garrisons' recent trip to England and received the young couple quite warmly. Recognizing a journalistic opportunity, Villard took notes on the conversation and sent an interesting and well-received dispatch to the *Chicago Tribune*. Later, in a coup reminiscent of his Civil War days, he and Fanny happened to be in Naples when Mount Vesuvius erupted. An Italian professor offered him the use of his observatory, an ideal vantage point, and the reporter was able to send to Chicago a vivid eyewitness account of the eruption. At this point he was treating journalism as something of an avocation, a by-product of his elegant travels with his bride, but he was prudent enough to keep his hand in the game.

Late in May 1868, after a European sojourn of nearly two years, the Villards sailed for Boston. Judging from the fact that they went to live with Fanny's parents and two of her brothers, George and Frank, at Rockledge—a comfortable enough place, perhaps, but no one's idea of genteel living—we may conclude that Villard's inheritance had proved less durable than he thought. In any case, he assented to Garrison's reiterated offer of rooms in the family home, and it was there that Fanny gave birth to their first child, Helen Elise, at the end of June.

Once again, Villard worked as a freelance journalist, writing articles and editorials for several newspapers (among them the Boston *Daily Advertiser*) and magazines. One of these was a new but already prestigious magazine called the *Nation*, whose literary editor was Wendell Garrison. With the exception of a long, prescient article on Bismarck, at that time hardly known in the United States, little of what Villard produced in this period was successful; his writing was conscientious, thorough, gloomy, and heavy as a stone, totally lacking in the immediacy of his Civil War pieces. His blinding migraines, now an almost continual source of torment, may have been partly to blame.

Ready for a change of direction, Villard took advantage of Garrison's connections to obtain an introduction to leading members of the American Social Science Association, an organization dedicated to liberal reforms. This society, founded in 1865 and based in Boston, counted among its members many of the country's leading intellectuals, scientists, and politicians, as well as a number of businessmen and industrialists. In short order Villard was invited to join the association, elected its secretary, and made the editor of its new quarterly, the *Journal of Social Science.* In the leading article he wrote for the first issue, Villard identified the "high aim" of social science: "the discovery and application of the immutable laws governing man and his social relations." The journal's task was to further and clarify this aim by opening avenues of inquiry and diffusing information.

In practice the pursuit of the society's elevated goals was parceled out among various committees, which concentrated on such broad areas as education, health, economy, and jurisprudence, with progress duly reported in the journal. In addition to this work, Villard devoted much time to fund-raising for the society, to programs for the assistance of newly arrived immigrants—he remembered his own early days on American soil—and especially to civil service reform. His work required a certain amount of traveling (usually to New York, but also to Chicago, Washington, Philadelphia) and brought him into frequent association with the kind of people he preferred: successful, prominent, wealthy, powerful, influential. Although his new job was unlikely to make him rich, it gave him the opportunity to pursue his interests in journalism and politics, to further the liberal causes he supported, and to increase his acquaintance with people at the highest levels of American society.

As always when he traveled, Villard wrote faithfully to Fanny, and as always, with great solemnity, he forswore traveling forever. "I don't believe you will have much to fear hereafter from my roaming propensities," he wrote from New York on January 8, 1869. "My wife and child seem to me now truly the greatest attractions in the world." One wonders that he was able to travel at all, for his letters are filled with the litany of his physical ailments—the noises in his head, his sudden fevers, his lengthy vomiting bouts, the disabling pains in his head and joints. He often visited doctors while traveling, though he balked at the expense; once again the Villards' finances were tight, and from time to time he slipped a ten-dollar bill into the envelopes he mailed to Fanny, hoping to tide her over until he returned to Boston.

Villard had found a way of moving in the best circles on a very modest salary. Late in October, on another trip to New York, he described for Fanny, nearly eight months pregnant, a dinner he had attended at the home of one George Cabot Ward, "the rich banker." After the dinner, a large party had adjourned to the home of Lawrence Godkin, the editor of the *Nation;* among them, and enraptured, was Henry Villard: "About thirty gentlemen of the highest social position were present—as fine a body of men as I have ever seen anywhere."

It was during the period of his secretaryship that Villard began a serious study of economics and finance, applying himself with more interest, determination, and thoroughness than he had ever been able to bring to his formal education. He eventually focused on banking, and especially on the relationship between banking practices and working class unrest, both in Europe and in the United States. He also began to ponder profitable ways of acting as a middleman between European investors, especially German financial institutions, and the American economy, in whose solidity, prosperity, and potential for expansion he never ceased to believe. Certain German banks, he learned, might be particularly interested in investing in American railroads.

The Villards' second child, a son they named Harold Garrison Villard, was born on December 3, 1869. The birth was difficult, and Fanny recovered from it slowly. On December 16, her twenty-fifth birthday, Harry had to carry her downstairs so that she could preside at the supper table. "I felt so old," she confided to her diary.

Fanny's diary entries from this period show how cozily domestic her Rockledge existence was, even when Harry was on the road. She attended her parents, admired her children, played the piano, took long walks, read her husband's ardent letters ("Adieu, sweet girl in blue"), and looked for the right cook or housekeeper (even middle-class households of extremely modest means, such as the Garrison-Villard household in Roxbury, employed servants). Villard, however, was not so well content as his wife. The harsh climate of Boston had aggravated several of his preexisting conditions, principally the se-vere catarrh that forced him to be miserably conscious of every breath, as well as a constant sensation of hearing noises inside his head. His condition worsened relentlessly; desperate measures seemed to be required; and in September 1870 he resigned from the association, kissed wife and children good-bye, and sailed alone for Germany.

The purpose of his trip was twofold. First of all, he hoped to ob-tain some effective medical treatment, for no American doctor and no home remedy—no pills, no powders, no poultices, no plasters, no concoctions of boiled daisies or camphor bark—had served to alle-viate his inflamed membranes, his constant coughing, his splitting headaches. Second, he wanted to discuss with the right people some of the business schemes that were taking shape in his busy imagina-tion. Impressed by Villard's work for the Social Science Association, Jay Cooke, an important American financier then engaged in pro-moting the Northern Pacific Railroad, had sought his advice on the subject of increasing German immigration to the railroad's lands; their extended correspondence had whetted Villard's interest in business matters and focused his attention on the future of railroads in America. At the same time, on Will Garrison's advice, Villard had entered into negotiations with an Englishman named William Law-son, who wanted someone to act as his agent in some large stock transactions. Although Villard's relationship with the vacillating Law-son was long, tormented, and ultimately frustrating, it brought him experience in stock brokerage, some tidy profits, and growing insight into the upper reaches of high finance. He would "prove a great noo-dle in business," he remarked to Fanny, if he couldn't make enough money to "live comfortably" and still manage to save at least $1,000 a year. Villard was beginning to discover in himself a talent for busi-ness on the grand scale.

The pain that this separation caused both Henry and Fanny was a main theme of the frequent letters they exchanged. In addition, she worried about his health and gave him earnestly detailed accounts of their children's everyday activities; equally earnest, he described his medical adventures and the progress of his business projects and spoke longingly and tenderly of the "babes." He stayed for some time in Würzburg, undergoing treatment—or, otherwise stated, the tortures of the damned—from a famous eye, ear, nose, and throat specialist, one Professor Troeltsch. While explaining his symptoms to the professor, Villard told Fanny, he was in such an agitated state that he burst into tears. Over the course of several weeks of "manipulations," Troeltsch diagnosed his condition as "catarrh of the left ear with accompanying nervous prostration," removed an enormous polyp from inside his nose, and punctured one of his eardrums three times in an attempt to relieve the pressure in his head. These painful operations, which Villard depicted in gruesome detail for Fanny's benefit, brought him some relief, though it proved to be only temporary. In any case, for a time the noises grew quiet, his coughing subsided, his headaches were more bearable, his digestive process less troubled.

The rest of his German sojourn was taken up with visiting relatives in the Palatinate and Bavaria and conferring with bankers in Berlin. He laid before these interested gentlemen a detailed, careful scheme, the product of much study and excogitation, for establishing mortgage banks in the United States to take advantage of the territorial and economic expansion that marked the nation's recovery from its attempted suicide.

The positive reception the Berlin bankers gave his ideas raised Villard's hopes and mitigated his health problems. Early in 1871 he sailed for Boston, eager to begin work on winning approval from the Massachusetts legislature for his mortgage bank charter. His association with the aggravating Lawson had at least proved lucrative enough for him to afford expensive medical care and an instructive four months in Europe. His health was by no means restored, but the thought of seeing Fanny and his children again enlivened him.

The mortgage bank scheme, alas, went the way of the Kansas

land scheme and the Colorado gold rush guide scheme, pretty good ideas that could have used a little luck. The only profit Villard drew from this one was the entrée it had given him into German financial circles. As his prospects declined, so did his health, and at Rockledge he sat brooding in the parlor while that enthusiastic valetudinarian, his father-in-law, questioned him closely about his multifarious symptoms and suggested various remedies, not eschewing quackery. Soon Villard was as sick as ever, and once again he thought he could be cured by an extensive sojourn on his native soil. Neither he nor Fanny could consider another lengthy separation—she was in the early months of her third pregnancy—and in the fall of 1871 they and their two children sailed for Germany.

In Villard's absence, the victors in the Franco-Prussian War had unified Germany at last; King Wilhelm of Prussia was now Kaiser Wilhelm of Germany, and Otto von Bismarck was the kaiser's Iron Chancellor. This was, of course, not the democracy that Villard and his friends had imagined when they dreamed of a united Germany, but he was much too sick for politics. The family spent the winter of 1871–72 in Wiesbaden, a town known for its hot springs, where they were joined on March 13, 1872, by their third child, Oswald Garrison Villard.

In April, having soaked at length in the waters of Wiesbaden, he felt healthy enough to set about the business of generating income. Before leaving America, Villard had proposed himself as a foreign agent for Wisconsin Central Railroad bonds, and the president of the Wisconsin Central, an acquaintance made during Villard's stint with the Social Science Association, had agreed; now the agent was on his way to Frankfurt, the financial center of Germany, to see if he could make his bright vision of America's railroad future enter some hard bankers' heads.

He was not immediately successful, but lack of persistence was never one of his problems. Eventually he persuaded one bank to purchase a quantity of Wisconsin Central bonds and pocketed a handsome commission, enough to allow him and his family, accompanied by two servants, to spend the summer of 1872 in Switzerland. Although Professor Troeltsch had warned him against mental strain,

Villard was hard at work while his family were on holiday. His ongoing struggle with Lawson over the extremely mutable terms of their agreement was conducted by mail, but other affairs required him to make frequent forays into Germany. He was still (though with diminishing hope) exploring ways to carry out his mortgage bank plan, he was still trying to float Wisconsin Central bonds, and he had a few other schemes, in all of which he featured as the broker, the intermediary between two worlds. He was talking himself into a new career.

In early fall Villard and his family moved for the winter to Heidelberg, a picturesque town situated not far from Speyer. Frankfurt, too, was within easy reach, and Villard was able to renew his assault on that city's bankers. He was by this time quite well known in Frankfurt's banking circles and seemed to be on the verge of closing some highly satisfactory negotiations when a sudden financial panic swept across Germany. Overnight it became impossible for anyone, no matter how well connected, to persuade the grim-faced money lords of Frankfurt that what they needed to do with their teetering golden piles was to tip a few of them in the direction of someplace called Wisconsin.

Villard saw months of hard work and high expectations dashed. Soon the migraines were worse, and the coughing fits, and the noises. One day shortly after Christmas, a great wave of malaise swept over him, leaving him nervous and trembling. At last, on December 28, Villard reached the culmination of several years of increasingly bad health: his eyes bulging, his face the color of blood, he fell full length to the floor in his Heidelberg residence and lay there, motionless and speechless, until the distraught Fanny could find enough people to shift his bulky frame and carry him to bed. Several doctors were summoned, and they all used the same words: *Apoplexie, Gehirnschlag.* The patient, thirty-seven, a tall stout man with a florid complexion, had suffered a stroke.

According to Fanny's diary, Harry's poststroke therapy included ice, mustard baths, belladonna, and aconite. As his condition improved it became clear that his mental faculties as well as his power of speech were intact, but his doctors thought it unlikely that his motor functions would return. They distressed Fanny by telling her that her husband, should he live, would probably dwindle into a vegetable state, and they warned Villard that he could never again perform mental labor without endangering his life. Years later, writing his memoirs, Villard made these doctors the subject of an outburst that is the definition of schadenfreude. "They themselves did not live long enough to see their predictions falsified," he chortled.

Before long he was moving about gingerly, regaining dexterity, growing calmer. His head, less troubled by noises and migraines, seemed rather better than it had before the stroke. Though his financial prospects looked decidedly bleak, Villard had the comfort of knowing that he would recover physically. In February 1873, while continuing to recuperate, he received an unexpected visit. The caller—someone he knew vaguely, a banking acquaintance—was the messenger of fate, and when he entered the room, Villard's life changed.

JAY GOULD.

Photograph c. 1875. Carbinet card by Sarony.

Collection of the New-York Historical Society.

17

Working on
the Railroad

I like to see it lap the Miles—
And lick the Valleys up—
And stop to feed itself at Tanks—
And then—prodigious step

Around a Pile of Mountains. . . .

EMILY DICKINSON,
"I Like to See It Lap the Miles"

V illard's unexpected visitor was an investor who had sunk a
great deal of good German capital into an American outfit
called the Oregon & California Railroad Company. Now he
was beginning to question the value of the bonds he had purchased
in such abundance and with such high expectations, for despite excellent prospects and spectacular initial reports, the Oregon & California had defaulted on its recent interest payments. The investor's
money, already seven thousand miles away, was threatening to move
definitively out of reach, and the perplexed gentleman needed wise,
well-informed counsel. He fondly hoped that Villard's activities on
behalf of the Wisconsin Central Railroad, his long residence in
America, his familiarity with the American West, and his fluency in
English—all of which were common knowledge in Frankfurt banking circles—might qualify him to be a source of such counsel. Speaking with some agitation, the caller presented his case to the
convalescent.

Interested but cautious—he knew little of Oregon, and nothing about the Oregon & California Railroad—Villard requested more information, studied the voluminous material made available by the bondholders' Protective Committee (which represented all the European holders of Oregon & California bonds), and some days later, after due consideration, gave his banking acquaintance an opinion concerning the health of his investment. Naturally, Villard pulled no punches, and so depressing was his diagnosis—the patient was gravely ill—that several more grief-stricken investors arrived at his door, among them the chairman of the Protective Committee. Impressed by Villard's seriousness and familiarity with the details of American railroad financing, the members of the committee formally invited him to join their number, but he didn't feel sufficiently recuperated to accept. By spring he was much improved, and the invitation was renewed. Having requested and received the assurance that "not much work was expected of me," Villard decided to join the committee.

It was thus, four months after suffering a stroke, that he embarked upon the most extraordinary of his several careers. As was so often the case in Villard's life, a fortuitous combination of circumstances, a piece of luck, put him in the right place at the right time; but he prepared for luck as others might prepare for trouble, and he was ready for luck when it came. Although he had, as he declared, "nothing resembling a regular training for business pursuits," his personality, his tastes, his experiences, his talents, and his ambitions all fitted him for the kind of success enjoyed by the self-made men he admired. With some truth, Villard gave credit for his accomplishments of the next ten years to "the training in enterprise, perseverance, and resourcefulness which I owed to my previous occupations," but this only partially explains the matter. Novalis, one of the German Romantics whose works Villard read so avidly in his youth, is the author of a famous aphorism—roughly translatable as "Character is fate"—that Villard's life seemed to exemplify. Passionate for success, he succeeded; driven to excel, he excelled; after dreaming so long of fortune and fame, he saw his dreams come true. Striving, for him, was a mode of being, but he strove purposefully, helping fate along by such astute measures as his prescient study of railroads and their financing in the early 1870s. Moreover, as even one of his severest critics admits, Villard was naturally "quick-witted, magnetic and eloquent," and he achieved success almost effortlessly because "he attracted friends and followers everywhere." For Oswald Garrison Villard, his father's spectacular "rise in the railroad world" could be attributed to "vision plus character, plus brains, plus unflagging energy, plus the belief that he could thus repay his debt to his adopted country."

Everything began calmly enough. While a delegation from the Protective Committee assigned to inspect conditions on the ground in Oregon was making the long round trip, Villard had little to do but continue his convalescence. The delegation returned with a discouraging report on the financial prospects of the Oregon & California, which confirmed this appraisal by defaulting on its next interest payment. Reaching a conclusion that he would later call "a great mistake," Villard and the committee decided against foreclosure—what would they do with an impecunious railroad operating in a foreign country an ocean and a continent away?—and sought to salvage the bondholders' investment by arriving at a compromise with the owner of the road, an idiosyncratic personage named Ben Holladay.

At this point Villard became more than a consultant to the bondholders; he was the natural choice both to draw up the compromise and to represent the committee in its American negotiations with Holladay. Working out the terms of the compromise required Villard to spend a good deal of time in Frankfurt between October 1873 and April 1874. During this period, as the quality of his work became known and his aptitude for it apparent, his reputation in banking circles grew, and he found himself (nothing loath) Frankfurt's resident expert on the American West, American business practices, and American railroad securities. Before long another group of worried gentlemen, investors in the faltering Kansas Pacific Railroad, approached him and asked him to represent them as well. The Kansas Pacific was seriously in arrears on its interest payments, and its bondholders wanted Villard to conclude arrangements for funding these payments with the owners of the road.

Thus charged with two missions on behalf of German capital investment in the United States, Villard sailed to America with his family in April 1874. Fanny and her three children, to her parents' great delight, moved back into Rockledge, while Harry's full agenda required his presence in New York. (Both Villard and the bondholders' committee seemed to have forgotten their assurances that his workload would remain light.) One of his first activities in the big, dirty, bustling city was a meeting with Ben Holladay.

Rough-hewn, untroubled by scruple, devoid of culture, Ben Holladay typified what might be called the buccaneer capitalism of his generation. He was born in 1819, another product of the log cabins of Kentucky, which appear to have possessed significant formative powers. Holladay couldn't read books, but he could read signs, and he had early foreseen the immense riches to be derived from providing transportation and scooping up government land grants in the expanding American West. By 1866 he was the "Stagecoach King" of the vast territory between Kansas and the Pacific Ocean, and after he sold his giant network of stagecoaches, freight wagons, steamboats, and riverboats to Wells, Fargo and Company a few years later, he went to Oregon with enough money to acquire politicians, newspapers, and a couple of railroads on the way to gaining control of a huge federal land grant.

But Holladay's new empire, like his boastfulness, his name-dropping, his flashy jewelry, his many mansions, his extravagant parties, was a façade that hid "a surprisingly shaky foundation. He was forever rearranging his holdings by creating or merging subsidiaries. His steamship and railroad interests were interlocked in a bewildering arrangement of double pledging their securities to creditors." With this system the ignorant, analphabetic Holladay had managed to fool some of "the shrewdest and most experienced bankers in Europe" into financing his hollow operation, a gaudy bluff whose goal was to monopolize the transportation business in Oregon while benefiting from the perquisites, privileges, and outright donations the government used to encourage such energetic entrepreneurs as himself.

Although Villard and Holladay shared some traits—both looked at Oregon and calculated its potential for profitability, both were naturally inclined to overreaching, each in his own way liked to display the symbols of his success—their manners and tastes clearly marked them as belonging to different classes. The aristocratic Villard's reaction to this uncouth man was predictably unfavorable; he found Holladay "illiterate, coarse, pretentious, boastful, false, and cunning." Holladay physically repelled Villard, and we may amuse ourselves by picturing their encounters: Villard sits tall and erect, while above his heavy mustache his nostrils flare in disdain; the shorter, portlier, much more elaborately bewhiskered Holladay shifts his chair ever closer and soon begins to slap Villard's wellborn knee with his meaty peasant's hand, punctuating his stream of inane conversation with iterations of his verbal tic, "Don't you know."

As it turned out, Villard did. He saw through Holladay's bluff almost at once, realized that he was in financial extremities, and meticulously set about stripping him of his power. Villard's keen observations of Holladay must have focused and encouraged his own mounting ambitions. If this mendacious boor, this transparent fraud, was able to command great masses of foreign capital, what might he, Henry Villard, a man of integrity and high purpose, expect to command? What financial weapons might he not wield? Despite various nagging ailments, he was comparatively healthy again, his energy was up, he was rested, well nourished, ready for action. In fact he was stouter than ever, and he wrote to Fanny about his dietary resolutions, which he would have occasion to renew: "I only hope that my waist shall steadily waste away henceforth until I shall be as slender as when you first knew me. May be you will fall in love with me again then." As he neared forty, Villard had lost the lean and hungry look of his war correspondent days. Now he was a highly placed, well-paid representative of important foreign financial interests, and his person, like his way of life, had grown stately.

In May 1874, accompanied by his German financial agent, an engineer named Richard Koehler, Villard set out for the West Coast. They traveled by special trains on lines belonging to the Wisconsin Central, whose interests Villard had once represented in Germany, and the Kansas Pacific, his next project after the Oregon & California. On the way to San Francisco, they crossed the Great Plains, which Villard had first seen as the sole passenger on the maiden journey of the Leavenworth-to-Denver stagecoach run, fifteen years previously, in 1859, when there were only five hundred miles of railroad track between the Mississippi River and the Pacific Ocean. Then the buffalo in their millions had roamed the plains, grazing their way south and then north in the ancient cycle of their great seasonal migrations; now the huge animals were nowhere to be seen. The only evidence of their recent presence was trainloads of their bones, which were being hauled to the East, where they could do some good. Later in 1859, when Villard drove a two-horse wagon out of Denver, bound for St. Louis, he left behind him a rough, ramshackle town of about two hundred scattered shanties and cabins. Now the population had climbed past forty thousand, and those hovels had long since disappeared. Villard was able to gauge with his own eyes the dimensions of the country's surging westward expansion.

Villard and Koehler stopped for several weeks in San Francisco to inspect Holladay's operation. The thriving town fascinated Villard, especially the Chinese section. In a letter to Fanny dated June 24, 1874, he described how Asian immigrants had "literally transformed a large part of San Francisco into a Chinese City, swarming with tens of thousands of hair-tailed Mongolians & containing tea-houses, opium-smoking rooms, joss houses, theatres. . . . I have spent hours in canvassing the Chinese & watching the curious life there."

In the course of his less exotic investigations—those into Holladay's books—Villard made the startling discovery that one of the Oregon & California's lines, against which Holladay had issued $3 million in bonds, was but an insubstantial thing; it had never been constructed, and Holladay had diverted the money to other ends, not all of which were apparent. The disclosure of this and other frauds perpetrated by Holladay and his lawyer, a refined but shifty individual named Latham, gained Villard increased prestige in European financial circles and increased his leverage in his struggle with the contemptible Holladay.

In mid-July Villard and Koehler left San Francisco for Portland.

The journey seemed calculated to highlight Holladay's unfulfilled promises to his investors: a five-day stagecoach run between Redding, California, and Roseburg, Oregon, covered a gap of some 250 miles in the Oregon & California's line. Although the long ride in the coach was oppressively hot and dusty, the pristine, rugged beauty of Oregon heightened the excitement that Villard always felt in the American West and made him glad of his journey. The land seemed timeless, boundless, inexhaustibly rich, infinite in its possibilities.

It was after midnight when the special coach carrying Villard and Koehler clattered up to the railroad platform in Roseburg, southernmost station on the Oregon portion of the Oregon & California line. Out of the shadows a large white figure moved toward them, billowing like a ghost, and called out, "Hallo, here are the Dutchmen!" Obnoxious, jovial, dressed in his nightshirt, Ben Holladay escorted his dusty guests to his private railroad car.

Early the next morning the special train started for Portland, about 180 miles away at the northern end of the long, broad Willamette valley, which lay lush and fertile in the hot July sun. Villard needed none of Holladay's irksome prodding to appreciate the grandeur and richness of the scenery they passed through, the mountain ranges to the west and east, the vast forests of Douglas fir, the enormous fields of wheat, the flourishing orchards. He felt, he said, "as though I had reached a chosen land," whose promise could not fail to result in prosperity. As he gazed out the window, Villard saw what his European constituents must do to salvage their investments: invest more! If rail and water transportation could be brought "under one honest, efficient, and permanent control"—Villard believed in benevolent monopoly—the state's development would accelerate, to the mutual profit of all concerned. Villard envisioned a bright and orderly future for Oregon, when its vast resources would be properly exploited and its timber, its farm products, and its people duly shifted about on a rational, integrated system of ships, steamboats, and trains. In the event, as he later admitted, his confidence in western Oregon's capacity for development and growth proved excessive, too sanguine for the region's real possibilities, but for the time being his hopeful vision remained intact, growing and evolving in his mind.

In Portland Holladay and Villard signed agreements; Villard affixed his name no fewer than 240 times. The compromise he and the bondholders had sought was achieved, and Villard hurried away, glad to be out of Holladay's unedifying company and never expecting to see Oregon again. After a brief stop in Boston to embrace Fanny and the babes, he sailed for Germany, where he submitted a long printed report to the committee in Frankfurt, attempting to convey to his colleagues some of his absolute faith in Oregon's future. He suggested that they should devise ways of attracting northern European immigrants to Oregon; the committee nodded agreement and commissioned Villard to set up an immigration bureau in New York. For people invested in Oregon railroads, promoting Oregon immigration was a way of securing future customers and their own prosperity.

Villard landed back in New York in the fall and learned that Holladay had welshed on various aspects of the compromise he'd signed and refused to comply with others; a year of work had gone for nought, and a grim Villard prepared for the unpleasant task of renegotiating the entire agreement. By the time the former Stagecoach King arrived in the East, where he habitually spent the winter, Villard, determined not to be thwarted again, had him bound so tightly with stout legal and financial cords that he twisted and whined and finally signed a new compromise of Villard's own devising. According to its terms, Holladay surrendered control of the Oregon & California, of another railroad, named the Oregon Central, and of the Oregon Steamship Company, the only regular connection (Portland–San Francisco) between Oregon and the rest of the world. It had been a long struggle, but Villard had finally succeeded in eliminating Holladay from the picture.

This success sent Villard back to Europe in the spring of 1875, seeking Holladay's creditors' consent to the new compromise. By the time he addressed his constituents, Villard had big plans to lay before them, plans not rich in detail but vast and sweeping: to corner

the transportation market in Oregon; to build it, expand it, and improve it, and by so doing make it profitable; and to increase efforts
to encourage immigration to Oregon from within the United States
and emigration to Oregon from among the industrious peoples of
Germany, Scandinavia, and England. The German investors agreed
to support Villard's plan; so did the English investors; and Villard was
appointed to manage the entire operation. For this grave responsibility he would, of course, be amply remunerated.

By November Villard was back in New York, intensifying the efforts of his Oregon immigration bureau, for which he personally
composed a variety of brochures and other advertising material for
national and international distribution. He was also deeply involved
in managing his Oregon companies as best he could from a continent away, and his intermittent, profitable, but inconclusive wran-
gling with the snarled affairs of the Kansas Pacific continued.

By May 1876, when Villard, once again in Portland, was elected
president of the Oregon & California Railroad, the Oregon Steamship Company, and a couple of other Oregon companies, he found
himself standing at the end of a rainbow. In the steady stream of
letters (at least one and sometimes two or three a week) he wrote to
Fanny during this period (1874–76), when he was so frequently away,
Villard revealed his slightly incredulous excitement as it dawned on
him how very much money he was going to make riding the railroads.
Brokering fees, dividends, stock profits, commissions, interest on investments, and other financial arrangements were bringing him a
princely and steadily growing income. He faithfully reported to
Fanny his recurring coups, calling her, for example, his "darling
greediness" and teasing her by implying that she was materially insa-
tiable. A more straightforward letter conveys to her, his obviously sympathetic and admiring audience, the joyous thrill of the man who has
ventured and gained:

> I knew you would be mad at me for not returning to-day, but I
> am sure that the wrath of my little wife will be appeased when I
> tell her that her great "schemer" has now in his pocket nine

thousand Dollars clear profit made this week and that he expects his labors to be eventually rewarded by more than as much more!

The days when, nervous about his own limited business experience, he would grant Fanny a bit of lordly praise for having ordinary common sense—in 1872 he had called her decision to send him a copy rather than the original of an important document "a great piece of smartness on your part which makes me think that thee will be a fine business-wifey yet"—were long gone. Fanny had become his confidante and collaborator, frequently acting as his secretary and consulted on all his most important decisions.

In the fall the Villards' plans to move the family to Oregon were canceled by complications in the affairs of the Kansas Pacific, whose already low earnings had been further reduced by several successive crop failures in the state. As in the case of the Oregon & California, Villard was the representative in America of the committee formed to protect the bondholders of the Kansas Pacific, almost all of them Frankfurt-based investors, from financial catastrophe. For the past two and a half years, however, Oregonian matters had claimed most of his time, and he had never been able to reach any satisfactory arrangements with the owners of the Kansas Pacific. Nevertheless, his unyielding and incorruptible efforts on behalf of the bondholders, his employers, had made him a conspicuous figure. The railroad, meanwhile, had fallen upon even harder times and was being forced into receivership. On November 3, 1876, the U.S. District Court for Eastern Kansas appointed Henry Villard and Charles S. Greeley joint receivers of the Kansas Pacific Railroad. Given the already extraordinary demands upon his attention, Villard was understandably reluctant to accept this appointment; but since he felt partially responsible for the plight of the railroad, he agreed to take the job. This meant, of course, more traveling: he had to inspect the Kansas Pacific's main line and branches, visit the stations, peruse records, statements, and other documents, and participate in an unending sequence of meetings and negotiations.

Meanwhile, there was the question of where he and his family should live. Villard's involvement with the Kansas Pacific had put at least a temporary end to the idea of their relocating to Portland, but it was clear to everyone, even Fanny's loving father, that the Villards could no longer continue at Rockledge. The harsh climate of Boston simply took too great a toll on Henry's health, which, despite his large and robust appearance, continued to be quite uncertain. His business activities, too, required him to spend a great deal of time in New York. Toward the end of 1876, Villard, Fanny, and their three children moved out of Rockledge and took up residence in the Westminster Hotel in New York City.

During the first half of 1877 Villard divided his time between New York and points on the Kansas Pacific line, but wherever he was, he continued working at a furious pace, conducting the tangled affairs of several enterprises at once and always pressing the European bondholders in the railroads he represented for more capital. He made large-scale plans for his railroads, plans that (he was convinced) would work, but they always required funds.

In the summer Villard took his family on a long journey to points west, intending to make stops in Colorado, California, and Oregon. Business, to be sure, was one reason for the trip, but what he really wanted was for Fanny and their children to share his experience of the great American Northwest, to feel the same excitement he felt and to see the enormity of the task he had set for himself. In addition to these motives, Villard still thought of moving with Fanny and the children to Oregon, and the trip was to serve as the family's introduction to their future home. In Denver, however, he caught an annoying cold, which incautious exposure to a chilly fog in Oakland turned to pneumonia several days later. One evening he felt well enough to dine with the family in their hotel dining room, but after dinner his fever rose, his pulse mounted, and once again Fanny watched horrified as her husband slipped into unconsciousness. Physicians were summoned, who arrived, ministered, and after a week despaired, telling Fanny that Harry had not an hour to live.

Fanny's diary entries, usually accounts of the weather, visits, shopping, and minor family occurrences, rarely penetrated below the surface of events or recorded anything like a personal insight or a reflective remark. Her entries for this period (July 24–August 3, 1877), however, though written with her usual calm objectivity, give some indication of the grief and helplessness she felt as Harry went into a sudden and seemingly irreversible decline. July 24: "Harry is dangerously ill." July 25: "What an anxious night I have passed." July 26: "Harry is alarmingly ill." July 27: "Dr. McNulty is so alarmed at Harry's condition that he decided to have a consultation." July 28: "In the afternoon he suddenly began to sink and would have died, had not the Dr. given him brandy and champagne at the critical moment. No one of the three doctors expected him to outlive the night." July 29: "Harry is stronger, but he talks wildly, orders us all away from him, tries to get up and is in a frightful condition." July 30: "Improved—weak." July 31: "Harry was fearfully weak & felt very much demoralized." August 3: "I felt very tired & weak from all the trouble. At ten o'clock I fainted away & was hardly myself 2 hrs. afterwards."

These entries raise some tantalizing questions—how did Villard feel about being treated by a doctor with so Irish a name? did the teetotaling Fanny arrive at a new appreciation of the revivifying effects of spiritous liquors?—but they afford a glimpse into the gravity of Villard's case and the nervous strain that figured so largely both in his condition and in the effect on Fanny of nursing him through it. Naturally calling on her father and brothers at such a time (her mother, many years an invalid, had died in January 1876), Fanny had telegraphed to them in despair with the news of Harry's hopeless state and imminent death. As before, however, some last resort of resilience in his constitution fooled his doctors, and his slow but steady recovery belied their direly considered opinion. By the fall he was well enough to travel, and the family returned to New York. Once again, death had approached Henry Villard, prepared to claim him, and then inexplicably turned aside. His sanguine temperament kept him from brooding excessively on the fragility of his health, especially when he was otherwise prospering, but his escape had been too narrow to forget entirely, and his various maladies began to accumulate morbid implications.

Meanwhile, a new problem had arisen, and Villard, as principal receiver of the Kansas Pacific Railroad, had to get healthy in a hurry. Jay Gould, a wealthy financial adventurer who had gained a controlling share of stock in the Union Pacific Railroad, was intent on absorbing its competitors, especially the Kansas Pacific. Unscrupulous, calculating, utterly grasping, Gould was also extremely intelligent, as the ingenious combinations by means of which he steadily enriched himself proved. Villard found him a much worthier opponent than Holladay and even accorded him a grudging respect; Gould's success was real, not hollow, however many companies he sucked dry, stockholders he defrauded, or associates he betrayed, and Villard admired Gould's daring, his skill, and the cultured opulence of his private life.

Calling upon his bondholders to stand firm, Villard successfully brought the Kansas Pacific through the rate war instituted by Gould to bring it low. Wearying of this, Gould, a wanly smiling, deferential, diminutive man, sought to open negotiations with his ponderous opponent. They spoke of Germany and Goethe, the Civil War, language acquisition, and the American economy, and each appraised the other's weaknesses and strengths. A two-year struggle ensued, which generally took the form of repeated attempts by Gould to capture the German bondholders' citadel, indefatigably defended by Henry Villard. Having failed to dislodge Villard and the Germans by buying up a great block of short-term Kansas Pacific bonds and suing to redeem them as soon as they came due, Gould tried a double cross: he and Villard signed a reorganization agreement favorable to the bondholders, and shortly afterward, taking advantage of Villard's temporary absence from his post at the Kansas Pacific (he was preparing for a European vacation after what he presumed was a job well done), Gould presented the bondholders with a different and much less favorable plan. Villard, furious, canceled his travel arrangements and returned to the fray.

Although Gould managed to get him dismissed as receiver, Villard continued to represent his German bondholders, stubbornly, incorruptibly withstanding virulent assaults on his character and refusing to be bought off, no matter how advantageous to him personally were the deals that Gould proposed. At last, early in 1879,

Gould appeared in Villard's office on Nassau Street in New York, declared himself weary of fighting, and agreed to comply with all the concessions and conditions that Villard's bondholders required.

This time Gould kept his word, and Villard's triumph over the man whom he variously called "the great gobbler up of railroads," "that most unscrupulous and most dreaded machinator," and "the most-feared man in Wall Street"—a triumph achieved through firmness, integrity, and complete fidelity to his employers' interests—made him a sensation in financial circles and brought him increased respect and prestige, not only on Wall Street but also in Frankfurt and London. Villard thought of this contest, so bravely won, as a bitter struggle with a reprehensible man, but in the world of high finance, angry grudges and moral disapproval yield to the prospect of profits: Villard and Gould continued to do business together, often as allies.

As Gould had anticipated, after he agreed to a settlement Kansas Pacific securities rose sharply. When he sold all his stock a few months later, he was said to have cleared $10 million. Villard, too, profited greatly from his successful resolution and reorganization of the Kansas Pacific's affairs. Now he was free to turn his attention back to his Oregon companies. With a glowing reputation, solid international backing, and grandiose future plans, he had become a force to be reckoned with at the topmost levels of American capitalism.

THOMAS ALVA EDISON.

Photograph of the exhausted inventor with the improved phonograph

after working seventy-two hours, June 16, 1888.

Schenectady Museum Archives.

18

Upgrade, Downgrade

Headaches and heartaches and all kinds of pain
They all ride along with the railroad train.

"CASEY JONES"
(American folksong)

W hen Henry Villard and his family returned to New York in the fall of 1877, after Villard's recovery from his brush with death, they moved into Westmoreland House, a decidedly upscale apartment building that stood on Seventeenth Street just above the northeast corner of Union Square. It was fitting that a man so interested in technological progress should move his family into the first apartment house in New York to install an elevator. According to his son Oswald, the Westmoreland was located in what was "the center of the business and fashionable life of the city." New York in those days was a tough and dangerous place with little resemblance to the gentle, law-abiding metropolis of today. Its streets were notoriously filthy, dimly lit, and foul smelling, and gangs of toughs roamed them at will; its whorehouses flourished, especially around the hotels; its government and police force seemed, like jackals, to glory in corruption. The Villards' neighborhood, nevertheless, was relatively calm and protected, and at night Seventeenth Street was "as quiet as a village thoroughfare save for a tiny one-horse, one-way street car, which ambled past the Westmoreland at decorous intervals, returning through Eighteenth Street." Now sufficiently wealthy to live the genteel life he'd always dreamed about, Villard did not stint. The family occupied two large apartments—a total of eleven richly furnished rooms—and employed a number of servants, including the coachman who drove their carriages (landau, victoria) and cared for their horses.

The newfangled elevator at the Westmoreland proved to be a source of trouble and sorrow for the family. One day the Villard children came into the lobby with some of their Garrison cousins, all bent on a delightful session of elevator riding. The elevator was on an upper floor, but Helen, seeing that the door was partly open, cried out excitedly, "It *is* here!" and stepped into the open shaft; her fall was broken by the large wheels at the bottom. Her brother believed that Helen's injuries and the shock to her nerves "laid the foundation of a life of semi-invalidism," and she was doomed to much suffering at the hands of a great many expensive doctors.

The period between 1874 and 1884 was the busiest of Villard's life. Nothing, not pneumonia or gout or any other of his numerous ailments, could extinguish his energy for very long, and it flamed in a dozen different directions. He bought, sold, haggled, negotiated, maneuvered, compromised, schemed. As his fortune mounted, railroads remained the main, but not the only, focus of his multifarious personal investments. He had never been thrifty, not even when he was indigent; now, with large sums at his command, he disbursed them ardently, as though driven by some demon of acquisition. He liked to think that his money was speeding the march of progress, and he was always on the lookout for the next big thing. The practical applications of electric power, for example, had begun to interest him greatly. He also considered making a return to journalism, not as a reporter this time but as the owner of a journal. In any case, by 1879 Villard was driving so many projects forward, incurring so much stress, making so many demands upon his reserves of nervous energy, willpower, and persuasiveness, however vast, that his body's intermittent yelps of protest grew into a protracted, clamorous wail; he rarely got through a week without some serious indisposition. Fanny's diaries of this time, along with accounts of drives, promenades, social calls, shopping, charitable work, and the occasional concert or play, are more and more occupied with Harry's illnesses, yet he was constantly on the go, forever leaving or returning, forever conscious of his business obligations but inexpressibly missing his wife and babes.

Paradoxically, he seemed to thrive on infirmity, and for several years most of what he touched turned to gold. He was not interested so much in amassing wealth (though amassing it gave him great pleasure) as in exploiting it, energizing it, putting it to work. Spending money—whether the immediate goal of the spending was mere display, or his and his family's personal comfort, or charity, or simply the accumulation of more money—was in the end the surest way to obtain the status and prestige that he considered his rightful due, the goal and motivation of all his striving. He could no longer offer these proofs of his worth to his adoring, abandoned mother or his aloof, unimpressed father, so he laid them all before Fanny. For her part, and despite her own father's exhortations in favor of closed purses and the simple life, she encouraged the steady stream of financial successes achieved by her husband and enjoyed without reservation the luxurious living they entailed.

In 1879, the German creditors of the Oregon Steamship Company, tired of waiting for their investments to show a profit, decided to act contrary to Villard's advice and sell out their interest. When Villard saw that they were resolved to abandon the field, he ceased all attempts at dissuasion and set about seizing the opportunity for himself. With the help of a somewhat obfuscating prospectus of his own composition—in characteristically authoritative and enthusiastic terms, it evoked the glowing future of the Oregon Steamship Company but said little about its uncertain present or troubled past—Villard easily formed a syndicate of American and British investors in New York, contributed $35,000 of his own money, and bought control of the steamship company from the Germans. This move was, as he said, a great relief to him; "the duty of satisfying a group of disappointed foreign bankers had gradually become very irksome."

In April Villard arrived in Portland, determined to increase his control over the transportation systems of western Oregon. To this end, he opened negotiations to purchase the Oregon Steam Naviga-

tion Company, a thriving operation active on the Willamette and Columbia Rivers, with assets that included more than a dozen riverboats, three portage railways, a small railroad, and much besides.
The company's owner and president, a former riverboat pilot named
John C. Ainsworth, was an intelligent man and a shrewd negotiator;
for $100,000 he sold Villard an option to buy the steam navigation
company. Back in New York and faced with the necessity of locating
several million dollars, Villard raised enough capital to cover the purchase price by means of an adroit maneuver, which may be considered the first "leveraged buyout," the first time anyone bought a
company with money borrowed against *its* assets, not his own. He
formed a new concern, the Oregon Railway & Navigation Company,
that would absorb both the profitable Oregon Steam Navigation
Company, the object of his desire, and the unprofitable Oregon
Steamship Company, which was already under his control. On the
strength of his option to buy the existing company, he was able to obtain loans and sell stock in the proposed new one, and long before
his option expired—much to the amazement of Ainsworth, who had
looked forward to pocketing his hundred thousand—Villard had in
hand the price of the Oregon Steamship Navigation Company. Thus,
mortgaging assets in a company not yet his, he managed to fund a
concern not yet in existence: the Oregon Railway & Navigation Company, which gathered Ainsworth's former enterprise into its embrace.

While Villard was away doing business in Portland during April
and May, William Lloyd Garrison, now in his seventy-fourth year, entered his final decline. Still mentally active and dedicated to his
causes, but increasingly weakened and suffering, Garrison at last
yielded to Fanny's insistence that he come to New York, live in her
home, and consult her doctors. On April 28, 1879, he arrived and
took up residence with his daughter and grandchildren in Westmoreland House. But he was beyond the help even of New York
physicians, and on May 23 he lay speechless in the room that Fanny
had prepared for him and feebly beat time as she and her four brothers stood around his bed and sang the old hymns he loved. The next

evening he died. All over the country, both black and white Americans mourned him as a champion of human rights.

Fanny's devotion to her father had been absolute, and his passing grieved her deeply, as it did her husband, whose experience of paternal love had come chiefly from Garrison. Moreover, Villard was worn out from his exertions in the rarefied atmosphere of high finance. In July he took his family to Europe and rested there for several months. When he returned to New York in late November, one of his associates was waiting at the dock with the news that shares of Oregon Railway & Navigation stock, issued as a bonus to bond subscribers five months previously and theoretically worth little more than the paper they were printed on, had increased mightily in value and were now selling well above par; Wall Street's confidence in Villard and the businesses he promoted seemed to be boundless. Like a gambler on a winning streak, he looked about him for other investment opportunities.

Oswald Garrison Villard recalled a spring evening in 1879 when his father told the three Villard children that he was suspending bedtime rules so that they could see "something very wonderful." After dark he led them to a nearby hotel, the Clarendon, where the first outdoor arc lights in New York were on display. As rapt as any of his children, Villard gazed up at the dazzling, sizzling, sputtering incandescence and saw it shining with possibility. In Christmas week of the same year, he made an excursion to Menlo Park in central New Jersey, site of the laboratory operated by the brilliant young Thomas Alva Edison, whose invention of the phonograph two years previously had brought him international fame. Villard was among the thousands who flocked to Menlo Park to see the first public exhibition of Edison's new incandescent lamps, which were already being called "the light of the future."

At thirty-two, Edison—born in Milan, Ohio in 1847—was a dozen years younger than Villard, mostly self-educated, and thoroughly unaristocratic, yet the railroad magnate and the inventor had much in common, enough to form a close and lasting relationship. Like Villard, Edison was filled with ambition and brashly self-confident; both of them were innovators who thought on the grand scale; to each of them, capital (of which neither could get enough) was like a piano or an artist's brush, a tool for giving form to imagination; each included in his makeup a good deal of the salesman and the showman; and both had their eyes fixed on a vision of the future.

Their visions, as it turned out, were compatible. Villard sought out the inventor, sized him up, appreciated Edison's forthrightness, his enthusiasm, his drive (qualities they shared), and encouraged him with a promise of support for his business enterprise, the Edison Electric Light Company. A few months later, having invested handsomely in the company, Villard again visited Edison in Menlo Park and commissioned him to install electric lights aboard the SS *Columbia*, a large ship then under construction in a Pennsylvania shipyard for Villard's Oregon Railway & Navigation Company. Villard and Edison thus collaborated on an innovation, the first ship ever to be illuminated by electricity, and one evening in May 1880, the newly launched *Columbia*, festooned and glittering, steamed down Delaware Bay and out into the Atlantic on its long maiden voyage, bound for San Francisco by way of Cape Horn.

The launch was the occasion for a grand ball given by the Villards at the Brunswick Hotel. "I celebrate myself," Walt Whitman joyously declared, and so too might Henry Villard, who delighted in commemorating his successes with parties, banquets, and balls, elegant and lavish affairs that quickly achieved the status of genuine society events and were eagerly attended by the wealthy and influential. The ball at the Brunswick was spectacular, but the most elaborate of Villard's celebrations was yet to come.

After two months and several thousand miles, the SS *Columbia* docked in San Francisco with all its lights still steadily burning; Edison's original light installation would remain unchanged and in good working order until the *Columbia* was renovated fifteen years later. Once again, Henry Villard had picked a winner. Until the end of his career he was Edison's staunchest supporter, the only one of his patrons, the inventor said, who "believed in the light with all his heart." Villard also believed in several other of Edison's bright ideas and became a frequent visitor at Menlo Park. They had much to say

to each other, the disheveled Edison rapping out his flat Ohio sylla-
bles in his high, hearty voice, and the soigné Villard responding in
his German-accented rumble. He particularly encouraged Edison's
ideas for an electric railway and watched the succession of ever-larger
electric trains that the inventor ran in the fields adjoining his laboratory. Both men dreamed of an electric locomotive that could
match the power and speed of the steam-driven kind, but cheaply
and silently. An apostle of progress, Villard put his money where his
faith was; at one crucial point, he saved Edison's company with a
timely check for $40,000. Within a year after meeting the inventor,
Villard was elected to the board of directors of the Edison Electric
Light Company.

The bewildering number and variety of Villard's projects during
this period extended to his domestic arrangements. Toward the end
of 1879, he discovered, admired, and bought an impressive brick
house and a hundred acres of land on a wooded hilltop (it would become known as Villard Hill) overlooking the Hudson River at Dobbs
Ferry, about twenty miles north of New York City. This magnificently
situated place, with views extending south to the Statue of Liberty and
north to West Point, was called Thorwood, and it would remain, despite other residences in other places, the Villards' true family home
for nearly fifty years. Villard prudently put Thorwood in Fanny's
name, and they hired the young architectural firm of McKim, Mead
and White to renovate and enlarge the house; this was the first of
many commissions that McKim and partners would receive from
Henry Villard. Eventually Thorwood grew into a great mansion at
least three times its original size, with six living rooms, a beautiful little library designed by Stanford White, and a white-and-gold music
room that was the work of Charles McKim.

McKim was connected to the Villards in various ways. Villard was
well acquainted with his father, James Miller McKim, a Presbyterian
minister who had been in charge of educating the ex-slaves of the
Sea Islands when Villard was a reporter at Port Royal in 1863. Moreover, Miller McKim had been a loyal and longtime ally of William
Lloyd Garrison in the abolitionist cause, and their two families were
very close; Charles's sister Lucy, one of Fanny's closest friends, was

married to Fanny's brother Wendell. Charles was indebted to Villard for having persuaded the stern Reverend McKim to allow him to go to Paris, no place for a young Presbyterian, and study architecture at the Ecole des Beaux-Arts in 1867. The Villards' magnificent country house was the happy result of great friendship combined with great talent; by the mid-1890s, McKim, Mead and White was the most prestigious architectural firm in the country.

With its large park, carefully laid out under Villard's direction, and its unsurpassed vistas, Thorwood seemed like paradise on earth to the Villards, especially the children. It was a spot of civilized wilderness where man and nature coexisted harmoniously, the kind of place where the protagonist of a novel by Karl Gutzkow might live; and indeed, as Villard watched the glorious sunsets over the Hudson he was much reminded of his native Palatinate and the Rhine. Villard had the motto "Peace Be Unto This House" cut into the stained-glass window above a landing overlooking the park as a permanent tribute to the peace he found there. Over the years many guests passed through Thorwood, for the Villards loved to entertain. Fanny organized concerts and recitals; Sunday dinners were generally large and festive—the family, including the children, dressed formally for them, whether there were guests or not—and there was no end of special occasions. The Villards' guests, like their hosts, tended to be liberal, cultured, irreligious, and international.

In fact, the family's carefree approach to religious matters scandalized their staid Presbyterian neighbors. While the latter were going to church on Sunday and keeping holy the Lord's day, the Villards were playing tennis and croquet. Worse, they refused to join any congregation at all in Dobbs Ferry. When, upon closer acquaintance, Fanny's blameless, upright, benevolent character was revealed, she caused her neighbors further consternation. How could one so obviously not of the elect lead a life so exemplarily moral?

Among the many dogs of Thorwood was one Brutus, a great mastiff who seemed to have chosen Villard through some kind of extrasensory dog apparatus that picks up waves beyond human perception. One day, without ever having laid eyes on Villard, Brutus ran away from home and came to him at Thorwood. Duly delivered back where, in the judgment of others, he belonged, Brutus returned to Villard's side at his earliest opportunity, undeterred by the homes, the bitches, and the two miles that lay between him and his alpha male. After this cycle repeated itself several times, Brutus's master ceded him to Villard. Oswald Garrison Villard remembered his father and Brutus walking on the grounds at Thorwood, "a wonderfully matched pair . . . both superb specimens of their type." In the evenings the family would sit in their favorite cozy parlor, and Brutus, lying at his master's feet as Villard perused the foreign newspapers, would disappear nightly under a pile of discarded pages.

Such idyllic scenes of domestic peace, however, were far from the rule in 1880, for Villard was busy strengthening and expanding his empire and continuing his steady ascent to the dizzying heights of transportation control in Oregon. Through a series of maneuvers and arrangements, the German creditors of the Oregon & California and its subsidiaries were eliminated, British (and some American) investors became the new bondholders, and Villard, a majority stockholder in the reorganized railroad, was elected its president. Like his holdings, his vision was expanding; now it embraced the continent. He perceived that in order to prosper, his system of railroads and water transport along the coast and in the valleys of the Columbia and Willamette Rivers required access to a transcontinental railroad, preferably one under his command. With all the main transportation lines of the vast Northwest under a common management, the region's immense wealth of natural resources could be properly and rationally exploited, to the profit of all concerned, particularly the man at the top. The chief obstacle to the execution of this grandiose project was the Northern Pacific Railroad Company.

     ■   ■   ■

The Northern Pacific—in the words of a historian, "the single greatest American corporate undertaking of the nineteenth century"—received a charter in 1864, authorizing it to construct a railroad from Duluth and St. Paul, Minnesota, to the Pacific Ocean, either at a port on Puget Sound in Washington or farther south, with a terminus at Portland and the Columbia River delta. This act of faith in the future of a country where a most violent civil struggle was raging had been signed by Abraham Lincoln himself. An enormous land grant (it eventually comprised 60 million acres), to be earned incrementally as the railroad built its way to the West, provided the incentive for pushing construction forward.

Despite the great boom in railroad building that had begun shortly after the Civil War and not yet subsided, there was still only one transcontinental railroad in the United States. This was controlled by the Union Pacific, with lines running to California from Omaha and Kansas City. A golden spike had been driven to mark the conjunction of the eastward and westward roads at a small town in northern Utah in 1869. This centrally located line, however, had little effect upon the isolation of the Northwest, which Villard was determined to relieve.

Under its current president, Frederick Billings, the Northern Pacific was following a policy of cautious expansion, trying not to build too far ahead of the population that alone could make the railroad profitable. The upright, intelligent, well-educated Billings, born in Vermont in 1823, was a relatively mild-mannered denizen of the railroad jungle, not a gorilla like Holladay or a hyena like Gould. He was as attached as anyone to his own interests and those of his company, but he was somewhat distracted by family problems in the early 1880s, and he perhaps underestimated the threat posed by Henry Villard.

Billings was neither temperamentally nor financially equipped to make a sudden lunge to the coast; Villard, on the other hand, was a gambler by nature, and his tendency to take risks had been enhanced by his recent financiering success. His network of transportation enterprises must have a connection to the rest of the country, for that meant immigration, development, trade, prosperity. To gain access to this lifeline, Villard was prepared to extend his own lines as far east as necessary. He believed—correctly, as it turned out—that he knew a sufficient number of the right people and enjoyed enough of a reputation to be able to raise large sums of money whenever he felt the need of them. He entered into a lengthy series of negotiations with Billings concerning construction programs, profit sharing, rights of way, proration, division of traffic and interests, spheres of influence, and so forth, but he could obtain no real satisfaction. None of the suggested compromises allowed Villard to retain what he considered a sufficient degree of control over railroad matters in Oregon and Washington.

In the summer, Villard made an exploratory trip into eastern Oregon and southeastern Washington, accompanied by two associates and advisers: George Pullman, the extremely successful developer of railroad shipping cars, and William J. Endicott, a wealthy Bostonian who had befriended Villard and backed him financially ever since his days with the American Social Science Association. The activity they saw and the potential they recognized on their excursion, particularly the region's future in grain production, persuaded Villard to begin constructing several branch, or feeder, lines to serve the main rail lines along the Snake River.

Expansion, both in construction and in holdings, was the name of the game for Villard in 1880; he built new lines, bought choice coal and timber lands near his existing or proposed lines, and snapped up anything that looked like a hindrance to his monopoly. For example, early in 1880 a trustee in the small Seattle & Walla Walla Railroad attempted to sell Villard some of its bonds; Villard's response was to purchase the entire railroad as well as the coal mine it served. His tentacles now extended to Puget Sound, all the more reason to achieve a transcontinental connection. He founded another new enterprise, the Oregon Improvement Company, designed to develop the natural resources of Oregon and Washington in cooperation with the Oregon Railway & Navigation Company. Once again the investors who followed Villard's fortunes eagerly bought up shares of the new company's stock, and the issue was an immediate success; in the following months the price per share moved briskly upward.

In the fall of 1880 a sudden infusion of capital took the Northern Pacific out of its defensive position. A syndicate headed by the powerful firm of Drexel, Morgan & Company bought $40 million in Northern Pacific bonds; now Billings and his railroad could build their own line all the way to the coast with no need of consulting Villard's convenience or of coming to any sort of compromise agreement with him. Villard saw with some alarm that the presence of this strong competitor would depress the value of stocks in his Oregon and Washington companies and make it harder for him to raise any additional capital to support them. The only way that he could see to avert such a catastrophe as this, and to make the Northern Pacific do what he wanted, was to become its owner.

Villard had bought the competition before, but the competition had never been anything like so imposing. A formidable task lay before him: first, he had to attract sufficient capital to buy a controlling interest in the stock of the Northern Pacific, and second, he had to accomplish this feat stealthily, otherwise he could easily be thwarted. Throughout the latter half of 1880 and into 1881, while Billings was dickering with his backers over routes, Villard, occasionally using surrogate buyers, purchased shares in the Northern Pacific. Then, early in 1881, having gone as far as he could on his own, Villard sent a confidential proposal to fifty-five friends in high financial places.

The proposal solicited subscriptions to a fund of $8 million. Subscribers were promised handsome profits, but no further information was given or security offered beyond Villard's pledge and signature. The nature of the enterprise would be revealed on May 15, 1881—this was later extended to the end of June—but for now Villard was asking his friends to bet on his hand without getting so much as a peek at any of the cards. This was, of course, not the way he put it in the prospectus.

Before carrying out this bold move, which became known in the annals of Wall Street as the "blind pool," Villard discussed it with a few close advisers. At least one of them, William J. Endicott, strongly advised him against trying to seize control of the Northern Pacific. Even if Villard's efforts were successful, Endicott pointed out, the road could not be made profitable for many years, the population it served was as yet far too sparse, Villard would not make enough to meet his obligations, and he would put himself under excessive nervous strain besides. These were wise and prophetic words, but Villard heeded none of them.

His status on Wall Street combined with the seductive mystery and novelty of his proposal to bring him, within twenty-four hours, subscriptions totaling more than twice the amount that he had requested. There was a rush on Villard's offices, where successful bankers and wily financiers, mighty capitalists all, loudly clamored for permission to place more of their funds at his disposal, no questions asked. A second subscription of $12 million generated similar levels of excitement and was paid up just as quickly. Moving carefully and quietly, by spring Villard had enough shares of Northern Pacific stock at his command to take control of the company. Billings, who was outraged at having been bushwhacked, put up a fight, and there ensued a brief struggle of moves and countermoves, including Villard's filing of a couple of civil suits. In the end Billings capitulated, sold his stock to Villard, stepped aside, and literally collapsed under the strain of his losing struggle.

This creative and masterly combination of ploys—the blind pool, which was and remains sui generis, followed by the first hostile takeover in Wall Street history—brought Henry Villard close to the pinnacle of his financial power and made him for a time one of the two or three most influential men in American finance. Hardly pausing, he plunged on. His next bold step, taken in June 1881, was to form yet another new corporation, the Oregon & Transcontinental Company, one of the first holding companies ever organized in the United States. Its purpose was to coordinate and harmonize the interests of Villard's various concerns—the Northern Pacific, the Oregon & California, the steamship lines, Oregon Railway & Navigation, and to some extent the Oregon Improvement Company—and to offer them shelter and protection in the event of inclement financial weather. The stock issue for the Oregon & Transcontinental was the next in Villard's string of successes, and it seemed to many, including, perhaps, himself, that he could do no wrong.

Meanwhile there were other things in the world to buy besides railroads. On July 1, 1881, Villard made a resounding return to American journalism by announcing his acquisition, five weeks previously, of the *New York Evening Post,* a daily newspaper, and the weekly magazine the *Nation,* which was to become the *Post*'s weekly edition. The timing of this purchase suggests that the ex-reporter's knack for being in the same place as the news had not deserted him; the next day, July 2, in a train station in Washington, D.C., one Charles Guiteau, disappointed in his hopes for a government office, shot down the person he held responsible for this outrage, President James Garfield. The mortally wounded president lingered for ten weeks before succumbing, and the news business throve.

Villard's grab of an important big-city newspaper—railroad baron acquires media outlet—may seem at first glance a recipe for slanted news, constrained reportage, and self-aggrandizing propaganda, but in fact his ownership of the *Evening Post* revealed him at his best: principled, liberal minded, judicious, even self-effacing. As his editors he chose his old friend Horace White, late of the *Chicago Tribune;* Carl Schurz, like Villard a German-American success story; and the British-born E. L. Godkin, founder and editor of the *Nation*.

Villard averred that he was "prouder" of having put together this impressive "combination of journalistic ability than of any of his business triumphs." Schurz, a refugee from the 1848 uprisings in Germany, had been an early and strong supporter of Abraham Lincoln, U.S. minister to Spain, a valiant Civil War general (Chancellorsville, Gettysburg, Chattanooga), a successful journalist and editor, a U.S. senator, and secretary of the interior. White and Villard—their acquaintance dated back to the days when they covered the Lincoln-Douglas debates as young reporters—had been business associates for years, and White was, moreover, a respected journalist of long experience, a liberal in his views, and an authority on economics, particularly banking and finance. As for Godkin, under his leadership the *Nation*—whose literary editor, Wendell Garrison, replaced him as editor of the magazine—had become one of the most prestigious and intelligent publications in the country. "In the ability with which [the *Nation*] discussed politics and social questions, the trenchancy of its style, and the soundness of its literary criticism, it was unapproached by anything else in American . . . journalism."

Having purchased these two highly respected organs and placed them in the hands of talented, experienced, large-minded men, Villard, with what one historian calls "rare generosity," assumed the

Evening Post's financial responsibilities but deliberately divested himself of any influence over the paper's contents. He wanted, he said, an absolutely independent newspaper devoted to truth and not to an ideology or a political party or a single viewpoint. Some rich men of Villard's day and perhaps even later used their newspapers to further their economic or other interests. Wishing to make sure that no such accusation could be leveled at him, Villard put his paper into a family trust whose trustees had "full authority . . . to protect the editorial department from all interference." The *Evening Post* flourished, printing influential articles on financial, political, and cultural subjects, and Villard realized healthy profits through righteous deeds. It is said that he never dictated a single editorial line in the *Evening Post,* which he owned (though it was recorded in Fanny's name) until he died.

At the age of forty-six, Villard had achieved enough success for several lifetimes, and he wasn't through yet. Now that he was rich as Croesus, with a fortune amounting to at least $6 million—equivalent to something in nine figures today—he turned to philanthropy, giving money to a great many institutions and organizations in both his native country and his adopted one. The Villard papers at Harvard's Houghton Library contain much evidence of his charity, including a clipping from the *Zweibrücker Zeitung* of August 9, 1881. This newspaper announced Villard's gift of 15,000 marks to the gymnasium in Zweibrücken, the very institution from which he had been expelled for political radicalism at the age of fourteen. The gift was accompanied by a letter to the officials of the school, which the *Zeitung* printed in full, and in which Villard declared his belief that the kind of education one received in a gymnasium was the "best foundation for material success, as well as for intellectual and moral development." He felt it his duty, he said, to share the fruits of his success— which he believed he owed chiefly to his gymnasium training—by giving others the opportunity to enjoy such advantages. He included a stipulation that the scholarships thus established must be awarded according to merit and need, with no distinctions based on place of birth or religious adherence. In closing he alluded to his own school days at the Zweibrücken gymnasium, which he always remembered with esteem and gratitude. We may imagine that Villard found the establishment of this scholarship fund particularly satisfying.

Their skyrocketing net worth persuaded Harry and Fanny that they should build themselves a mansion in New York City worthy of their position. For Villard such a dwelling would be a symbol of all that he had achieved in the nearly three decades since he first landed in New York, penniless and alone, and had to depend for his lodging on the generosity of strangers. In April he purchased a large lot extending from Fiftieth to Fifty-first Streets on the east side of Madison Avenue, facing the east end of St. Patrick's Cathedral. He had in mind something in European style, an elegant town house with a courtyard, and naturally he discussed his ideas first with Fanny, and then with Charles McKim.

When, that is, he had the time. At the meeting of the new Northern Pacific board of directors in September, Villard was elected president of the railroad, replacing Frederick Billings, who had resigned at the end of June. Charming, courteous, and cooperative with the man he had defeated, Villard appointed Billings chairman of the railroad's executive committee.

Villard's rise had been meteoric, and now he was in a position to carry out his first priority: to push "with the utmost energy" the construction of the Northern Pacific's main line in order to effect a transcontinental rail connection for the Pacific Northwest. Assessing Villard's impact on this region, a historian states that "the decade after 1875 could accurately be described as the age of Henry Villard"; another writer, waxing metaphorical, declares, "For a decade the fiery Villard blazed across the Northwest like a comet." He shone with particular intensity after gaining command of the Northern Pacific in September 1881.

The entire Western half of the country was in a state of rapid development and uncontrolled expansion, and Villard was imbued with the spirit of the times. He drove his various companies into a veritable blitz of frenetic construction, not only on the Northern Pacific's transcontinental line but also on branch lines, particularly in Washington and Oregon. His Northern Pacific crews were working from both ends of the route, digging, hacking, blasting, building, and leaving their tracks behind them. The vast distance those tracks would ultimately cover stretched from St. Paul, Minnesota, to Portland, Oregon, and Washington's Puget Sound ports, Seattle and Tacoma, by way of North Dakota, Montana, and Idaho. The pace and scope of Villard's operations exacted a heavy price. In his first year as president, expenditures on the Northern Pacific exceeded receipts by more than $10 million.

Billings and other advisers urged caution, but Villard overrode them and plunged ahead, not only urging forward the work on the main road but also undertaking the construction of yet more tributary roads, as well as ordering the erection of a terminal and hotel in Portland and several station buildings along the line. Meanwhile, to maintain the confidence of his stockholders, he disbursed dividends that his companies could ill afford. For an extended period, however, his enterprises prospered, and his prosperity drew national attention and admiration. In 1882, in what amounted to a financial celebrity profile, the *Boston Herald* offered this analysis of Villard and his success: "He has really earned his millions by perception, discretion and power of combination. To make money is naturally his object, but it is not his sole object, and he understands that money may be made at too high a cost."

Villard's most important architectural commissions in Portland and elsewhere went to McKim, Mead and White, and a distinctly unimpressed Stanford White found himself traveling the hinterlands on his way to meetings with the railroad magnate. White admired the natural beauties of the great Pacific Northwest, but he failed to share Villard's vision of the towns and their prosperous future. Tacoma, for example, was for White "a God-forsaken place at the end of Puget Sound" whose main features were "board shanties and tree stumps." White preferred the refinements of urban life (they were to prove his undoing; in 1906 the husband of Evelyn Nesbit, one of the girls whom Stanny had delighted to push in his famous red velvet swing, shot him dead) to the simpler provincial pleasures; moreover, he found Villard slightly pompous and thought that he was treated altogether too royally by the people whose towns and communities he visited. "Tuesday I saw his royal highness Mr. Villard," White wrote to his wife. "I do not know whether the papers have been full of him and his party in New York: but here you think of nothing else. The whole air is full of it; if he was a King there could not be more of a row."

Throughout his frequent travels between 1881 and 1883, Villard wrote to Fanny with his habitual diligence. Part of what he reported to her was his growing celebrity, for his business triumphs, his sudden rise to prominence, and his furious determination to open up the Northwest had made him famous; wherever he went, crowds greeted him and speeches were expected of him. In his letters he assured Fanny that notoriety was something he shrank from and expressed surprise that he could be thought so wonderful by all these strangers. Like traveling, fame was an unwelcome aspect of his business life, an occupational hazard that he accepted with a sigh of resignation loud enough for Fanny to hear. Toward the end of 1882, his letters to her became most solicitous of her health, for she was in her fourth pregnancy, carrying the child who would be their last, the child of their mature years, eleven years younger than Oswald, his next older sibling.

All during this period, the crews working the western and eastern portions of the Northern Pacific's transcontinental line moved the tracks, sometimes by circuitous routes, toward their destined convergence. In two years, with as many as twenty-five thousand men working for him, Villard saw to the construction of two thousand miles of railroad, about half of that on the main line. In the west the road extended from Portland beyond the confluence of the Columbia and Snake Rivers, up through eastern Washington to the little hamlet of Spokane, and then east into Idaho and the northern Rocky Mountains, stopping at Lake Pend Oreille. After Villard took command, the workers began building east from the lake and down into Montana along the Clarks Fork River. From the east they took up the line where it first struck the Yellowstone River in eastern Montana, eight hundred miles away from Lake Pend Oreille, and followed the river west toward Billings and the mountains. Behind them the road stretched back east across the Badlands, through Bismarck and Fargo, and then southeast across Minnesota to St. Paul. As the workers approached Billings, the civilizing rails passed within forty miles of the site near the Little Bighorn River, where not very many years previously (1876) another overreacher, Gen. George Armstrong Custer, had gone too far. Along much of the route, soldiers of the regular army protected the striving crews from possible Indian attacks.

Indians were actually among the least of Villard's worries. As expenses and cost overruns mounted, he employed various expedients to maintain cash flow and keep the men on the job. He bought or formed new companies, including a company to build terminals, and a railroad, the St. Paul & Manitoba, that extended into Canada. He floated new bonds, shifted assets from one enterprise to another, dipped into his own resources, pledged his personal credit. His personality, his great capacity for enthusiasm, made him susceptible to the "boom psychology of the time." In his case the result occasionally verged on megalomania, as when he talked—to the unreceptive Billings, among others—of creating a transportation monopoly "from Puget Sound to the Golden Gate," of absorbing the Union Pacific, of gaining a foothold in western Canada.

The construction gangs toiled on, blasting tunnels, grading mountains, building bridges and trestles, taming as best they could the long stretches of dense forest, rugged wilderness, impossible terrain, splitting into two groups during blizzards, when one group shoveled snow while the other laid track, and taking their chances with the lightning of the summer storms. When other workers refused certain tasks or demanded rates he considered exorbitant, Villard turned to cheap labor, particularly Chinese coolies, whom he imported by the boatload—he boasted of having as many as fifteen thousand of them in the field when Northern Pacific construction was at its peak—and who offered employers inestimable advantages: they worked harder and more efficiently than their Caucasian counterparts, often performing jobs that others found too hazardous, and they did so for less money. After the manner of empire builders everywhere, Villard paid little heed to the plight of the many whose labors turned his vision into reality. Hundreds of them were buried in unmarked graves near the tracks they died building; as for the thousands and thousands of survivors, most of them Chinese, when work or money ran out they were simply discharged, strangers in a strange and hostile land, to make their way as best they might. For Villard, who looked beyond the fates of individuals, these were painful but unavoidable facts, worthwhile sacrifices to achieve a greater good.

According to a railroad historian, in financial matters Villard was "reckless and careless as only a visionary can be," and his "incomparable gift for raising funds was diminished by a tendency to buy properties at inflated prices." A fellow magnate described him as "an *honest* 'wild man'" who made "extravagant and lengthy" acquisitions *"to feed a short system."* In 1882, the Northern Pacific's finances seemed "so disarrayed . . . that some thought Villard would not last out the year."

All during the period 1881–83, Villard matched his frenzy of expansion with a tireless promotional effort, international in scope and designed to attract the most desirable railroad workers and settlers to the big empty lands served by the Northern Pacific. True to his Northern European way of viewing things, Villard confined his advertisements to hundreds of newspapers in the United States, Canada, Germany, Scandinavia, England, and Holland; to this day the ethnic makeup of the region reflects his influence. He established emigration agencies abroad and stocked them with brochures and other publicity offering cheap land, good jobs, and limitless opportunities in the vast American Northwest; and he made sure that he and his businesses stayed in the news. Traveling mostly in his private railroad car, he made a dash from New York to Portland that set a record for speed and symbolized the headlong lunge that his career had become. Promoting himself and promoting his enterprises blurred into a single activity.

His philanthropic endeavors also continued apace. Perhaps his most significant gifts were two generous endowments, first to the University of Oregon and later to the University of Washington, which in both cases allowed the universities to remain in operation after the legislatures of their respective states (such were the times) failed to provide for them. Villard Hall on the Eugene campus of the University of Oregon, still standing today, was one of the academic buildings that its namesake's assistance made possible.

The historical dimension of Villard's influence on the development of the Northwest was apparent even to his contemporaries. The Oregon paper *The Guard* (August 13, 1881) commented, "It is remarkable how little has been done for the advancement of this coast by our millionaires. . . . We are glad to note an exception to this class. Mr. H. Villard['s] . . . conduct is very different from that of Stanford and the C.P.R.R. nabobs, who have never given anything to charitable or educational institutions, or otherwise, and have extracted the utmost farthing from the people of California." None was more convinced of his significance than his wife. Together they believed that Villard's business operations, unlike those of such men as Ben Holladay and Jay Gould, sprang from a selfless desire to improve people's lives, not from any considerations of profit, status, or power, and that such righteousness deserved both the garland of praise and the crown of success. Fanny wrote Harry several letters that begin with the salutation "Dear Railroad King" or some variation thereon, and they sometimes referred to themselves as the duke and duchess of Oregon, surprising imagery for a former radical antimonarchist and the daughter of a champion of equality. It may be objected that they were joking, but these two seldom joked, particularly about themselves, and even when they did, the point was the underlying seriousness of the matter at hand.

Perhaps unaware of her husband's mounting financial difficulties or else fully convinced that he would surmount them, Fanny wrote from her desk at Thorwood on April 17, 1883:

> My dearest Railroad King!
>
> What a world of business you must be living in! . . . You have a right to feel happy and proud at the triumphant success that has crowned your efforts. I think your son Harold has a fair appreciation of it, for he is learned indeed as regards your steamers, your railroads, your stocks and your superiority in point of character over all "Railroad Kings." . . . I am the adoring wife of the president of the N.P. Road—that is enough for me!

In a hastily written note, Henry sent back a message from Portland: "Dearest Darling . . . I love your letter."

Two weeks later, a strangely abstract letter from Fanny expressed
in awestruck tones uncomplicated by nuance the sense they both
had of his exalted undertaking:

> My dearest Railroad King,
>
> Your second dispatch from Walla Walla brings the good news
> of your enthusiastic reception by the people en route. It must
> indeed be gratifying to you to have such genuine appreciation
> of all your great efforts on their behalf, shown you. It is pleasant
> too, to know, that outward applause is gladly given, where the
> highest and noblest of motives enter into human conduct,
> whether in connection with material prosperity or simply the
> moral arena. The influence of such a work as yours upon the
> general tone and improved morality of the people, whom you
> may half be said to govern, can only be dimly imagined, never
> actually known. My estimate upon your labors, you know, and I
> have always been taught to judge all things by the highest moral
> standards possible.

It was clear that such selfless benevolence merited a monument
more substantial than heightened public morality, and indeed, as
Fanny sat in Thorwood composing this letter, work on the Villards'
imposing Manhattan residence was well advanced. One year before,
in April 1882, Villard had commissioned McKim, Mead and White to
design and build a unified complex of six elegant dwellings on his
Madison Avenue property. Several aggressively swank Vanderbilt
mansions stood nearby, on or just west of Fifth Avenue. Tastefully
emulous, Villard wanted his home to transcend its less fashionable location and magnify its owners through classical restraint rather than
ostentatious display. In this he succeeded, and time has justified him:
his mansion is still nobly standing, while the Vanderbilts' great homes
have long since fallen in New York's assault on its past.

The Villard Houses, as they have always been called, reflect their
namesake's European background and his lifelong insistence on the

most elegant accommodations possible. He knew generally what he wanted: brownstone, spare ornamentation, understated splendor, classical proportions, harmonious lines, a front courtyard. He desired the last of these, he said, to break the monotony of New York houses (which all fronted directly on the street in an unbroken line), to "secure privacy and get rid of tramps, and to live in a quiet and secluded way." Joseph Wells, the unsung genius of McKim, Mead and White, worked closely with Villard on the exterior design of the building. In giving shape to his employer's ideas, Wells drew inspiration from two Roman palazzi—the Farnese and, more extensively, the Cancelleria, both magnificent products of the High Renaissance in Italy. Wells's design, distinguished, serene, timeless, resulted in "one of New York's great landmarks," an "opulent and awe-inspiring . . . brownstone palace." Distinctive touches included the ground-level loggia, formed by five graceful arches, across the rear of the courtyard, and the elegant little second-story balconies that overlooked it. A contemporary critic called the composition "very quiet, a little cold, perhaps a little tame but . . . extremely refined."

As they worked together perfecting the design for the house, Wells and Villard, despite significant disparities in age and temperament, improbably became friends. Born in Boston in 1853, the year Villard first landed in New York, Wells was noted for keeping an amiable disposition half concealed beneath a façade of mordant humor and epigrammatic wit. His ironic sensibility found expression in his notebooks, where he recorded the following warning: "To all great men who wish their littleness to remain hidden, my advice is: Never sit for a bust or portrait, or build a house." Such sentiments notwithstanding, the architect and the railroad baron remained close, and when Wells died young of tuberculosis, in 1890, only one New York newspaper ran an obituary: the *Evening Post*.

Five of the six separate dwellings enclosed within the palazzo that Wells designed for Villard would be sold to the latter's business associates; he and his family were to occupy the most splendid of the six, which took up the entire four-story southern wing of the complex. This wing, entered from the courtyard, covered a portion of Villard's plot measuring sixty feet along Madison Avenue by a depth of a hundred feet on East Fiftieth Street. The Villards spared no expense on the inside of their future home; the amenities included the latest Edison electric fittings, a hydraulic elevator, and a voracious coal-burning central heating system. Fanny's diary entries show how enthusiastically she joined in the project of furnishing her new mansion. (December 18, 1882: "Magnificent weather. Shopped, shopped, shopped!") Stanford White, who excelled at interior design and decoration, had charge of this aspect of the work. He was assisted by several of the best artists and artisans in America: the sculptor Augustus Saint-Gaudens, the stained-glass artist and muralist John La Farge, and the master woodworker Joseph Cabus, among many others. Together they produced one decorative *coup de scène* after another; a striking example was the extraordinary bronze-doré clock, depicting the signs of the zodiac, that White and Saint-Gaudens designed for the wall facing the grand staircase, whose yellow marble steps were four yards wide. With its columned doorways, triple drawing room (where Fanny and Henry inserted their initials in mother-of-pearl on one pilaster column), two-story music room, and monumental carved fireplace, its noble staircase and twelve-hundred-square-foot dining room, its costly imported materials, its marbles and mahoganies, marquetries and mosaics, its abundance of elaborate, harmonious decoration, Villard's palace was indeed fit for a Renaissance duke or king, though perhaps not for a quiet and secluded life. (Here, as at Thorwood, Villard expressed his yearning for tranquility; he had the word PAX inscribed in the vaulted entrance hall.) Villard played an important role in the production of this outstanding architectural achievement, and it gave him, at least for a time, unique status among the oligarchs of the Gilded Age.

In the spring of 1883, while armies of workers were carrying Villard's grandiose plans to fruition in New York City and the distant Northwest, Fanny was approaching her term. On May 22, as the worst thunderstorm in living memory thrashed the lower Hudson Valley, she gave birth at Thorwood to her fourth child, Henry Hilgard Villard, whom the family would call Hilgard. His arrival took his big brothers by surprise; neither Harold, thirteen and a half, nor Oswald, eleven, had noticed that anything unusual was about to happen, and no one had seen fit to apprise them of the family's imminent blessing.

Shortly after Hilgard's birth, his father received some unsettling news from his chief engineer: the cost of completing the Northern Pacific would exceed previous estimates by at least $14 million. Recent expenses, particularly those necessitated by the extremely difficult and costly work along the Clarks Fork River, were considerably higher than revenues, and any rapid improvement of the situation seemed to be out of the question. Villard was shocked by these revelations; he had somehow failed to notice the ominous figures and the daunting projections. Nevertheless, though the cards were running against him, he believed the game could still be won, and he resorted to the tactics that came most naturally to him. Incapable of folding, too impatient to check, he bet some more.

The leading crews at both ends of the Northern Pacific's converging tracks were now engaged in an exhausting struggle against the most demanding and dangerous terrain of the entire route, rugged, mountainous terrain capable of eroding vast piles of capital. Villard ordered his engineers to press on, to increase the pace, to keep spanning the rivers and leaping the canyons and drilling and blasting the tunnels and spiking down the tracks. He would not wait through another winter; the Northern Pacific must become a transcontinental road now, this summer, and he would make its completion such an *event*, such a cause for general rejoicing, that even the most nervous investor would think the success of the road assured. In Villard's ever-sanguine prognostications, the extravaganza he planned would cause a rise in his stocks, his capacity for fund-raising would continue undiminished, armies of clean-limbed, hard-working immigrants from northern Europe would arrive and settle industriously along the transcontinental route, and soon things would be booming. There was, moreover, the pleasure to be derived from reiterated acknowledgments of his historical significance, even if such tributes were orchestrated by himself. The key to all these happy results was to make the celebration spectacular and unforgettable. Like all Villard's plans, this one required the disbursement of a great deal of money.

About $300,000, to be precise, perhaps $4–5 million in today's dollars. Outlays began in late June, when the Northern Pacific sent out 350 engraved invitations, addressed to some of the most distinguished and prominent personages in the United States, England, and Germany. Recipients included former president Grant and the governors of all the states traversed by the railroad; various senators, congressmen, members of Parliament, and other politicians; British noblemen, German scientists, assorted bankers, writers, journalists, ambassadors, diplomats, industrialists, and businessmen. The Northern Pacific invited these luminaries to join its president, Mr. Henry Villard, in an excursion to celebrate the completion of its transcontinental line with the driving of the last spike in Gold Creek, a tiny outpost sixty miles west of Helena, Montana; the excursion would then continue on to the Pacific coast. The railroad made all travel arrangements for its guests, wherever they might be; transatlantic accommodations for the scores of European invitees were particularly luxurious. Almost all those who received an invitation accepted. Most of them assembled in New York, and after some preliminary festivities there and in Chicago, Villard transported his guests to St. Paul at the end of August. A parade, a grand banquet, and much speechifying immediately preceded the start of the excursion proper, shortly after midnight on September 3, 1883. Mr. Villard's show was on the road.

"Villard's grand celebration," according to one historian, "was extensive, dramatic, and in retrospect quite foolish." Additional adjectives suggest themselves: injudicious, desperate, irrational. His recent attempts at getting an infusion of cash through second mortgages and debenture bonds had not been successful, so he had further exposed himself by heavily investing his own funds in the Northern Pacific and borrowing more against his personal credit—in short, by raising the stakes. Faced with stunning cost overruns, insufficient traffic, and mounting evidence of an approaching downturn in the U.S. economy, with his advisers prophesying doom, his finances in an impenetrable mess, and stocks in all his companies declining in price, Villard chose to spend a significant proportion of his dwindling resources on a lavish, interminable party whose purpose was to promote himself, his railroad, and their heroic accomplishments. This was denial on the transcontinental scale, and the resulting spectacle—a man on a narrow ledge above an abyss, doing somersaults and remarking upon the fineness of the weather—contained elements both heroic and pathological.

It took four long trains—all designated "double first class," with right-of-way over all other trains—to convey Villard and his guests to their destination. Each train had well-stocked dining rooms and bars, plush seats, and the latest Pullman sleeping cars, with beveled glass mirrors, mahogany panels, and richly appointed toilet rooms. Everywhere the trains passed, there were celebrating crowds, elaborate decorations, marching bands, flower girls, artillery salutes, toasts, and endless speeches. Having apparently decided that the bitter cup of fame, once tasted, must be drained to the dregs, Villard spoke at every opportunity. He often sounded like a visiting politician, touting his past accomplishments, expressing his faith in the future, and declaring his support of the people, and progress, and hard work. Grant spoke as often, but more briefly; in one town his entire speech consisted of a single sentence: "Boys, you should remember that this is not a campaign year." There were dozens of other speakers, including (in Bismarck) Sitting Bull, chief of the Sioux, the conqueror of General Custer. Now pardoned but temporarily in U.S. custody, the chief responded to Villard's invitation to say a few words in Lakota with a brief address that was translated by an army interpreter. His version of the chief's words was blandly courteous, but others familiar with the Lakota tongue asserted that Sitting Bull, with the forceful eloquence for which he was renowned, had passionately decried land thieves, and all their works, and all their pomps. After his speech, the chief sold autographs at $1.50 apiece.

Surrounded by the nineteenth-century equivalent of hype, Villard proudly rolled along on his brand-new tracks, some stretches of which were bearing the weight of a railroad car for the first time. With him in the leading train were Fanny and their four children, Jane Whelon (three-month-old Hilgard's nurse), and a clutch of notable Germans. The predominantly English passengers in the second train included the British minister, Lionel Sackville-West, and his lovely young daughter Victoria. (Later, as Lady Sackville, Victoria had a daughter, a second Victoria Sackville-West, known as Vita, who became a prolific writer and Virginia Woolf's close friend.) Journalists were relegated to the fourth car, and so they hit every town at the end of the party and had to get their reports on the festivities from more or less competent witnesses.

As the trains rolled across the empty plains, they passed isolated herds of buffalo, survivors of a holocaust, and some of the gentlemen amused themselves by potting at the beasts through the open windows of the moving cars. The Europeans, who had never seen buffalo before, seemed particularly keen, but were good sports about taking turns. In Greycliff, Montana, near the Crow Indian Reservation, the passengers left the train to gaze in wonder at a group of three thousand Crow assembled on the plain in front of their encampment. It was a confrontation heavy with symbolism: the defeated people had agreed to provide some entertainment for their conquerors, who were celebrating their continuing conquest. As Villard had requested, a contingent of young Crow warriors in headdresses and fierce war paint, about three hundred strong and not all of them sober, performed a wild, howling war dance, complete with throbbing drums and menacing gestures. This performance thrilled some of the spectators and caused others, particularly the Germans, great consternation. Perhaps they, whose uncivilized ancestors fought the Romans so long and so bitterly, recognized the authentic malevolence of the barbarian warriors as they raged in the scalp dance. After the ceremony a young Crow came up to Victoria Sackville-West and wished to get into her carriage, suggesting, without much ado, "You go. Me go." She rejected his suit, but never forgot it.

High in the Rockies, Villard's makeshift tracks, built because two long tunnels through the mountain were still unfinished, showed how close to the edge of disaster his recklessness and haste had brought him. At the first tunnel, engines had to pull the passenger cars up the ascent (which was more than double the grade the government allowed) two by two, over the Continental Divide, and then down a steep descent via a series of breathtaking switchbacks. Things were much the same at the second tunnel, except that by then it was night, and according to the German journalist Nicolaus Mohr, a member of the party, "It was too dark to see, but we guessed that we were being pulled along terrifying cliffs. From time to time we caught sight of a light far down below us and by the sounds of creaking wood we could tell we were creeping across deep chasms." On the way down two cars separated, and at the bottom one slammed into the other, jarring the whole train and doing a great deal of damage; one of the cars had its roof and one side ripped off. A terrible fear seized Villard as he jumped from the train, hurting his foot, and he ran limping to the wrecked car. Fortunately it held several unflappable English persons, who picked themselves up off the floor laughing and told Villard that there was, quite honestly, no harm done. The car carrying Frederick Billings, of all people, had also been tossed about, but the quantity of flying glass had missed him, and no one else on the train was hurt, either. Villard breathed a heartfelt sigh of relief, and his excursion continued.

At Gold Creek, the last-spike ceremony was the climax and consecration of all that had gone before. Three thousand people—cowboys, Indians, ranchers, miners, adventurers, farmers—watched and listened as no fewer than eighteen dignitaries spoke, including Villard. Frederick Billings, in a magnanimous effusion, declared, "There were brave men before Agamemnon. There have been last spikes and last spikes, but there was never a more significant last spike driven on the continent than this one; never one which had more work and faith behind it; never one with a greater future before it." As time passed, the crowd, in the manner of crowds, grew restless, and some of its number sought to calm themselves with liquor. At last the speeches were over; two competing crews, demonstrating "the speed and precision with which rails were laid," hammered down the last twelve hundred feet of track; their headlong efforts drove the crowd into a frenzy of excitement. The supreme moment arrived, amid the shriek of train whistles, the roar of cannon, and the shouts of the spectators. With a gesture of resignation, the Sioux chief Iron Bull handed the last spike to Villard. Baby Hilgard touched it, and then Villard and Fanny and Grant and Billings and a couple of others all struck the spike that fastened the final track on the transcontinental line to the earth. The military band played "God Save the Queen," "Die Wacht am Rhein," and "Yankee Doodle"; the assembled multitude, perhaps thinking that now at last there would be food and drink, went into ecstasies of cheering and stomping. It was about eighteen minutes past five, Montana time, in the afternoon of September 8, 1883, and Villard stood at the pinnacle of his career. But his balance was wobbly, and he wouldn't stay there long.

As the trains moved westward, amid widespread jubilation, Villard continued to wave and doff and bow and speak, but the bad news had already reached him: his stocks were still falling, all across the board, and nothing, not even the reiterated festivities of the last-spike excursion, looked like stopping them. "Festive" barely describes the celebrations that took place in Portland, the western end of the transcontinental line. Years later, in his history of Oregon transportation, Villard could not refrain from a reference to what he called, without undue modesty, "the greatest event in the history of Portland—the great celebration of the opening of the Northern Pacific as a through line, and the magnificent welcome extended to me and to the hundreds of guests who accompanied me across the continent." At the time his accomplishments seemed to him, in his heart of hearts, less unequivocally wonderful. In Tacoma and Seattle the hero's welcomes and the outpourings of admiration continued, but none of these blandishments could distract him for long. He was in a panic to get back to New York and see what he could do about averting catastrophe.

On September 15, while Villard was still in Seattle, an article in the *New York Herald*'s financial section described the previous day's stock market activity, which had resulted in a slight drop:

> The decline . . . probably would not have occurred at all had it not been for a general stamping upon the Northern Pacific properties, about which, for an hour or two, the scalpers of the

Board Room executed a regular war dance. Their viciousness emanated from reports that a very damaging statement of the company's affairs, prepared by an expert, was shortly to be made public.

The vivid imagery suited the interests of a man who had just sponsored such a dance. This story, and other stories like it, preyed on Villard's mind as he and his family hurried home.

Fanny's diary entries from the final days of the excursion are blithe and bland; they suggest either that she too had well-developed denial skills or that her husband had not yet revealed to her what his enormous public relations effort had been conceived to dissemble. In Tacoma, on September 13, Fanny described how "Harry walked proudly at the head of his company to the tune of the music." The next day, in Seattle, they were met by "the most enthusiastic reception of all," and the daughter of the president of the university, which Villard had recently saved from collapse, welcomed him with a speech "so touching, we all felt moved to tears." Despite Fanny's tone of blissful ignorance, Villard's mounting stress must have communicated itself to her in some way; on the trip back to New York she horrified both him and their children by fainting dead away in a Chicago department store.

The return to the real world made Villard sick, too. His obsession had drained him, physically, mentally, and financially; his great transcontinental excursion, while it had added to the sum of his glory, had not accomplished its larger purpose of attracting investors; the complicated structure that his energy had built, that his willpower and charisma had sustained, was threatening to fall down around his ears. The thought made his head pound—he already had a bad cold—and he moved closer to the catatonic despair that lay in wait for him on the other side of every failure. While Fanny stayed at Thorwood with the older children and the "transcontinental baby," as she called Hilgard, her weary husband tried to reconquer Wall Street, which had surrendered to him so willingly not very long ago but was now, to his further detriment, in the throes of a panic.

As his stocks continued to fall, Villard sought assistance—that is, capital—from many sources, but he had lost his magic touch. He darted and dodged, devising mortgage plans, shuffling figures, investing more of his own money, executing various frantic maneuvers designed to calm his stockholders. His disillusioned friend Endicott looked on sadly. "I cannot quite make up my mind," he told Villard, "whether it is you or Barnum that has the greatest show on earth."

According to Fanny's diary, it wasn't until October 17 that she learned anything specific about her husband's distress: "Harry told me of the terribly anxious time of it he has had, owing to the swindling operations at the stock market and the terrible depreciation in his stocks." Could he have failed to tell her anything before this, or she to notice that something was amiss? In any case, their troubles deepened. After a celebration dinner hosted by his departing German guests at Delmonico's, Henry confided his despair to Fanny: "My darling, I have had a very trying time of it yesterday in a business way and wished all evening I had the comfort of your presence. . . . I must confess I did not feel like feasting and it cost me an effort to keep my countenance. Well, there is an end to all our troubles! May it come soon for us." Villard's fortunes were buoyed only temporarily by some of his loyal German friends, who staked him to $20 million against a second mortgage on the Northern Pacific. By the middle of December the road was still operating at a deficit, and bankruptcy loomed.

The Villards valiantly kept up appearances throughout the fall. In order to be near Henry's work and their new house, which was approaching completion, they moved into the Buckingham Hotel on Fifth Avenue. They attended operas, dined out fashionably, oversaw their workers. But in late November, at the end of his rope, Villard capitulated and asked Endicott and two other friends to examine his accounts and advise him as to what he should do. At midnight on December 17, Endicott roused him in his suite at the Buckingham to give him the verdict: he must resign immediately from the presidency of both the Oregon & Transcontinental Company and the Oregon Railway & Navigation Company, his two prize creations, and prepare to do the same at the Northern Pacific. Meanwhile a syndicate (headed by Endicott) would see about clearing up the very large mess that he had made.

Villard felt betrayed. It surprised him (though it will not surprise the reader) to discover that people who had supported him when he was making money for them withdrew their support when he stopped. Even insiders in his companies had used their knowledge and sold their stocks to save their own personal skin, while he had stood firm and lost a goodly portion of his. He accepted Endicott's terms, however—he really had little choice—and the next day, by way of economizing in their newly straitened circumstances, the Villards moved out of the Buckingham and into their new mansion. Though not quite finished, it was certainly fit for habitation, and there the family passed an unsociable, gloomy December. They missed the Vanderbilts' lavish ball on the eleventh, nor did they attend the Astors' Christmas party; outdoors the sound of sleigh bells seemed to mock their misery, but home was no better. "The house, beautiful as it is, is only trying to us," Fanny wrote in her diary on Christmas Eve. A few weeks later, to his lasting chagrin, Villard was forced to resign from the presidency of the Northern Pacific as well. His letter of resignation cited two factors in his decision: "nervous prostration" and the best interests of the company. His fall was now nearly complete; he contemplated it amid the splendors of his new home, whose foundations had developed a distinct tremor.

The newspapers, of course, were mad for this story. Even the least experienced cub reporter could see rich possibilities in the tale of a man who within a period of twenty-four hours had lost control of two major corporations and moved into a palace. Rumors flew; anonymous sources, both real and contrived, provided good copy; reporters were rebuffed and therefore free to use their imaginations. A few papers were sympathetic, many others weighed Mr. Villard's business practices and found them wanting, and still others were obviously delighted that so proud a man had got his comeuppance. There was much speculation: about half a million dollars' worth of bonds that he had supposedly stashed away in Fanny's name; about what percentage, if any, of his personal fortune he had really lost; about whether or not he was in his right mind. Insulting crowds began to gather on Madison Avenue, many among them disgruntled investors in Villard's companies who had no carved marble fireplaces or stained glass to comfort them in their loss.

On January 5, an interview with Henry Clews, a man whom Villard admired and respected, appeared in the *World*. Clews couched his opinion of the matter in frankly funereal terms, and Villard must have winced at what he read. Villard's resignation, Clews declared solemnly,

> makes a sorry ending of a life that only a few months since had so bright a promise. No man ever came to Wall Street with so much encouragement; no man ever had such confidence placed in him; no man ever had more financial power given to him; no man ever has, apparently, so abused such a position. It may be from ignorance and it may be from wilfulness, and this can be ascertained only by an accurate knowledge of that gentleman's present financial status.

Villard read the newspapers, listened to the crowds, and edged closer to a breakdown. More than anything else, the accusations of dishonesty grieved him, because they seemed monstrously unjust; wouldn't a dishonest man have avoided losing so much money? He refused to defend himself publicly or grant any sort of interview and sank further into despair. Toward the end of January, Frederick Billings, who thought the reports of Villard's losses exaggerated, came to get the truth from him in person. Billings's biographer memorably paints the ensuing scene: "The two men, one exhausted and on the verge of hysteria, the other in a state of high exasperation and anxiety, shouted at each other amid the new paint and varnish." Villard was, of course, far from having lost *everything*—he had had too much for that—but he was able to convince Billings that his losses had been substantial enough to deserve sympathy, and the two parted without animosity.

Despite Clews's asseverations, accurate knowledge of Villard's financial plight was not forthcoming. It seems likely that he lost about $5 million, not enough to satisfy those who thought he should lose all, as had some of the investors whom he had led to ruin, but enough to shield him from accusations of gross deception. The thought gave him little comfort. For its part, the press described the Villards' tragic dive into the abyss of bad finances so dramatically that they attracted a great deal of sympathy for their plight. Commiserating letters poured in, and L. P. di Cesnola, the director of the Metropolitan Museum of Art, found it in his heart to make an offer probably unique in the history of museums: he proposed to return the Villards' $1,000 subscription.

As she watched her husband sliding deeper and deeper into despondency, Fanny turned to the man whose ebullience and confidence were the equal of Villard's on his best days: Thomas Edison. The inventor arrived at the mansion with a draft for $40,000, the repayment of the advance that Villard had given him at a crucial stage in his work on the electric locomotive; more important, he brought a bright vision of the future to the man who had often shared his visions:

> When Mr. Villard was all broken down and in a stupor caused by his disasters in connection with the Northern Pacific, Mrs. Villard called for me to come and cheer him up. It was very difficult to rouse him from his despair and apathy, but I talked about the electric light to him, and its development, and told him that it would help him win it all back and put him in his former position.

Fanny had chosen her man wisely. Edison gave Villard the glimmer of hope—an electric glimmer—that started him on the road to recovery and would lead him once again to pots of gold.

As the weeks passed it became obvious that Henry, Fanny, and the children would be compelled to abandon their dream house, which they were no longer able to afford and which had, in any case, become an oppressive symbol of Villard's folly. At the end of April, after a quiet residence of four and a half months on Madison Avenue—one wonders how much time they had spent, altogether, in the triple drawing room—they moved back to Thorwood. The town house was transferred to trustees and stood empty for two and a half years; the Villards never saw the inside of their former home again.

Not even Thorwood, it turned out, was far enough from Wall Street. Once again, Villard felt the need of recovering from a mighty blow on his native ground. Besides that, now that he was feeling somewhat better, he had some new proposals for his German friends. Having sustained no losses on his account, they retained their confidence in him, and he wanted to talk to them about the Edison Electric Light Company.

Early in June, Villard sailed away from New York, intending to stop in England before going on to Germany. One writer states that Villard "fled to Europe, leaving a trail of disillusionment in his wake," along with a "formidable backlog of debts, unpaid bills, muddled contracts . . . ill-advised purchases . . . personal animosities and conflicting financial interests." He also left behind, at least for a while, Fanny and the children, preferring to lick his wounds in relative solitude. As his health and self-esteem returned, he began to think of himself as a man with a grand vision whom less farsighted men had betrayed and abandoned for mere gain. Only little by little, and then imperfectly, would he come to realize that he had fulfilled his evolutionary function in the economic jungle. It had taken a freewheeling, gambling entrepreneur like himself to open up the Pacific Northwest; the problems of further development would have to be addressed by more disciplined, more meticulous, more technical minds than his.

HENRY HILGARD VILLARD.

Photograph of young Hilgard, c. 1889, by Sarony.

Sophia Smith Collection, Smith College.

19

The Vanity of Human Wishes

O child of paradise,
Boy who made dear his father's home,
In whose deep eyes
Men read the welfare of the times to come,
I am too much bereft.
The world dishonored thou hast left.
O truth's and nature's costly lie!
O trusted broken prophecy!
O richest fortune sourly crossed!
Born for the future, to the future lost!

RALPH WALDO EMERSON
"Threnody"

ccompanied by Wendell Garrison, Villard settled into his voyage of recuperation. As so often in his life, he was seeking solace in transportation, in motion, traveling away from painful memories and into the future, and the farther he got from the scene of his disasters, the higher his spirits rose. His ultimate destination was Germany, where he planned to visit relatives and friends, confer with potential investors, and find a suitable residence for himself and his wife and children. First, however, the two brothers-in-law passed a few days in London.

The receptions that greeted Villard in both England and Germany proved to be wonderfully restorative. A lavish dinner in London featured testimonials and expressions of gratitude from those British citizens who had been his guests on the great last-spike excursion, and he was given a gold loving cup inscribed with their names. Still smarting from the stinging blows inflicted upon him by the American press, Villard found balm for his wounds in the deferential, respectful treatment he received in the British newspapers.

Once he reached Rhenish Bavaria, Villard's rehabilitative journey became a triumphal progress. Although news of his transcontinental extravaganza had intrigued the citizens of his native region, to them Villard was chiefly known as a philanthropist. He had frequently extended his bounty to the province in general and to his two hometowns of Speyer and Zweibrücken in particular, giving money to schools, libraries, historical societies, and museums, setting up funds for scholarships and loans to benefit poor people, providing disaster relief, building a hospital and nursing school (*Diakonissenanstalt*) in Zweibrücken that was to grow into one of the largest institutions of its kind in Germany. Villard's unstinting generosity had earned him the gratitude of his former countrymen, and when they learned of his imminent arrival they turned out in force to demonstrate their feelings. Villard proudly described several particularly heartwarming scenes in a long letter to Fanny:

> The papers had announced my movements and in consequence crowds of people waited at every station and cheered me as the train passed. On arriving at Speyer, I was welcomed with an address by the burgomaster on alighting from the car. He headed a deputation of forty gentlemen in dress coats and white ties, among them several old friends. I was conducted to a carriage and as I came out of the station buildings I saw a crowd of thousands welcoming me with continued "Hochs," and waving hats and handkerchiefs. We led a long procession of carriages which moved slowly through the streets. . . . Every house was decorated with flags and many with flowers, garlands and inscriptions. The side-walks and windows were lined all along the route with enthusiastic people. Altogether it was an overwhelming reception—the more so as I had not expected such an ovation in the least.
>
> After supper I was serenaded by the united singing societies

of the place. . . . Then we had a reception and it was nearly midnight before I got to bed. . . . The next morning at 9 a.m. I commenced receiving deputations from the gymnasia, charitable and other institutions which I had assisted.

Villard's letter goes on like this for several pages. He was the guest of honor at a banquet presided over by the provincial governor and "attended by 150 representative men of Rhenish Bavaria." There were toasts, a "most eloquent and flattering speech" delivered by the governor, an expansively grateful reply from Villard. After the banquet he was conveyed to a public park, "where all Speyer had assembled to honor me once more with an illumination, fireworks, music and no end of enthusiasm."

There was likewise no end of adulation. These scenes repeated themselves the next day in Kaiserslautern, whither Villard had been transported by special train. He was assured, more than once, that "the king himself would not have had as hearty a reception." The celebrations culminated in Zweibrücken, where a crowd of thousands greeted him at the station on the evening of his arrival and a torch-lit procession led him through the festive streets, which were lined with citizens clamoring at the sight of him. He was serenaded to sleep and applauded upon awakening, and when he left Zweibrücken a couple of days later, thoroughly feted, toasted, and hoarse from having been called on so often to "say a few words," another crowd gathered around his departing train and cheered it out of the station.

No physician could have prescribed a better way to banish the lingering physical and mental effects of Villard's business debacle. The ovations "formed a most soothing and flattering compensation" for his recent "bitter trials," and all his old zest returned to him. Having decided that he and his family would live in Berlin, former capital of Prussia and now, thanks to Otto von Bismarck, capital of a united Germany, Villard quickly made arrangements to lease a large, comfortable apartment and returned to America in August. Two weeks later he sailed back to Germany, this time in the company of Fanny and their four children. By October they were settled in

Berlin, where they would spend what Villard later called a "most grat-ifying" two years.

Villard's surviving sister, Emma, had lived for more than ten years in Berlin with her husband, Gen. Robert von Xylander, and the city was also home to several other relatives, friends, and veterans of the last-spike excursion. The Xylanders had been Villard's honored guests during that memorable trip, and now they returned the favor by introducing the Villards into the capital's most glittering social cir-cles. Mr. and Mrs. Villard quickly became acquainted "with official society and with the leaders in science, art, literature, and finance, and their families." Villard, of course, was something of a lion in such groups, from which he received admiration for his accomplishments, honor for his exploits, and sympathy for his misfortunes. Once again he was comfortable, reassured, respected, important, and like an old champion he began to think about making a glorious comeback and regaining his rightful title.

In 1884, during the reign of Emperor Wilhelm I and under the expert guidance of his chancellor, Bismarck, Germany was the dom-inant power on the continent, the most dynamic, the strongest eco-nomically and militarily, the most technologically advanced. German education was the best in Europe; German industry was in full ex-pansion; German culture, particularly music and literature, was in full bloom. The zeitgeist, perfectly suited to Villard's temperament and tastes, was energetic and vital, ambitious and confident.

As always, Villard sought the company of intelligent, cultured, suc-cessful, and powerful people. He and Fanny frequently entertained guests in their salon, and some of the leading figures in Germany availed themselves of the Villards' hospitality. One important regular visitor was Werner von Siemens, an inventor, an electrical engineer, and the pioneering head of Germany's first electric company, who shared with Villard and Edison the conviction that the future of elec-tric power was immeasurably great. A wide range of other guests—scholars, scientists, statesmen, artists—included Theodor Mommsen, the noted historian of ancient Rome, and Joseph Joachim, the greatest violinist of his day.

Mommsen was famous for his liberal politics but he was sufficiently conservative to believe that they did not apply to women. One memorable evening, while seated at the Villards' table, he chose to regale the company, including his suffragist hostess, with his opinions on gender issues. The proper place for women, he opined, was in the home, fulfilling their homely duties, for they were unfit to meddle in the intellectual sphere; knowing this, German men tolerated no silly aspirations on the part of their women and preferred them simple, domestic, and beautiful. The normally sweet-tempered Fanny, who found the women of Germany unlovely, unfashionable, and uncharming, replied angrily that Herr Professor Mommsen's countrywomen might well be simple and domestic, but that they would have to work hard to meet his third requirement. Oswald Garrison Villard, the source of this story, unfortunately fails to record Villard's reaction to the symbolic clash that was taking place in his dining room between the Old World and the New, between his past and his present, between a representative of his father's patriarchal generation and the American feminist whom he himself loved and admired above all women.

The Villards' friendship with Joachim proved more satisfactory. The music-loving Fanny, whose German was by now quite good, delighted in the conversation of an artist so eminent and so intelligent, and she and Villard attended many recitals and concerts at which the maestro performed as a soloist, played with his fellow members of the Joachim-DeAnha String Quartet, or conducted the Berlin Philharmonic Orchestra. His programs included much new music, including works by Johannes Brahms and Gustav Mahler. Except for Hilgard, who was still too young, each of the Villard children played a musical instrument—Helen and Oswald the violin, Harold the cello—and Joachim was even induced to listen to Helen's playing and recommend a teacher for her. We can imagine the poor girl, whom years of more or less constant discomfort had rendered reticent and inward, getting ready to submit her fiddling to the judgment of her parents' friend, the finest violinist in the world. In fact Helen and her brothers were accomplished amateurs, and with Fanny on piano they performed chamber concerts for the pleasure of family and friends.

All of the Villard children profited from their two years' stay in Berlin. It was true that young Hilgard, a bright, lovable little boy, the focal point of the family's affection, seemed occasionally susceptible to bouts of illness that struck without warning. In this he resembled his father, and like his father he rebounded quickly from such crises, even though some of them were quite severe and one at least, like a dire premonition, struck terror into the hearts of his family. But Hilgard's powers of recovery and his sunny, affectionate, uncomplaining nature were enough to persuade his parents that there was nothing seriously wrong with him.

Wherever Henry Villard was, whether in some backwater frontier town or in one of the centers of European civilization, he inevitably encountered powerful people who stood at the peak of the social pyramid. In Berlin, his family background and international fame— to say nothing of his natural magnetism—facilitated his access to the very highest levels of German society. Villard and Fanny could count among their acquaintances Kaiser Wilhelm's son Crown Prince Friedrich and Friedrich's wife, Princess Victoria, named after her mother, the reigning queen of England. This was a decidedly progressive royal couple, and the Villards frequently encountered them, not only at banquets, balls, and various official functions but also on the frozen pond in the *Thiergarten,* democratically ice-skating among their future subjects. The princess, who knew of and admired Villard's charitable activities on behalf of schools in the Palatinate, sought his help in setting up the first girls' high school in Germany. (A forceful and resolute woman, Princess Victoria was instrumental in forming and focusing the enlightened views of her husband, and much good was expected of his reign. In the event, however, Kaiser Friedrich III succumbed to throat cancer little more than three months after his father's death in 1888, and the throne passed to his son, the autocratic, militaristic, self-deluded Wilhelm II, who was to play such a significant role in facilitating the cataclysm that was World War I.)

Proposals and requests of various kinds came Villard's way during his stay in Berlin. The Turkish government tried to recruit him to supervise the building of a railroad system through the wilds of

Anatolia; a private group wanted him to take over the financing and building of a long line in German East Africa, from the seacoast to the interior. Villard had no inclination to venture quite so far from civilization as he knew it—according to his memoirs, the idea of living for years with his family in such outposts was "utterly repulsive to him"*—but he had other, more agreeable possibilities. The directors of the Deutsche Bank, for example, often applied to him for information on American investment opportunities and were clearly thinking about employing him as their agent. Villard bided his time, enjoying his leisure while carefully considering his best move. In April 1885, on the occasion of his fiftieth birthday, he could look back over a working life of adventure and accomplishment, but he wasn't through yet.

From the wreck of his enterprises, Villard had salvaged the presidency of the Oregon & California Railroad. This office required him to make frequent trips to London, but running a far-flung, complex business operation by remote control, with no possibility of personal, on-site involvement, failed to hold his attention. At the end of 1885, Villard resigned from the O&C, and thus he was free from all major business obligations when the Deutsche Bank made him a most attractive offer.

The bank wanted Villard to represent them in New York, not as a banker—for which position he had neither interest nor training—but as an investor, charged with identifying and acquiring solid, profit-making securities in America's public and corporate sectors,

---

* The final section of Henry Villard's two-volume *Memoirs,* published a few years after his death, shifts from the leisurely first-person narrative of the seven previous sections to a hurried third-person account. In the preface to the first volume, we are told that Villard, in failing health, "devoted his last summer to a compendium of the period from 1863 to 1900 written in the third person." If true, this is very strange; Henry Villard was a man of distinctly first-person tendencies, and his *Early History of Transportation in Oregon,* purportedly written during the same period, is couched in the first person. Why would he switch to a third-person narrative for his own autobiography? It seems likely that the final section of the *Memoirs* was compiled by (though for inscrutable reasons not attributed to) Villard's sons Harold and Oswald, who based their work on letters, newspaper articles, family memories, their father's other writings (both published and unpublished), and his voluminous papers, thus preserving, for the most part, Villard's own words.

with a particular emphasis on railroad securities. In other words, armed to the teeth with German capital, Henry Villard could return to the railroad wars. He was well rested, formidably backed, and famished for vindication. He believed that his reappearance in New York under these auspices would "be tantamount to his complete rehabilitation," and he couldn't wait to make Wall Street and its denizens—colleagues, friends, and enemies alike—feel his weight. Villard agreed, in principle, to the bank's offer; arrangements and negotiations began.

Early in February 1886, while in Berlin, the Villards had signed a deed of sale, conveying one of the Villard Houses (457 Madison Avenue) to Harris C. Fahnestock. In September, just before sailing for New York, the Villards received a cable from Whitelaw Reid, who offered to buy their south wing at 451 Madison Avenue, the place they had for four and a half months called home. It was Reid who, as Villard's colleague and rival in their war correspondent days, had so decisively scooped him at Shiloh; now Reid was scooping up his house. Reid had married an heiress, and this step proved to be a better means of securing long-term residence in the most lavish of the Villard Houses.

The Villards returned to New York late in October 1886. They spent a few weeks at Thorwood, rejoicing to be back in that lovely place. Then, on November 19, they moved into their Manhattan residence—they thought of it as their "winter-quarters"—the three lower floors of the extraordinary Louis C. Tiffany mansion, which stood (until it was pulled down in 1937) at the corner of Seventy-second Street and Madison Avenue. Fanny, grown used to stately, orderly Berlin, complained to her diary that "the filth of New York is appalling" (as it no doubt was), but the family was apparently quite content to be tenants in the Tiffany house, and they would continue to spend the winters there and the other seasons at Thorwood for the next several years.

Hilgard's fragile health was much more troubling to his parents than the dirty streets of New York. The child ate little, dark circles discolored the pale skin around his eyes, and a bad cold became a persistent, racking cough. To compensate him for his enforced confinement to the house, Hilgard was given a pet dog, a friendly, frisky terrier puppy whom he named Tommy Dot. Little boy and little dog formed an immediate attachment.

One evening not long after they moved into their luxurious winter quarters, the Villards were at home to three hundred guests, who came to welcome Henry and Fanny back to the United States. Among the guests was Thomas Alva Edison, who provided some high-tech entertainment: the new, improved version of his so-called talking machine, the Edison phonograph, the first device capable of reproducing recorded sound. A popular soprano named Lilli Lehmann sang into something that looked like a giant funnel, which surmounted a revolving cylinder; this cylinder was then placed into another machine, and at the flip of a switch there came crackling out into the huge drawing room an attenuated, scratchy version of Miss Lehmann's lovely voice. However low its fidelity, the inventor's newest contraption thrilled the assembly. Relishing the astonishment of his other guests, Villard beamed approval at his brilliant friend and protégé. Edison, it was clear, was a man whose ideas had the potential to change the world, and incidentally to generate enormous profits, and Villard wanted to be instrumental in actualizing that potential. He had never liked to confine himself to one area of business activity; his work for the Deutsche Bank occupied only a part of his busy mind. Ever since his conversations with Edison's German counterpart, Werner von Siemens, Villard had been maturing a grandiose plan to consolidate Edison's various companies, ally them with Siemens's enterprise, and dominate the worldwide expansion of the electrical industry.

The sale of the Villards' Madison Avenue mansion to the Whitelaw Reids in 1886 had at last cleared away Villard's remaining debts and provided him with sufficient capital to make some investments of his own. Always willing to put his and his clients' money in the same place, but older now and more inclined to mature reflection before doing so, Villard reopened his old offices in the Mills Building downtown and began a careful study of the stock market. His credentials (which proved him to be a man with masses of good German capital at his command), along with the vivid memories of his former spectacular successes, gained him a respectful reception in the leading brokerage houses and mostly good-natured treatment from the press.

Determined to make his mark with his first move, Villard spent months in calculation, meditating upon figures and graphs and ledgers and documents like a chess master brooding over a crowded board. He waited so long that his German backers, peeved by the thought of their languishing capital, began to mutter and stir, and the eager anticipation of the players on the street turned to disappointed shrugs; there would be no comeback after all. Finally, in the spring of 1887, Villard moved from contemplation to action: he bought several million dollars' worth of the prime mortgage bonds issued by a small Western railroad. As in the old days, there was a precipitous rush to back his choice, and the market value of the bonds rose steeply. Within a few days he resold them at a significant profit— the name, after all, of the game—and it looked as though his old magic had returned.

This was an immensely satisfying coup, but it proved to be merely the springboard that Villard used to vault once more into what his *Memoirs* call "his former position before the public." Like a lover repenting her faithlessness, the goddess Fortune leapt back to his side and wrapped him in her embrace. And soon, as though to prove her intentions honorable, she placed within his hands the means of regaining everything he had lost.

At the end of August, Elijah J. Smith called upon Villard in his New York offices and without much ado launched into an urgent plea for help. No request could have been sweeter to Villard's ears, for Smith was his successor as president of both the Oregon & Transcontinental Company and the Oregon Railway & Navigation Company, the enterprises that Villard had conceived and founded. The humiliation of having been forced in 1883 to resign from the presidency of his two creations still rankled in his heart. To be begged and cajoled to salvage those very companies seemed like the stuff of fantasy. And yet. Villard must have leaned back in his chair to savor the moment as Smith, at some length, explained what he was proposing.

The crisis of 1883, which Smith felt no need to address in detail, had greatly reduced the power and prestige—in short, the clout—of the Oregon & Transcontinental. Although the company still held a significant number of Northern Pacific shares, the management of the Oregon & Transcontinental could neither come to a satisfactory financial settlement with the Northern Pacific nor even obtain representation on its board of directors. Smith and his Oregon & Transcontinental associates had therefore decided to buy up yet more Northern Pacific shares, enough to gain control of the railroad at its annual board election, which was scheduled for the fall. Alas, they had overextended themselves in this effort, and a proposed bond issue for the Oregon Railway & Navigation Company, from which its agent, the Oregon & Transcontinental, hoped to derive fresh funds, had fallen millions of dollars short of its goal. The upshot of all these developments was that Smith's two companies were sliding into receivership, and that it would cost $5 million to put on the brakes. In return for securing this sum, Villard would get the unpurchased bonds and twenty thousand shares of Railway & Navigation stock, control of the two Oregon companies, and sufficient proxies for the Northern Pacific election to place whomever he liked on the railroad's board of directors.

"What a revolution of the wheel of fortune!" Villard's *Memoirs* exclaim. Struggling to maintain his objectivity in a matter that stirred his emotions so deeply, Villard cabled the terms of the proposal to his German backers and urged them to make their decision without delay. The response was almost immediate, and within thirty-six hours the entire sum was at his disposal. So quick a transaction was unheard of, and once again Henry Villard had succeeded in dazzling Wall Street and the financial press. Not by some painstaking series of maneuvers, but in what amounted to a lightning flash, Villard had made his dramatic return to railroad affairs in the Pacific Northwest; he was, once again, the "Railroad King." The *Boston Herald* proclaimed that "Henry Villard is the man of affairs par excellence in this country. Jay Gould is the monster money machine, Villard the genius of financial operations."

Despite the crash of 1883, Villard had managed to retain the trust of many of his former backers, but this trust carried with it, he knew, grave responsibilities. Although he was flattered by the encomiums in the newspapers and the congratulations that came pouring in from all over America and Europe, the memory of what had happened to him the last time he stood on the heights remained fresh in his mind. "He had received too severe a lesson," we read in his *Memoirs,* "as to the fleeting character of quickly acquired wealth and the fickleness of public favor to be very eager to expose himself again to a like fate." Like many hard lessons, however, this one would have to be learned more than once.

After days of deliberating, Villard resolved to occupy no administrative or executive position at any of the three companies, not even as a director on the board of the Northern Pacific. He would remain in the background, operating as a financier and nothing more. Predictably, this admirable resolve aroused a storm of protest from all concerned; ardent representations were made to him regarding his experience, his expertise, his duty; and against his better judgment he bowed to the pressure. He resumed the leadership of his two Oregon companies and returned to his former seat on the board of the Northern Pacific. He was determined to clear up the railroad's financial mess, put an end to bickering both internal and external, and settle down to the business of making large profits for his clients, his stockholders, and himself. Eventually he would look upon his decision to "burden himself again with corporate responsibilities" as "the greatest mistake he ever made." Now, however, despite his misgivings, he seemed wholeheartedly back in the game, participating in hard and hectic negotiations, elaborating complicated plans, asserting his control.

At the same time, Villard was furthering his electrical agenda. Naturally inclined to view the big picture, he was farsighted enough to realize, long before most of the industrialists and big businessmen of his day, that the world would sooner or later run on electricity, and that current was destined to replace steam. He had never, even in his darkest days, relinquished his stock in Edison's original company, resolutely holding on as the shares he'd purchased at thirty-three and a third dollars rose past four thousand.

Now, having interested Werner von Siemens in the idea of German-American cooperation in promoting electricity, Villard approached Thomas Edison. Before there could be any international combinations, Villard explained, all of the Edison light and manufacturing companies, over which the inventor himself had long ceased to exercise any control, must be consolidated into a single new corporation, for which Villard proposed the name of Edison General Electric Company. The firm would design, manufacture, and distribute electrical appliances, provide municipalities with electricity, and encourage Edison's genius by providing him with the capital necessary to produce new inventions.

Like Villard, Edison was a man with a large vision constantly thwarted by shorter-sighted men unwilling to risk the sums necessary to turn the vision into palpable reality. The inventor had already spent too much time beseeching the cautious, conservative directors (including the Morgan group) of his various companies to fund their expansion, and he saw in Villard a kindred spirit, a man of audacious imagination. Edison and his associates quickly agreed to Villard's proposals, leaving it to him to conduct the enervating negotiations required to effect the consolidation. Villard was also in contact with his German investors: Werner von Siemens, acting through the Deutsche Bank and backed by his large and immensely successful firm, Siemens & Halske; and the General Electricity Company of Berlin, an important electrical manufacturing and contracting company.

Villard, however, was not the only financial entrepreneur fascinated by electricity and Thomas Edison. The redoubtable J. Pierpont Morgan, too, had visited Menlo Park, spoken with the inventor, admired his work, disapproved of his personal hygiene. He had even had "one of the first isolated [lighting] plants" that Edison produced installed in his own home. Convinced of electricity's future, but also convinced that it was not yet at hand, Morgan had made some preliminary investments and proposed to take control of this "promising industry" in the fullness of time, when and if it became sufficiently profitable. Since Drexel, Morgan & Company, the banking syndicate effectively commanded by Morgan, controlled the finances of Edison's enterprises—to Edison's great chagrin; the conservative bankers continually rejected his funding requests—Morgan could watch the progress of the new industry that Edison had called into being and choose the moment of least risk and greatest profit-making potential.

Recognizing that Morgan's threatening presence could not be ignored, Villard included Drexel, Morgan when putting together his international electrical combination, the Edison General Electric Company. In April 1889 the two German companies and Edison's consolidated company formed a conglomerate, Edison General Electric, with capital of $12 million, more than 60 percent of which was held by Villard and his German friends. Drexel, Morgan provided most of the rest. Their interests thus joined, the potential rivals Morgan and Villard eyed each other warily. Unlike the vast majority of the magnates of the Gilded Age, Morgan was at least as well educated, cosmopolitan, multilingual, and cultured as Villard. He was, furthermore, the heir of a good family and a handsome fortune, which had grown colossal under his shrewd guidance. Morgan, Villard knew, was a worthy opponent, and he would be a formidable competitor for control of Edison General Electric. In 1889, backed by the Deutsche Bank, which had provided the bulk of EGE's capital, Villard became its first president. He had conceived, formed, and financed a huge multinational corporation, brought about "one of the biggest consolidations ever carried out under the laws of New Jersey," and taken command of the whole operation, which still thrives today as General Electric. Morgan and his associates managed, quite profitably, EGE's initial stock offering, and the great man bided his time.

Meanwhile the railroad wars were heating up again, and Villard had to shift his concentration for a while to the Northwest. For a man who had wished to avoid the stress of responsibilities, who had sought to stand out of the spotlight, he seemed particularly busy and highly visible.

The railroad struggle was a contest for territorial domination that pitted the Northern Pacific, now effectively controlled by Villard and his allies, against the Union Pacific, whose president was Charles Francis Adams Jr. Adams's distinguished family tree included two presidents (his grandfather and his great-grandfather); his brother Henry was a prominent historian and writer, author of *The Education of Henry Adams* and *Mont-Saint-Michel and Chartres,* among other works. Villard and Adams, who were the same age, had known each other since long before their railroad days, when both were active in the American Social Science Association in Boston. They had, in addition, certain personal characteristics in common. According to one historian, Adams's "prickly ego found salve in taking the high ground with those who exploited his shortcomings. Ironically, he shared this characteristic with Villard, whose own ego was as vulnerable as it was massive." As railroad rivals, each of them seems to have felt a more or less grudging respect for the other. Adams admired Villard's persistence, his large-scale ideas, and considered him the "biggest man of the crowd." On the other hand, when frustrated by his opponent, Adams could refer to Villard, with all conviction, as "a vagabond Teuton and a Yankee swine."

In the background of this struggle, looming next to J. P. Morgan in the periphery of Villard's vision, hovered another rival for business success, the competent and dangerous James J. Hill. Hill's Manitoba line, soon to be consolidated into the Great Northern Railroad, lay to the north of the Northern Pacific and was stretching steadily westward from Crookston, in northeast Minnesota. Unlike Villard and almost everyone else in the industry, Hill built cautiously, cheaply, and efficiently, availed himself of no federal assistance, and made sure to build to markets big enough to support his advance. He had already announced his intention to build to Spokane and on to Puget Sound. While the Union Pacific and the Northern Pacific faced off, Hill continued his line's inexorable westward movement in what many consider the greatest of all the great American railroad-building feats.

The aim of every railroad chieftain was to dominate—or better yet, monopolize—the railroad traffic in his region. Villard and Adams both recognized the threat that Hill posed; the Northwest hardly seemed big enough for two east-west lines, let alone three. Fearing that the Union Pacific and the Northern Pacific might destroy each other in a protracted struggle, Villard called a truce and entered into negotiations with Adams to settle the many differences between their two roads.

The negotiations proved to be particularly arduous and lengthy. At one point, thinking an agreement had been reached and tormented by gout, Villard went to Karlsbad, Germany, for a cure, only to be called home, gout or not, by the news that Adams had reneged on the deal. Later, Adams built lines into Northern Pacific territory; Villard retaliated by constructing a line that threatened the Union Pacific's monopoly of the mining traffic in Montana. At last the struggle came down to control of Villard's creation and pride, the Oregon & Transcontinental, the holding company that owned the bulk of Northern Pacific stock. The O&T's extensive Northern Pacific holdings made it the decisive battleground; whoever controlled the Oregon & Transcontinental controlled the destiny of the Northern Pacific Railroad.

At the insistence of his German backers, Villard had reluctantly resumed the presidency of the Oregon & Transcontinental. When he learned that the Union Pacific was maneuvering toward a hostile takeover, he began to prepare his defenses, spurred on by the information that Hill and several of his heaviest moneymen intended to join the serried ranks of those who were trying to swallow up the Oregon & Transcontinental. Both sides scrambled for leverage in the company's upcoming board elections by obtaining proxies and snapping up shares of Oregon & Transcontinental stock, which as a consequence of being sought after more than doubled in price. The struggle between these combatants involved rapid deployment, massed formations, enormous transactions, all reported in the financial press as though from the front lines of a war zone and followed eagerly by the nation's finance and railroad buffs. Villard called the seesaw battle "the bitterest fight" of his life, and when in the end he was triumphant, when his forces at last controlled the boardroom of the Oregon & Transcontinental, he felt not elation but disgust, self-reproach, exhaustion. The months of frenetic effort, the endless palaver, the surreal pressure, the public notoriety—it added up to too high a price, no matter how valuable his stocks were. This last battle proved to him "how well founded his fears had been of the disagreeable consequences to himself personally of his return to power, and he could not help upbraiding himself, even after the struggle was over, for not having followed his own better judgment and remained a private business man."

Although circumstances later caused Villard to sell his interest in the Oregon Railway & Navigation Company, whose management had chosen to throw in their lot with his rivals—the Union Pacific and the group led by James J. Hill—Villard's railroad successes continued throughout 1889. Swiftly and inevitably, he rose to the top in the Northern Pacific hierarchy. In September he was elected chairman of the finance committee, and a month later, yielding once more to the importunities of his friends, he agreed to take over as chairman of the board. The railroad was prospering, earnings were rising splendidly, but the Northern Pacific's financing was haphazard, and large additional expenditures (repairs, improvements, construction of new stations and branch lines) were required. With his power and prestige at their height, Villard was able to consolidate all the Northern Pacific's existing mortgages and obtain a generous amount of operating capital by negotiating what was at the time the largest railroad mortgage ever created. This mighty instrument, conceived and worked out in much of its detail by Villard himself, authorized the issue of a total of $160 million worth of Northern Pacific bonds. When Villard complained of rheumatism to James G. Blaine, an old friend, Blaine replied that any man who floated a mortgage worth $160 million should expect a touch of misery in his back.

His railroad prospering and protected, his electrical business humming toward a future of limitless possibility, his clients and supporters well content, Villard by 1890 was once more an immensely successful man. The continued excellence of the *Evening Post* enhanced his stature, and the recovery of his fortune enabled him to resume his charitable activities at their former level. The vessel of his domestic and family life, expertly piloted by Fanny's loving hand, was sailing tranquilly on. Despite her charitable work and her political activities, despite the concerts and lectures and discussion groups she attended and the endless round of social calls she paid and received, Fanny found time to fill the house with music and flowers, to keep herself abreast of developments in literature, the arts, and current affairs, and to excel as the charming hostess to a large international circle of acquaintances and friends, among them some of the most interesting and accomplished people in the world. As for the Villards' children, Helen had been introduced to society in 1887; there were two hundred guests at her coming-out party. Her health seemed improved, and now there was even the occasional young man. Harold and Oswald were students at Harvard. Little Hilgard, ever attended by Tommy Dot, coddled by his mother and his sister, by Jane, his nurse, and by Peck, his maid, had turned out to be a precocious, sensitive, remarkably sweet-tempered child, wry and grave by turns in his conversation, and gracious in his manners. He had a certain quality that made everyone he met, young or old, desirous of his good opinion. Though never robust, he had been enjoying an extended period of good health—longer than a year—when he began to cough in February.

      ▪   ▪   ▪

E ternal vigilance was the price of railroad barony. Early in 1890, Villard saw that his serenity was in danger of being disturbed by the continuing alliance of Adams's Union Pacific and Hill's Great Northern. An exclusive agreement between them was blocking the Northern Pacific's access to miles and miles of Union Pacific track in Oregon and Washington. In typically aggressive fashion, Villard (backed by some of his numerous German supporters) countered by offering to buy a majority interest in one of Hill's railroads, the St. Paul & Manitoba, the purchase of which would give the Northern Pacific more room to move.

There followed meetings, exhortations, haggling. Villard had charts and figures to prove that his purchase of Hill's railroad would serve both their interests. Hill hemmed and hawed, sought advice, said maybe, then no. Late one evening a few days later, two of Hill's lieutenants, fresh from dinner with him, appeared at the Tiffany house and told Villard that Hill was ready to sell. Skeptical but not hopeless, Villard asked that Hill come to his office at ten o'clock the

following morning to draw up the necessary papers. The two gentlemen, made sanguine by conviviality, assured Villard that Hill would
be there, but the next day Villard waited in vain. Though he had half
expected this, he was nonetheless chagrined. When he called Hill's
offices the next day on one of the new, hand-cranked telephones, he
was told that "Mr. Hill had slipped away again." Mr. Hill would continue to slip away. A rueful passage in the *Memoirs* asserts that this
scheme to buy Hill's railroad, had it been carried out, would have
marked the crowning achievement of Villard's whole career. But Hill
was a shrewd, sinuous opponent, and he could never be brought to
do anything that might work to Villard's advantage.

This contest, and others like it, went on into the spring, but the
Northern Pacific continued to thrive despite the harsh competition.
At the same time, Villard was forming a new corporation, the North
American Company, designed to absorb and reorganize the Oregon
& Transcontinental. Edison General Electric, though likewise flourishing, required some of his attention as well. The turmoil and excitement of big business, however, could not distract him from what
was increasingly on his mind: the failing health of his darling
youngest son.

Hilgard's February cough had by March evolved into whooping
cough, and then into a bronchial infection so severe that pneumonia
seemed inevitable. For weeks his bony little frame was racked by
paroxysms of coughing and vomiting that brought him to the brink
of death as his family looked on in despair. His doctors were the best
available, however, and gradually he began to recover. By the middle
of May, his appetite and some of his color had returned, and he and
Tommy Dot were enjoying the delights of spring on the beautiful
grounds at Thorwood. This respite, however, proved to be both temporary and brief. Hilgard's seventh birthday party on May 22 was a
great success, but it was, as Fanny later wrote, "the last rejoicing of
the kind."

Hilgard began to grow weaker, more easily tired, and several
times Villard had to carry his exhausted son home from a short walk
while a cold fear gripped his heart. Soon Hilgard's face began to take
on an ominous radiance. On June 3, Thorwood was the scene of the

wedding of the daughter of T. F. Oakes, the president of the Northern Pacific and one of Villard's oldest friends. At this event Hilgard, all unconsciously, vied with the bride for the focus of attention. Sitting there with a slight smile on his wan face, he replied serenely to the many guests who came up to him and wished him well. The next day he was violently ill, and from then on his decline was steady, except for a few interruptions that gave him some measure of relief and those who loved him a few vain hopes. Although feeble and wasted, he insisted on spending a couple of his last days fully dressed and sitting up in his favorite armchair, "erect and determined," his mother wrote, "like a martyr." On the morning of June 6, however, he stayed in his bed, never to rise from it again. Physicians came, treated, and prescribed, but it was clear to them and to the Villards that whatever was draining away Hilgard's life was beyond their reach. On June 10 Hilgard's anxious father, called to the city on business that he could not ignore, sadly kissed his son good-bye. Later that day the doctors told Fanny that Hilgard was suffering from peritonitis and that he could not live. Her urgent message to Henry brought him back in the small hours of the night to his son's bedside. Helen and Fanny were there; Harold and Oswald had been summoned from Cambridge and were on their way. With the dreadful attention of a man watching his worst fears come true, Villard joined his wife and daughter around Hilgard's bed. The tiny figure was still, pallid, softly panting. Shortly after daybreak, as the carriage bringing Harold and Oswald was rolling up the drive, the piteous sounds of Hilgard's breathing slowed and stopped. By the time his brothers rushed into the room, he was dead.

Two days later, Hilgard's small coffin lay amid flowers in the parlor at Thorwood, on the very spot where Miss Oakes and her husband had plighted their troth ten days before. A large, grief-stunned crowd of relatives and friends listened while Carl Schurz delivered an eloquent eulogy, touching in its heartfelt sympathy and unmitigated by religious consolation. On June 21, 1890, Hilgard was finally consigned to the family resting place in Sleepy Hollow Cemetery, an old and historic graveyard in Tarrytown, New York. From the grave, if you looked up and away toward the high ground overlooking the river, you could see Thorwood. The final note of pathos on Hilgard's burial day was added by Tommy Dot, who that evening, like a dog in a mythic tale, at last gave up searching for his friend and laid himself down and died.

His young son's death was beyond all comparison the greatest grief in Villard's life, and (death elicits clichés) he never got over it. The family consoled itself as it could, but it was soon apparent that Thorwood's evocations were too melancholy to be borne. Villard arranged his multifarious business affairs as best he might, and early in July the family sailed for Europe.

RARE PHOTOGRAPH OF HENRY VILLARD,
FANNY GARRISON VILLARD, HELEN VILLARD, AND
THE DEVOTED MASTIFF BRUTUS, LYING AT HIS
MASTER'S FEET, AT THORWOOD, C. 1898.
Alexandra Villard de Borchgrave Private Collection.

20

Sleepy Hollow

Über allen Gipfeln	*On the mountains*
Ist Ruh,	*Perfect peace,*
In allen Wipfeln	*In the treetops*
Spürest du	*Noises cease,*
Kaum einen Hauch;	*No more ado;*
Die Vögelein schweigen im Walde.	*The birds have silenced their song.*
Warte nur, balde	*Just wait, before long*
Ruhest du auch.	*You'll be quiet, too.*

GOETHE
"Wandrers Nachtlied"
("Wanderer's Night Song")

For several weeks the sad family moved from place to place, visiting Ireland, England, France, and the Black Forest in southwest Germany before settling down for an extended stay in Freiburg, an old town at the edge of the forest not far from the Rhine. Shortly after taking up residence in Freiburg, Villard left Fanny and the children there and proceeded to Berlin. While in the capital, he fell into conversation with a friend, Ludwig Bamberger, a liberal leader in the Reichstag. They talked, naturally, about politics, which is tantamount to saying that they talked about Bismarck.

Prince Otto von Bismarck-Schönhausen had recently lost the position he had occupied for nearly twenty years: chancellor of the German empire. In his previous job, premier of the kingdom of Prussia, the brilliant, amoral Bismarck had provoked three separate wars. Nasty but brief, they had achieved his political objectives—chief among them the unification of Germany under Prussian (that is, his own) domination—at the bargain price of fewer than a hundred thousand killed and maimed. Thereafter, for the better part of two decades, Bismarck, standing deferentially behind the imperial throne, had ruled Germany and cowed the rest of Europe. Then, in March 1890, this ardent if disingenuous defender of the monarchist principle was dismissed by someone who believed in it with all his heart, the young Kaiser Wilhelm II. In the struggle for supremacy in Germany, the greatest statesman in Europe had been brought low by a popinjay, who was also his sovereign. Until he died, some eight years later, the bitter memory of his humiliation burned in the old man's mind like a blister; in the summer of 1890, his wound was still fresh.

In the course of his conversation with Bamberger, Villard proclaimed that he had never met Bismarck, not for want of opportunity but for want of inclination; as far as Villard was concerned, the ex-chancellor was politically and morally objectionable. Agreeing that Bismarck was "both selfish and unprincipled," but calling him "the greatest man of our age, and one of the most interesting," Bamberger counseled Villard to secure himself an invitation to the prince's country home. Villard's application received a prompt and cordial reply—the ex-chancellor would be delighted to meet a fellow countryman who had accomplished so much in a foreign land—and within forty-eight hours Villard was on a train bound for Friedrichsruhe, a village about ninety miles northwest of Berlin.

If we did not live in a time when the seduction of principle by celebrity is a common spectacle, we might wonder why a pacifist republican would deliberately seek the company of a warmongering monarchist opposed to every liberal idea. But Bismarck was also a famous man who for better or worse had shaped the course of history, and Villard was a former newspaperman with a pronounced taste for associating with the powerful. Except for the prince's doctor, Villard was his only guest, and during the course of the financier's brief stay (two nights), he and his host held several long, private conversations.

They ranged over a wide variety of topics, including the gout (Bismarck identified Villard as a fellow sufferer by the latter's swollen hands), American politics and national characteristics, and Villard's railroad experiences, but there was one subject to which the ex-chancellor obsessively returned: his recent fall from power. Bismarck's "cutting sarcasm and bitter denunciation" apparently shocked his guest, who wrote that the old man's "language became a perfect diatribe when he referred to the present Emperor and some of his ministers, whom he held responsible for his removal. His expressions regarding them were not only amazing, but embarrassing to me, as I had close social relations with many of the ministerial objects of his scorn." Uncomfortable but starstruck, Villard fell to admiring the prince's countenance as he railed, particularly his "wonderful eyes."

> They seemed incapable of expressing affection, and their steel-like hardness only inspired awe for the towering intellect, the irresistible will, the defiant courage, the fiery energy of their owner. To watch the lightning changes of expression mirrored in them, reflecting the strong emotions evoked by humbled pride, wounded ambition, and thwarted selfishness, and, above all, by the loss of his absolute sway, was indeed an enviable privilege.

Villard's sense of privilege, which reveals more about him than it does about Bismarck, kept him from flinching at some of the old man's more unsettling pronouncements, such as his confident assertion that the German state would eventually have to extirpate by force the evil represented by the Social Democrats. The prince and his guest parted with expressions of lasting gratitude on one side and promises of renewed welcome on the other, and Villard left Friedrichsruhe quite satisfied with his new acquaintance and rightly convinced that Bismarck would seek revenge for his humiliation as long as he lived. Upon returning to Freiburg, while the details were still vivid in his mind, Villard wrote a full account of his visit to the Iron Chancellor.

A few weeks later, a sudden telegram from America filled Villard with "the gravest anxiety": his North American Company was in serious trouble. The recent passage in the U.S. Congress of the Sherman Silver Purchase Act was, contrary to the predictions of its supporters, causing a rapid tightening of the money supply. (The controversy over whether to adopt gold or silver as the standard, or basis, for the national currency now seems quite deadening and inconsequential, especially since neither is used today, but this issue vexed American politics in the most lively fashion throughout the final quarter of the nineteenth century. In general, big-time capitalists, including Eastern financiers like Henry Villard, favored the sound money, secure investments, and stability they considered inherent in the gold standard; with the enthusiastic support of the silver-mining interests, farmers, ranchers, homesteaders, and other small-timers, particularly in the South and West, preferred the freer financial conditions and more accessible credit that they believed the silver movement would bring.) This new "stringency . . . in the money market," as Villard called it, made it impossible for North American to meet upcoming obligations to the tune of $2 million, and the directors of the company were facing the awful prospect of selling stock at catastrophic losses when they turned to him for help.

Most reluctantly, Villard set out for the banking houses of Frankfurt and Berlin, where his eloquent pleading and categorical assurances quickly raised the necessary sum. Within forty-eight hours he wired $2 million to North American; the fledgling company was getting off to a shaky start. A few weeks later, in late November, the first rumblings of the impending worldwide financial earthquake shook North American to its foundations, which the recent influx had shored up but not secured. To his immense chagrin, Villard found himself back in Frankfurt, facing his hastily reconvened banking friends, assuming the supplicant position, and asking once again for enough money to save his company from bankruptcy. This time, embarrassingly enough, he needed even more capital than he had requested the last time, and it took two days of intense begging and bargaining before he finally succeeded in prying away an additional $3 million from his unwilling supporters. His success came at a heavy price: he left Frankfurt knowing that he had pushed these men too far to retain their former trust.

The downward spiral that was to culminate in the great crisis of 1893 began spinning in the fall of 1890, when Baring Brothers, the prestigious London banking house, failed. The panicky directors of the North American now began to entreat Villard to return home and take over the reins of the company; only he could help it weather the steadily worsening financial conditions. Villard held out as long as he could, but eventually he felt compelled to capitulate, and in December the family returned to New York.

Villard found the North American nearly insolvent and his status on Wall Street, that fickle thoroughfare, greatly reduced. Once again, his *Memoirs* tell us, he was the victim of injustice.

> His absence in Europe left him free from all responsibility for the new catastrophe, but he suffered just as much abuse as though he had been directly instrumental in bringing on the disaster, instead of having strained every nerve to save the company. This second breakdown utterly disheartened him, and he made up his mind then to resign all his corporate positions and absolutely retire from all business pursuits just as soon as possible.

His efforts to kick the business habit, however, would go on for more than two years.

Meanwhile, there was work to be done. He spent much of 1891 in New York, gauging the financial waters, considering the results, and developing the strategy that would save his German investors from the effects of the 1893 crash. In the fall, he embarked with Fanny on his last official tour of the Pacific Northwest, traveling, of course, on the Northern Pacific. Villard was often called on to speak during this tour, and whenever he did so he warned his audience of troubles on the way, the consequences, he said, of the Sherman Silver Act. Keep out of debt, he admonished the crowds, be wary of new ventures, and prepare for the worst. Although he was enthusiastically received and respectfully listened to, critics ridiculed him in print as "a croaker and a pessimist." Villard returned to New York depressed, filled with apprehension about the future of the Northern Pacific. Events would prove his apprehension and his pessimism amply justified.

For diversion from these dreary forebodings, there was the elaborate New York social scene, a whirl of dinners and operas and banquets and balls. The highlight of the 1891 Christmas season was the fantastically lavish coming-out party that Jay Gould threw for his daughter. Among the hundreds and hundreds of guests were such eminences as John D. Rockefeller, J. P. Morgan, and Andrew Carnegie, all of whom, like Villard, were linked to Gould, slippery though he was, by present or former business ties.

In spite of railroad matters and the delights of New York society, Villard managed to save a portion of his attention for the Edison General Electric Company. Patent fights, lawsuits, and other impediments slowed the company's progress in 1891, but Villard, its president, retained his complete faith in Edison and the future of electric power. Furthermore, the performance of Edison General Electric stock gave him no reason to regret having steered so many of his German investor friends toward electricity instead of railroads. There were, nevertheless, some pressing matters to attend to, and Edison was being difficult about cooperating.

Edison could light up a city, but some of his business decisions suggest that he was much in the dark. He adamantly opposed the use of the newly developed alternating current, refusing to concede its advantages over the direct current he preferred. "The use of alternating current instead of direct current is unworthy of practical men," he huffed to Villard, who in this matter was more practical and farsighted than he. Villard was likewise unable to get Edison even to consider a merger with one of EGE's chief competitors, the Thomson-Houston Company of Lynn, Massachusetts, which was busily developing the high-voltage potential of alternating current. Villard, the entrepreneur, sought to put an end to costly competition by absorbing Thomson-Houston. Edison, the naive believer in free enterprise, thought competition meant progress and should be encouraged; moreover, he believed alternating current was dangerous and would prove impractical. At first, he had a point; there *were* some accidents in the early days—the words "electrocute" and "electrocution," after all, were coined around 1889—and a persistent folk belief that under certain circumstances a person whose house was powered by alternating current could be shocked to death by switching on the lights. But great strides in safety had been made, the methods of generation and protection were steadily being improved, and Villard saw what Edison could not see, that a system capable of delivering a great deal of power over long distances was destined to supersede a system that delivered considerably less power over considerably shorter distances. Having reached an impasse, Villard decided to ignore Edison's wishes—they were unreasonable and unscientific, and besides that, the inventor's financial share in his own company was only 10 percent—and opened secret negotiations with Thomson-Houston.

The president of Thomson-Houston was a former shoe salesman named Charles A. Coffin. Like almost all electric companies, Thomson-Houston had succeeded by imitating some of Edison's discoveries, stealing a couple of his ideas, and then adding a few innovations of their own. Under Coffin's aggressive management, Thomson-Houston had solid backing, excellent scientists and engineers, and a policy of steady expansion. Villard found Coffin a hard bargainer, and their negotiations stretched out over a long period of time. The pretense of secrecy was stubbornly maintained—Coffin instructed the supervisor of a plant Villard was scheduled to inspect not to reveal the financier's identity—but on Wall Street the rumors naturally started swirling. Prices of electrical products were falling, and Villard appeared to be in trouble.

All the while, J. P. Morgan had been buying Edison General Electric stock and was poised to take over control of the company. Like Villard, Morgan saw that a big merger was what EGE needed, and as EGE's banker he attempted to facilitate matters with Thomson-Houston. To Morgan's surprise, Coffin refused the deal, citing as his reason the incompetent management of the Edison company; a practical man, he had no intention of submitting his firm to what he saw as the vagaries of Villard, Edison, and their associates. Morgan, nothing daunted (he was inclined to believe that Coffin's assessment of Villard's performance was correct), saw his chance and countered Coffin's refusal to sell out to EGE by proposing instead to sell EGE to him. "To Morgan it made little difference," Edison's biographer writes, "so long as it all resulted in a big trustification for which he would be the banker." Coffin and Morgan agreed upon a consolidation, and thus Villard, who had sought to circumvent Edison, found that Morgan had circumvented them both.

The new company, the General Electric Company, was chartered in April of 1892; Charles Coffin was its first president, a position he was to hold for nearly thirty-five years. The removal of Edison's name reflected the reality of the new company, from which Edison was effectively frozen out. "Something died in Edison's heart," his secretary said. The inventor was forever embittered by this turn of events but with typical confidence looked forward to bigger and better things, to developing dazzling new inventions while unburdened by the corporate yoke.

Villard, too, the founder of Edison General Electric, was like his friend the inventor rather brusquely pushed aside to make way for the new company. On February 20, 1892, the *New York World,* citing the usual authoritative sources, asserted that "a courteous resignation" on the part of the president of Edison General Electric "would be courteously received." Villard's resignation was duly delivered, and except for some personally owned stock, his connection with the electric company was completely severed; Coffin did not even offer him a seat on the board of GE.

Although totally defeated in the struggle with Morgan, Villard saw to the happiness of his German backers; they were able to sell their EGE stock at a profit of 200 percent, and frothing steins were lifted in his name. Nevertheless, the whole disagreeable affair served to strengthen Villard's resolve to retire from active involvement in business. His plunge into presidential politics in the latter half of 1892 was in part a way of withdrawing for a while from the strenuous disappointments of the business world.

Villard's urgent desire to see the repeal of the Sherman Act led him in the election year of 1892 to involve himself in a national political contest for the first time in nearly four decades. The incumbent president, a Republican named Benjamin Harrison, favored silver and high tariffs, both anathema to Villard, who withdrew his longtime support from the Republican Party and turned to the Democrats. The candidate he considered most likely to promote the gold standard and lower tariffs was former president Grover Cleveland, a large, pink gentleman from upstate New York whom Harrison had defeated in 1888.

Villard's love for the excitement of high-stakes politics was undiminished, and he threw himself with great energy into the process. He had set himself a daunting task: many members of Cleveland's own party opposed him, and the ex-president himself, having tasted both victory and defeat, was extremely reluctant to become a candidate again. According to Villard's *Memoirs,* it was he who, after much urging, finally persuaded Cleveland to run and he who lobbied leading Democrats to accept Cleveland's candidacy and give him the party's nomination. Once that was secured, Villard worked unstintingly on Cleveland's behalf, raising money for the Democrats, canvassing his vast acquaintance, and organizing a group called German-Americans for Cleveland. Villard's efforts were rewarded by Cleveland's squeaky electoral college victory (Harrison, whose running mate was none other than Whitelaw Reid, won the popular vote) in the 1892 election.

A few days later, Villard celebrated his candidate's triumph with a large party, at which President-elect Cleveland was the guest of honor. The other guests included "leading Independents and Democrats from all over the country," active, well-heeled gentlemen dedicated to prosperity, both theirs and the country's. In his opening speech at this grand affair, Villard congratulated the president-elect on his successful campaign and then proceeded, not too subtly, to remind him of what his supporters expected him to do in the way of currency and tariff reform; Cleveland, Villard roundly declared, had "the finest opportunity since Washington and Lincoln of bestowing great benefits upon the Republic." Like most successful politicians, Cleveland too knew how to sing in the high rhetorical key, and he responded with "the most feeling utterance he had ever made," which "moved the gathering deeply." At that emotional moment, it seemed to Villard and his other guests that Mr. Cleveland was prepared to effect the reforms that they desired.

This elite assembly attracted the attention of the press, which was immediately filled with reports that Villard was destined for an important role, perhaps even a cabinet post, under the new regime. In fact, Villard asked nothing more from Cleveland than "leave to discuss pending public issues freely with him." Villard liked the idea of acting as consultant to people in high places, of operating behind the scenes without strictures or obligations. When Cleveland suggested to him the possibility of an appointment as United States minister to Kaiser Wilhelm's government in Berlin, Villard was pleased, flattered, grateful, and categorical in his refusal. The reasons he gave showed his good judgment, demonstrated his proud sense of his own integrity, and proved that the spirit of 1848 was still alive in him. He was not eligible for the position in question, he told Cleveland, because he had contributed to his campaign, because he had a vested interest in Wall Street, and "because he had never learned to bow down before kings."

Cleveland consulted Villard, among others, on cabinet and important diplomatic appointments, but the public issue that Villard most wanted to discuss with the president-elect was the repeal of the hated Sherman Act. Throughout the winter and up until Cleveland's inauguration in March 1893, Villard repeatedly urged him to make the establishment of the gold standard his first presidential priority. Cleveland, Villard insisted, must agree to call a special session of Congress immediately after the inauguration to bring about the repudiation of the silver standard and the repeal of the Sherman Act. Unable to make the vacillating Cleveland see the critical importance of this measure as clearly as he did, Villard agreed to the new president's suggestion that he present the matter to the cabinet after the inauguration; the president promised to abide by their decision. Though Villard gave an impassioned speech, he won the support of but a single cabinet member, the secretary of agriculture, who favored an unconditional and immediate return to the gold standard. Disgusted and defeated, Villard withdrew from political activity. Soon he would have what he called, in his densest syntax, "the sorry satisfaction of seeing all he had feared and prophesied as to the impending panic and its effect upon the fate of Mr. Cleveland's administration come to pass." When the financial panic of 1893 (up to that time the worst economic crisis in the history of the country) struck later in the year,

President Cleveland did indeed call a special session of Congress to repeal the Sherman Silver Purchase Act, but by then most of the damage was already done.

After his failed appeal to President Cleveland's cabinet in the spring of 1893, Villard was determined that his working days were over. Exhausted and frustrated from many months of futile pitches and unsuccessful pleading of one kind or another, he realized that his powers of persuasion, of energy and will, had waned irrevocably, and he felt both unwilling and unable to rise to the challenge of the hard times to come. In June he resigned from both the Northern Pacific and its holding company, the North American. Villard foresaw that the railroad was bound to go under in the coming storm, but he did not feel responsible. To his manner of thinking, the collapse was due to circumstances, some of them global, well beyond his control, and much of Northern Pacific's debt was in fact owed to him. He also foresaw that he would be blamed for the company's failure. "It seemed a hard fate indeed," he complained, sounding for all the world like an injured prince, "that he should have to pass twice through the same ordeal and receive such punishment for once more loyally uniting his personal fortunes with the same ill-starred company." There was no contemplating the possibility that some policies or misjudgments of his might have contributed to the Northern Pacific's exposed situation.

In any case, his resignations came not a moment too soon; Fanny had long feared that he might again collapse under the constant pressure of what he called "his corporate duties," and she and the children considered his retirement long overdue. Although the immediate future of American business looked pretty bleak, Villard was well prepared for the deep recession that plagued the national economy in the latter half of 1893, and his personal fortune was not appreciably affected. Relieved of his business burdens and financially secure, he settled down to the life of a wealthy retiree. It took him a while to learn how to make the best use of his newfound leisure.

Appointed to chair a Chamber of Commerce committee charged with providing for the proper entertainment of certain foreign guests (among them a Spanish princess) of the United States government, Villard prepared a lavish program that included a great parade through the streets of New York, a banquet at the Waldorf, and a ball at Stanford White's exuberantly designed Madison Square Garden, then in the early years of its brief life. Great was the chairman's dismay, however, when he learned that Congress, although it had indeed extended formal invitations to these important personages, had voted no appropriations for their entertainment. Thus, to his amazement, Villard found himself working day and night, lobbying and fund-raising, negotiating and organizing, just as he'd been doing before he decided to retire. When the ordeal was over, the lesson he drew from it echoed one he had learned long ago, back in his vagabond days: "Americans, however hospitably inclined they may be, do not care to bother with foreigners who do not speak their own language."

As predicted, the financial crisis struck, stocks plunged, interest rates on loans skyrocketed, and the Northern Pacific slid into default. Called upon to help set up the receivership, Villard made several astute recommendations but then announced his intention to withdraw definitively from business and go abroad for several years. "His usefulness as a financial adviser and leader were obviously entirely gone," he told the board of directors. "It would positively injure the work of the committees if he played a leading part in it." Though it served his purpose to say these things, he had small doubt that they were true. Amid howls of protest and "some exciting scenes," Villard would consent to do no more than recommend a receiver before making good his escape. "I'm out of it, now," he told the reporters.

As it turned out, the receiver, Edward D. Adams, did a magnificent job, reorganizing the Northern Pacific so successfully that it began to turn a profit and its stocks moved up. This outcome eventually provided Villard with some compensation for the abuse, as he saw it, to which he had been subjected. In the meantime, though, the pleasures of travel beckoned, and Henry, Fanny, Helen, and Oswald sailed for Gibraltar in November 1893. There they began a long, leisurely tour of the Mediterranean, including much of North Africa, before moving on to Greece, Constantinople, Vienna, Lake Constance, Lake Geneva, Italy, and other places. Except for a threat of litigation that managed to vex him thoroughly before it dissolved into air, Villard's travels were untroubled by business cares. The family spent Christmas 1894 with Emma and Robert von Xylander, who now lived in Munich, and there were many pleasant evenings in the company of a wide circle of family and friends. Villard was having no trouble adapting to a life of leisure.

When Villard and family returned to New York in May 1895, many observers thought he would return to the Wall Street battlefields, but they had mistaken their man. He did not wish, ever again, to be responsible for other people's money, and he wanted to devote his time "to what he considered higher and nobler objects, such as he had followed before he became a business man." This meant, in practice, that he intended to return to the literary life that he had fancied for himself ever since he was a boy. He began to read extensively and to make real progress on the memoirs that he'd been working on, in a desultory way, for the past twenty years.

Another factor confirming his resolution to withdraw into the obscurity of a scholarly life was his growing deafness. This was a condition that he shared with Edison, who experimented with electrical hearing aids and a phonograph (turned, apparently, to some frightening volume) that was supposed to massage any ear applied to it. Villard gladly accepted such a phonograph from Edison, but remained hard of hearing until he died. He and Edison nevertheless continued to be good friends. Edison said of him, "He was a very aggressive man with big ideas, but I could never quite understand him." What Edison found particularly hard to understand was Villard's consistent failure to laugh at his jokes. Anyone who has ever heard old recordings of Thomas Alva waxing humorous will be sympathetic to Villard's point of view.

For all Villard's blindness to the inventor's comic talent, Edison esteemed the older man's willingness to make the conceptual leap and his power to envision future possibilities. Some of Villard's projections—the world electricity cartel was a good example—tended to fantasy, but that was how creative intelligence worked. In an interview he gave nine years after Villard's death, Edison praised his late friend's ability to perceive the implications of ideas, an ability that

Edison had found to be unique among members of Villard's profession. "Most men have no imaginations. Wall Street men, in particular, have no imaginations," the inventor declared crustily. He made an exception for Henry Villard, who had frequently backed Edison's projects when no one else would. For example, only Villard had seen a future for Edison's electric trolley; all the other company directors had voted against it. "Imagination in Wall Street?" Edison, still indignant, growled at the interviewer. "Why, there is more imagination among hardware men."

The Villards divided their residence, as before, between Thorwood and their winter quarters in the city. For three years, from 1895 to 1898, they did little traveling. Villard was much occupied with various writing projects, especially of the autobiographical kind, and he also began an intensive study of the Civil War that included burrowing in archives and visiting battlefields with maps and official accounts in his hands. He continued his philanthropies (he was a benefactor of Harvard Law School, among others) and maintained a lively interest in politics and current events.

In 1898, encouraged by leaders and patriots and newspapers—not including the *Evening Post*—the great majority of the American people were clamoring for their soldiers to go forth and do battle with villainous Spain. Villard recognized the sound of naked imperialism, and when he and Fanny could stand "the war-racket" no longer, they sailed for Europe and did not return to the States until after peace was concluded at the end of 1898.

In 1899, Henry and Fanny made one final, unofficial tour over the Northern Pacific. There were receptions, applause, expressions of public gratitude all along the line, especially in Washington and Oregon. The University of Oregon, which Villard had rescued and continued to support, gave him a particularly heartfelt welcome. Before returning to New York, the intrepid couple took an Oregon Steamship Company vessel to Alaska, which neither of them had ever seen. Back in New York, Villard interrupted his memoirs in the middle of a detailed description of the battle of Chattanooga and turned to a historical work that would be published after his death as *The Early History of Transportation in Oregon*.

Although Villard continued to present the appearance of a healthy man, his big body, never as sound as it looked, was moving like the century toward its ineluctable end. In 1897, heart trouble had joined rheumatism and gout among the forces ranged against him. He seemed to know that his extended journey to the Northwest in 1899 would be the last of his travels, and he gave it the last of his energy. He continued his reading and writing projects, however, mostly in his beautiful library at Thorwood. On March 30, 1900, he delighted in the birth of his first grandson, Henry Serrano Villard, born to Harold and his wife, Mariquita, and held him at his christening. Then, in early October 1900, he was disabled by a mild stroke, the first of a series. The next day, October 3, 1900, Fanny wrote in her diary that Harry had "talked very sweetly to us all in the evening in his chamber." Under that entry, in another ink, is a later addition: "It was like a farewell & so it turned out to be."

Throughout October Villard seemed to improve, but he was subject to scary relapses. Gradually he became immobile. He was pushed about in a "rolling chair," and on October 22 he had to be carried downstairs for what turned out to be his last drive. As they drove through Thorwood's beautiful park, he said, "I feel like one risen from the dead." His good days grew fewer and farther between, and as she sat by his bedside Fanny saw how close he was to the end and steeled herself. After the first of November he spoke no more, though his eyes sometimes expressed a kind of mute, nervous fright. On November 9, as a bad storm raged around Thorwood, Fanny put into her diary a few sentences of sad resignation: "Terrible day of storms & high wind outdoors, and inside, the gradual going out of Harry's life." The following night, she wrote, she "sat by Harry's deathbed till my heart was ready to break." A little past midnight on November 12, with Fanny, Harold, and Oswald at his side (Helen, now married and living in Dresden, could not get home in time), Henry Villard died.

The cause of death, the doctors said, was an apoplectic stroke. Three days later, the funeral service was held at Thorwood and attended by a large group of mourners that included Thomas Edison, Carl Schurz, Charles McKim, and Horace White. The Mendelssohn

Quartet, with organ and violin accompaniment, sang "Ein feste Burg," someone read a selection from scripture, and Reverend T. C. Williams called the deceased "a modern man in every sense" and "an idealist in action," with a "genius for interesting men." On November 15, 1900, Henry Villard joined his son Hilgard in Sleepy Hollow Cemetery. The monument created by Karl Bitter, the noted architectural sculptor, presides over his grave today.

The donations and bequests in Villard's will included the Harvard Law School, Harvard, Columbia, Oregon and Washington State Universities, the German Society of New York, the American Museum of Natural History, the Metropolitan Museum of Art, the orphan asylum in Zweibrücken, the hospital and training school in Speyer, the Red Cross Hospital in Munich, the Children's Hospital in Berlin, and several scholarship foundations in universities, art schools, and German gymnasiums. Thorwood continued to be Fanny's home and the favorite resort of her children and grandchildren until, like her husband and her youngest son, she died there, in 1928.

HENRY VILLARD.

Photograph of a portrait, c. 1890, that hung in
Villard Hall at the University of Oregon.
The portrait was stolen and never recovered.

Alexandra Villard de Borchgrave Private Collection.

Epilogue

uring Henry Villard's visit to the venerable Otto von Bismarck in 1890, the prince asked him a rhetorical question: hadn't he encountered a great deal of prejudice against foreigners in America? Villard, who sought the company of great men but was little given to deference, contradicted his host's expectations by declaring that energy and enterprise prevailed among Americans as among no other people on earth. A man's birth, his ethnic origin, were not so important as his abilities, and anyone who had those in sufficient measure would win the esteem and admiration of his fellows. Though perhaps not strictly true, Villard's answer to the question was the answer of an American; indeed, his very reaction to Bismarck's query was quintessentially American. Villard had long since left behind him the perennial racial anxieties of the *Volk*, along with other impediments, and become a man of the New World.

Like the cornflower, Villard throve best in America, but his roots were European. The qualities he shared with his new countrymen—his independence, brashness, drive, competitiveness, his gambling, winner-take-all propensities, his self-reliance, his faith in possibilities, his straight talk—were conditioned by his Old World upbringing and education. Temperamentally American, culturally European, he was an instance of that rare and interesting phenomenon, a man equally at home in two cultures.

Just as he always returned to Europe, to his beginnings, for rehabilitation and renewal, so he harbored throughout even his most intense years of business activity his fond boyhood dreams of the quiet, contemplative, literary life. He would probably have been con-

tent to remain a newspaper correspondent, exercising his large powers of observation and expression, turning out the occasional book,
always confidently planning some deeper, stronger work. But when
he realized that he could achieve in business the kind of success he
wished for his writing, he was able to transfer his creative energy to
financial matters with a flair that approached the artistic. The blind
pool, the unprecedented capital maneuverings, the innovative investment arrangements, the transcontinental gala—all of these had
about them a pronounced operatic air, a feeling for the flourish.
Like most capitalists, he sought to eliminate competition, but he did
so not by slowly strangling or crushing rivals (as so many of his contemporaries did) but by swooping upon them, suddenly, irresistibly,
con fuoco, and carrying them away.

When circumstances finally permitted, he returned to literary
pursuits and tried to become a writer again. As he sought to put his
life down on paper, he found that his most interesting, most intense
experiences had taken place during the Civil War, which had provided him with a unique opportunity to exercise, all at once, his fearlessness, his spirit of adventure, his energetic curiosity, and his
writing talents. When his *Memoirs* reach first Manassas, the big battle
at Bull Run that opened the war, Villard's focus begins to shift. His
autobiography quickly metamorphoses into a military history, a
painstakingly thorough account of the battles he witnessed; and the
drama of his subject—himself—fades into the background of a
larger drama. So completely did he lose himself that he left time for
only a perfunctory treatment of his great business successes and failures, with which he clearly identified less strongly.

In a similar manner, his attitude toward wealth was markedly im-
personal; money was a tool, a means to various ends, and there were
many accomplishments greater than its mere accumulation. The literary and intellectual excellence of the *Evening Post*, the visions that
Edison inspired in him, the transformation of the Pacific Northwest—these were all triumphs of the imagination, and his financial
triumphs seemed to him less significant.

He was often fortunate in his associations, never more so than in
his choice of a wife. Fanny elicited his best qualities and provided the

solid mooring necessary for so volatile a man. Villard attracted and impressed a wide range of extraordinary people, who recognized his innate courtesy, admired his abilities, sought his opinion. His attitude toward influence, however, resembled his attitude toward money: it was something to be used, pragmatically and conscientiously, to reach a higher goal.

It was this tendency toward idealism that set Villard apart from most of the tycoons of the age, who seemed more thoroughly at home in the material world. His life, fascinating in itself, merits attention also because to the basic American saga of the penniless immigrant lad, animated by dreams of material success, who lifts himself up by his bootstraps until he stands upon a proud pinnacle all his own, it adds some welcome elements of refined aspiration. For Henry Villard, success lay in acquiring not great riches but a great name.

Notes

THE MAIN SOURCES for the life of Henry Villard are his own auto-biographical writings, which occupied him for many years, especially during the period from about 1892 until his death, in 1900. The present work is chiefly based on these writings, beginning with the *Jugend-Erinnerungen: 1835–1853*, written in German under the name of Heinrich Hilgard-Villard and published in 1902 by the Hermann Bartsch Printing House of New York. These "Memories of Youth," never translated into English, come to an end on October 18, 1853, the day when the young adventurer first stepped onto American soil. *Memoirs of Henry Villard, Journalist and Financier,* two volumes written in English and published by Houghton, Mifflin and Company in 1904, cover the balance of Villard's life. Unless otherwise indicated, all unattributed quotations in the present text come from these posthumously published autobiographical volumes.

The Henry Villard and Fanny Garrison Villard Papers, a collection stored in the archives of the Houghton Library at Harvard University, contain a vast array of letters, diaries, and other documents indispensable to a study of the life of Henry Villard. Publication of this material is by permission of the Houghton Library, Harvard University, and the authors of the present biography gratefully acknowledge the unfailing courtesy and cooperation of Tom Ford and the Houghton staff.

Material from the Villard Papers, as well as from the many other sources we have used, are referenced in the following notes. Sources are identified in an abbreviated form; for fuller information, see the Bibliography.

1. REBELLION

3   *more than fifty revolutions:* Robertson, *Revolutions,* vii.

13   *Friedrich Hecker:* Discussed ibid., 167–70.

14   *Engels on "amateurishness":* Ibid., 174.

20   *a noted psychoanalyst:* Erikson, *Young Man Luther,* 43.

21   *one sardonic historian:* Kevin McAleer, *Dueling,* 137.

2. THE SORROWS OF YOUNG HENRY

27   *"a mother's heart":* Gutzkow, *Aphorismen,* in *Gutzkows Werke,* 2:443.

31   *the general cacophony:* Burrows and Wallace, *Gotham,* 653ff. This monumental work has provided us with many statistics, descriptions, and facts concerning nineteenth-century New York.

31   *more than three million immigrants:* Ibid., 736ff.

31   *economic boom of the early 1850s:* Ibid., 712ff.

31   *third-largest:* Ibid., 475.

32   *"kein König da":* Nadel, *Little Germany,* 17.

32   *Freethinking intellectuals, et al.:* Ibid., 98.

33   *largest circulation:* Burrows and Wallace, *Gotham,* 739.

33   *Crystal Palace:* Batterbury, *On the Town,* 76.

33   *newspapers from October 18: New York Daily Times,* October 18, 19, 20, 1853.

35   *Astor House . . . "most prestigious":* Burrows and Wallace, *Gotham,* 436.

38   *a year of wandering:* Our account of Henry Villard's *Wanderjahr* is based on an unpublished fragment of a first draft of his *Memoirs.* The fragment, a manuscript containing 119 pages and entitled "First Experiences in America," is in the Henry Villard Collection at the Houghton Library, Harvard. The holograph original is designated bMS Am 1322 (642); its microfilmed reproduction is Film 98–1695. Direct quotations from this manuscript fragment are not further identified in these notes.

3. THE LURE OF THE LAW

53   *fertile upland:* Wyman, *Immigrants,* 63.

53   *"major German center":* Ibid., 63.

53   *Ten percent:* Ibid., 49.

54   *"I can truthfully say":* Theodor Erasmus Hilgard to his mother, private family archive.

54   *"noblemen, doctors":* O. G. Villard, " 'Latin Peasants,' " 7.

56   *"most all infidels or rationalists":* Quoted in Wyman, *Immigrants,* 70.

56   *"skeptics and loose moralists":* Ibid., 70.

57   *"Outwardly Belleville":* O. G. Villard, " 'Latin Peasants,' " 18.

4. THE SOLITARY SALESMAN

69 *"plantation discipline"*: William Cullen Bryant, *New York Evening Post;* quoted in Mayer, *All on Fire,* 453.

5. QUEST FOR RECOGNITION

80 *"Old Public Functionary"*: McPherson, *Battle Cry,* 156.

83 *Chief Justice Taney:* Our discussion of the Dred Scott case is based on McPherson, *Battle Cry,* 170ff.

6. THE REPORTER AND THE RAIL-SPLITTER

97 *among those with sufficient insight:* From the *New York Times,* July 12, 1858 (quoted in Oates, *With Malice,* 162): "Illinois is from this time forward, until the Senatorial question shall be decided, the most interesting political battleground in the Union." Note the ominous military metaphor.

97 *"one long running rebuttal"*: Fehrenbacher, *Prelude,* 17.

98 *"If slavery is not wrong"*: Quoted in Johannsen, *Lincoln-Douglas Debates,* 7.

98 *ethically equal:* Fehrenbacher, *Prelude,* 24.

98 *made journalistic history:* Angle, *Created Equal?,* xxiv.

99 *a small cannon:* Sparks, *Lincoln-Douglas Debates,* 49.

99 *Illinois River canal boats:* Donald, *Lincoln,* 215.

100 *another Democratic newspaper: Philadelphia Press,* August 26, 1858, quoted in Sparks, *Lincoln-Douglas Debates,* 127.

100 *a Republican newsman: Chicago Press and Tribune,* August 23, 1858, quoted in Sparks, *Lincoln-Douglas Debates,* 135.

102 *Carl Sandburg wrote: Lincoln,* 2:399.

104 *a profoundly spiritual man:* See, for example, Wolf, *Chosen People,* 192; Randall and Current, *Lincoln,* 4:375.

7. ALL THAT GLITTERS

107 *Halstead wrote:* "Some Reminiscences," 61.

8. THE EVE OF '61

123 *"the best accounts"*: Hesseltine, *Three,* xvii.

123 *"among the 'historians'"*: Halstead, "Reminiscences," 61.

123 *"ardent beverages"*: Hesseltine, *Three,* 142.

124 *"irrepressible conflict"*: Quoted in McPherson, *Battle Cry,* 198.

127 *"hundreds of thousands"*: H. G. and O. G. Villard in Henry Villard, *Lincoln on the Eve,* v.

129 *"passional attraction"*: Quoted in Catton, *American Heritage,* 55.

129 *"Mr. Lincoln's personal appearance"*: Henry Villard, *Lincoln on the Eve,* 17.

130 Lincoln's *"conscientiousness"*: Ibid., 35–36.

130 *December 16:* Ibid., 39, 41.

130 *dispatch of January 19:* Ibid., 48–49.

131 *on February 9:* Ibid., 64.

133 *"His face was pale"*: Ibid., 71.

133 *waspish sketch:* Ibid., 74.

133 *a biographer:* Donald, *Lincoln,* 274.

134 *"merciless throngs"*: Henry Villard, *Lincoln on the Eve,* 78.

135 *"march of triumph"*: Ibid., 82.

135 *"The President's remarks"*: Ibid., 84.

135 *"standing upright"*: Ibid., 94.

136 *on February 20:* Ibid., 97.

9. LOOK AWAY, DIXIELAND

141 *"Chevalier" Wikoff:* Donald, *Lincoln,* 324.

10. FIRST BLOOD

158 *Lt. Bayard Wilkeson:* Crozier, *Yankee Reporters, 360–61.*

158 *the anonymous correspondent: New York Herald,* July 24, 1861, 8. Reporters killing soldiers was apparently not considered front-page news.

158 *"small army of Northern correspondents"*: Catton, *American Heritage,* 492.

159 *a distinguished historian:* Ibid., 93.

162 *"Not a sound is heard"*: *New York Herald,* July 20, 1861.

163 *from a cornfield:* The scene that Villard and Coffin witnessed at Bull Run is described in Crozier, *Yankee Reporters,* 101–2.

11. THE SLAUGHTER OF THE INNOCENTS

172 *"defeated to the end of time"*: Spore, "Sherman," 31.

174 *Halstead later claimed:* Ibid., 31.

175 *in his [Sherman's] autobiography:* Sherman, *Memoirs,* 234.

175 *members of Villard's family:* Verbal statement of Oswald Garrison Villard to the anonymous author of an unpublished biography of Henry Villard in the possession of Alexandra de Borchgrave.

175 *"in sorrow, consternation, and doubt"*: Long and Long, *The Civil War Day by Day,* 153.

177 *Grant's appearance:* See Keegan, *Mask,* 202–29.

178 *severed his connection:* On Villard's switch from the *Herald* to the *Tribune,* see Crozier, *Yankee Reporters,* 211.

179 *"produced, man for man":* Kluger, *Paper,* 102.

181 *"I conversed freely":* New York Tribune, April 5, 1862.

188 *"In the camps, as in the newspapers":* Quoted in Starr, *Bohemian Brigade,* 105.

189 *"unsupported romance":* Grant, "Fragment on Shiloh," in *Memoirs,* 1012.

190 *"powerful, gloomy narrative":* Crozier, *Yankee Reporters,* 217.

190 *"celebrated and controversial":* Starr, *Bohemian Brigade,* 103.

191 *Greeley never forgave:* Gay to Villard, January 31, 1864, in Starr, *Bohemian Brigade,* 104.

12. TRAMPLING OUT THE VINTAGE

193 *"a shuffler of papers":* Catton, *American Heritage,* 209.

200 *"a new record for confusion":* McPherson, *Battle Cry,* 519.

200 *acoustic shadow:* Ibid., 520.

202 *another future commanding general:* In 1884 Sheridan succeeded Sherman as supreme commander; Sherman had succeeded Grant in 1869.

203 *"most influential paper":* Starr, *Bohemian Brigade,* 98.

206 *"The President particularly liked":* Ibid., 160–61.

210 *"its old, old difficulty":* Catton, *Glory Road,* 45.

211 *"mulish and intractable":* Quoted in Starr, *Bohemian Brigade,* 165.

215 *loosed a storm:* Nevins, *Evening Post,* 322.

216 *the worst defeat:* Donald, *Lincoln,* 399.

217 *"the big Bavarian":* Starr, *Bohemian Brigade,* 164.

13. FREE AT LAST

220 *"remarkable expense accounts":* Nevins, *Evening Post,* 251.

220 *the account he submitted a few months later:* Ibid., 251.

220 *"the most execrable measure":* Quoted in McPherson, *Battle Cry,* 566.

223 *"My Business is Circumference":* Dickinson, *Selected Letters,* 176.

224 *"No officer in this regiment":* Higginson, quoted in McPherson, *Negro's Civil War,* 169.

225 *series of raids:* Ibid., 169.

227 *"a metal fortress":* Crozier, *Yankee Reporters,* 311.

228 *a rebel teamster:* O. G. Villard, *Fighting Years,* 3.

229 *"the only one worth reading":* Charles Nordhoff, *Harper's Monthly,* June 1863, quoted in Starr, *Bohemian Brigade,* 264.

14. COME IN AND SHUT THE DOOR

234 *"an authentic American hero"*: Mayer, *All on Fire*, xiii. The authors of the present work acknowledge a profound debt to Mr. Mayer's magnificent biography for much of the material on William Lloyd Garrison and his family presented herein.

235 *"all on fire"*: Quoted ibid., 120–21.

236 *"the pinnacle of his career"*: Ibid., 445.

237 *"No American before Garrison"*: Ibid., 445.

238 *"I wish my children"*: Ibid., 552.

238 *"especially Fanny"*: F. G. Villard, *William Lloyd Garrison*, 6–7.

239 *"the very picture"*: This quotation and several of those that follow are based on an unpublished fragment originally intended for publication in Henry Villard's *Memoirs* and formerly included (as HVP B157) among the Henry Villard Papers in the Houghton Library at Harvard University. Unfortunately, this manuscript can no longer be found among the Villard Papers—it apparently went missing in the late 1940s or early 1950s—and the present authors have never seen it. Our only source of quotations from it is an unpublished anonymous biography of Henry Villard (hereinafter referred to as "Anonymous Biography"). See note for p. 175.

239 *a letter to her dear friend*: Fanny Garrison to Lucy McKim, Fanny Garrison Villard Papers, bMS Am 1321 (825).

240 *"an awfully nice girl"*: Anonymous Biography.

240 *"She was very lovely"*: Ibid.

240 *in her diary*: Fanny Garrison Villard's diaries are in bMS Am 1321 (900) and (901), Fanny Garrison Villard Papers.

241 *"yield to the impulse"*: Anonymous Biography.

242 *white apron pockets*: Ibid.

242 *"eye-lids droop"*: Ibid.

242 *as his son explained*: O. G. Villard, *Fighting Years*, 5.

243 *his first letter*: Henry Villard Papers, bMS Am 1322 (629).

15. WAR FEVER

246 *"for greenbacks"*: Halstead, "Some Reminiscences," 63.

252 *too sick to witness*: Henry Villard's *Memoirs* suggest that the only action he personally witnessed at Chattanooga was the Union's seizure of Orchard Knob during the first day (November 23) of the three-day battle. Although von Willich's troops certainly took part in the storming of Missionary Ridge on November 25, Villard breaks off his narrative the day before this final assault, merely indicating that his recurring indisposition forced him to abandon field work in November. It seems highly unlikely that Villard, had he

been an eyewitness to the thrilling events on Missionary Ridge, would have neglected to record them, and virtually impossible that he could have remained with Von Willich's troops without witnessing the battle. It may be conjectured, therefore, that Villard's bad health forced him to withdraw from the front lines on November 24, 1863.

253 *"without bothering to explain"*: Starr, *Bohemian Brigade*, 63.

253 *"I left the* Tribune *without regret"*: Henry Villard to Francis J. Garrison, April 5, 1864, Henry Villard Papers, bMS Am 1322 (541).

253 *"Mr. Greeley's chameleon policy"*: Hill to Sydney H. Gay, in Starr, *Bohemian Brigade*, 291.

254 *"occasions when you have served us"*: Sydney H. Gay to Henry Villard, January 31, 1864, Henry Villard Papers, bMS Am 1322 (153).

254 *"a variety of circumstances"*: Henry Villard to Francis J. Garrison, April 5, 1864, Henry Villard Papers, bMS Am 1322 (541).

258 *"I left the army"*: Henry Villard to Francis J. Garrison, August 10, 1864, Henry Villard Papers, bMS Am 1322 (541).

259 *"You are somewhat mistaken"*: Francis J. Garrison to Henry Villard, August 18, 1864, Henry Villard Papers, bMS Am 1322 (136).

259 how *"gratifying"* it would have been: Henry Villard to Francis J. Garrison, September 14, 1864, Henry Villard Papers, bMS Am 1322 (541).

259 *Frank's long reply:* Francis J. Garrison to Henry Villard, September 25, 1864, Henry Villard Papers, bMS Am 1322 (136).

260 *a German legal document:* This document, in bMS Am 1322 (636), Henry Villard Papers, is discussed in Fuchs, "Henry Villard," 134. The original German statement concerning the "various counterclaims" refers to *"verschiedene seinem Vater an ihn zustehende Gegenforderungen."*

16. IN SICKNESS AND IN HEALTH

264 *astounded father wrote his son:* W. L. Garrison, *Letters,* 5:276–77 (May 25, 1865).

265 *Villard also wrote a letter:* Henry Villard to Wendell Garrison, May 25, 1865, Henry Villard Papers, bMS Am 1322 (546).

266 *Garrison handed Villard a long letter:* William Lloyd Garrison to Henry Villard, August 10, 1865, Henry Villard Papers, bMS Am 1322 (147).

267 *gave as good as he got:* Henry Villard to William Lloyd Garrison, August 16, 1865, Henry Villard Papers, bMS Am 1322 (542).

267 *a letter dated October 30:* Henry Villard to Fanny Garrison, October 30, 1865, Henry Villard Papers, bMS Am 1322 (629).

269 *a farewell letter so like Polonius's admonitions:* W. L. Garrison, *Letters,* 5:418–19 (July 6, 1866).

271 *"And now my own, dearly beloved":* Henry Villard to Fanny G. Villard, August 1, 1866, Henry Villard Papers, bMS Am 1322 (629).

272 *"He told me":* Henry Villard to Fanny G. Villard, August 3, 1866, Henry Villard Papers, bMS Am 1322 (629).

272 *he knows . . . that she will do her duty:* Henry Villard to Fanny G. Villard, August 8, 1866, Henry Villard Papers, bMS Am 1322 (629).

272 *"the little girl will then have a chance":* Henry Villard to Fanny G. Villard, August 22, 1866, Henry Villard Papers, bMS Am 1322 (629).

273 *"vindicate your womanhood":* W. L. Garrison, *Letters,* 5:456–60 (February 19, 1867).

274 *a letter to his wife:* Ibid., 5:489–92 (May 24, 1867).

275 *"painful sacrifice":* Henry Villard to Fanny G. Villard, May 25, 1867, Henry Villard Papers, bMS Am 1322 (629).

276 *"I realize very well":* Henry Villard to Fanny G. Villard, July 14, 1867, Henry Villard Papers, bMS Am 1322 (629).

277 *"was never nearer to my heart":* Henry Villard to W. L. Garrison Jr., September 4, 1867, Henry Villard Papers, bMS Am 1322 (629).

278 *"The worst is come!":* Henry Villard to Fanny G. Villard, September 2, 1867, Henry Villard Papers, bMS Am 1322 (629).

278 *"What I felt":* Henry Villard to Fanny G. Villard, September 7, 1867, Henry Villard Papers, bMS Am 1322 (629).

279 *article on Bismarck:* Henry Villard, "Karl Otto von Bismarck-Schönhausen."

280 *the "high aim" of social science:* Henry Villard, "Historical Sketch."

280 *"I don't believe":* Henry Villard to Fanny G. Villard, January 18, 1869, Henry Villard Papers, bMS Am 1322 (629).

281 *"About thirty gentlemen":* Henry Villard to Fanny G. Villard, October 29, 1869, Henry Villard Papers, bMS Am 1322 (629).

281 *"I felt so old":* Diary of Fanny G. Villard, December 16, 1869, Fanny Garrison Villard Papers, bMS Am 1321 (900).

283 *"catarrh of the left ear":* Henry Villard to Fanny G. Villard, November 16, 1870, Henry Villard Papers, bMS Am 1322 (629).

17. WORKING ON THE RAILROAD

290 *"not much work was expected of me":* Henry Villard, *Early History,* 37.

290 *"Character is fate":* Novalis, *Heinrich von Ofterdingen,* part two. In the phrase in question, the author speaks of his conviction that *"Schicksal und Gemüt Namen eines Begriffs sind."*

291 *"quick-witted, magnetic":* Josephson, *Robber Barons,* 238.

291 *"vision plus character":* O. G. Villard, *Fighting Years,* 13.

291 *"a great mistake":* Henry Villard, *Early History,* 39.

292 *"a surprisingly shaky foundation":* Schwantes, *Signatures,* 56.

293 *"I only hope that my waist":* Henry Villard to Fanny G. Villard, May 23, 1874, Henry Villard Papers, bMS Am 1322 (630).

295 *"here are the Dutchmen!":* Henry Villard, *Early History,* 43.

295 *"a chosen land":* Ibid., 43.

295 *"under one . . . control":* Ibid., 47.

297 *"I knew you would be mad":* Henry Villard to Fanny G. Villard, April 2, 1875, Henry Villard Papers, bMS Am 1322 (630).

298 *"business-wifey":* Henry Villard to Fanny G. Villard, January 12, 1872, Henry Villard Papers, bMS Am 1322 (630).

299 *Fanny's diary entries:* Diary of Fanny G. Villard, July 23–August 3, 1877, Fanny Garrison Villard Papers, bMS Am 1321 (900).

302 *"the great gobbler":* Henry Villard to Fanny G. Villard, April 2, 1875, Henry Villard Papers, bMS Am 1322 (630). The "machinator" phrase comes from Villard's *Memoirs.*

302 *"most-feared man":* Henry Villard, *Early History,* 80.

18. UPGRADE, DOWNGRADE

305 *"fashionable life of the city":* O. G. Villard, *Fighting Years,* 24.

305 *"as quiet as a village":* Ibid., 26.

306 *"laid the foundation":* Ibid., 26.

309 *"something very wonderful":* Ibid., 28–29.

309 *"light of the future":* Josephson, *Edison,* 224.

310 *"believed in the light":* Ibid., 293.

313 *"superb specimens":* O. G. Villard, *Fighting Years,* 42.

313 *"greatest . . . corporate undertaking":* Winks, *Frederick Billings,* 187.

315 *Seattle & Walla Walla:* Armbruster, "Boom," 3.

317 *literally collapsed:* Winks, *Billings,* 248.

318 *"unapproached by anything else":* Nevins, *Evening Post,* 443.

318 *"rare generosity":* Ibid., 444.

319 *a clipping: Zweibrücker Zeitung,* no. 185, August 9, 1881, 2.

320 *"the decade after 1875":* Schwantes, *Signatures,* 56.

320 *"like a comet":* Klein, *Union Pacific,* 559.

321 *"a God-forsaken place":* Quoted in Baker, *Stanny,* 97.

321 *"his royal highness":* Quoted in Lowe, *Stanford White's New York,* 109.

323 *"boom psychology":* Winks, *Billings,* 263.

323 *Chinese coolies:* Discussed in Armbruster, "Boom," 20.

324 *"reckless and careless":* Klein, *Union Pacific,* 560.

324 *"incomparable gift":* Klein, *Union Pacific,* 444. The fellow magnate, quoted by Klein, was John Murray Forbes of the Chicago, Burlington and Quincy.

325 *Fanny wrote from her desk:* Fanny G. Villard to Henry Villard, April 17, 1883, Fanny Garrison Villard Papers, bMS Am 1321 (876).

326 *a strangely abstract letter:* Fanny G. Villard to Henry Villard, April 30, 1883, Fanny Garrison Villard Papers, bMS Am 1321 (876).

326 *the Villard Houses:* They now form part of the Helmsley Palace Hotel; the restaurant Le Cirque occupies the main floor of the Villards' former residence.

327 *"quiet and secluded way":* Quoted in "The New York House of the Future," *Real Estate Record and Guide* 28 (December 1881), 1208, cited in Shopsin, *Villard Houses,* 30.

327 *"one of New York's great landmarks":* Lessard, *Architect,* 113.

327 *"opulent and awe-inspiring":* Shopsin, *Villard Houses,* 21.

327 *"very quiet, a little cold":* Mariana Van Rensselaer, *Century Magazine,* February 1886, quoted in Baker, *Stanny,* 107.

327 *"To all great men":* Quoted in Shopsin, *Villard Houses,* 42.

330 *"quite foolish":* Winks, *Billings,* 254.

332 *"You go. Me go.":* Alsop, *Lady Sackville,* 62.

333 *Nicolaus Mohr:* Mohr, *Excursion,* 153.

334 *"the greatest event":* Henry Villard, *Early History,* 98.

335 *Fanny's diary entries:* Entries for September 13, 14, 24, 1883, Fanny Garrison Villard Papers, bMS Am 1321 (900).

336 *"you or Barnum":* Quoted in Winks, *Billings,* 261.

336 *"swindling operations":* Diary of Fanny G. Villard, October 17, 1883, Fanny Garrison Villard Papers, bMS Am 1321 (900).

336 *"I have had a very trying time":* Henry Villard to Fanny G. Villard, "N. Y. Tuesday Evening 1883," Henry Villard Papers, bMS Am 1322 (632).

338 *Billings's biographer:* Winks, *Billings,* 261–62.

339 *a bright vision of the future:* Josephson, *Edison,* 293.

340 *"formidable backlog":* Klein, *Union Pacific,* 560–61, 564.

340 *evolutionary function:* This analysis is based on Buss, "Henry Villard," 163ff.

19. THE VANITY OF HUMAN WISHES

344 *long letter to Fanny:* Henry Villard to Fanny G. Villard, July 18, 1884, Henry Villard Papers, bMS Am 1322 (631).

346 *Theodor Mommsen:* Fanny's set-to with the professor is recounted in O. G. Garrison, *Fighting Years,* 67–68.

350 *"winter-quarters":* F. G. Villard and Henry Villard, *Story of Our Little Boy,* 66.

350 *"filth of New York":* Diary of Fanny G. Villard, October 24, 1886, Fanny Garrison Villard Papers, bMS Am 1321 (900).

355 *"one of the first . . . plants":* Josephson, *Edison,* 292. We have based much of

our account of the interactions between J. P. Morgan, Thomas Edison, and Henry Villard on this authoritative work.

355 *"promising industry"*: Ibid., 292.

356 *"one of the biggest consolidations"*: Ibid., 353.

357 *one historian:* Adams's opinions of Villard are quoted in Klein, *Union Pacific,* 572, 566, 573.

357 *Unlike Villard and almost everyone else:* See Klein, *Union Pacific,* 569.

361 *"the last rejoicing of the kind":* Fanny G. Villard and Henry Villard, *Story of Our Little Boy,* 116. Not long after Hilgard's death, the Villards published this small book in his memory. The style of the book suggests that it was mostly, if not completely, Fanny's work, though Villard must have been an active collaborator. We have followed this book's account of Hilgard's last days.

362 *"erect and determined":* Ibid., 118.

20. SLEEPY HOLLOW

366 *"selfish and unprincipled":* Our account of Villard's visit to Bismarck follows his own, in Henry Villard, "A Visit," 664–70.

370 *"The use of alternating current":* Quoted in Josephson, *Edison,* 359. The following section on Edison is largely based on pp. 359–65 of this book.

374 *categorical in his refusal:* O. G. Villard, *Fighting Years,* 70.

376 *"I'm out of it, now":* Armbruster, "Boom," 18.

377 *"a very aggressive man":* Quoted in Josephson, *Edison,* 294.

377 *In an interview:* New York World, August 22, 1909. This front-page article, strikingly entitled "Fill Up the East River Now and Dig Another," discusses various grandiose plans for which Edison could get no backing.

379 *Fanny wrote in her diary:* Our account of Villard's death follows Fanny's diary entries, especially those for October 3, October 22, and November 9, 1900, Fanny Garrison Villard Papers, bMS Am 1321 (900).

379 *the funeral service:* Our account follows the obituary notices in several daily newspapers, particularly the *New York Times,* November 13, 1900.

Bibliography

Alsop, Susan Mary. *Lady Sackville: A Biography.* Garden City, N.Y.: Doubleday, 1978.

Angle, Paul M. *Created Equal? The Complete Lincoln-Douglas Debates of 1858.* Chicago: University of Chicago Press, 1958.

Armbruster, Kurt E. "Boom and Bust: Henry Villard and Puget Sound." Paper delivered at the 52nd Pacific Northwest History Conference, Victoria, B.C., April 15–17, 1999. Mr. Armbruster's book *Orphan Road: The Railroad Comes to Seattle* (Washington State University Press, 1999), from which most of the material in his paper was taken, appeared too late to be consulted for the present work.

Baker, Paul R. *Stanny: The Gilded Life of Stanford White.* New York: Free Press, 1989.

Batterberry, Michael and Ariane. *On the Town in New York: From 1776 to the Present.* New York: Chas. Scribner's Sons, 1973.

Burrows, Edwin G., and Mike Wallace. *Gotham: A History of New York City to 1898.* New York: Oxford University Press, 1999.

Buss, Dietrich G. "Henry Villard: A Study of Transatlantic Investment and Interests." Ph.D. diss., Claremont College, 1976.

Catton, Bruce. *Glory Road.* Garden City, N.Y.: Doubleday, 1952.

———. *The American Heritage Picture History of the Civil War.* New York: American Heritage/Bonanza Books, 1960.

———. *The Coming Fury.* Vol. 1 of *The Centennial History of the Civil War.* New York: Doubleday, 1961.

Crozier, Emmet. *Yankee Reporters 1861–1865.* New York: Oxford University Press, 1956.

Dickinson, Emily. *Selected Letters.* Edited by Thomas H. Johnson. Cambridge: Harvard University Press, 1986.

Donald, David Herbert. *Lincoln.* New York: Simon & Schuster, 1995.

Erikson, Erik H. *Young Man Luther.* New York: W. W. Norton, 1958.

Fehrenbacher, Don E. *Prelude to Greatness: Lincoln in the 1850's.* Stanford, Calif.: Stanford University Press, 1962.

Fuchs, Thomas. "Henry Villard: A Citizen of Two Worlds." Ph.D. diss., University of Oregon, 1991.

Garrison, William Lloyd. *The Letters of William Lloyd Garrison.* 6 vols. Edited by Walter M. Merrill and Louis Ruchames. Cambridge: Harvard University Press, 1971–81.

Grant, Ulysses S. *Memoirs and Selected Letters.* New York: Library of America, 1990.

Gutzkow, Karl. *Gutzkows Werke.* Edited by Peter Müller. Vol. 2. Leipzig: Bibliographisches Institut, 1911.

Halstead, Murat. "Some Reminiscences of Mr. Villard." *American Monthly Review of Reviews* 23 (January 1901): 60–63.

Harris, Brayton. *Blue & Gray in Black & White: Newspapers in the Civil War.* Washington: Batsford Brassey, 1999.

Hesseltine, William B., ed. *Three Against Lincoln: Murat Halstead Reports the Caucuses of 1860.* Baton Rouge: Louisiana State University Press, 1960.

Hilgard, Theodor Erasmus. Letter to his mother. October 8, 1843. Unpublished document in private family collection.

Hilgard-Villard, Heinrich. *Jugend-Erinnerungen, 1835–1853.* New York: Hermann Bartsch Printing House, 1902.

Hirsch, Helmut. "Theodor Erasmus Hilgard, Ambassador of Americanism." *Journal of the Illinois State Historical Society* XXXVII, no. 2 (June 1944): 164–72.

Johannson, Robert W., ed. *The Lincoln-Douglas Debates of 1858.* New York: Oxford University Press, 1965.

Josephson, Matthew. *The Robber Barons.* New York: Harcourt, Brace, 1934.

———. *Edison.* New York: McGraw-Hill, 1959.

Keegan, John. *The Mask of Command.* New York: Viking, 1987.

Klein, Maury. *Union Pacific: The Birth of a Railroad 1862–1893.* Garden City, N.Y.: Doubleday, 1987.

Kluger, Richard. *The Paper: The Life and Death of the New York Herald Tribune.* New York: Knopf, 1986.

Kunhardt, Philip B., Jr., et al. *Lincoln: An Illustrated Biography.* New York: Knopf, 1992.

Lessard, Suzannah. *The Architect of Desire: Beauty and Danger in the Stanford White Family.* New York: Dial Press, 1996.

Long, E. B., and Barbara Long. *The Civil War Day by Day: An Almanac 1861–1865.* Garden City, N.Y.: Doubleday, 1971.

Lowe, David Garrard. *Stanford White's New York.* New York: Doubleday, 1992.

Mayer, Henry. *All on Fire: William Lloyd Garrison and the Abolition of Slavery.* New York: St. Martin's Press, 1998.

McAleer, Kevin. *Dueling: The Cult of Honor in Fin-de-Siècle Germany.* Princeton: Princeton University Press, n.d.

McPherson, James M. *Battle Cry of Freedom: The Civil War Era.* New York: Ballantine Books, 1989.

———. *The Negro's Civil War: How American Blacks Felt and Acted During the War for the Union.* New York: Ballantine Books, 1991.

Mohr, Nicolaus. *Excursion through America.* Chicago: R. R. Donnelly & Sons Co., 1973.

Nadel, Stanley. *Little Germany: Ethnicity, Religion, and Class in New York City, 1845–80.* Urbana: University of Illinois Press, 1990.

Nevins, Allen. *The Evening Post: A Century of Journalism.* New York, 1922.

Oates, Stephen B. *With Malice Toward None: The Life of Abraham Lincoln.* New York: Harper & Row, 1977.

Randall, J. G., and Richard N. Current. *Last Full Measure.* Vol. 4 of *Lincoln the President.* New York: Dodd, Mead & Co., 1945–55.

Robertson, Priscilla. *Revolutions of 1848: A Social History.* Princeton: Princeton University Press, 1952.

Sandburg, Carl. *Abraham Lincoln: The Prairie Years.* New York: Harcourt, Brace, 1926.

Schwantes, Carlos A. *Railroad Signatures Across the Pacific Northwest.* Seattle: University of Washington Press, 1993.

Sheehan, James J. *German History 1770–1866.* Oxford: Clarendon Press, 1989.

Sherman, William T. *Memoirs of General W. T. Sherman.* New York: Library of America, 1990.

Shopsin, William C., et al. *The Villard Houses: Life Story of a Landmark.* New York: Viking, 1980.

Sparks, Edwin Erle, ed. *The Lincoln-Douglas Debates of 1858.* Springfield: Illinois State Historical Library, 1908.

Spore, John B. "Sherman and the Press." *Infantry Journal,* November 1948, 31.

Starr, Louis M. *Bohemian Brigade: Civil War Newsmen in Action.* Madison: University of Wisconsin Press, 1954.

Stich, Dr. H. *Heinrich Hilgard (1835–1900).* Zweibrücken: Hilgard-Stiftung, 1907.

Strouse, Jean. *Morgan: American Financier.* New York: Random House, 1999.

Villard, Fanny Garrison. *William Lloyd Garrison on Non-Violence, Together with a Personal Sketch by His Daughter.* New York, 1924.

Villard, Fanny Garrison, and Henry Villard. *The Story of Our Little Boy: In Memory of Henry Hilgard Villard, 1883–1890.* New York: G. P. Putnam's Sons, n.d.

Villard, Henry. *The Past and Present of the Pike's Peak Gold Regions.* 1860. Reprinted, Princeton: Princeton University Press, 1932.

———. *Lincoln on the Eve of '61: A Journalist's Story.* Edited by Harold G. and Oswald G. Villard. New York: Alfred A. Knopf, 1941.

———. "Historical Sketch of Social Science." *Journal of Social Science* I:5–16.

———. "Karl Otto von Bismarck-Schönhausen." *North American Review,* January 1869, 165–221.

———. "A Visit to Bismarck." *Century Illustrated Monthly* 67 (March 1904): 664–70.

———. *Memoirs of Henry Villard, Journalist and Financier, 1835–1900.* 2 vols. Boston and New York: Houghton, Mifflin, 1904.

———. *The Early History of Transportation in Oregon.* Edited by Oswald Garrison Villard. Eugene: University of Oregon Press, 1944.

Villard, Oswald Garrison. *Fighting Years.* New York: Harcourt, Brace, 1939.

———. "The 'Latin Peasants' of Belleville, Illinois." *Journal of the Illinois State Historical Society* XXXV, no. 1 (March 1942): 7–20.

Henry Villard Papers and Fanny Garrison Villard Papers. Houghton Library, Harvard University.

Winks, Robin W. *Frederick Billings: A Life.* Berkeley: University of California Press, 1998.

Wolf, William J. *The Almost Chosen People: A Study of the Religion of Abraham Lincoln.* Garden City, N.Y.: Doubleday, 1959.

Wyman, Mark. *Immigrants in the Valley: Irish, Germans, and Americans in the Upper Mississippi Country, 1830–1860.* Chicago: Nelson-Hall, 1984.

Photo Credits

lard de Borchgrave Private Collection.

Page 1. Bacharach, c. 1761. Alexandra Villard de Borchgrave Private Collection.

Page 1. Anna Margarethe Engelmann (1742–1825). Alexandra Villard de Borchgrave Private Collection.

Page 2. Friedrich Theodor Engelmann (1779–1854). Courtesy of Mary E. Armstrong, Frankfort, Michigan.

Page 2. Gustav Leonhard Hilgard (1807–67). Alexandra Villard de Borchgrave Private Collection.

Page 2. Katharina Antonia Elisabeth "Lisette" Hilgard. Alexandra Villard de Borchgrave Private Collection.

Page 2. Henry Villard before his wedding day, January 1866. Alexandra Villard de Borchgrave Private Collection.

Page 3. Henry Villard, 1877. Photograph by Rockwood, 17 Union Square, New York.

Page 3. Henry Villard, his mother, sister Emma, and Robert Hilgard. Alexandra Villard de Borchgrave Private Collection.

Page 3. Harold, Helen, and Oswald Villard, 1876. Photograph by Rockwood, 17 Union Square, New York. Sophia Smith Collection, Smith College.

Page 4. Four special trains for the Villard last-spike excursion.

Alexandra Villard de Borchgrave Private Collection.

Page 4. Pavilion at Gold Creek, Montana, September 8, 1883. Alexandra Villard de Borchgrave Private Collection.

Page 5. Waterfall outside St. Paul. Alexandra Villard de Borchgrave Private Collection.

Page 5. Crow Indians. Alexandra Villard de Borchgrave Private Collection.

Page 5. A thousand feet of unfinished track. Alexandra Villard de Borchgrave Private Collection.

Page 6. Villard House, detail of mantel frieze, 1885. The New-York Historical Society. Unidentified photographer, McKim, Mead and White Collection. Negative no. 73833.

Page 6. Villard House, music room, 1885. The New-York Historical Society. Unidentified photographer, McKim, Mead and White Collection. Negative no. 73834.

Page 6. Fanny Garrison Villard holding Hilgard. Alexandra Villard de Borchgrave Private Collection.

Page 6. Villard House, triple drawing room, 1884. Alexandra Villard de Borchgrave Private Collection.

Page 7. Werner von Siemens. Landes Archive, Berlin, Germany.

Page 7. Prince Otto von Bismarck. Landes Archive, Berlin, Germany.

Page 7. Fanny Garrison Villard and Oswald. Photograph by Hof Photograph, G. Th. Hase & Sohn, Karlsplatz, 4, Freiburg, Germany. Sophia Smith Collection, Smith College.

Page 7. Henry Villard with his first grandson Henry Serrano Villard and his son Harold. Alexandra Villard de Borchgrave Private Collection.

Page 8. Fanny Garrison Villard with her grandchildren. Alexandra Villard de Borchgrave Private Collection.

Page 8. Birthplace of Henry Villard, Speyer. Alexandra Villard de Borchgrave Private Collection.

Page 8. Harold Garrison Villard. Sophia Smith Collection, Smith College.

Page 8. Thorwood. By permission of the Houghton Library, Harvard University, bMS Am 1322 (642), Folder 1.

Page 8. Karl Bitter's funerary monument for Henry Villard in Sleepy Hollow Cemetery. Courtesy of Katharine N. Villard.

Index

Page numbers in *italics* refer to illustrations.

About the Authors

ALEXANDRA VILLARD DE BORCHGRAVE is the great-granddaughter of Henry Villard. She is a distinguished photographer who has taken portraits of notables such as George Bush, Henry Kissinger, and Anwar Sadat. Her work has appeared on the cover of *Newsweek* and other major international publications. Active in the Washington community, she is married to Arnaud de Borchgrave, president and CEO of United Press International.

JOHN CULLEN graduated with a Ph.D. in English literature from the University of Texas. His translations from German and Italian include Christa Wolf's *Medea,* Adolf Holl's *The Left Hand of God,* and Susanna Tamaro's *Follow Your Heart.* He lives in upstate New York.